# Curriculum Development for Education Reform

Acquisitions Editor: Christopher Jennison
Cover Design: Initial Graphic Systems, Inc.
Electronic Production Manager: Eric Jorgensen
Publishing Services: Interactive Production Services
Electronic Page Makeup: Interactive Composition Corporation
Printer and Binder: R. R. Donnelley & Sons Company
Cover Printer: The Lehigh Press, Inc.

Curriculum Development for Education Reform

Library of Congress Cataloging-in-Publication Data
Henson, Kenneth T.
    Curriculum development for education reform / Kenneth T. Henson.
        p.    cm.
    Includes bibliographical references and index.
    ISBN 0-673-99222-5 (hardcover)
    1. Curriculum planning--Handbooks, manuals, etc.  2. Educational
change--Handbooks, manuals, etc.   I. Title
LB2806.15H46   1995
795'.001--dc20                                                  95-2581
                                                                  CIP


94  95  96  97    9  8  7  6  5  4  3  2  1

# Curriculum Development for Education Reform

Kenneth T. Henson
Eastern Kentucky University

HarperCollins*CollegePublishers*

Historically, every school has had a core of hardworking teachers who have been content to remain in their classrooms and devote their expertise and energy to educating their students. During times of emergency, such as preparing for accreditation visits, these teachers always surface as the leaders who do the job that must be done. Because these teachers provide the leadership for improving their schools, their efforts must be recognized.

But current reform movements in every state are demanding constant and total involvement of all educators. As in the past, teachers are giving time and energy to meet these demands. This book is dedicated to all the teachers who are giving their best to improve our schools and to all the tens of thousands of central office curriculum and instructional leaders, principals, and college and university professors who are dedicated to helping teachers meet this challenge.

# BRIEF CONTENTS

# CONTENTS

# PREFACE

The primary purpose of this book is to help the reader develop and improve curriculum development skills and use these skills to implement education reform practices. Since the author does not assume that all reform practices are good, this book provides the reader with the foundations needed to make judicious decisions regarding both the implementation of reform practices and the value of the practices. Most reform practices have both strengths and limitations. The readers are provided with opportunities to review the merits and the criticisms of each popular reform practice and are urged to weigh the pros and cons carefully so that they can make their own value judgments about the worth of each to their local school district.

Another theme of this book is multicultural education. Throughout the country, teachers encounter students of many and varied backgrounds. Many of these students leave their marks on the schools' honor rolls and lists of valedictorians and salutatorians. Yet, because of language barriers and troubled home environments, many minority students have low expectations of themselves. Successful curriculum development in the 1990s must be aimed at helping all students succeed.

Through the use of case studies, this book provides opportunities to apply curriculum foundations and practices to some of the many problem situations faced by today's students, situations which challenge all contemporary teachers.

The tone is intentionally encouraging because lasting improvements in the schools require the support of those who enroll in this course: designated curriculum directors, administrators, instructional supervisors, and teachers—*especially* teachers, since successful reform requires an unprecedented level of teacher involvement and leadership. But the encouraging language should not—must not—be interpreted as uncritical support for all education reform or as a failure to recognize the weaknesses that characterize many of these reports. On the contrary, the author's concern about the many unsound practices recommended by the nation's reform reports was clearly expressed in his *USA Today* article, "Reforming America's Public Schools" (1986; see Appendix A) and in *America's Public Schools in Transition* (Stinnett & Henson, 1982), which contains major sections entitled "America's Battered Schools" and "America's Battered Teachers."

Simple, quick-fix solutions usually take place in an environment of ignorance. And any improvements usually disappear quickly. Sound curriculum development requires the development and implementation of theories based on a solid knowledge of educational foundations. Consequently, good curriculum development is seldom quick or easy. So the overriding theme of this book is sound curriculum development for lasting school reform.

## Instructor's Manual

A five-part instructor's manual is available. Part I introduces the reader to the book's pedagogy. Part II provides chapter outlines that can easily be made into transparencies. Part III provides multiple-choice test items for each chapter. Part IV is a key to the multiple-choice test items. Part V provides essay test items for each chapter.

Kenneth T. Henson

## Acknowledgments

I gratefully acknowledge the following people for their help in this project:

Robert Alley, Wichita State University;
Anita S. Baker, Baylor University;
Marlow Berg, San Diego State University;
Joseph A. Bosco, State University of New York;
Andrea Bowman, Central Washington University;
Robert J. Harder, Washington State University;
Jim Henderson, Kent State University;
Barbara Johnson, Michigan State Department of Education;
James Johnson, Hofstra University;
Richard D. Kimpston, University of Minnesota;
E. John Kleinert, University of Miami;
Georgia Langer, Eastern Michigan University;
John W. McLure, University of Iowa;
Robert Oana, Bowling Green State University;
Sharon Pate and James Leming, Southern Illinois University;
Gerald Ponder, University of North Carolina at Greensboro;
Daisy F. Reed, Virginia Commonwealth University;
Robert A. Roth, California State University, Long Beach;
Edmund C. Short, Penn State University;
Jay Thompson, Ball State University;
Robert Williams, Indiana State University; and
John L. Wright, Greenville College

# TO THE STUDENT

Newspapers, magazines, books, and reports regularly describe problems in our schools. Legislators and educators are suing their states for failing to provide the type of education needed to prepare students for the twenty-first century. Schools and teachers are being measured, not by their own performance but rather by the performance of their students on national exams. The people are calling for a national curriculum. To say the least, these are exciting and challenging times.

As a twenty-first-century educator, you are no longer restricted to teaching the textbook content to the students in your classrooms. The teacher's role has moved from the classroom to the total school (restructuring), to the community, and to the world (reform). Your job is to prepare your students to ask new types of questions, think new kinds of thoughts, dream new dreams, and reach new goals. In effect, you must play a major role in shaping the future.

To be sure, this new role requires mastering content, and knowledge of the principles of curriculum development is an indispensable part of this content. But, if indeed you are to use this course and this book to prepare for the type of education reform that is already moving rapidly throughout the world, you will need content *and more*. You must have the courage and stamina to seek the answers to many questions: What is it about education reform that perplexes me? (After all, nobody fully understands all the reform elements.) Which reform practices in my district do I support? What insights do I have about learners that I can use to contribute to designing a new type of educational system? What is wrong with our current system? What is right with it? What is wrong with our world? How can I help change it? What are my strongest feelings? How can I use the answers to these questions to increase the impact I can have on shaping our schools and our world?

What have been my greatest learning experiences? What made them so? Who is the best teacher I have ever had? Why? Exactly how did that teacher reach me? What is the difference between knowledge and wisdom? What are my fondest memories from elementary school? Secondary school? What were my most traumatic experiences? How can I best use these memories and experiences to help others? How is each discipline different? Does each discipline have a best route to mastery? How can this route be discovered? For what disciplines is each teaching method best suited? What other kinds of questions should I be asking myself so that I can ride the crest of the reform wave and experience success instead of wallowing in dissatisfaction?

How can I remain passionate about reform and yet avoid falling prey to the politicians' empty rhetoric and to the flawed recommendations that characterize so many of the reform reports? How can I keep my concern for the welfare of every student of every nationality and every social level as the reason and guide for all of my decisions? How can I help all students realize their strengths, their self-worth, and their importance and obligations to the community? What is it about me that makes me different from any other human being that has ever lived, and how can I understand and harness this uniqueness to direct my energies and those of my colleagues to make a positive difference in our schools and in our world?

Kenneth T. Henson

# Chapter 1

# INTRODUCTION

## OBJECTIVES

This chapter should prepare you to:

- Explain how the hidden curriculum can affect the academic and social development of minority students.
- Develop a working definition of curriculum.
- Criticize the reform reports from an educational perspective.
- Describe some events that have led recently to an improved image of American education.
- Improve your ability to influence your colleagues' points of view.

## EASTWOOD MIDDLE SCHOOL

Eastwood Middle School, in the town of Madisonville, is in many ways a typical American middle school. Its 26 teachers and 425 students in grades 5 to 8 make it average in size. Its culturally diverse student body and its predominantly white administration and faculty contribute to its typical qualities. Since Eastwood Middle serves a working-class population, the students do not always receive the level of encouragement they need to convince them to try to achieve their maximum potential. On the contrary, those who do receive encouragement at home are told to "get an education so that you can get a good job." Unfortunately, like other communities, Madisonville has its share of broken homes, single parents, and latchkey children.

Madisonville also has its right and wrong sides of the tracks. There are several pockets of ethnic groups, and Madisonville residents are stereotyped according to their subcommunities, each with its own ethnic culture.

As is true of schools throughout the country, Eastwood Middle School is the hub of the community, not in the sense of being a meeting place for citizens to gather but because it is the one place that the community's youth from all backgrounds come together.

Eastwood Middle School is located in a state where education reform is occurring at record speed. Each week brings new dimensions of reform. During two years of rapid reform, the schools in this state have been introduced to such innovations as curriculum alignment, nongraded primary curriculum, site-based decision making, alternative testing, performance evaluation, research-based teaching, educational technology, and valued outcomes. A new tax increase has financed these and other changes in education.

To say that teaching in Eastwood Middle School during the past two years has been an exciting experience would be the understatement of the year. Highlighting the motivation for Eastwood teachers to pursue reform has been a series of articles in the local newspaper on a continuing "school reform" theme. Eastwood's senior faculty members remember times when about the only news items about local schools were stories on the decline of standardized test scores, failure of the schools to enforce discipline codes, or an occasional drug bust. Drug problems initially shocked this small midwestern community, but as alcohol and drug problems increased, they grew to be seen as an unfortunate sign of the times.

But good things have been happening at Eastwood—and recently. Even the television news programs have featured special stories on some of the curriculum reforms at Eastwood. Yes, the senior faculty members would agree that it was time for some positive stories about their school, and the reform stories are welcomed and appreciated.

However, education reform at Eastwood Middle School has its problems. As with all schools, Eastwood has its share of naysayers, faculty members who announce daily in the teachers lounge that the reform won't work. Some of the reasons they give for predicting the early demise of the education reform movement are:

- "It will never work. Sure, all the reform elements sound great in theory, but once they move from the drawing board to the real world, they won't work."

- "The recent infusion of money that is fueling this education reform movement will soon run out, and when this happens, reform will stop."

- "This school reform movement is just another fad. The legislators are using it to build their own support base. Once they stop getting publicity, they'll withdraw their support."

- "The principal is using the reform movement to get another feather in her cap. She'll press for its implementation just long enough to get all the media coverage she can get, and then she'll find another way to get publicity."

- "We teachers are being enticed under pretenses to go along with all the reform issues. We are receiving more and more work assignments with no more pay, and all of us are already overworked. Soon we'll come to our senses and say, 'Enough's enough'."

- "This reform is holding us teachers accountable for the performance of *all* our students, and let's face it, some students will never succeed. The movement was doomed to fail before it started."

Although these naysayers are in the minority in terms of numbers, they are a loud and determined group. The principal often muses over how much this group of teachers could contribute to reforming the school if they channeled all their energy positively.

Like most schools, Eastwood also has its group of innovators who are standing ready to take on new challenges. These faculty members seem to thrive on challenges, and they appear to be tireless. Instead of being exhausted from overwork, these teachers seem to derive energy from working hard. Eastwood's principal wishes that this group had more members.

The majority of Eastwood's teachers are somewhere between these two extremes. They hear the rumblings and they read and hear about the success stories. Caught in the middle between the two points of view, they are waiting to see whether they should invest their energy and time in the reform movement. They know that successful reform will require a big commitment of everybody's time and energy. They want to improve their schools, but since their daily and weekly schedules are already taxing, before making personal investments in the reform, they want to be sure that the reform movement will not run out of steam or money before it succeeds.

Susan Carnes has just completed her undergraduate studies and has accepted her first full-time teaching assignment at Eastwood. After serving on the faculty for only two months, Susan can see the political forces at work. In addition to the distinct social groups, she has noticed that different individuals have their own reasons for wanting the education reform movement at Eastwood to succeed or fail.

Carlos Garcia is a soft-spoken, polite science teacher who seems immune to the daily gossip. He is a good listener who seems to empathize with all the complainers and yet never complains. It seems clear, though, that when the chips are down, Carlos will support the administration and the reform practices.

At the other extreme is Irene Watson, whose tongue seems to be loose at both ends. Irene is a large, boisterous teacher who demands attention wherever she goes. Even in faculty meetings when all 26 teachers are present, Irene speaks up every time anyone else speaks. It is as though she believes that her right to express her opinion is at least equal to the rights of all other 25 teachers combined. Susan is amazed that the rest of the faculty members permit one individual to dominate them. Apparently, they are willing to accede to her overwhelming personality just to avoid the unpleasantness that would surely follow if she did not get her way.

This bothers Susan. After all, these are supposed to be professional people, and professionals are supposed to have some autonomy and to be able, in the case of professional teachers, to put the welfare of the students ahead of concerns for themselves and their colleagues. Susan doesn't see concern for the students as a force behind any of the decisions made by this faculty. In fact, she doesn't see that any efforts are being made to address the needs of the minority students.

But two months is a short time to be on a faculty, and Susan is sure that she has much more to learn about the school and her new colleagues. She can tell that her success depends on her ability to learn more about both. Susan believes that, as a professional, she is committed to helping the local reform efforts succeed if, indeed, these efforts will improve the situation of the students at Eastwood. Anyhow, since this is the state's decision and since she is a state employee, she has concluded that perhaps it is up to her to find ways to make the reform serve the students.

Susan wonders whether she should express her position on the local school reform issue and perhaps seek out others who are also committed to its success. Also, Susan desperately wants to talk to someone about the school's multicultural needs. Just having a peer to talk to and being able to share her feelings would bring her some much-needed relief, and yet she wonders whether this would lead to friction with those who oppose reform.

As can be seen from this description of Eastwood Middle school, curriculum reform does not come easy. Most faculties are divided over change of any kind, and reluctance is common, especially when heavy commitments of time and energy are required. Intelligent, school-wide involvement with education reform will require a good grasp of the meaning of curriculum and familiarity with the development of the current wave of school reforms. This chapter begins by examining several definitions of curriculum and then discusses some flaws in current reform practices.

## DEFINING *CURRICULUM*

The term *curriculum* comes from a Latin word meaning "racecourse." When used in education, curriculum has many meanings. Traditionally, the word has meant a "list of courses." But through the years the term has expanded, taking on several additional meanings. Curriculum developers who have a clear intellectual grasp of several of these meanings can perform a wider range of curriculum development activities and can do so more effectively than one who has only a vague idea of what is meant when the word curriculum is mentioned.

Some definitions of curriculum are much more general than others. This is true even for definitions provided by the same author (Taba, 1962), for example:

• Curriculum is a plan for learning.

• A curriculum usually contains a statement of aims and of specific objectives; it indicates some selection and organization of content; it either implies or manifests certain patterns of learning and teaching, whether because the objectives demand them or because the content organization requires them. Finally, it includes a program of evaluation of the outcomes.

## A Program of Studies

In its early application to American education, curriculum meant a program of studies. Zais (1976) points out that when asked to describe a curriculum, a layperson is likely to list a sequence of courses. This connotation of curriculum is seen in most college catalogs, which often define sequence of courses to describe a particular program of studies.

## A Document

Some educators define curriculum according to its intended purpose, which is to improve instruction. For example, James McDonald defined curriculum as "planned actions for instruction" (Foshay, 1969). Such a definition implies that curriculum is a document. When an accrediting team makes a site visit, the chair or another team member may ask to see the science curriculum. Usually, this person will expect the school officials to produce a document describing the school's science program.

## Planned Experiences

To other educators, the term curriculum means a school's planned experiences. Saylor and Alexander (1966, p. 5) distinguish between the school's actual activities and its planned activities: "Curriculum encompasses all learning opportunities provided by the school" versus "A curriculum plan is the advance arrangement of learning opportunities for a particular population of learners." Saylor and Alexander say that a curriculum guide is a written curriculum plan.

Others have also defined the curriculum as experiences:

A sequence of potential experiences is set up by the school for the purpose of disciplining children and youth in group ways of thinking and acting. This set of experiences is referred to as the curriculum (Smith, Stanley, & Shores, 1957).

All the experiences that children have under the guidance of teachers (Caswell & Campbell, 1935).

The curriculum is now generally considered to be all of the experiences that learners have under the auspices of the school (Doll, 1989).

This point of view with its emphasis on experiences rather than content, reflects the thinking of the Progressive Education Era (1920s to 1940s), when the curriculum emphasis shifted from subject-centered to student-centered.

## Social Implications

The concept of curriculum can be expanded even more, to include changes in social emphasis, for example:

- [Curriculum is the] learning experiences and intended outcomes formulated through systematic reconstruction of knowledge and experience, under the auspices of the school, for the learners' continuous and willful growth in personal-social competence (Tanner & Tanner, 1980).

If we are to achieve equality, we must broaden our conceptions of curriculum to include the entire culture of the school—not just subject matter content (Gay, 1990).

## Curriculum as an End

The preceding definitions portray curriculum as content to be learned or experience to be had as a means toward an end. In contrast, other definitions present curriculum as the end unto itself.

Curriculum is all the planned learning outcomes for which the school is responsible (Popam & Baker, 1970).

## Lack of Consensus

At this point, the logical mind strives to impose some order on the definition of curriculum. Unfortunately, this is not possible, because, the development of curriculum theory has not followed a straight, logical path. Wiles and Bondi (1993, p. 15) give some explanation of the lack of systematic theoretical curriculum evolution:

As we approach the twenty-first century, theoretical dimensions of curriculum development remain suppressed by a dependence on economic sponsorship, political conservation, and the failure of educators to gain consensus for any significant change in the schooling process.

So, instead of wrapping up this discussion by giving a precise definition of curriculum, we offer a series of definitions given by Oliva (1992, pp. 5–6).

- Curriculum is that which is taught in school.
- Curriculum is a set of subjects.
- Curriculum is content.
- Curriculum is a program of studies.
- Curriculum is a set of materials.
- Curriculum is a sequence of courses.
- Curriculum is a set of performance objectives.
- Curriculum is a course of study.
- Curriculum is everything that goes on within the school, including extra-class activities, guidance, and interpersonal relationships.

- Curriculum is that which is taught both inside and outside the school directed by the school.
- Curriculum is everything that is planned by school personnel.
- Curriculum is a series of experiences undergone by learners in the school.
- Curriculum is that which an individual learner experiences as a result of schooling.

Figure 1.1 shows various definitions of curriculum arranged in pairs for the sake of comparison, showing some of the extreme diversity in the ways curriculum is viewed.

## The Hidden Curriculum

The curriculum that we have been attempting to define, though varied in many respects, has at least one implied commonality: it is visible. Whether it is a document or an ongoing set of activities, it is visible. But, like the moon, curriculum has a face that is never completely exposed; or, if you please, every curriculum has a hidden dimension. The more obscure, less visible part of the curriculum is referred to as the *hidden curriculum*. Wiles and Bondi (1993, p. 9) refer to the hidden curriculum as the *unplanned* curriculum. Schubert (1986, p. 105) says that the hidden curriculum is that which is taught implicitly, rather than explicitly, by the school experience. McNeil (1990, p. 308) says, "The hidden curriculum refers to unofficial instructional influences. . . ."

The task of grasping a clear concept of the hidden curriculum is difficult. Not so difficult, though, is the ability to see that the hidden curriculum is a powerful force in any school, a force that may reinforce the school's, state's, and local reform efforts and the school's stated mission, or it may militate vigorously against the reform and mission, or it may support some parts of local reform practices and the school's mission and may work against other parts of the reform and mission.

The socialization process that comes from the school itself, as a community, is much a part of the hidden curriculum. In some schools, this process teaches that competition is the road to success in the United States; in other schools, students learn that cooperation is preferred. In some schools, students learn to appreciate diversity; in others, students learn to avoid students with different backgrounds. These are just a couple of the hundreds of lessons taught in every school by the hidden curriculum.

The nature of the hidden curriculum is more covert than overt; this may or may not be intentional. Apple (1979, p. 14) defines the hidden curriculum as "the tacit teaching to students of norms, values, and dispositions that goes on simply by their living in and coping with the institutional expectations and routines of schools day in and day out for a number of years."

One danger of the hidden curriculum is its prejudicial influence on students, in particular, where multiculturalism is concerned. Oliva (1992, p. 551) addresses this concern:

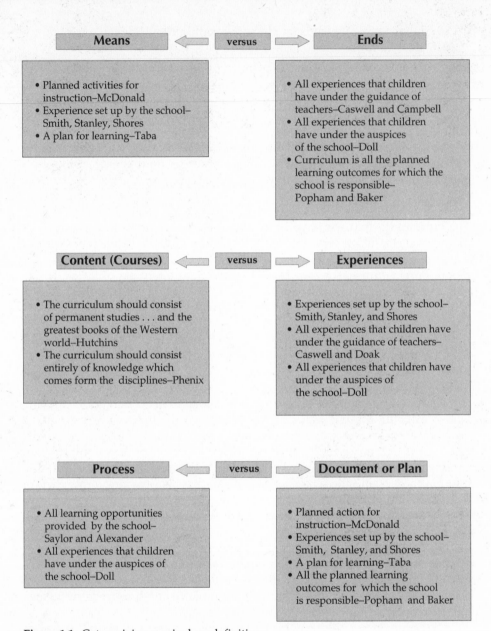

**Figure 1.1** Categorizing curriculum definitions.

Multiracial committees and entire faculties find that, in order to eliminate negative attitudes and conflicts, they must analyze all aspects of the school, including the 'hidden curriculum'—the school climate, social relationships among individuals and groups, values and attitudes held by both student and faculty, pressures on student conduct, unspoken expectations, and unwritten codes of conduct.

# EDUCATION REFORM

Curriculum development has been described as a messy process. Wynne and Ryan (1993, p. 135) have said, "Curriculum is one of education's biggest, sloppiest, and slipperiest concepts." One reason curriculum development is complicated is that it is aimed at facilitating teaching; yet teaching, itself, is an enormously complex and fluid process. Such problems in changing the curriculum have contributed to its remaining "archaic," a description applied by many people. Des Dixon (1994, p. 365) offers his description of today's curriculum:

> Today's curriculum is largely Victorian, a late 19th-century expression of the industrial revolution as applied to the education industry. We have tinkered with it but we have not changed it.

Another factor which complicates curriculum development is the environment in which it occurs—a highly complex environment that is constantly changing. To be effective, the curriculum must be designed and modified to reflect the changes in the society at large, changes in the local community, changes in the local school, and changes in the students. Failure to consider and adjust for these changes is tantamount to learning how to operate a car without ever driving it in traffic.

## Some Criticisms of Education Reform Reports and Practices

Since the role of today's teachers in curriculum planning is expanding beyond their own classrooms, teachers cannot choose to ignore education reform. Therefore, it behooves all teachers to understand as much as possible about the overall national reform movement and about the particular reforms (practices) that are occurring in their own state.

Curriculum developers of the 1990s need to have an awareness of some of the history of the education reform movement of the 1980s. This wave of education reform was started in a sporadic fashion, with a few states introducing reform legislation. It has its origin in a climate of dissatisfaction and lack of confidence in local school boards and local educators (Des Dixon, 1994). It would be comforting to know that this recent wave of reform had its origin in research, but nothing could be further from the truth; the 1980s and 1990s reform wave was born in a climate of politics. As Cook (1994, p. 48) says, "this reform movement is all about power and who has it; those inside the schools or those outside." Actually, Governor William Winter of Mississippi is credited with having introduced the first bold statewide education reform movement. Winter's major concern was with improving the state's economy, which he believed would be possible only through improving education. His Accountability in Instructional Management (AIM) program required all teachers to get together with fellow faculty members in their discipline and design a grades 1–12 curriculum. In every school and in all disciplines, each curriculum was to include objectives, content, teacher activities, student activities, materials, and test items *for every day's lesson.* Mississippi teachers were given five years to develop this new curriculum.

But soon after this process was under way in a few states, an explosion occurred. Dissatisfied with the performance of American students on standardized achievement tests, then Secretary of Education Terrel Bell established the National Commission on Excellence in Education. In 1983 this commission released its report, *A Nation at Risk,* to the President and to the public at large. From a humanist perspective, even the basis for this report (i.e., putting concern for test scores ahead of concern for the total welfare of students) was flawed. (This type of flaw is evident in other reform reports.) More specifically, the test scores of American students were compared to those of students in other nations. One erroneous assumption in making such a comparison was that our schools have the same purpose as schools in other nations. Although we might argue that we live in an international community and therefore must strive to be competitive on the world labor market, educators must consider some questions: Is this really the most important purpose of our schools? Is performance on such tests adequate for measuring the many functions of our schools?

Another flaw in the thinking of education reform reports is their conclusion that American schools are inferior to schools in other nations based on standardized test scores, when, in fact, American students who have taken these tests have competed against the top few percent of selected students in other countries who have gone on to pursue formal secondary education programs. Throughout this century, American schools have attempted to educate all of the country's youth. Granted, no country has reached perfection in this goal, but more important, until recently no other country has aspired to this goal. Furthermore, our schools have been successful in retaining an increasing number of students. For example, in 1920 about 22 percent of the 25 to 29 year-olds were high school graduates. By 1985 the percentage of students graduating had risen to 87 (Schlechty, 1990).

A third flaw of most of these reports is their overemphasis on science and mathematics while completely ignoring other subjects. Tanner (1994, p. 296) addresses this concern. Referring to the reform reports, he says:

> our educational and curricular priorities are skewed to favor the development of an elite in the sciences and mathematics.

For a discussion of the proposals made in several 1980s reform reports, see Appendix A.

## A Positive Turn

After a decade of negative reports, some reports have exposed the intentional misuse of testing to portray the schools negatively. Consequently, Gough (1993, p. 108) predicts an upturn in the public's perception of American education:

> But the public's perception of our profession took a turn for the better in 1991. That's when the first "Bracey Report" on the condition of education (titled "Why Can't They Be Like We Were?") appeared in the pages of the *Kappan*. That's also when the third draft of a report on The Condition of American Education, written by researchers at the Sandia National Laboratories, began to circulate informally throughout the education community—and then beyond it, to a broader audience.
>
> The Sandia researchers, employees of the Department of Energy, had no vested interest in defending education. They wanted only—as Robert Huelskamp, one of the three systems' analysts who conducted the study, points out in this issue—to take a close look at the education system that "develops future scientists, engineers, and mathematicians." But the Sandia researchers found, in the process, essentially the same thing that Gerald Bracey had found: the schools were not in the state of collapse that some critics had claimed.
>
> Those critics dismissed Bracey and other educational researchers who published similar analyses (e.g., David Berliner and Richard Jaeger) as "apologists" for the system. But it was harder for them to dismiss the findings of the Sandia analysts, who were, after all, disinterested outsiders. Thus the Sandia study helped shift conventional wisdom. The "oh-ain't-the-schools-awful" refrain quickly began to give way to today's more realistic assertion that the schools are doing just about as well as they ever did. This new view allows the critics and the proponents to join forces and to focus on the all-too-real problems that plague many school systems.
>
> For years, the National Assessment of Educational Progress (NAEP) has been called "the nation's report card." Isolated results on this test have been used as evidence of the deterioration of American schools. Yet, when viewed over a 20 year span, Bracey (1991) reported, "They are very stable." While the performance of white students has remained constant, the performance of Afro-Americans and Hispanics have actually risen.
>
> With all the hoopla over our schools graduating illiterates, the writing scores on the nation's report card "have not changed since 1974." The greatest alarm set off in the bulk of the reform reports focuses on the declining math scores; yet, the NAEP math scores have remained constant since 1973. Science scores are slightly below their level at the time this testing began in 1969. Another major test of the performance of American schools is the Standardized Achievement Test. Bracey (1991) has said that, "Since 1997 when the National

Center for Education Statistics (1990, Vol. I) reported the results as "stagnation at relatively low levels," of achievement, every one- or two-point change in SAT scores has been front-page news. Less has been made of the fact that blacks, Asian-Americans, Native Americans, Mexican-Americans, and Puerto Ricans *all* scored higher on the SAT in 1990 than in 1975."

Another important fact which the public seldom sees is how the population who takes the Standardized Achievement Test (SAT) is determined. Since the test is taken voluntarily and since it is used for college admission, the annual audience is whoever shows up on Saturday morning to take it. Considering the increase in the number and diversity of students who take this test, it is remarkable that the scores have held steady. For example, when the test was initiated, in 1941, the subjects were 10,654 mostly white, male students headed for Ivy League and other prestigious private universities. During the 1988–90 school year, one and a quarter million students (1,025,523), of which 27 percent were minorities, took the test. Furthermore, 52 percent were females and historically females have not scored as well as males on the SAT.

## Narrow Views

Since the National Commission on Excellence in Education released *A Nation at Risk*, in 1983, over 400 national- and state-level reform reports have followed. Most share the flaws that characterized the parent report, and most have additional flaws. Naturally, the reports represent the interests of their authors. Most reform reports have been written by committees whose interests (or agenda) have ranged from economics to defense. Because the reports have been written by special-interest groups and because most of the groups are politically based, many of the reports are narrow in their perspective. Whatever the purposes of our schools—and there is no implication that there is, could ever be, or should be universal agreement on their purposes—American schools do not have the sole purpose of producing competitive workers, or superior soldiers, or world-competitive economists. Thus, because many of the reports view the purpose of the schools in the light of the mission of their interest group, they are too narrow.

## Overall Purposes

Another flaw in many of the education reform reports concerns the overall intended purpose of the reports, that is, the reasons for their existence and their intended effects. The language used is significant. Most of the reform reports use inflammatory language which does not suggest an honest effort to inform or enlighten the public but rather an attempt to excite and alarm. For example, the parent report, *A Nation at Risk*, (p. 5), which set the tone for the later reports, says, "If an unfriendly foreign power had attempted to impose on America the mediocre educational performance that exists today, we might well have viewed it as an act of war." This report also says that American schools are "drowning in a rising tide of mediocrity." Another major report, *Action for Excellence: A comprehensive plan to improve our schools* (Education Commission of the States, 1983), which appeared at about the same time, speaks of "a need for survival" and uses such terms as *emergency* and *urgency*. Intentional or not, the use of exaggeration and inflammatory language misleads the public.

## Unsound Recommendations

Many of these reports are flawed in terms of their recommendations. Because most of the reports were written by laypeople, most of whom are not educators, many of their recommendations are not educationally sound. For example, *A Nation at Risk* recommended both a longer school day and a longer school year. In other words, the critics were saying that the performance of the schools is mediocre (meaning "terribly poor"), so give us more of it. Most of the reports call for more math and science at the expense of the arts and humanities. Most appear to address the secondary curriculum on an assumption that whatever is good for secondary students and teachers is good for their elementary counterparts.

Few of the early reports addressed the fact that a large number of students are on drugs. Few addressed the fact that teachers are overworked. Few mentioned the need to discover ways of motivating students. Until recently, few of the reports mentioned the problems in society that must be addressed and overcome before the schools can reach their academic goals. Hodgkinson (1991, p. 10) lists some of these conditions:

- Since 1987, one-fourth of all preschool children in the U.S. have been in poverty.

- Every year, about 350,000 children are born to mothers who were addicted to cocaine during pregnancy. Those who survive birth become children with strikingly short attention spans, poor coordination, and much worse. Of course, the schools will have to teach these children, and getting such children ready for kindergarten costs around $40,000 each—about the same as for children with fetal alcohol syndrome.

- Today, 15 million children are being reared by single mothers, whose family income averages about $11,400 in 1988 dollars (within $1,000 of the poverty line). The average family income for a married couple with children is slightly over $34,000 a year.

- Twenty percent of America's preschool children have not been vaccinated against polio.

- The "Norman Rockwell" family—a working father, a housewife mother, and two children of school age—constitutes only 6% of U.S. households today.

- One-fourth of pregnant mothers receive no physical care of any sort during the crucial first trimester of pregnancy. About 20% of handicapped children would not be impaired had their mothers had one physical exam during the first trimester, which could have detected potential problems.

- At least two million school-age children have no adult supervision at all after school. Two million more are being reared by neither parent.
- On any given night, between 50,000 and 200,000 children have no home. (In 1988, 40% of shelter users were families with children).
- In 1987, child protection agencies received 2.2 million reports of child abuse or neglect—triple the number received in 1976.

See Table 1.1 for a summary of the criticisms of education reform.

## Positive Outcomes

With so many flaws in the way that education reform has been dealt with, one must wonder whether the overall results of education reform can be positive. This is a complex question whose answer depends to a great extent on teachers and other curriculum developers. When 11,000 public school teachers and administrators were asked whether, if properly implemented, the reform efforts in their state would improve the students' education, approximately two-thirds (63.7 percent) said yes (Kentucky Association of School Administrators, 1993). Some of the reform practices represent much improve-

Table 1.1   Summary of criticisms of education reform and implications for curricularists

| Criticism | Implications for Curricularists |
| --- | --- |
| Faulty conclusions | Curricularists must expose the myths that commonly develop when people are misinformed. |
| Promotion of the narrow goals of reform committees | Curricularists must constantly remind the public that the goals of education are many and varied. |
| Educationally unsound recommendations | Curricularists must use the research and literature to expose recommendations that are educationally unsound. |
| Failure to involve teachers, administrators, and professors in the development of educational reform. | Curricularists must find ways to become involved not only in the implementation of but also in the developmental stages.  This includes lobbying local legislators, attending general sessions, and writing letters to offer time and expertise. |
| Lack of research base | Curricularists must use the research and literature to guide their own work. This requires being a wise consumer of others' research and being involved in research studies. |

ment over current practices, yet ultimate success depends on the degree of support given by teachers.

Not all the outcomes of the reform reports have been negative. For example, the reforms have reaffirmed the importance of education in the public's mind. Consequently, in several states the level of financial support has been raised. Equally important, increased public awareness of the importance of education has raised the overall level of parent support. Increased parent participation is a necessity for maximum academic gains.

The education reform reports are also focusing teachers' attention on the broad curricula of the school as a whole. Historically, most teachers have not been concerned with curriculum development beyond their own classroom. Involvement in their school's total curriculum should enable teachers to avoid both lack of consistency and duplications between their classes and others, particularly in the classes students take during the years just prior to and just following a particular teacher's class.

## Administrators

During the 1980s and 1990s the level of involvement of school administrators in curriculum and instruction has reached heights unprecedented since the days of the one-room school. Research on effective schools has made educators aware of the need for administrators—particularly building principals—to be at the center of instructional and curriculum planning. Terrel Bell (1993, p. 597) has said, "It is futile to even try to improve a school if the leadership is lackluster."

## Other Changes

The reform movements are rapidly changing the roles and lives of teachers, administrators, parents, counselors, designated curriculum leaders, instructional supervisors, and students. Thousands of representatives from all these groups are responding to the demands of education reform in many ways, ranging from desperate panic in efforts to meet the reform challenges to absolute refusal to comply with reform requirements.

## Teacher Education

Teacher education colleges and departments have three major responsibilities in the education reform movement. First, they must prepare students who will be knowledgeable about the major reform practices in their state and skilled in implementing them. Effective implementation of school reform will place two requirements on teachers, designated curriculum directors, instructional supervisors, administrators, parents, and counselors: These educators and parents must (1) be comfortable with and confident in their ability to carry out the reforms, and (2) acquire and maintain a positive attitude toward the reform movement. Teacher education colleges and departments must provide their students with the opportunities to develop these necessary understandings, skills, and attitudes.

The second role of education colleges and departments is to help teachers assess the value of each reform practice for their school and students. Frankly, some of the reform practices should never have been implemented. Clark and Astuto (1994, p. 513) explain:

> Many of the reform initiatives that are currently most popular could be dismissed as ridiculous on their face if they were not devised and supported by apparently credible advocates.

The reform reports have used a lot of rhetoric. Many speak of needed "excellence" and increased "rigor." Some reports have convinced the public that the underlying cause of the perceived failure of American schools is weak teachers. Interestingly, a decade after *A Nation at Risk* was published, its initiator, Terrel Bell (1993, pp. 595,597) said:

> We have foolishly concluded that any problems with the levels of academic achievement have been caused by faulty schools staffed by inept teachers and by fixing the schools we can attain the levels of success we so desperately need in this decade.

Bell continued by saying:

> We also know that teacher leadership of and involvement in school improvement must become a more integral part of our plans.

But the reports have already affected the mind-sets of the public, and the public believes that our teacher education curriculum needs more rigor. Consequently, when the president of the National Council for Accreditation of Teacher Education (NCATE) polled the public (1990), two-thirds said that student performance would be improved if teachers were required to meet higher professional training standards. Although this unproven postulate may be true, educational research has shown that teachers suffer more from lack of knowledge and expertise in pedagogy than from a lack of more content knowledge.

The third major role of education colleges and departments in education reform is to help in-service teachers, administrators, curriculum developers, instructional supervisors, and counselors gear up to the reform requirements of their state. Teachers, in particular, hold the key to the success or failure of reforming the schools. Clark and Astuto (1994, p. 520) explain, "No one can reform our schools for us. If there is to be authentic reform in American education, it must be a grassroots movement."

## Identifying True Weaknesses

Current education reform efforts have resulted from perceived weaknesses in American schools. Although, as already stressed, some of these perceptions are dead wrong, some are not; some of the reform reports identify major weaknesses that permeate the schools. Separately and collectively, these weaknesses prevent American students from reaching their maximum potential. Correcting the condition will require some major curriculum adjustments within and beyond the classroom which, in turn, will require changing the ways teachers and other educators use the curriculum development process in their classrooms and in the school at large.

As you prepare to launch your own program to contribute to education reform, a logical way to begin your reform efforts is by examining the weaknesses in the current educational system. The following paragraphs discuss some of the areas that many educators say need to be improved.

## The Lack of a Research Base

At a time when the National Council for Accreditation of Teacher Education is requiring a sound knowledge base and a sound theoretical model, there is evidence that the public schools are ignoring these all-important issues. According to Egbert (1984, p. 14), "Teachers ignore research and overestimate the value of personal experience." When teachers ignore research, they forfeit the opportunity to bring maximum improvement into their classrooms. Brown (1990) has said that teachers do not base their planning on the factors that affect achievement. Too often, the major goal of teachers is to cover the required topics. This attitude has carried over to the students. The desperation of teachers to cover the material does not go unnoticed by students. Stefanich (1990, p. 50) explains, "They [students] view learning only as the acquisition of knowledge."

Teacher education colleges and departments must assume major responsibility for graduating students who are prepared as both conductors and consumers of research. These skills are prerequisite to developing an appreciation for research.

The relationship between the role of the schools and the way educators view research is ironic. From the perspective of the reconstructionist, a major role of the schools is to lead or shape society; yet society seems to be leading the schools in the use of research. It is unthinkable that the advancements that have been made in industry, architecture, business, agriculture, engineering, medicine, or any other profession could have come about without the major role of research.

Graduate curricula for educators reflect the importance of research to education in that almost all graduate degree programs require one or more courses in research, and most advanced graduate programs require all candidates to conduct their own research studies, usually in the form of a major thesis or dissertation. Unfortunately, such courses and assignments are too often viewed as obstacles to be overcome rather than tools to be developed and used in the schools. Even more critical, many undergraduate teacher education programs are devoid of research, either as a subject to be studied or as a project to be carried out.

## The Need for Structure

One theory that has been developed to explain the drop in American students' standardized test scores is the way students store new information (Van Gulick, 1990). This theory, *constructivism*, is explained by Markle, Johnston, Geer, and Meichtry (1990, p. 53):

> Constructivists describe learning in terms of building connections between prior knowledge and new ideas and claim that effective teaching helps students construct an organized set of concepts that relates new and old ideas.

If students are to learn to connect new information with existing understanding this will happen in response to purposeful planning by teachers. As Markle et al (1990) explain, teachers must give assignments that require students to describe the process they use to explore new content in relation to what they already know.

Although schools have many varied purposes (discussed in detail in Chapter 3), one major purpose recognized universally is to educate. One perception of education is that it is the process through which individuals learn to alter their environments and alter their own behavior to better cope with life situations. This process involves acquiring new information and changing that information into meaningful knowledge. Indeed, this is the purpose of curriculum content. *Content* may even be defined as the information that is selected to be changed later into useful knowledge. Similarly, activities are selected to become meaningful experiences to students. These processes will be discussed further in Chapter 7.

## QUESTIONS

1. What characteristics make some definitions of *curriculum* more useful in curriculum development than others?
2. What must teachers and others know about the process of curriculum development in order to enhance their school's reform efforts?
3. What must teachers and others know about education reform in their state in order to promote sound reform through curriculum development?
4. Considering your experience in schools, the definitions in this chapter, and your role in education, how would you define *curriculum*?
5. What are the strongest evidences of the power of the hidden curriculum that you have witnessed?
6. What would you find helpful to your efforts in conducting research at your school?
7. What must teachers and others know about human behavior, politics, and the nature of schools to garner the support of their colleagues in education reform?

8. What political factors in your school might inhibit or promote reform?

9. Among the reform practices or policies in your state, what features can you identify that will serve students' needs?

10. Can you identify features in reform efforts in your area that can be used to meet the special needs of minority students? If so, what are these features, and how can they be used more effectively toward this end?

11. Describe any elements in your school's hidden curriculum that militate against the success of minority students or education reform. For each element, tell how you might alter the effect of the hidden curriculum.

12. How can your faculty increase its political influence on education reform in your state and district?

## SUGGESTED FURTHER ACTIVITIES

1. Select a topic in your teaching field and identify and list the major concepts in a week's lessons.

2. Research the literature on effective schools and make a list of the qualities common to these schools.

3. Select an important concept in your teaching field, preferably one that students find difficult to comprehend, and devise a step-by-step method to help students relate this concept to prior knowledge.

4. Examine the list of definitions of *curriculum* in Figure 1.1. Choose one of these definitions or create your own definition.

5. Assess your reasons for taking this course and identify at least two important professional aims or goals that will give you direction and motivation throughout the course.

6. Examine the list of reasons the Eastwood Middle School naysayers give as to why teachers resist school reform and restate each reason, making it a reason to support school reform.

7. Interview a local school superintendent, principal, or counselor and get a list of the major education reform laws in your state. Select one or more of these practices that you would like to support. Between now and the end of this course, build a strong case of support for this reform practice.

8. Develop a strategy to increase your faculty's political influence in your community and state.

## BIBLIOGRAPHY

*Action for excellence: A comprehensive plan to improve our nation's schools* (1983). Denver, CO.: Education Commission of the States.

Apple, M. (1979). *Ideology and curriculum*. Boston: Routledge & Kegan.

Beauchamp, G. A. (1981). *Curriculum theory* (4th ed). Itasca, IL: Peacock Publishers.

Bell, T. H. (1993). Reflections one decade after 'A Nation at Risk.' *Phi Delta Kappan, 74*(8), 592–600.

Bracey, G. W. (1991). Why can't they be like we were? *Phi Delta Kappan, 73*(2), 104–117.

Brown, D. S. (1990). Middle level teachers' perceptions of action research. *Middle School Journal, 22*(2), 30–32.

Caswell, H. L., & Campbell, D. S. (1935). *Curriculum development*. New York: American Book Company.

Clark, D. L. & Astuto, T. A. (1994). Redirecting reform: Challenges to popular assumptions about teachers and students. *Phi Delta Kappan, 75*(7), 513–520.

Cook, A. (1994, January). Who's story gets told? Rethinking research on schools. *Education Week, 13*(17), 48.

Des Dixon, R. G. (1994). Future schools and how to get there from here. *Phi Delta Kappan, 75*(5), 360–365.

Doll, R. (1989). *Curriculum improvement: Decision making and process* (7th ed.). Boston: Allyn & Bacon.

Egbert, R. L. (1984). The role of research in teacher education. In R. L. Egbert & M. M. Kluender (Eds.), *Using research to improve teacher education*. Lincoln, NE: American Association of Colleges for Teacher Education.

Foshay, A. W. (1969). Changing interpretations of the elementary curriculum. In H. G. Shane (Ed.), *The American elementary school*. Thirteenth yearbook of the John Dewey Society.

Fullan, M. G. (1993). Why teachers must become change agents. *Educational Leadership, 50*(6), 12–17.

Gay, Geneva (1990). Achieving educational equality through curriculum desegregation. *Phi Delta Kappan, 72*(1), 61–62.

Gough, P. B. (1993). A view from the outside. *Phi Delta Kappan, 74*(9), 669.

Henson, K. T. (1986). America's public schools: A look at the reports. *USA Today, 114*, 75–77.

Hodgkinson, H. (1991). Reform vs. reality. *Phi Delta Kappan, 73*(1), 9–16.

Hutchins, R. M. (1936). *The higher learning in America*. New Haven: Yale University Press.

Kentucky Association of School Administrators (1993).

Macdonald, J. B. & Leeper, R. R. (Eds.) (1965). *Theories of instruction*. Alexandria, VA: Association for Supervision and Curriculum Development, 5–6.

Markle, G., Johnston, J. H., Geer, C., & Meichtry, Y. (1990). Teaching for understanding. *Middle School Journal, 22*(2), 53–57.

McNeil, J. D. (1990). *Curriculum: A comprehensive introduction.* New York: HarperCollins.

National Center for Education Statistics, *The condition of education 1990, Vol. 1. Elementary and Secondary Education.* Washington, DC: U.S. Department of Education, p. 9.

National Commission on Excellence in Education (1983). *A Nation at Risk.*

National Council for Accreditation of Teacher Education (1990). Standards, procedures, and policies for the accreditation of professional units. Washington, DC: NCATE.

Oliva, P. F. (1992). *Developing the curriculum* (3rd ed.). New York: HarperCollins.

Phenix, P. H. (1962). The disciplines as curriculum content. In Harry Passow (Ed.). New York: Columbia University Teachers College Press.

Popham, W. J., and Baker, E. L. (1970). *Systematic instruction.* Englewood Cliffs, NJ: Prentice-Hall.

Saylor, J. G., and Alexander, W. M. (1966). *Curriculum planning for modern schools.* New York: Holt, Rinehart, and Winston.

Schlechty, P. C. (1990). *Schools for the 21st century: Leadership imperatives for educational reform.* San Francisco: Jossey-Bass Publishers.

Schubert, W. H. (1986). *Curriculum: Perspective, paradigm, and possibility.* New York: Macmillan.

Smith, B. O., Stanley, W. O., and Shores, J. H. (1957). *Fundamentals of curriculum development: Renewal.* New York: Harcourt, Brace, Jovanovich.

Stefanich, G. P. (1990). Cycles of cognition. *Middle School Journal, 22*(2), 47–52.

Taba, Hilda (1962). *Curriculum development: Theory and practice.* New York: Harcourt, Brace, Jovanovich.

Tanner, D. (1993). A nation "truly" at risk. *Phi Delta Kappan, 75*(4), 288–297.

Tanner, D., & Tanner, L. N. (1980). *Curriculum development: Theory into practice.* New York: Macmillan.

Van Gulick, R. (1990). "Functionalism, information, and content." In W. G. Lylcan (Ed.). *Mind and cognition.* Cambridge, MA: Basil Blackwell.

Wiles, J. & Bondi, Joseph (1993). *Curriculum development: A guide to practice* (4th ed.). New York: Macmillan.

Wynne, E. A. and Ryan, K. (1993). *Reclaiming our schools: A handbook on teaching character, academics, and discipline.* New York: Macmillan.

Zais, R. S. (1976). *Curriculum principles and foundations.* New York: Harper & Row.

# Chapter 2

# SOCIAL AND TECHNOLOGICAL FOUNDATIONS

*Life at school and life outside school are simply too far apart. We need to go back, then, and build up anew from the foundations of democratic values, social realities, and our knowledge of human growth and development.*

LOUNSBURY, 1991, P. 3

## OBJECTIVES

This chapter should prepare you to:

- Apply the statement "The school is a microcosm of the community and of society at large" to curriculum development.
- Identify a unique goal of American schools and explain how this goal has helped shape curricula.
- Give an example of how a school's culture affects its curriculum.
- Defend the need for multicultural education in schools.
- Explain how the education reform practice "teacher empowerment" has enhanced teachers' ability to change the entire school.
- Assess your technological comfort level.
- Broaden your ability to apply technology to curriculum development at your school.
- Apply technology to multicultural concerns.

## LINDA BLEVINS' FIRST YEAR OF TEACHING

Linda Blevin was in her senior year in college before she began to consider the job options that her major offered. She had chosen economics because she enjoyed studying it. Upon graduating, Linda accepted the first position for which she had been interviewed, in the home mortgage division of a local bank.

Linda found that her major had prepared her well for this job. From the beginning, she found the work easy. But by the end of her second year, she was extremely bored. Linda spent each day involved with paperwork, and she missed being around people. She decided to return to school and obtain a master of arts in teaching (MAT) degree. Since she lived in the inner city and depended on the city buses for transportation, Linda felt fortunate that a university extension center was located only a few blocks from her apartment.

The program had a major classroom observation component which was designed to permit students to observe in a number of different classrooms. In the first school she visited, the student body was composed of 90 percent minority students. About half the students were Afro-Americans, but as she looked about in each classroom, Linda saw that a number of other ethnic groups were represented in most classes.

Linda was shocked by the first class she visited. The lack of order and control was surprising, but the teacher was more of a surprise than the students. Marvin Watts was a cigar-smoking, overweight white man who, Linda quickly deduced, had been hired because of his size and self-confidence. It was immediately obvious that the man feared nothing. In one of their first conferences, Watts told her that his goal was to get through each day and each school year. "You see," he said, "It would be different if these kids wanted to learn, but they don't. Hey, half of them are on dope or booze. The other half will drop out. Look at it this way, teachers are hired to keep these kids off the streets and out of the prisons, which, as you know, are already overfull.

"Let me give you a little advice. Today you hear all this reform jargon. Let me tell you something: Most of these reports were written by politicians who have no idea what the real world is all about. I mean, have you seen the Goals for 2000? Give me a break. Half of these kids are on crack, and even they aren't as spacey as the President and the governors responsible for that report. The schools will be drug-free by the year 2000! Yeah, sure they will. They talk about turning over the school to the parents and site-based councils. Most of these kids don't *have* parents. Those that do don't speak enough English to order a meal at McDonalds. Could you imagine asking them if they think the curriculum should be integrated? They would probably think they had been insulted. And they're supposed to help their kids with their education. That's a joke. The kids who do have parents go home and help them!"

Linda noticed two Asian students who sat at the same table each day. Neither paid any attention to Watts as he lectured in a monotone. She could understand their choosing to ignore Watts, for that was her own method of tolerating his dull lectures, but she didn't understand why he was willing to ignore them, until she had an opportunity to ask.

"It's simple," Watts replied, "They don't understand a word of English. The sup will probably ship them to another school if he ever gets around to it. Right now, they're just as well off here as they would be anywhere else."

At first, Linda was appalled at this attitude. In a way Watts was OK. At least he was honest. But how could he be so irresponsible? Linda was angry. Later, her shock and anger melted into concern. All she could think about were the waste and the unfairness to these students. If they didn't prepare for the future while here at school, how would they ever improve their lot in life? Linda knew the answer to that question.

Linda also noticed that she could count the different ethnic groups in any room because the members of each group seemed to be drawn to each other like drops of oil on water. Watts showed no concern over how the students arranged themselves in groups.

Once she overcame her shock at the lack of respect these students showed to the teacher, and to each other, Linda began to notice that none of the strategies she had learned about in her recent college courses were evidenced in any of the classrooms in this school. It was as though topics such as curriculum alignment, valued outcomes, research-based teaching, metacognition, research-based curriculum, authentic assessment, performance evaluation, and, yes, cultural pluralism had never penetrated the walls of this school or the heads of any of its teachers.

Back at the university, Linda was able to relate each topic she studied there to the classrooms she had observed. She could see that, once she graduated, and if she decided to remain in this community (and that was a big if ), the culture of the schools would militate against her efforts to implement the curriculum and instructional strategies she was learning. Although she wanted to help bring about change, she wondered whether she could fight the powerful forces of tradition that permeated this school and community.

Knowing that first-year teachers are often viewed with a jaundiced eye, Linda wanted to avoid being perceived as an overzealous novice who expects to save the world. She believed that she needed a strategy that would provide gradual, long-lasting improvement for all students without alienating her fellow teachers. But she didn't know how to begin developing such a plan.

Maximum effectiveness of all school personnel, including teachers and other curriculum developers, requires an understanding of the context in which a school resides. First, context refers to a school's physical surroundings. A school located in a small, rural community does not have the advantages and disadvantages of an urban ghetto school. Maximum effectiveness in either setting requires planning to (1) capitalize on the resources of the community and (2) overcome the community's weaknesses.

## SOCIAL FOUNDATIONS

We are taught that a school is, theoretically, a microcosm of the local community and of society at large. Most teachers in urban schools find little comfort in this statement. But, as Wood (1990, p. 33) reminds us, our schools are microcosms of good communities only when we work to make them so:

> We take for granted that our schools are communities, when, in fact, they are merely institutions that can become communities only when we work at it.

Shouse (1992, p. 105) expresses this relationship another way:

> The world is an enlarged school, or the school is an epitomized world, as you please to say it. But there must be a distinction. The social conditions under which these things are done constitute the dividing line between school world and non-school world.

Although people tend to think of the uniqueness of each school as arising from the subjects taught and the activities pursued, these comments by Shouse assure us that the uniqueness comes from these elements and more.

Each school, like each community, has its unique culture. *Culture* has been defined as "an invisible framework of standards representing beliefs and values that are perceived as having worked well in the past" (Kowalski & Reitzug, 1993, p. 159) and as simply, "the way we do things around here" (Tice, 1994, p. 48). Culture is the social glue that binds together the many elements of a school or a society. A school's culture can make the school an enjoyable place to be or it can make the students' world a constant nightmare. It can welcome ethnic diversity, or it can harbor and nurture prejudices. It can stimulate minds, or it can anesthetize entire beings.

Each generation must examine the culture of its schools and of its communities. Teachers and other curricularists must realize that the culture and the curriculum of a school are tied to the culture of the community and society. Cohen (1990, p. 518) explains:

> First, the curriculum has not just now gone public. Decision making about curriculum has, at least intermittently, been public and political in the U.S. from the outset, though education and researchers and many professionals convinced themselves for a time that it ought not to be. In fact, political controversy over curriculum is as old as public education.

Lieberman (1990) provides some examples of community changes that conservatives usually talk about (poverty, hopelessness, deteriorating urban life, and a growing multicultural population). Lieberman cautions educators to look beyond the effects these changes have on content and also to consider the effects that community changes have on the culture of a school and on the culture of the classrooms.

## Importance of Society-School Relationship

The relationship between the school and society is important in at least two general ways. First, many Americans believe that the school has some responsibility for shaping society. The degree to which the school should affect society is a value judgment. Social reconstructionists believe that schools are responsible for improving the society totally and continuously. But social reconstructionists are extremists, and many people question the idea that the school's role in changing society is so potent.

At the opposite extreme are those who believe that the school's primary role is to conserve society. These people would have society return to the "good ol' days."

Whether one believes that the schools should change society or should preserve society, most people recognize that the schools should affect society. Perhaps most people would agree that the schools should protect some qualities and change others.

The second major relationship between the school and society is the sum total of effects that society has on the schools. Oana (1993, p. 5) has poignantly expressed the powerful influence the community has on the schools:

> The problem is, today's schools, no matter how much they change, cannot cope with all the social ills its clients bring to their doors each day.

For teachers to think that it is possible to ignore society and shape their curricula as they, the teachers—the professional educators—know it should be shaped is to be blind to reality. As Apple (1990, p. 526) has bluntly stated, "Whether we recognize it or not, curriculum and more general educational issues in the U.S. have always been caught up in the history of class, race, gender, and religious relations."

A clear understanding of the relationship between the schools and the society begins with the realization that the school is an institution that was created by and for society, and furthermore, that the school is an institution that is supported by the society. Teachers and other educators who refuse to recognize that the community owns and supports the schools will inevitably get into trouble. In his book *The Water Is Wide*, Pat Conroy (1972) illustrates this point clearly. Describing his failure to understand this relationship, Conroy, when a first-year teacher, refused to heed the advice of his supervisor who forbade him to take his islander students to the South Carolina mainlands to celebrate Halloween. His students had never been trick-or-treating and he thought they should have the opportunity to experience this custom first hand. But, cautioning him not to make the trip, the supervisor told him, "Son, I can replace you just as easily as replacing a light bulb." And he did. Conroy, an excellent teacher who loved his students and his job, was fired. As an instrument of society, the school must work for and with the community.

It would be simple if the teacher's responsibility were only to the employer, (i.e., the society), but it isn't, because the school was also created for another purpose: to serve the students. Thus teachers must serve two masters: the society and the students. The two are not always compatible. On the contrary, serving society may be, and frequently is, in direct conflict with the teacher's responsibility for serving the students.

## How the School Influences the Society

The tension between the need to serve the society and the need to serve the students can be seen by examining the school's purposes. Some of the traditional and still important purposes of the school are citizenship, intellectualism, and vocational preparation (see Figure 2.1).

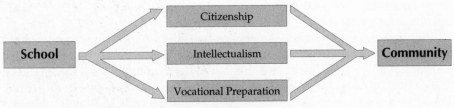

**Figure 2.1** Some ways schools influence society.

## Citizenship

More than 2000 years ago Aristotle stressed the need to guide the development of citizenship in youth. To Thomas Jefferson, an educated citizen was indispensable to a democratic society. Remember Thomas Jefferson's famous words:

> If a nation expects to be ignorant and free in a state of civilization it expects what never was and what never will be.

The Seven Cardinal Principles of Secondary Education, which apply also to elementary schools, affirm citizenship as an important aim for the nation's schools. Indeed, one of the seven principles *is* citizenship. Although few people would question the value of this aim for American schools, many disagree over what the aim encompasses. Some of the more generally accepted responsibilities of schools in developing citizenship are the:

teaching of social studies

development of national allegiance

acquiring of skills

development of a desire to protect society

development of a desire to improve society

development of social responsibility

development of moral values

Some of these responsibilities might be met indirectly through the hidden curriculum (discussed in Chapter 1).

## Intellectualism

In his familiar quote, Jefferson used the word *ignorant*, the opposite of *intellectual*. The pursuit of wisdom is as old as philosophy itself, and, as we shall see in Chapter 3, wisdom and philosophy are inseparable. During the golden age of Greece, the belief in the value of knowledge for the sake of knowledge was common. Throughout the civilized world, intellectualism is still prized. In the United States, a country that has always been known for its strong emphasis on pragmatism, intellectualism is often viewed suspiciously unless it leads directly to practical ends.

But through their history, Americans have been dedicated to serving individual students. Their values are reflected in the percentage of the nation's youths served by its schools, and they are reflected in the Goals for 2000. The first of these goals is for *all* children in the United States to be ready for school. The second goal is to raise the high school graduation rate to 90 percent by the year 2000.

Mary Antin, the daughter of European immigrants, understood this unique, education-for-all goal of American schools. Mary Antin was unable to speak English, but this did not prevent her from attending the Boston public schools. Later, reflecting on her experience, she wrote (1912, p. 186):

> Education was free . . . it was the only thing my father was able to promise us when he sent for us; surer, safer than bread or shelter. On our second day I was thrilled with the realization of what this freedom of education meant. A little girl from across the alley came and offered to conduct us to school. My father was out, but we five between us had a few words of English by this time. We knew the word school. We understood this child—who had never seen us until yesterday, who could not pronounce our names, who was not much better dressed than we—was able to offer us the freedom of the schools of Boston. No application made, no questions asked, no examinations, rulings, exclusions, no machinations, no fees. The doors stood open for every one of us.

This historically unprecedented commitment to all students, coupled with the belief that intellectual superiority is essential to maintaining national security and a strong national economy, has given contemporary Americans a revived appreciation for the indispensable need for intellectualism in the schools. The language used in the reform reports of the 1980s and early 1990s reflects this feeling. Two of the most frequent adjectives used in the more than 400 reports are *rigor* and *excellence*.

## Vocational Preparation

The first American school was established to prepare young men for entrance into Harvard College, where they would study for the clergy. The vocational role of the school was reaffirmed in 1918 by the Seven Cardinal Principles of Secondary Education, which were written for all grade levels including elementary. In the United States, the vocational force is so strong that students at all levels often give as a reason for taking particular classes the fact that it is required for graduation; and their reason for wanting to graduate is to increase their ability to get a job and earn more money.

During the 1980s and early 1990s, the impact of business and industry on the curriculum increased substantially. Apple (1990, p. 526) addresses this influence:

> The public debate on education and on all social issues has shifted profoundly to the right in the past decade. The effects of this shift can be seen in the number of trends now gaining momentum nationally . . . the often-effective assault

on the school curriculum for its supposed biases against the family and free enterprise . . . and the consistent pressure to make the needs of business and industry the primary concerns of the education system.

But the role of the worker has changed drastically during the past decade, shifting from Taylorism (breaking each job down into small parts and closely supervising the worker to ensure that each function is performed precisely according to instructions) to group problem solving. Arthur Wirth (1993, p. 1) has described a major contrast between the aims of educators during the early 1990s and the world-connected, group-oriented, problem-solving skills that future work will require of employees. He says:

> Under Secretary Bennett's banner of "back to basics" and test score account-
> ability, the 1980s produced the hyper-rationalization that Arthur Wise warned
> us about in *Legislated Learning: The Bureaucratization of the American Classroom.*
> For example, an action by the Texas legislature made Texas teachers subject to
> a $50 fine if they were caught teaching reading without an approved textbook,
> and legislators in Florida passed a law making basal materials "the only legal
> means to provide reading instruction." With regard to role models, we were
> given Joe Clark, the New Jersey principal who got improved performance with
> a bullhorn, a baseball bat, and school expulsions. The Report Card on Basal
> Readers (Goodman, et al, 1988, p. 33), funded by the National Council of
> Teachers of English, said that the style of the 1980s was based, more than any-
> thing else, on control: "to control reading, to control language, to control learn-
> ers, to control teachers. And this control becomes essential to tight organiza-
> tion and sequence. Any relaxation of the control in any of these elements
> would appear to undermine the whole system." What was being described
> was, in short, the centralized model of bureaucratic control. Just as so many of
> the corporate giants in industry had eventually discarded this model, the
> movement to adopt it in education faltered. At the end of the 1980s Lauro
> Cavazos (Cooper, 1989), Bennett's successor, acknowledged, "We tried to im-
> prove education by imposing regulations from the top down, while leaving
> the basic structure of the school untouched. Obviously, that hasn't worked."

In contrast, modern businesses are turning away from the race to outpro-duce international competition and are using satellites, facsimile machines, and computer modems to solve problems. Robert Reich's book *The Work of Nations: Preparing Ourselves for 21st Century Capitalism* (1991, p. 224—233) iden-tifies four worker skills that will be required in the future:

- Abstraction—the capacity to order and make meaning of the massive flow of information, to shape raw data into workable patterns
- System thinking—the capacity to see the parts in relation to the whole, to see why problems arise
- Experimental inquiry—the capacity to set up procedures to test and eval-uate alternative ideas
- Collaboration—the capacity to engage in active communication and dia-logue to get a variety of perspectives and to create consensus when that is necessary.

## How the Society Influences the School

Both society and the schools are in a continuous state of change. The relative power of social forces affecting the schools shifts, and the relative power that the schools have to shape society also waxes and wanes, requiring teachers and other curriculum directors to be constantly aware of the society-school relationship. Although the relationship between the schools and society is symbiotic, the schools have the responsibility for monitoring the social forces that affect them and for seizing the opportunities the schools have to affect the community. Stated differently, at any time, teachers, administrators, and other curriculum developers should be able to foresee obstacles and opportunities and should change the curriculum accordingly.

Too frequently, school personnel have remained passive and reactive, going about their daily business without concern for the world around them. The result, of course, is that instead of presenting a steady positive image of their profession, educators always seem to be reacting and defending themselves and the schools.

At this time, some important changes teachers and other curriculum developers should be extremely concerned over and should be adjusting the curriculum to accommodate are: (1) poverty, (2) breakdown of the family, (3) drug abuse, (4) multiculturalism, (5) opportunities to use classroom research, and (6) opportunities to use technology in the curriculum.

Since the early 1980s the states have dramatically increased the requirements made on elementary and secondary curricula. The first time a governor pushed through a major statewide education reform law was in 1982, when Mississippi governor William Winter called a special legislative session to deal with education reform. The result, House Bill 4, required several major changes in Mississippi's schools. As Pipho (1992, p. 278) notes:

> The bill called for a state-supported kindergarten program, changes in the compulsory attendance ages, a teacher aide program for reading in the first three grades, salary increases for teachers, fines for parents who did not comply with compulsory attendance laws, changes in school accreditation and teacher certification, the establishment of a large board of education to choose a state superintendent of education, and increases in sales and income taxes to raise $110 million in new funds to pay for the reform package.

This bill, which brought about the Accountability in Instructional Management (AIM) program (mentioned in Chapter 1), required every district in the state to develop a new grade 1–12 curriculum in every subject. Since this first school reform step, every state in the country has put forth massive efforts to change its elementary and secondary schools. In every state, successfully changing the schools—if it occurs—requires changing the curricula.

Education reform is making monumental changes in the way programs are developed. Most of these changes are long overdue, for example, increasing the level of involvement of teachers and parents in curriculum development. The benefit of involving teachers and parents in planning is substantiated by research. O'Neal, Earley, and Snider (1991, p. 123) report that:

> Research has constantly indicated that parent and family involvement is critical to the academic success of many children.

To better meet the needs of children and teenagers, some states' education reform programs are creating child care and teen centers. This approach is supported by research. Even the practice of validation through research is part of many reform programs; some state reform programs require teachers to select and use methods that have been validated by research.

Solomon (1989, p. 63) has offered some specific suggestions for teachers to use to guide parents who want to help their children. Referring specifically to helping parents help their children with their homework, Solomon says:

> Teachers should encourage parents to: (1) set a definite time for study each day with a beginning and ending time and no interruptions; (2) provide the proper environment; (3) provide the materials needed; (4) require the student to organize school materials including books, notes, assignments, and papers; (5) require a daily list of homework assignments; and (6) provide support and guidance if the child becomes discouraged or frustrated.

If parent involvement in curriculum development is to occur, it must be planned for from the outset.

## Societal Forces that Affect the Curriculum

At any given moment, there are many forces working to keep the school curriculum the way it is and many counterforces aimed at changing it. Many of these forces come from various components of society. Some of the most important forces that are always at work are tradition, textbooks, laws, religious beliefs, multicultural concerns, poverty, the expansion of knowledge, and growth in technology (see Figure 2.2).

### Tradition

One of the oldest and strongest forces in any society is tradition. Although we might think of tradition as being a dominant force in primitive societies, it is also a major influence in civilized societies, including our own culture.

When teachers try to introduce change at their schools, often the first resistance they hear is the voice of tradition.

"But we've never done that at this school."

"It will never work."

"They won't like it." (*They* is seldom defined).

"The administration will never buy it."

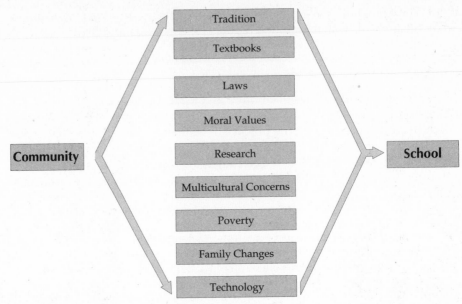

**Figure 2.2** Some ways society influences the schools.

Often, tradition is a stumbling block to progress. New ideas are not given a chance because of fear of failure or a fear of the unknown.

Lowell C. Rose (1991, p. 128), executive director of Phi Delta Kappa, pinpointed the paralyzing effect that tradition has on schools when he said:

> Schools are cautious and confusing places where teachers, principals, and students try to create islands of safety and sanity for themselves and are reluctant to leave those safe shores for parts unknown.

Since teachers, principals, students, and even the school itself are part of the community at large, it is not surprising that the powers of tradition are at work inside the school as well as in the outside community.

But tradition affects the schools in positive ways as well. It acts as a stabilizer, preventing "change for the sake of change"; in doing so, it protects the tried and proven. For example, consider the massive reform movements that are reshaping the curricula in all states. Some necessary questions are: Is this particular reform practice good? What evidence is available to show that it works? What evidence suggests otherwise? Do we really need this reform? Why? One commonly heard answer is: "Because the Japanese are doing it." But is this a sound reason for change? In explaining the views of traditionalists, McNeil (1990, p. 4) tells us:

> Americans place a premium on innovation and creativity. Thus it is a mistake for educators in the United States to respond to competition from Japan by initiating the Japanese curriculum with its emphasis upon shaping a whole population to a high level of rigorous discipline and its focus upon the same basic

academic subjects for all. Although in Japan the average amount of learning is higher, the range of knowledge is narrower, and Japanese educators themselves are uneasy about Japan's emphasis on rote learning at the expense of critical thinking. Instead of adopting curriculum so that pupils score higher on multiple-choice examinations, Americans should be concerned with maintaining their advantage in creativity, problem-solving skills, and innovation.

For further examination of change for the sake of change, see the case at the beginning of Chapter 5.

## *Textbooks*

Through the years the textbook has been the number one curriculum determiner. There are multiple reasons for the textbook's ability not only to survive for almost 400 years but to remain the most powerful curriculum determiner throughout the centuries. One explanation for this success and longevity is the textbook's availability. One has only to teach or study abroad to realize that in the United States the textbook is so accessible that it is taken for granted. Teachers and students alike are expected to have their own copies of the textbooks used in their classes. This makes the issuing of reading assignments very easy.

A second advantage that has contributed to the textbook's impact is organization. Most textbooks are organized so that the content in each chapter builds on the content in previous chapters. This makes organization of the class easy for teachers who use required textbooks. Even in classes where a syllabus is required, the textbook often provides the pattern for the sequencing of the syllabus.

A somewhat different service provided by the textbook is the opportunity it offers for teachers to demonstrate their expertise. By mastering the stable content in the textbook and then lecturing, chapter by chapter, the teacher can demonstrate expertise in content and organization. (This is in no way a criticism of teachers who wish to have their expertise recognized. In fact, when students are aware of a teacher's expertise, the teacher gains power. Further, students expect and want their teachers to have mastery over the content they teach.)

The textbook also makes test construction easy and defensible. By requiring a text, and then using the text to construct the tests, a teacher can defend the questions on the tests. Even when the teacher fails to address some of the topics in class, the teacher is still protected. When questioned about the content validity of the test, the teacher can respond, "It was taken from the assigned readings in the text."

Clearly, some of these qualities are true strengths of the textbook; other qualities are of questionable value. Notice that no attempt is being made here to describe the textbook as being good or bad, and no attempt is being made to present a balanced analysis of the strengths and weaknesses of textbooks. Rather, we are offering some of the reasons why the textbook has had, and in all probability will continue to have, a powerful influence on the curriculum in American schools.

## Laws

The influence of textbooks on the school may go unnoticed by many people, but this is not true of laws. The states make most of the laws that set requirements at each grade level. The federal government decides how many units (also called *Carnegie units*) of each subject are required for graduation from high school. Each state has latitude in placing these required units at different grade levels and in adding other graduation requirements. The federal government is having an increasing influence over the curriculum.

The power of legislation affecting schools is not constant. During one era, federal laws may be the dominating social force on schools. During another era, state laws, local developments, or other influences may dominate. For example, during the mid-1950s, the *Brown v. Board of Education* decision, which required integration in the public schools, was perhaps the strongest force affecting the curriculum. In 1975 Public Law 94-142 (Education for all Handicapped Children) dominated. During another era, increased funding or the absence of funding may be the overriding force shaping the schools. For example, during the 1980s, lack of finances caused the school year to be shortened in parts of West Virginia and Florida. The Elementary and Secondary Education Act of 1965 was the most influential of any law on education in the 1960s.

## Moral Values

Ever since the first American school was established to prepare students for admission to a divinity college, religion has been a force shaping the curriculum. At times, the question of how much influence religion should have on the curriculum has caused controversy in the community. On some occasions, the controversy has been so serious as to draw the attention of the entire nation, as was the case with the Scopes trial (or the so-called monkey trial) in Tennessee in 1925.

A deterioration of the moral fiber in the United States has made the moral responsibilities of schools a special concern to some educators. For example, John Lounsbury (1991, p. 5), a longtime leader in the National Middle Schools Association, says:

> I believe further that unless America can be brought to a deeper appreciation of the place of values, attitudes, and the affective domain in public education, reform efforts will fall short of the success so desperately needed in this last decade of the twentieth century. Unfortunately people continue to talk about training, performance on tests, mastery of discrete subjects, and grades, as if these were the beginnings and ends of education.

Education in its fullest sense has to involve heart as well as mind, attitude as well as information, spirit as well as scholarship. That our nation is suffering from moral leukemia is hard to deny. Our easy sophistication and ample affluence have encouraged much inconsequential living that does little to enable humankind, but much to advance hedonism. Eisenhower rightly warned us that "A people that values its privileges above its principles soon loses both." And we are dangerously close to that time. Our educational practices have compounded that decline problem by over-emphasizing the knowledge acquisition objective of education and virtually ignoring any official way the more important behavioral objectives, other than to report on "conduct," defined simply as the absence of overt misbehavior.

Lounsbury is not alone in his perception of society's moral decline. The schools must share some of the blame for the current state of affairs because they no longer emphasize character development as they did for more than two hundred years. Audrey Cohen (1993, p. 791) addresses this concern:

Today, with parts of the American education system in disarray, the entire nation is politically, socially, and economically under siege. How many of our current problems, we must ask, derive from too many years of a bankrupt or near-sighted approach to learning? The focus of education—elementary, secondary, and postsecondary—has steadily narrowed decade by decade. The commitment to education as a training in character has vanished.

Lounsbury (1991, p. 5) gives some examples of values that are prized by civilizations throughout the world, values that he says should be everyday features in our schools; yet he warns against the schools dictating particular values.

We need classrooms in which beauty is savored, truth honored, compassion practiced, and fellowship honored; classrooms where creativity is encouraged, where youngsters are assisted in dreaming of a better life; classrooms that are laboratories of living rather than places where teachers stand and talk and students sit and listen. . . . The school must not attempt to dictate a particular set of values, but must assist young adolescents in exploring their values, attitudes, and standards.

These comments exemplify the paradox involved in the curriculum's role in teaching values. Morality is indispensable and merely to provide definitions of *value* is not enough. Theodore Roosevelt said, "To educate a man in mind and not in morals is to educate a menace to society."

G. A. Davis (1993, p. 32) gives credence to Lounsbury's words of caution:

Schools always have taught values and always will. Values relating to patriotism, hygiene, and health, appreciation for the sciences, the arts, one's culture, and education itself are common substance for effective education in the classroom. Other values are equally non-controversial and warrant teaching: honesty, responsibility, trustworthiness, a sense of fairness, and respect for the rights and property of others. Recently, values pertaining to cocaine use, AIDS prevention, and gang violence have become high priorities in many districts.

Although some of these values can be considered to be religious values more than others, and each of us has stronger feelings about some beliefs than others, most teachers would probably agree that the schools share some of the responsibility for influencing these values.

Perhaps the cry for more emphasis on values and morals could be described as a cry for a return to basics. For, indeed, at the beginning of the century socialization was deemed by many people to be a more important function of the schools than intellectual development. As Schlecty (1990, p. 18) says, "By the early twentieth century, and perhaps even more so by the 1930s, many thought that the "real" purpose of schools was to serve as an engine of social reform. Certainly, the practices in many of today's schools would be shocking to those who hold the schools accountable for the welfare of society.

## The Future

### Research

This book stresses the need for research-based decisions in education, but therein lies a trap. The design of most educational studies is correlational, not causal. Consequently, research findings do not always lend themselves to linear application. A second trap can be the tendency of consumers to focus on research that supports a favored practice. Special effort is needed to report and use studies that question the favored positions.

Of equal concern is the contemporary practice of focusing only on studies that examine effects on test scores. Interestingly, when W. J. Burke spent a sabbatical leave interviewing national teacher of the year finalists from a seven-year period, he learned that all 54 finalists attributed their success to their relationships with students and, in particular, to their ability to transmit a sense of efficacy to each student. Burke wrote in his 1967 book *Not for Glory*:

> I could close my eyes and re-create the sights and sounds, the words, faces and atmosphere of those adventures in friendship. My micro-scopic examination of fifty-four separate school systems encouraged me to believe that nothing in American life can match the vigor and importance of the classroom confrontation of minds. Therein lies our future. There is no turning back. The kinds of teachers I met are not content to look upon education as something finished. No teacher, no American, can afford that luxury.

The qualities Burke describes do not appear on test scores. Such widespread testimony of the need to consider non-test-related measures of achievement is too convincing to be ignored.

Eisner (1985, p. 27) perceives the dependence on quantitative test scores to be so extreme that he used the term *scientism* to describe the current overemphasis on tests. Scientism refers to the belief that everything that exists can be understood through the same methods, that there is only one legitimate way to verify knowledge of the world, and that unless something can be quantified it cannot be truly understood or known. In fact, Eisner lists "Faith in scientism as applied to education" as one of the six major forces affecting the curriculum.

Unfortunately, a broad focus will result only if curriculum workers insist on gathering and using qualitative data in their decision making. Every nation, every state, and every institution needs a stabilizer to keep it on course and headed in a chosen direction. Tradition is a common example of such a stabilizer. Without such a stabilizer, we will discard the good along with the bad as we take up first one practice and then another.

## Multicultural Concerns

In recent years, no social issue has concerned educators more than multicultural issues. Multicultural education became a major concern during the 1960s and remained a central focus of curriculum attention throughout the 1970s. Interest waned during the 1980s but has increased to become a leading issue of the 1990s (Reed, 1994). One way to view the multicultural concerns of teachers is to recognize that students from minority backgrounds live in two very different worlds. The lack of harmony between these worlds (or cultures) can cause continuous problems for minority students. Each culture has certain expectations of the student; these expectations can be mutually exclusive; and the demands can be imposed directly or indirectly. Indirect expectations are perhaps the more difficult because they consist of conflicting forces, which make conflicting demands on students. Glatthorn (1993, p. 381) explains the results of these opposing or conflicting forces:

> The best way to think about these children and youth is not to consider them "disadvantaged" or "culturally deprived," but to see them as individuals experiencing *cultural discontinuity*. As used by contemporary scholars, cultural discontinuity is the clash of two cultures: people with a particular set of cultural values and norms find themselves in an alien world with very different values and norms.

The degree of discontinuity these students feel varies depending on their ages, sex, and the particular group to which they belong. To cushion the effects of cultural discontinuity, these students adjust their behaviors and develop protective coloring. Ross, Bondy, and Kyle (1993, p. 232) explain:

> In order to protect their sense of collective identity as a cultural group, the minority persons develop certain ways of behaving (i.e., walking, talking, dressing) which separate them from "white people's ways." Being successful in school is likely to be regarded as "acting white".

Teachers who understand that these conflicts exist can learn more about the difficulties these students face by helping them become involved with the curriculum and helping them to accept the curriculum by modifying it to make it resemble the "practical" learning that happens outside the school. As

Darling-Hammond (1993, p. 755) explains, unless teachers understand that students' backgrounds, needs, and perspectives toward education are different, the needs of all at-risk students will go unmet.

> Concerns about "at-risk" children—those who drop out, tune, out, and fall behind—cannot be addressed without teachers who are prepared to understand and meet the needs of students who come to school with varying learning styles, and with differing beliefs about themselves and about what school means for them.

The movement toward multicultural education has grown rapidly and would have grown even faster if there were not widespread confusion over the meaning of the term multicultural. Stringfield (1991, p. 262) expresses concern over the ambiguity in definitions of such terms in textbooks:

> Upon examining seven textbooks in foundations, I found significant differences in terminology. Many terms in social foundations are confusing. For example, two textbooks define "cultural pluralism" as a way of describing a society made up of many cultural groups coming together to form a unified whole while another defined it as "acceptance and encouragement of cultural diversity within a larger society." Several textbooks did not mention the term, although one mentioned cultural diversity. Terms such as "multicultural education," "multiethnic education," and "global education" are also unclear. (See Table 2.1.)

Whatever definitions are used to talk about this problem, society is suffering from a lack of human productivity among minorities. Put simply, when any young person fails to reach the level of potential of which he or she is capable, society suffers the consequence. Maximum human productivity requires tolerance, a quality which is still lacking in our society. Hugh B. Price (1992), the vice president of the Rockefeller Foundation, says that, without the quality of tolerance, our society simply will not survive. The overlap of social and nonsocial factors that pressure the curriculum is clearly and abundantly evident. By presenting the traditional stereotypes of minorities, textbooks retard the curriculum changes needed to address ethnic and gender minority issues in positive and appropriate ways.

If tolerance is to be developed, our curricula must be adjusted to promote it. But the multicultural role of schools must go beyond the development of tolerance; future curricula must promote an appreciation for diversity. Each ethnic group should learn to value the uniqueness of other ethnic groups, and all groups must see the strength that diversity offers our nation.

Human rights must remain a major concern of all teachers, for all teachers share the responsibility for promoting among students an appreciation for others' rights. But students cannot be taught to appreciate and protect the rights of others through didactic methods. Ricardo Garcia (1994) suggests the use of social contracts such as the one shown in Box 2.1. He says that such a contract can be used like a blueprint to guide the management of classroom behavior.

**Table 2.1    Summary of effects of society on schools**

| Elements in Society | Implications for Curricularists |
| --- | --- |
| Tradition | Impedes and deters change. Curricularists must find ways to protect cherished beliefs and yet to continue to improve the curriculum. |
| Laws | Introduce change. Curricularists are compelled to protect the rules of the school and the laws of the land. |
| Religious beliefs | Protects accepted beliefs. Curricularists must assume that certain accepted values are promoted without imposing one dissemination on students. |
| Research | Curricularists can use research to assure that proposed changes are worthwhile. |
| Multicultural changes | Create a need for curricularists to make certain that the needs of minority students are met. |
| Poverty | Creates major learning obstacles for at least one-fourth of all students. |
| Changes in the family | The general deterioration of the family creates a need for the school to find other ways to motivate students and demonstrate the importance of education in today's world. |

An examination of the demographic shift in cultures in the United States shows that, by the year 2000, the ethnic majority that we know today will no longer be the majority. Every major metropolitan area will have a "minority majority." But the teaching majority of today will continue to dominate the teacher ranks.

The National Council for Accreditation of Teacher Education (NCATE) requires the development of a "multicultural perspective," which it defines as a "recognition of (1) the social, political, and economic realities that individuals experience in culturally diverse and complex human encounters, and (2) the importance of culture, race, sex, gender, ethnicity, religion, socioeconomic status, and exceptionalities in the education process"(1990, p. 65).

Because this statement is broad and general, it is subject to as many interpretations as it has readers. It should not be surprising that for several years,

## Box 2.1

## Social Contract

*The classroom operates as a community of scholars who are engaged in learning. The individual's right to learn is protected and respected by all scholars. Scholars should initiate learning and teachers should initiate instruction, balancing the rights of individuals with the rights of other individuals in the community.*

Right To Exist, or safe occupancy of space. The classroom is a physically safe learning environment. The teacher:

- does not allow students to physically harm each other or engage in other risky behavior that endangers any student.

Right To Liberty, or freedom of conscience and expression. The teacher:

- allows students to assert their opinions.
- fosters respectful student dissent as a means for rational understanding of issues and divergent opinions.
- fosters students' self-examination of their ethnic or cultural heritages. Teachers should help students become "ethnically literate" about their own individual cultural backgrounds and those of others.

Right To Happiness, or self-esteem: The classroom is an emotionally safe learning environment, fostering high self-esteem among students. The teacher:

- does not allow name-calling, elitist, racist, or sexist slurs, or stereotypical expressions in the classroom.
- disciplines students equitably ensuring that minority and majority group students are punished similarly for the same infractions.
- shows cultural respect by using linguistically and culturally relevant curriculum materials and instructional strategies, and telling the students that their languages and cultures are welcome in the classroom community.
- encourages students to understand their differences and similarities.

*Kappa Delta Pi Record 30(2): 70 © 1994 Kappa Delta Pi.*

more institutions failed to receive NCATE accreditation because of not fulfilling the multicultural standard than for any other reason. A 1992 review of 132 programs found that over half of the schools failed to meet the NCATE multicultural standard (Ovando, 1994).

A special handicap faced by many minority students is the language barrier. The United States trails most of the civilized world in the teaching of foreign languages. Outside the United States, more than half the world's population is bilingual. Ovando (1994) and Sizer (1990) recommend requiring that all students be proficient in two or more languages. Too often, foreign students are ignored because they speak little or no English. Perhaps the first thing needed to improve the education of these students is a change in attitude.

Several myths must be dispelled. For example, the common belief that learning an additional language interferes with one's native language must be disproved (Ovando, 1994). Another common myth is that success in learning a language is proportional to the time spent studying the language. Time-on-task is only one of many factors that affect learning a language or any other subject.

In addition to fostering appropriate attitudes, schools should make policy changes that promote language development and the academic success of students who are handicapped by a language barrier. For example, it should be made clear that these students are fully academically accountable. Academic success requires a special kind of language development—that of an academic vocabulary, which requires about five to seven years. Policy should ensure that these students are given the necessary support during this developmental period.

Our universities have failed to meet multicultural expectations in their education of future teachers. Doyle (1990, p. 9) explains:

> Learning to teach is treated as a mysterious but largely unproblematic process that occurs within teachers as they absorb information, emulate models, and extract lessons from practice. In turn, teaching is construed as largely algorithmic, i.e., the process of applying precepts or utilizing teaching skills in a variety of contents is seen as reasonably self-evident and direct, thus, something that can be routinized. To become a teacher, then, one must simply know the precepts and skills and have the opportunity to practice under "real" conditions.

Scott (1993, p. 2) says that students need an opportunity to develop their own theories based on experiences in multicultural classrooms:

> What is needed for teacher evaluation is a conceptualization of teacher education pedagogy in which theory and practice are interactive. "Practice draws theory" as much as "theory draws practices." Such a pedagogy would require that prospective teachers have sufficient practice to build principles of action, an understanding by theory to guide decision-making, and the recognition that teaching situations are multi-faceted ones in which there is seldom a perfect match between theory and practice. By defining teaching as dilemma-driven, teacher educators can better prepare teachers to cope with situations where there is often no one right way, or even best way, to act.

Kowalski et al (1994) suggest the use of the case study as a mechanism for preparing students to react wisely to dilemma situations. Case studies seem well suited to this role since they can be used to help individuals make judicious decisions.

The definitions of case studies vary. Merseth (1990, p. 54) uses three criteria:

1.  A case study is a descriptive research document based on a real-life situation, proven, or incident.

2.  In the presentation of a case study, every attempt is made to provide an unbiased, multidimensional perspective.

3.  A case study describes a situation requiring analysis, planning, decision-making, and/or action.

But Kowalski et al have not restricted their conceptions of case study to real-life situations. Although most of the cases these authors use are real experiences, they say that the literature and research support the use of contrived cases, which they call *armchair cases*. They say that each case must contain both relevant and superfluous information and must end in a problem situation.

When combining the case study method with simulations or games to prepare students for multicultural settings, teachers should remember that the most common mistake they make when using any type of simulation or game is not removing themselves from the center of the activity. Students need room to make mistakes and should be given only the minimum help needed to recognize their mistakes.

During the 1980s, feedback on effective school and teaching research prompted the use of direct instruction. Indeed, this approach was undeniably found to correlate with high achievement test scores. Unfortunately, it does not lead to the type of thinking needed for twenty-first-century living. Cohen (1993, p. 791) explains:

> And despite the lip service paid to the ideal of creating a spirit of inquiry, education is increasingly directed toward teaching students not how to inquire but rather how to digest the results of other people's inquiry.

## Poverty

Throughout their existence American schools have been challenged by poverty. The Franklin Academy, with its practical and relevant curriculum, lost its position as the most popular school in the country because it charged tuition, and the vast majority of families could not afford to send their children to the academy. Throughout the twentieth century, many schools have been too poor to afford their students even such basic necessities as textbooks, pencils, paper, and chalk.

In the environments surrounding the schools, poverty has taken its toll on millions of children. Today, one child in four lives in poverty. Extreme poverty often manifests itself in malnourishment, high rates of mortality, and even suicide. The number of behavioral problems correlates with the degree of poverty.

Such circumstances pressure educators to try to design the curricula to help our youth overcome the harm they suffer daily as a result of poverty. Knapp and Shields (1990) identify some ways that curricula in impoverished areas should be altered: (1) Maximize time on task, (2) set high expectations, (3) strengthen the involvement of parents in support of instruction, (4) plan content in small, discrete parts structured in sequence, (5) use whole-group or small-group formats, and (6) integrate the curriculum, giving students in all subjects opportunities to write, read, and discuss.

## Changes in the Family

Through the years, the strong family unit has been a profound strength in American culture. Yet the typical concept of family has changed radically in recent years. In 1989 a survey by the Massachusetts Mutual Life Insurance Company (Seligmann, 1989) asked 1200 randomly selected adults what the word *family* meant to them. From a list of definitions, only 22 percent picked the traditional definition of "a group of people related by blood, marriage, or adoption." About 75 percent selected "a group of people who love and care for each other."

The majority of today's youths have no concept of the traditional family that existed throughout the first half of the twentieth century, that is, a mother and father, the father the breadwinner for the family and the mother a homemaker who did not have a job outside the home.

Contemporary curricula must reflect these changes. Homework assignments must be compatible with the reality that most of today's youths do not have the support of the traditional family, for example, a quiet, lighted study area, ample time to give to homework assignments, and parents who are available, willing, and able to help them understand their assignments. Perhaps more important, most of today's youths have no adult role models at home who read books for information and pleasure, no parents to encourage them and remind them of the importance of education.

Most contemporary youths do not receive strong motivation and encouragement outside the classroom. Yet motivation is essential to learning. Campbell (1990) says that motivation is more: It is learning. Correctly designed, tests can be used to motivate students' interest in content. Markle, et al (1990, p. 56) have said: "The power of tests and other evaluation procedures to shape students' perceptions of their teachers' expectations cannot be overestimated." As teachers fulfill their new education reform roles—using valued outcomes, alternative assessment, performance evaluation, and portfolios—many new ways of motivating students will be available to those who are cognizant of the need to use evaluation and other means to motivate students.

## TECHNOLOGICAL FOUNDATIONS

The power of technology to change the curriculum is almost beyond comprehension. This was dramatically shown in 1957, when the USSR launched *Sputnik*, the world's first satellite to be placed in orbit. Americans were embarrassed to find that, at least temporarily, they had lost the space race. But beyond feeling embarrassed, they were terrified. Spurred by the fear that the country would be attacked, families and individuals built bomb shelters in their backyards and basements.

In 1959 thirty-five scientists, educators, and businesspeople assembled at Woods Hole, Massachusetts, to determine an appropriate response to this emergency. Their charge was to change the curriculum in the public schools as needed to win the space race. The fact that the USSR launched a satellite into orbit before the United States could achieve this feat paralyzed the public with fear. Advances in technology were the cause of all this.

The general results of the Woods Hole Conference were that content became interdisciplinary and major concepts were identified in each discipline. Themes, concepts, and principles replaced facts. Almost 40 years later, the need for such technologically induced changes in the curricula in American elementary and secondary schools remains strong.

### The Microcomputer

In recent years, nothing has had a greater impact on curricula in secondary and elementary schools than the microcomputer. An increased use of educational technology has characterized the education reform movement in most states. Ironically, in many states the increase in the availability of technology in the public schools has surpassed the availability of technology in teacher education colleges, and the availability and use of computers in the home and throughout the rest of the community have exceeded that in school. Often, students graduate from college and take teaching jobs in schools that are far better equipped with microcomputers than their colleges were, but still not equipped well enough to meet all the students' and teachers' needs. As Lewis (1994, p. 356) warns, "This gap between the schools and the rest of society will only widen as the technology available to students outside of schools continues to increase their access to information."

The problem goes beyond an imbalance in number of computers and beyond a lack of availability of up-to-date computers in public schools and teacher education colleges and departments: Many schools and colleges face critical shortages of quality software. Software shortages in teacher education colleges and departments are preventing the colleges from introducing their students to good software. The unfortunate result is that many teacher education majors are graduating and taking jobs only to learn that many of their students are more technologically advanced than their teachers are.

Paradoxically, as the microcomputer and other technological developments challenge education, these inventions also offer exciting solutions to the very problems they have created. Responding to an interviewer's question about areas of progress in education today (Dagenais, 1994, p. 52), Robert Anderson said: "Probably the most dynamic force impacting education today is the implementation of technological advancements." Indeed, if educators took advantage of these developments, there would be a cause for celebration.

The technological skills that today's teachers must have just to get by are considerably greater than those needed a decade ago. At a minimum, today's teachers should be preparing all students to write programs and use databases and spreadsheets. Rock and Cummings (1994) state the role that the future demands of teachers. Teachers need to feel comfortable with technology. Until using the technology becomes second nature, they cannot effectively change their teaching strategies. Furthermore, methods teachers should be requiring teachers to write programs in their disciplines that will draw upon their problem-solving skills and help develop creativity. For example, students can be taught to use the computer to create open-ended scenarios. Prospective English teachers might write introductions to stories available on software and then, in the classroom, ask their students to create various endings. Each scenario can be designed to help students develop particular skills, including advanced levels of thinking. Elementary science teachers might begin a story involving an imaginary field trip to an unfamiliar environment. The introduction could stir students' imaginations so that they could complete the story with their own embellishments.

A social studies teacher could begin a story about problems urban dwellers have because of their cultural backgrounds. The software could be designed to help students analyze the problems from the viewpoints of different cultures. Once the stories are completed, role playing, simulations, and discussions that will place students of varied backgrounds into cooperative working relationships can be next. A follow-up assignment might be for the students to use the computer to develop a profile of their value systems, listing their own beliefs, which came to light during the previous exercises.

Teachers who believe in integrating the disciplines know that such programs can be used in various disciplines. English writing assignments can easily focus on science, social studies, and so forth. After giving each of her fourth graders a computer to use to prepare writing reports, Edinger (1994, p. 58) reported that the computers increased the students' sense of efficacy and enabled them to revise their draft reports . . . at a remarkably sophisticated level.

Chapter 6 discusses the various levels of the educational taxonomies and gives examples of objectives at each level in each domain. By designing computer activities at the upper levels of the taxonomies, teachers can effectively use the computer to meet one of the schools' most critical needs—raising the level of student thinking.

The use of computers in the school started late, but once started, it advanced rapidly. In the early 1980s approximately 10 percent of the public schools had microcomputers; only a decade later, over 90 percent of the schools had computers (Rothstein, 1990). Another study reported that, by 1986, 95 percent of the high schools had computers (Becker, 1986). But there are still millions of teachers who do not have access to a computer for their individual use.

The expansion in numbers of computers in the schools has been paralleled by the growth in the number of ways computers are being used to provide quality instruction. Good computer-assisted instruction includes presenting information, guiding the learner, providing practice, and evaluating student learning (Alessi & Trollip, 1991).

A major contributor to the improvement in the use of computers in instruction has been improvements in the quality of software. Good software motivates students to create charts, to do writing assignments, and to produce other work that requires higher-level thinking. But Siegel and Davis (1986) say that commercial developers will probably not improve the quality of software as quickly as they should, as evidenced by the large number of computer books that teach amateurs how to program and the comparatively small number that tell how to select educationally sound software. California's State Department of Education funds the California Instructional Video Clearinghouse and the California Software Clearinghouse which review software for accuracy, instructional design, curricular match, content accuracy, interest level, and technical quality (Bakker and Piper, 1994). Hopefully other states will soon provide these services.

At least two implications for curriculum change are clear: (1) Future curricula must help future teachers assess software to ensure that their selections are educationally sound, and (2) curricula must go beyond technological literacy and aim for technological competency. Armstrong et al (1993, p. 326) explain:

> Today, technological literacy is no longer enough. Our society is insisting that employees be "technologically competent." This refers to a level of understanding that goes well beyond technological literacy. Competence suggests the presence of confident ability to use and extend present technologies and to adapt quickly to new technologies as they emerge.

Curricula must also change to alter teachers' perceptions. According to Geisert and Dunn (1991, p. 223): "Some teachers acknowledge still having computer phobia and remain apprehensive about using computers as either an instructional or management tool." Curricula in the elementary and secondary schools must offer nonthreatening opportunities for teachers to develop computer competency and must give teachers the computer time needed to become comfortable using computers in their lessons.

## Other Technological Developments

The microcomputer revolution is part of a much broader technological revolution which includes a number of other inventions. Several of these innovations are contributing to curriculum development and will certainly contribute more as newer developments occur. Paradoxically, although some schools do not have the funds required to make their students technologically current, a significant advantage offered by the technology is its ability to save money over time. Some of the more promising developments include CD-ROM, on-line data systems, electronic bulletin boards, interactive videos, and interactive distance-learning systems.

### CD-ROM

With CD-ROM enormous amounts of information are stored on a small disk. Consider the problem that rural teachers have in obtaining library materials for courses such as this curriculum course. With CD-ROM, hundreds of journals are now available to teachers through university centers. Such systems are incredibly user-friendly. A teacher can simply select a disk containing the desired journal and immediately call to the screen any issue of the journal printed within the previous three or four years. Hard copies of appropriate articles can be printed. This extremely useful technological innovation is already available in many university-extended campus centers, as well as in many school district curriculum centers.

### On-Line Data Systems

On-line data systems enable the user to access information from distant sources. Until the latter half of the 1980s users of such systems had to pay a fee to tap into the information pools and a separate fee for each minute the system was in use. Today, many on-line data systems are available through monthly subscriptions. An increasing number of local libraries subscribe to on-line data systems, making them accessible to virtually everyone.

In the near future, on-line data systems will use cable television lines and fiber optics. This will allow teachers in many school districts to make assignments on an almost unlimited array of topics (Armstrong et al, 1993).

### Electronic Bulletin Boards

Electronic bulletin boards are bulletin boards connected to computers. Currently, many schools are providing their teachers with modems, permitting them to tie into electronic bulletin boards. This service will allow teachers to share information with other teachers at local schools and universities. For example, a university professor of science education would be able to share information with the science department in a public school. Consider the possibilities: Teachers and professors would be able to collaborate on classroom research, students at one school would be able to work with students at another school, and so on. Foreign language students are already using this system to "post letters" to students in other countries.

For several decades, British elementary and secondary students have shared their on-going science projects through television. Electronic bulletin boards can provide American students a means of sharing their projects with other American students or, indeed, with students in countries throughout the world.

## Interactive Videos

At your local shopping mall, you may have seen cameras set up so that young people can demonstrate their musical and acting talents publicly through participating in a contest. If so, you have some idea of the motivational power that interactive videos have for young people. The interactive video is an exciting educational tool that has unique qualities. For example, unwanted material can be edited out. This flexibility is important to teachers who use videos in their classrooms. The video also offers a flexibility that is important to students: It does not require an on-site teacher; once recorded, the video can be used independently. Furthermore, the ability to freeze and play back information makes the lesson student-paced.

Interactive video offer teachers an opportunity to involve students in curriculum development. Chapters 4, 7, and 10 stress the need for students to be involved in identifying major concepts in their subjects. By using interactive video, students can help create scripts, edit material, and even present the material.

Consider the potential that this technology offers for bringing together students of varying ethnic backgrounds and students from different disciplines to work on cooperative assignments that are exciting to all students.

The power of video has been widely recognized. Texas, Florida, and West Virginia have approved their use for instruction and Texas has approved Optical Data System's "Windows on Science" in lieu of textbooks (Hancock and Betts, 1994). At Mansfield High School in Texas the power of video for instruction in biology was measured against traditional teaching. After 18 weeks an impressive gain in achievement was seen among students using video over their traditionally taught counterparts (Rock and Cummings, 1994).

## Interactive Distance Learning

Distance learning has been available in some school districts for over three decades. Early distance learning used satellite disks. A satellite disk was required on both ends to provide an uplink for the sender and a downlink for the receiver. This system is still being used throughout the country.

Recently, the interactive dimension has been added to distance learning, allowing a two-way exchange of ideas. For example, extension courses have been taught for a longtime by distance learning. Now, many distance-learning classrooms have learner stations which enable students to communicate orally and visually with the instructor and with students at other locations.

Currently, several states are developing "backbones," or major communications lines, that run the length of a state. Backbones will enable several users to share distance signals, which should result in considerable savings and increased availability.

The microcomputer has become a communications devise for literally millions of students and teachers, worldwide. Extensive computer networks facilitate such communication. For example, one single network (Internet) links together more than 15 million computer stations in over 134 countries (Pawloski, 1994).

This cursory review of technology will be dated as soon as this book is published; however, its purpose is not to teach the content but to challenge teachers and other curriculum developers to think about their own educational needs and those of their students and to consider how technology can best be used to meet these needs.

Many readers of this book are already knowledgeable consumers of technology, and this is good. For those who have not caught the excitement offered by this rapidly developing field, take the advice of Geisert and Dunn (1991), who said that the importance of knowing how to be an effective computer user in this day and age is too critical to let a lack of technological training get in the way; you are challenged to explore one or more of these or other technological advancements and the potential they offer for your future curriculum development activities.

Mecklenburger (1990), who directs the National School Boards Association Institute for the Transfer of Technology in Education, argues that teachers must think beyond just using new technology.

At any time, there are forces in a community that have an impact on its schools. Some of the more influential of these forces are tradition, textbooks, laws, moral values, research, multicultural concerns, poverty, family changes, and technology. As shown in Figure 2.3, schools exert pressure on their communities as they prepare future citizens for their roles in the world of work and promote intellectualism. Ideally, a homeostasis exists between these groups for when this balance is upset, problems develop between the school and the community.

**Figure 2.3** A balance is maintained between the forces schools and communities exert on each other.

## SUMMARY

Carefully planned, each school can be a microcosm of the community. Like the community, the school has its own culture, which must be considered when curricula are developed. The curriculum developer must remember that the school is a creation of the community and is supported by the community. This means that the curriculum must serve the needs of the community.

Curriculum developers must also serve the needs of the students. With the breakdown of the traditional family and the increase in poverty and diversity in the late twentieth century, this job has become more challenging.

Forces are constantly at work within the schools and outside the schools; some forces press for change, and others press to maintain the status quo. Through the years, the textbook has been the major curriculum determiner, although it has many severe limitations. Recently, education reform laws have dominated all other forces, using strategies that involve parents and teachers and requiring teachers to use research-validated materials. Teachers and other curriculum developers must take the responsibility for examining local reform practices and for protecting the interests of their students.

Advocates of multiculturalism recognize the need to protect cultural diversity, yet confusion over definitions has contributed to the ineffectiveness of their efforts. The nation suffers from the lack of contributions from minority members, many of whom are not qualified to compete for, or productively pursue, lifelong careers.

The number of computers in the schools has greatly expanded during the past decade. Today, over 90 percent of elementary and secondary schools have computers, yet many teachers still suffer from computer phobia and from not having computers available. Teachers and other curriculum directors must be prepared to take advantage of the new technological advances as they occur.

## QUESTIONS

1. What do you believe Shouse means when he says that the basic difference between the school world and the outside world is not in the activities themselves?
2. Why does a curriculum developer need to be familiar with a school's culture?
3. Should the fact that the community owns the schools give local citizens the right to dictate to the schools? If so, what types of issues should the community dictate and what types should it not dictate?
4. In your opinion, what is the most important step a school can take to develop good citizens?

5. What do you believe is the strongest force affecting school curricula? Explain your answer.

6. Should curriculum development courses focus on education reform? Why or why not?

7. How does tradition contribute positively to the schools? How does it contribute negatively?

8. In what ways have teachers' technological needs expanded?

9. Describe one area in which multiculturalism needs improving.

10. How can a curriculum developer adjust the curriculum to better meet the needs of poor children?

11. What uncertainties do you have about making computer assignments?

12. How have education reform programs empowered teachers and parents to significantly change the schools?

13. If your school could influence the community to change any way you wished, what change would you desire most?

14. If your school were a person, what would he or she be feeling?

15. What does it mean to think of your school as a school as opposed to a training site or a factory?

## SUGGESTED FURTHER ACTIVITIES

1. From all the courses you have taken, examine your course syllabi for multicultural objectives. Make a list of these objectives. Place an X next to each objective which you believe would be appropriate for future classes that you will teach.

2. Study your school's community and make a list of multicultural resources. Include such items as field trips and guest speakers.

3. Research the literature for as many definitions as you can find for *cultural pluralism, cultural diversity*, and *multicultural education*. Then write your own definition for each of these terms.

4. Interview a professor of computer education at your college. Make a list of the computer skills required for all undergraduate students in teacher education.

5. Interview two history teachers, asking them how they think the school can best develop citizenship in the students.

6. Select the method you prefer, for example, lecture, inquiry, discussion, simulation, or case study, and write an activity for your students that will help them develop good citizenship traits.

7. Develop a project to assign to your students to help them become more sensitive to world problems.

8. Write a computer assignment based on a multicultural problem in an urban setting.

9. Write a computer assignment that links your disciplines to at least three other disciplines.

## BIBLIOGRAPHY

Alessi, S. M., & Trollip, S. R. (1991). *Computer-based instruction, methods and development.* Englewood Cliffs, NJ: Prentice-Hall.

Antin, Mary (1912). *The promised land.* Boston: Houghton Mifflin.

Apple, M. W. (1990). Is there a curriculum voice to reclaim? *Phi Delta Kappan, 71*(7), 526–530.

Armstrong, D. G., Henson, K. T., & Savage, T. V. (1993). *Education: An introduction* (4th ed). Chap. 13. New York: Macmillan.

Bakker, H. E. & Piper, J. B. (1994). "California provides technology evaluations to teachers." *Educational Leadership, 51* (7), 67–68

Barth, R. S. (1990). A personal vision of a good school. *Phi Delta Kappan, 71*(7), 512–516.

Becker, H. J. (1986). *Instructional uses of school computers: Report from the 1985 national survey.* Baltimore, MD: Johns Hopkins University, Center for Social Organization of Schools.

Berlinger, V. W., & Yates, C. M. (1993). Formal operational thought in the gifted: A post-Piagetian perspective. *Roeper Review, 15*(4), 220–224.

Berman, Sheldon (1990, November). Educating for social responsibility. *Educational Leadership, 48*(3), 75–80.

Brimfield, R. M. B (1992, Summer). "Curriculum: What's curriculum?" *The Educational Forum, 56*(4), 381–389.

Burke, W. J. (1967). *Not for glory.* New York: Cowles Education Corporation.

Burrello, L. C., & Reitzug, U. C. (1993). Transforming context and developing culture in schools. *Journal of Counseling and Development, 71*(6), 669–677.

Butzin, S. M. (1992, December). Interpreting technology into the classroom: Lessons from the Project Child experience. *Phi Delta Kappan, 74*(4), 330–333.

Campbell, L. P. (1990, September–October). Philosophy = methodology = motivation = learning. *The Clearing House, 64*(1), 21–22.

Cohen, A. (1993). A new educational paradigm. *Phi Delta Kappan, 74*(10), 791–795.

Cohen, D. (1990). More voices in Babel? Educational research and the politics of curriculum. *Phi Delta Kappan, 71*(7), 518–522.

Conroy, Pat (1972, reprint 1991). *The water is wide.* New York: The Old New York Book Shop.

Cooper, K. (1989). Education secretary calls for restructuring of public schools. *Center Daily Times,* May 23.

Dagenais, R. J. (1994). "Professional development of teachers and administrators: Yesterday, today, and tomorrow/The views of Robert H. Anderson." *Kappa Delta Pi Record, 30*(2), 50–54.

Darling-Hammond, L. (1993). Reforming the school reform agenda. *Phi Delta Kappan, 74*(10), 756–761.

Davis, G. A. (1993). Creative teaching of moral thinking: Fostering awareness and commitment. *Middle School Journal, 24*(4), 32–33.

Doyle, W. (1990). Case methods in the education of teachers. *Teacher Education Quarterly, 17*(1), 7–15.

Edinger, M. (1994). "Empowering young writers with technology." *Educational Leadership, 51* (7), 58–60.

Edwards, J. L. (1994). Get started on technology. *Education Digest, 59*(5), 46–47.

Eisner, E. W. (1985). *The educational imagination* (2nd ed). New York: Macmillan.

Eisner, E. W. (1990). Who decides what schools should teach? *Phi Delta Kappan, 71*(7), 523–526.

Garcia, R. L. (1994). Human rights in the pluralistic classroom. *Kappa Delta Pi Record, 30*(2), 70.

Geisert, G., & Dunn, R. (1991, March–April). Effective use of computers: Assignments based on individual learning style. *The Clearing House, 64*(4), 219–223.

Glatthorn, A. A. (1993). *Learning twice.* New York: HarperCollins.

Goodman, K. S. et al (1988). *Report card on basal readers.* Katonah, NY: Richard C. Owen.

Gough, P. B. (1990, June). Good news and bad news. *Phi Delta Kappan, 71*(10), 747.

Hancock, V., & Betts, F. (1994). "From the lagging to the leading edge." *Educational Leadership, 51* (7), 24–27.

Hill, P. T. (1990, January). The federal role in education: A strategy for the 1990s. *Phi Delta Kappan, 71*(5), 398–402.

Hirsch, Herbert (1991, Spring). Book review. *The Educational Forum, 55*(3), 285–288.

Holt, Maurice (1993, January). The educational consequences of W. Edwards Demming. *Phi Delta Kappan, 74*(5), 382–388.

Knapp, M. S., & Shields, P. M. (1990, June). Reconceiving academic instruction for the children of poverty. *Phi Delta Kappan, 71*(10), 753–758.

Kochan, F. K., & Herrington, C. D. (1992, Fall). Restructuring for today's children and strengthening schools by strengthening families. *The Educational Forum, 57*, 42–49.

Kowalski, T. J., & Reitzug, U. C. (1993). *Contemporary school administration: An introduction.* New York: Longman.

Kowalski, T. J., Weaver, R. A., & Henson, K. T. (1994). *Case studies on beginning teachers.* New York: Longman.

Lewis, A. (1994). Reinventing local school governance. *Phi Delta Kappan, 75*(5), 356–357.

Lieberman, A. (1990). Navigating the four C's: Building a bridge over troubled waters. *Phi Delta Kappan, 71*(7), 531–533.

Lounsbury, J. H. (1991). A fresh start for the middle school curriculum. *Middle School Journal, 23*(2), 3–7.

Markle, G., Johnston, J. H., Geer, C., & Meichtry, Y. (1990, November). Teaching for understanding. *Middle School Journal, 22*(2), 53–57.

McNeil, J. D. (1990). *Curriculum: A comprehensive introduction (4th ed).* New York: HarperCollins.

Mecklenburger, J. A. (1990, October). Educational technology is not enough. *Phi Delta Kappan, 71*, 20.

Merseth, K. J. (1990). Case studies and teacher education. *Teacher Education Quarterly, 17*(1), 53–62.

National Council for Accreditation of Teacher Education (1990).*Standards, procedures, and policies for the accreditation of professional education units.* Washington, DC: National Council for Accreditation of Teacher Education.

Oana, R. G. (1993). *Changes in teacher education: Reform, renewal, reorganization, and professional development schools: A professional development leave report.* Bowling Green, OH: Bowling Green State University.

O'Neal, Michael, Earley, Barbara, & Snider, Marge (1991). Addressing the needs of at-risk students: A local school program that works. In R. C. Morris (Ed.), *Youth at risk* (pp. 122–125). Lancaster, PA.: Technomic Publishing.

Ovando, C. (1994, March 18). Curriculum reform and language minority students. Presentation delivered at the 1994 Professors of Curriculum meeting. Chicago.

Parker, W. C. (1990, November). Assessing citizenship. *Educational Leadership, 48*(3), 17–22.

Pawloski, B. (1994). "How I found out about Internet." *Educational Leadership, 51* (7). 69–73.

Pipho, Chris (1992, December). A decade of education reform. *Phi Delta Kappan, 74*(4), 278–279.

Ponder, G. A., & Holmes, K. M. (1992, Summer). Purpose, products, and visions: The creation of new schools. *The Educational Forum, 56*(4), 405—418.

Price, H. B. (1992). Multiculturalism: Myths and realities. *Phi Delta Kappan, 74*(3), 208–213.

Reed, D. F. (1994). Multicultural education for preservice students. *Action in teacher education, 15*(3), 27–34.

Reich, R. B. (1991). *The work of nations: Preparing ourselves for 21st century capitalism.* New York: Knopf.

Riley, M. N. (1992, November). If it looks like manure. *Phi Delta Kappan, 74*(3), 239–241.

Rock, H. M. and Cummings, A. (1994). "Can videodiscs improve student outcomes." *Educational Leadership, 51(7),* 46-50.

Rose, L. C. (1991, October). A vote of confidence for the schools. *Phi Delta Kappan, 73*(2), 121–128.

Ross, D. D., Bondy, E., & Kyle, D. W. (1993). *Reflective teaching for student empowerment.* New York: Macmillan.

Rothenberg, D. (1993). Multicultural education. *Middle School Journal, 24*(4), 73–75.

Rothstein, P. R. (1990). *Educational psychology.* New York: McGraw-Hill.

Sagor, Richard (1990, November). Education for living in a nuclear age. *Educational Leadership, 48*(3), 81–83.

Schlechty, P. C. (1990). *Schools for the 21st century: Leadership imperatives for educational reform.* San Francisco: Jossey-Bass Publishers.

Scott, P. (1993). *Case studies in teacher education: Reflection on diversity.* Unpublished manuscript. Tallahassee, FL.

Seligmann, J. (1989, Winter–Spring). Variations on a theme. *Newsweek, 22*(2), 38–46.

Shouse, J. B. (1992). The school has captured the world. *The Educational Forum, 57*(1), 104–106.

Siegel, M. A., & Davis, D. M. (1986). *Understanding computer-based education.* New York: Random House.

Sizer, T. R. (1990). *Horace's Compromise: The dilemma of the American high school.* Boston: Houghton-Mifflin.

Snider, R. C. (1992, December). The machine in the classroom. *Phi Delta Kappan, 74*(4), 316–323.

Solomon, S. (1989). Homework: The great reinforcer. *The Clearing House, 63*(2), 63.

Stinnett, T. M., & Henson, K. T. (1982). *America's public schools in transaction.* New York: Columbia University Teachers College Press.

Stringfield, J. K. (1991). The Humpty Dumpty school of communications in education. *The Educational Forum, 55*(3), 261–269.

Tice, T. N. (1994). Research spotlight. *Education Digest, 59*(5), 48–51.

Tishman, S., Jay, E., & Perkins, D. N. (1993). Teaching thinking dispositions: From transmission to encultration. *Theory Into Practice, 32*(3), 147–153.

Wirth, A. C. (1993, January). Educational work: The choice we face. *Phi Delta Kappan, 74*(5), 361–366.

Wood, G. H. (1990, November). Teaching for democracy. *Educational Leadership, 48*(3), 32–37.

# Chapter 3

# HISTORICAL AND PHILOSOPHICAL FOUNDATIONS

## OBJECTIVES

This chapter should prepare you to:

• Evaluate the Seven Cardinal Principles of Secondary Education in terms of their relevance for today's schools.

• Discuss colonial legislation and its effect on today's schools.

• Give evidence of the Progressive Education Movement in today's curricula.

• Compare and contrast the influence of John Locke and John Dewey on today's curriculum.

• Trace the development of curricula from the colonial days to the present and relate this history to contemporary education reform.

• Give examples of three philosophical constructs in your fellow teachers' reactions to education reform.

## DIANE WORLEY'S GRADUATE CURRICULUM PROJECT ON SCHOOL REFORM

As Diane Worley completed her student teaching semester and her teacher education program, she reflected on the past four and a half years which she thought would take forever to finish but which surprisingly had passed so fast. At first she had been confused by the rumble over school reform in her state, but now she was glad that she had taken advantage of every opportunity to learn all she could about these activities. Having accepted her first teaching assignment and enrolled in her first graduate class, a curriculum development course, Diane was determined to use both her school experience and her curriculum course to continue learning about school reform.

Education 501, Foundations and Principles of Curriculum Development, proved to be an excellent avenue through which Diane could pursue her newest professional goal. The course required each student to conduct an independent research project, prepare a written report, and make an oral presentation of the report to the rest of the class. The written report was due two weeks prior to the final class meeting.

Diane had little difficulty in choosing her topic, "The Relationship Between the History of American Education and Contemporary School Reform," and her professor readily approved it.

As with most research studies, the first and most difficult task is delineating the project so that it is manageable. Dianne listed the following points:

- *The effect of American legislation on school reform.* This would involve survey-ing such legislation as the Old Deluder Satan Act, the Northwest Ordinance, and the Kalamazoo case, examining the goals of these laws, and comparing those goals to the goals of current school reform.

- *The effect that textbooks have had on the curricula in American schools throughout their history and the effect they are having in current reform efforts.* This would involve reviewing such books as the Bible, *McGuffey's Readers*, required classical literature, and the contemporary textbooks which Diane would use in her classes during this first year of teaching.

- *The relationship between the Seven Cardinal Principles of Secondary Education and the Goals for 2000.*

- *The relationship between the goals of the Progressive Education Movement and those of contemporary school reform.*

- *The implications of the recommendations made at the Woods Hole Conference on current reform goals.*

- *The causes of the development of the junior high school and middle school and a comparison of those causes with the current school reform efforts.*

- *The relationship between the current priorities of middle-level education and the Goals for 2000.*

- *A survey of the major curriculum changes over the past 250 years and a com-parison of the trends revealed with the goals of current school reform.*

Diane found that just reflecting on these issues and the simple act of making the list were both stimulating. She imagined the many charts that she could use to visu-ally show relationships in new and provocative ways. This project would enable her to make a unique contribution to education reform in her school and would also equip her with some of the tools needed to implement education reform.

Within a few days, Diane Worley had settled into her new school environ-ment. She enjoyed each part of her new world. Naturally, this included the lunch period and the lounge which provided about the only opportunities she had throughout the day to socialize with her fellow teachers. The lounge was especially interesting because of the differences she could see among the teachers. Although she expected to see more agreement among professional teachers than she had seen among her fellow college students, such was not the case. In fact, compared to her college peers, these teachers seemed to have even more pronounced differences in opinions. But the part she liked most was that her new peers seemed free to express their views without fear of pressure to agree with their colleagues or without feeling that they needed their colleagues to agree with them.

Diane also enjoyed being treated as a professional. Her principal and the administrative staff treated her the same way they treated teachers who had taught for many years. "What a contrast," she thought, "from the way I was treated as an undergraduate student." It was surprising to realize the degree to which others' perceptions of her had changed in only a few weeks.

To Diane, the best part of her new teaching career was the relationship she had with her students. She believed that nothing equaled the joy she felt from the meeting of minds engaged in purposeful learning. Soon though, Diane was to learn that not everyone shared her love for the pursuit of knowledge. Or perhaps it was that her love of her chosen methods of inquiry was grossly misunderstood.

The challenge came early in the first grading period when Diane introduced the term *concept*. Since some students seemed a little confused, Diane decided to give some examples. She carefully lifted her desk chair and placed it on the center of her desk. She began by asking the students to name the object on the desk. Although several of the older students seemed embarrassed to respond, everyone said that it was a chair. Then she asked how they knew it was a chair. The students began naming its parts: "It's a chair because it has a seat, four legs, and a back." "What would it be if these parts were disassembled?" Diane asked. After a lengthy discussion, the students concluded that it would no longer be a chair but just a collection of chair parts. "Then, a chair is more than something physical?" Diane concluded, with a questioning tone. The students agreed. Diane felt that she was really getting the idea of the meaning of concept over to these students. However, at this point the district instructional supervisor happened to pass by. Seeing the chair on the desk, the supervisor decided to pause long enough to see what was going on.

The supervisor, Ms. Sterling-Austin, was more than intrigued by this novel approach. In fact, after the lesson, she questioned this teaching style very rigorously.

Many teachers have lost the passion for teaching that Diane has. Negative reports, articles, and radio and television programs on education reform have caused many contemporary teachers to feel underappreciated. An awareness of the history of American schools and an ability to apply history and philosophy to curriculum development should help readers assess local reform practices.

## HISTORICAL FOUNDATIONS

### The Migrations

Certainly one of the most colorful characters in history was England's King Henry VIII, noted for his political cunning, lust, bad temper, and selfishness, among other qualities. When the Roman Catholic Church refused to sanctify Henry's marriage to Anne Boleyn, he established his own church, the Church of England, which today remains the major denomination in England. James I, who became king in 1603, made life difficult for certain Protestant groups. Finally, in 1620, a Protestant group migrated to Holland. Meeting even greater opposition there, they left for America. By this time another group of Protestants had left England for America, and by 1630 both groups had arrived in the area that was to be named Massachusetts.

Contrary to popular belief, these people, known as the *Puritans*, were not seeking religious freedom for all—they were seeking religious freedom for Puritans. According to their strict laws, the role of the church was to interpret the will of God, and the role of the state was to enforce it. The church building commonly served also as the courthouse, where civil laws were made and offenders were tried and sentenced. Since the civil law and the church were inseparable and since obedience to God required a knowledge of His laws, an institution was needed to guarantee that each citizen possessed this required knowledge.

### Early Schools

#### The Latin Grammar School

In 1635 the first Latin grammar school, forerunner of our modern schools, appeared. Designed after the English schools, Latin grammar schools aimed at preparing young men of the elite for entrance to a newly founded college at New Towne (later Cambridge, Massachusetts). Among the Puritan immigrants were more than a hundred graduates of Oxford and Cambridge universities. Steeped in a tradition that prized quality education, these highly educated settlers were determined to provide equally excellent educational opportunities for their sons. Thus, the General Court of Massachusetts appropriated 400 pounds for a new college.

In 1638 a young minister who was dying of tuberculosis willed his library of four hundred books and half of his estate (worth almost 2000 dollars) to the new college. In honor of John Harvard, the new institution was named Harvard College.

#### The Dame Schools

By 1642 every home was required to teach reading, Puritanism, and the laws of the colony. Thus the first American "public schools" were not really schools at all, at least not in the sense of a schoolhouse staffed by professional teachers. Although they were commonly called *dame schools* or *kitchen schools*, they were actually citizens' homes. Some wealthy citizens met the requirements of the law by hiring tutors from abroad and transporting them to America. But since this option was unaffordable for most people, the groups of early settlers got together and designated one of the women to teach the neighborhood children. Because household help was dear and the teachers' pay was meager or nothing at all, these "dames" often taught the children at the kitchen table while they prepared the family meals. Thus came the names dame school and kitchen school. The curriculum for these schools often consisted of no more than a few simple laws of the colony, a few Biblical rhymes, and some Biblical readings. Inspectors visited each house to ensure that the teaching was being done. Ultimately, of course, this system was expensive and ineffective, it was soon replaced by the public school.

The main motivation for the Puritans' long, expensive, and dangerous journey to the New World was their desire to build a new community to worship God. Worried that the devil was constantly engaged in efforts to take advantage of their children's ignorance and mislead them, they wasted little time before passing a law to help their children escape the devil's snares or delude the devil. The law, called the *Old Deluder Satan Act*, passed in 1647, required Massachusetts towns to erect and maintain schools. Communities of 50 or more families had to teach reading and writing; those with a 100 or more families had to establish a Latin grammar school and hire a teacher. The curriculum of this school was highly classical and dominated by Latin and Greek.

## *The Franklin Academy*

The following century was characterized by expansion; surveyors were needed to build roads, navigators were needed for the growing trade, mathematicians were needed for business, and so forth. Thus a need developed for a very different type of school, one with a less classical and more practical curriculum. In 1750 Benjamin Franklin responded to this need by opening the Franklin Academy in Philadelphia. In many ways the academy was the very opposite of the Latin grammar school: It was both secular and practical, offering subjects such as mathematics, astronomy, surveying, bookkeeping, and navigation. Because of its practical emphasis, by the end of the Revolutionary War, the Franklin Academy had superseded the Latin grammar school as the most numerous secondary school in the new United States. The content, strengths, and weaknesses of the three early schools are summarized in Table 3.1.

## The Public School

The Franklin Academy's practical curriculum enabled it to replace the Latin grammar school; yet it had one weakness—it was private and many parents could not afford its tuition. The Revolutionary War kindled a spirit of freedom and caused citizens to realize the value of education to a democratic society. In 1779 Thomas Jefferson proposed three years of free public education to all citizens of Virginia. However, 42 years passed before the Boston School Committee established the country's first public high school, in 1821. The

**Table 3.1  Curricula of Early Schools**

|  | Dame School | Latin Grammar School | Franklin Academy |
|---|---|---|---|
| Content | Puritanism, Colonel law, reading | Latin, Greek, religion | Astronomy, bookkeeping, mathematics, navigation, surveying |
| Outstanding Strength | The only school available | Availability | Practical |
| Outstanding Weakness | The teachers were housewives and mothers | Impractical | Charged tuition |

Boston English Classical School, later named the Boston English High School, was established to prepare youth for employment; yet, for many, it served as an entry to the university. Since these early high schools served these two distinctly different purposes, the curricula in individual schools varied greatly; most were very pragmatic, but some, located in college communities, were highly classical.

By 1860 half of the nation's children were in school. The commitment of the government to education was reconfirmed in 1787 by the Northwest Ordinance, which reserved a parcel of land in every township to be sold to finance public education. Further support came in 1874 in the Kalamazoo case, which gave citizens in every town the right to levy taxes to support their secondary schools.

## Goals for the Early Elementary School

Since the time of the establishment of the forerunners of modern elementary schools, the curriculum has been expanding constantly. The first Latin grammar schools had the single purpose of preparing elite young men for Harvard and the ministry, and the dame schools continued this religious emphasis, with a broadening of their curricula to include colonial law and reading. These changes were not as bold as they might sound, since colonial law and God's word were one and the same and since reading was added to prepare the youth to read the Bible.

## Goals for the Early High School

The last quarter of the nineteenth century set some definite trends that are still prevalent in high school education. The once small schools began to grow in enrollments. Teachers and administrators joined to form the first unified coalition of organized educators, the National Education Association (NEA). The NEA assumed leadership in determining the goals for the early high schools.

In 1892 its Committee of Ten stated that the purpose of the school was to pre-pare students for life, yet it recommended that all students be taught the col-lege preparatory subjects. Three years later the NEA reinforced the college preparatory goal with its Committee on College Entrance Requirements. During this same quarter century, regional associations were formed to inspect and accredit high schools.

The new century brought further clarification of the goals of the high school. In 1918 the NEA's Commission on the Reorganization of Secondary Education listed the following seven principles, formally known as the *Seven Cardinal Principles of Secondary Education,* as the main goals for both secondary and elementary schools:

1. Health
2. Command of fundamental processes (development of basic skills)
3. Worthy home membership (contributing family member)
4. Vocational efficiency
5. Citizenship
6. Worthy use of leisure time
7. Ethical character

Many educators consider this list of broad goals (which actually applies to both elementary and secondary schools) as the most important aims ever set forth for American education. Although the list contains only seven entries, the breadth and nature of these goals have caused them to remain relevant even though society has constantly changed.

## Experiential Education

From the beginning of public schools in America until 1875 (about 250 years), the school curriculum has been largely determined by one type of textbook or another. Initially, the main texts were the Bible and the hornbook, a sheet of parchment or paper, used in the dame schools, covered by a sheet of transpar-ent hornlike material to protect the paper from becoming soiled.

In the 1690s the first basal reader, called the *New England Primer,* was pub-lished. It, too, was a blend of religion and morals. Rhymes, called *catechisms,* were used to teach religious doctrine and language skills. "The sin of man, the wrath of God, the judgment of a fiery hell, and the salvation of a resurrected Christ permeated it from cover to cover" (Walker, 1976, p. 6).

In 1782 Noah Webster's book, known as the *Blue Back Speller,* was pub-lished, adding spelling to the curriculum. During the next 60 years, 24 million copies were sold. The intentions of the book were to provide moral and non-sectarian religious guidance, to provide valuable knowledge, and to motivate the students' interest.

During these first 250 years, instruction centered around recitation. Students studied, memorized, and recited their lessons until the material was committed to memory; those who failed received corporal punishment. This method was openly challenged by Francis Parker, who had been orphaned at the age of 8 and was apprenticed to a farmer until the age of 21. Parker discovered that life on the farm was very educational, but he found school to be so hateful and unbearable that he attended it only about eight weeks every year. Instead of turning his back on education, though, Parker decided to improve it. He believed that if education could be acquired so pleasantly in the fields, woodlands, and pastures, it could also be enjoyed in the schools. His dream was to become a great teacher; little did he know that the fulfillment of his dream would bring about a revolution of American education.

In 1875 this huge bearded man was elected superintendent of schools in Quincy, Massachusetts, a suburb of Boston. Through the teachers' meetings he established, Parker gave his 40 teachers not advice and knowledge but questions and demonstrations. He did not tell them how to teach; he *showed* them. He gave them not only a technique but also a spirit; he made them want to put life into their curriculum. To create a natural learning environment, Parker substituted games and puzzles for recitation and rote memorization. In the lower grades he instituted singing, playing, reading, counting objects, writing, and drawing. Above all, he wanted the experiences at his schools to be happy ones. Reversing the traditional teaching process, which began with rules and definitions, he gave students real-life problems that made them seek out the rules or generalizations.

This system, which became known as the *Quincy System*, gained national attention. In his own words Francis Parker told how enthusiastic the community had become over its schools: "Throughout the centuries of Quincy's history, its people have ever manifested a deep interest in education, and I believe that I am right when I say that at no time in the past has this interest been greater than it is in the first year of the new century [of Independence]" (Campbell, 1967, p. 83).

The Quincy System was the forerunner of other innovative experiments in education, for example, the Gary Plan, the Dalton Plan, and the Winnetka Plan. The *Gary Plan* was developed by William A. Wirt, the superintendent of schools in Gary, Indiana, where the elementary and high schools were designed as miniature communities. Unlike other schools, which had self-contained classrooms, the Gary Plan was open; students moved freely from one place to another throughout the day in platoons. Like Parker's system, this one was experimental and student-centered. The *Dalton Plan*, developed in Dalton, Massachusetts, in 1919, was significant in that it was a highly individualized program. Using contracts, students followed their own program. The plan involved students and teachers in the development of curricula. The *Winnetka Plan*, developed in 1919 by Carleton Washburne, superintendent of schools at Winnetka, Illinois, was also a highly individualized program. Stressing self-expression and creativity, it even used self-instructional materials to teach the fundamentals. The features of these experimental student-centered curricula are shown in Table 3.2.

**Table 3.2  Early Twentieth-Century Student-Centered Curricula**

| Quincy System | Gary Plan | Dalton Plan | Winnetka Plan |
|---|---|---|---|
| Games and puzzles | Miniature communities | Student contracts | Self-instructional materials |
| Student and teacher involvement in planning | Platoons | Student and teacher involvement in planning | Self-expression and creativity |

These programs were important in two ways: First, they changed the way Americans thought about education—it no longer had to be textbook-oriented and dominated by recitation. Students could become the focus or center of the learning experience, and school could be enjoyed, as student activity was not stifled, but encouraged. The belief of the seventeenth-century philosopher, John Locke—that experience is the basis of all understanding—was finally being implemented. Second, these programs were important because they led to several national movements in education.

## Progressive Education

The experience-based movement that Francis Parker had started in 1875 moved vigorously into the twentieth century. Before his death in 1902, he took a position as head of a normal school in Chicago, which later merged with the University of Chicago, where John Dewey was head of the philosophy and psychology department from 1894 to 1904. Professor Dewey established a school on the university's campus to serve as an experimental laboratory to study educational processes. This laboratory school was like any other school except that it was accessible to the professors and students so that they could conduct on-site research on teaching practices. Within a few years, almost every state in the nation had at least one university laboratory school.

Fifty years later, most of these laboratory schools were still operating, but recently the high school grades have been eliminated from most of them. As the century draws to an end, all but about a hundred of the laboratory schools have closed. Ironically, many of the survivors are now playing a major role in education reform by being forerunners in implementing school reform in their states, by serving as professional development schools, and by acting as role models through implementing education reform practices.

During the first quarter of the twentieth century, true concern for the student was evident. The Progressive Education Movement was child-centered, as opposed to subject-centered. Though often confused with permissive education, the Progressive Education Movement did not espouse permissiveness. The concept of progressivism is much more akin to pragmatism, for during this era, secondary school curricula became much more practical, offering agriculture, home economics, and other vocational subjects.

Progressivism meant more than pragmatism or practicality; it also meant that students helped plan the curriculum and sometimes selected their own individualized learning activities. The arts, sports, and extracurricular activities were added to the school program. Progressive educators' belief in the democratic process led them to involve parents, students, and teachers. For 50 years the progressive trend was well accepted by students, who perceived the curriculum as highly relevant. From 1933 to 1941 the Progressive Education Association sponsored the Eight-Year Study, a survey of the effects of such a general education on learners. This comprehensive lognitudinal study followed students from 30 experimental high schools through high school and college. The graduates of the experimental schools equaled their counterparts in the attainment of subject matter, and they outperformed them in attainment of academic honors and grades. Furthermore, students who had had freedom of choice in their curricula proved to be significantly superior in intellectual curiosity, creativity, drive, leadership, and extraclass activities. They also proved to be more objective and more aware of world events. Unfortunately, because of timing alone, the results of the Eight-Year Study were lost in history; they were made public just as the country plunged into World War II.

## The Junior High Movement

As the twentieth century approached, the typical elementary school included grades kindergarten (K) through 8, and the high school included grades 9 through 12. Common knowledge held that the purpose of grades 7 and 8 was to review the content covered in K through 6. Many people saw this use of the seventh and eighth grades as a waste of time, but it was difficult to prove that this was so, because American schools had no nationally accepted goals.

During the next 30 years, several national committees were established to set goals and measure the degree to which schools were meeting them. The first of these was the NEA's Committee of Ten, which reported its conclusions in 1893. The committee established that the major purpose of secondary education was preparation for life, not just for college. Accordingly, it recommended that grades 10 through 12 of high school (i.e., secondary school) be extended downward to include grades 7 through 12. This would make it possible to teach some secondary school subjects earlier.

In 1895 another major NEA report was issued (see Stinnett & Henson, 1982; Armstrong, Henson, & Savage, 1993). The NEA's Department of Superintendents Committee of Fifteen also wanted secondary school content to be lowered into grades 7 and 8, but it did not recommend changing the 8–12 grade pattern—in fact, it opposed this change. But four years later the NEA's Department of Secondary Education issued a report produced by its Committee on College Entrance Requirements suggesting a 6–6 grade system, but with an alteration: the upper 6 was to be divided into a 3–3 pattern. This, along with the recommendation of several other committees, promoted the idea that a junior high school was needed to meet the instructional needs of seventh-, eighth-, and ninth-graders.

Curricularists would find it comforting to think that concern for improving the curriculum for this age-group was the main cause for the development of the junior high school, but that would be an oversimplification. Many factors collectively caused the development of the junior high, and some of them had nothing to do with concern for the quality of the curriculum and instruction. Evidence that the junior high school resulted from causes other than educational can be seen in the fact that the early junior high schools were built *before* the goals for junior high were identified.

But there was some real concern for meeting the educational needs of this age-group. The NEA was quick to warn that merely regrouping the old elementary and secondary grades would not meet the needs of adolescent learners, and it provided a list of features needed to make a "real junior high school" (NEA *Research Bulletin*, 1923):

- A building of its own, housing grades 7, 8, and 9 or at least two of these grades
- A separate staff of teachers
- Recognition of individual differences among the students
- A reform of the progression of studies traditionally offered in these grades
- Elective courses to be chosen by the students
- Student activities designed for the needs of early adolescents

Research on the nature of adolescence seemed to demand a special school for these students (Hall, 1904).

Several existing conditions also contributed to the development of the junior high school. These included needs to (1) relieve overcrowded high school classrooms caused by the post–World War I population boom, (2) reduce the high dropout rate, and (3) make more efficient use of the time spent in school.

From the start, junior high schools have varied in many ways. About half the early schools were located in high school buildings, about one-third were housed in elementary schools, and the rest were located in separate buildings. The types of instruction in these schools were equally diverse. Therefore, it is not surprising that the majority of studies found little or no difference in the scholastic attainment of junior high school students and their counterparts in the traditional high schools.

Many studies were conducted to determine the effect of the junior high pattern on the socialization and psychological welfare of the students, but the bulk of these studies found little difference between junior high school students and high school students in grades 7 through 9. By the middle of the twentieth century, studies of the junior high school produced results that were disappointing to proponents who anticipated that these schools would be significantly superior to the high schools.

## The Middle School Movement

Widespread dissatisfaction with the junior high schools combined with several other factors to give rise to a new kind of school—the middle school. By 1950 many critics of the junior high believed that it had lost sight of its original purpose: to serve the unique needs and interests of the adolescent. They believed that the junior high school had gradually become a miniature high school. It is important to note that educators were dissatisfied with the junior high school's failure to attain its goals, but they were not dissatisfied with the goals themselves.

The time was ripe for a new type of school to replace the junior high school. Thus emerged the middle school, defined by Alexander and George (1981, p. 3) as "a school of some three to five years between the elementary and high school focused on the educational needs of students in these in-between years and designed to promote continuous educational progress for all concerned."

Although middle schools grew out of concerns over several junior high school problems, many positive forces also contributed to the development of the middle school. Alexander and George (1981, p. 14) offer three important objectives of the middle school:

1. To provide a program especially adapted to the wide range of individual differences and special needs of the "in-between-ager."

2. To create a school ladder arrangement that promotes continuity of education from school entrance to exit.

3. To facilitate, through a new organization, the introduction of needed innovations in curriculum and instruction.

### History and Status of Middle Schools

The first middle school was opened in Bay City, Michigan, in 1950. Middle schools grew modestly in number for about 15 years, but by the mid-1960s there was rapid growth. By 1980 the number of middle schools in the United States had reached 5000. With such rapid expansion, it is not surprising that middle schools vary greatly. Some middle schools encompass grades 5 through 8, some have grades 6 through 8, and some 5 through 7. Some use interdisciplinary team-teaching, but most do not. Less than half the middle schools use flexible scheduling. Failure of states to pass legislation defining the role of the middle school, as well as local concerns and priorities, has undoubtedly contributed to the failure of middle schools to reach their goals. Another problem has been the general failure of middle school principals to adjust their own perceptions and concepts of the middle school. Only a small minority of principals have received special training. Fortunately, middle school teachers have made more progress in adjusting their attitudes toward the middle school student. Unfortunately, the humanist attitude of the middle school teacher has not always resulted in changing his or her behavior.

Middle school teachers should realize that their role carries the responsibility for helping attain the general goals of the middle school. Some of these goals are:

1. To help students progress intellectually, socially, physically, and emotionally
2. To enhance the student's self-image
3. To provide opportunities for success
4. To promote active learning
5. To encourage exploration
6. To provide security

An understanding of the nature of the middle school student will help teachers and other curriculum developers who want to contribute to the goals of the middle school. For instance, middle school students are active by nature. Klingele (1979, p. 33) offers the following description of middle school students:

- Middle school students, by their very nature, need and desire a variety of challenging and flexible learning activities.
- Middle school students both desire and are capable of accepting variable amounts of responsibility for learning.
- Middle school students learn variable degrees of content, at different rates, and at different times.
- Middle school students will learn more and better when actively involved in the learning activity.
- Middle school students learn through various learning styles—no one style is necessarily effective for all students.
- Middle school students learn best in environments characterized by a respectful, warm, informal, and personalized climate.

Clearly, a major responsibility of curriculum developers who plan for this age-group is to find many and varied ways of encouraging all students to participate in their education, but this does not always happen. All too often the school practitioners, both teachers and administrators, have strayed from the purposes for which the middle school was originally designed. Lately, this situation has led to considerable criticism of middle schools.

## Goals of the Middle Schools in the 1990s

Throughout the years, the original student-centered goals for middle schools have been refined. As might be expected, the list of goals has grown. The National Middle School Association's list of priority events for middle schools during the 1900s shown in Figure 3.1 makes it evident that the early concern for providing for the uniqueness of the middle-level students has prevailed. Notice the particular emphasis that is given to meeting this goal through curriculum development.

### Transescence

Middle schools exist in varying grade patterns. Some span grades 5 through 8, whereas others include as few as two grades (often 5 and 6, 6 and 7, or 7 and 8). Because most junior high schools include grades 7 through 9, students there are usually at the adolescent stage; most schools cater to the preadolescent. *Transescence* is a term that refers to the preadolescent to early adolescent ages.

There is relatively little in the literature about the transescent student; few studies have focused on this age-group. Transescence is difficult to define because it is tied to our history and to our culture. For example, being a 12-year-old in the United States is different from being a 12-year-old in Japan. Both 12-year-olds have a few physical characteristics in common, but identifying other similarities is difficult because of the many different expectations of this age-group caused by different cultural environments. Furthermore, being a 12-year old in the 1990s is different from what it was to be a 12-year old in the 1950s. In a sense, it is not possible to discuss adolescence outside a socio-historical perspective. From a psychological perspective, during adolescence an integration of past experiences, a development of a sense of individuality, and a growing awareness of personal destiny all take place.

As youths enter the preadolescent ages, they may become less focused, and their attention spans may grow shorter. They often develop a keen sense of interdependence. But as we consider such "typical" characteristics, we must remember that many individual members of this age-group are perfect "nonexamples" of the stereotype. For instance, we might well think of middle school as a time of change (from child to adolescent and from reliance on home guidance to increased reliance on peer guidance), but a study of primarily middle-class suburban students reported that "stability, not change, is the overriding characteristic in the psychological patterns of reaction of these older adolescents" (Offer, 1969, p. 222).

Although the terms *transescence* and *adolescence* are almost impossible to define, teachers of middle and junior high school students are quick to say that there is something unique about the preadolescent and early adolescent. This uniqueness makes teaching this group a real challenge—and extremely satisfying. The young adolescent is sometimes described as lonely and vulnerable (Konopka, 1973). Teachers of this age-group are often surprised to learn how important teacher approval is to their students. And many of them find it very rewarding to teach this age-group because of the opportunity they have for influencing the lives of their students.

Another challenge to curriculum developers is determining the level of intellectual expectations to set for these students. Research has shown that

Priority 1    Middle-level schools are recognized as a legitimate level of education, along with elementary and secondary schools.

Priority 2    Both curriculum and instruction become more relevant to the developmental characteristics of middle-level students.

Priority 3    Teams are organized or reorganized into interdisciplinary teams with shared responsibility for the same group of students.

Priority 4    Universities and colleges (nationwide) offer state approved middle-level certification programs.

Priority 5    Public acceptance of the middle school philosophy leads to a vision that supports the growth and development of middle-level schools.

Priority 6    In-service/re-education of existing middle-level and non-middle-level certified faculty is increased to implement and maintain knowledge of the middle-level child.

Priority 7    Cooperative learning and other heterogeneous strategies will replace current grouping and tracking strategies.

Priority 8    A majority of middle-level schools adopt interdisciplinary teaming and advisor-advisee programs.

Priority 9    State/local policy makers recognize the need for adequate funding of middle-level education.

Priority 10   Curriculum will be more integrated and interdisciplinary throughout the middle school program.

Priority 11   Programs to develop skills in resisting peer pressures, to help form values, and to teach the causes and effects of substance abuse are increased.

Priority 12   Parents and schools form partnerships to meet the needs of the whole child.

Priority 13   Middle-level professionals are major student advocates, serving as connectors for students from elementary to middle school and from middle school to high school.

Priority 14   Collaboration and cooperative problem-solving replace competition as the driving philosophy of middle-level instruction.

Priority 15   The "integrity" of the middle school program is preserved.

Priority 16   Leaders are faced with developing plans that allow for continued growth and development of middle-level schools and the middle school movement.

**Figure 3.1** The NMSA Delphi Report-Priority Events
*Source:* Jenkins, D.M., and Jenkins, K.D. (1991, March). "The NMSA Delphi report: Roadmap to the future." *Middle School Journal,* 22(4): p. 29. Reprinted by permission.

only a few individuals in this age-group have developed the ability to function well at the formal operations level (Stefanich, 1990).

## Curriculum Needs of Middle-Level Students

Studies show that there is a hiatus in brain growth between the ages of 12 and 14 (Epstein, 1976). One can therefore conclude that the curriculum should allow students to use the mental skills they have already developed rather than designing curricula that require them to acquire new skills.

Paradoxical demands are made on curricula designed for middle-level students. For example, attempts to make students feel secure and well adjusted may remove "the springs of their intellectual and artistic productivity" (Hudson, 1966). Eichorn (1980, p. 67) says: "The mercurial nature of the transescent requires a fluid but structured atmosphere. It [their curriculum] should provide students with the security of structure, but it should be sufficiently elastic to permit students to explore learning and socialization in a manner consistent with individual needs." Since youths in the middle years are seeking greater independence, there should be provision for activities that allow students to accept challenges, and there should be support from the teacher to help them meet those challenges.

Winn, Regan, and Gibson (1991, p. 265) introduce another challenge that faces middle-level teachers and other curriculum developers—another mercurial quality of transescents: "One main characteristic of the learner during the fifth through the eighth grades is that his or her strategies for learning are unpredictable. Because the move from concrete operations to formal operation occurs during this time, the learning vacillates between the two as the shift is occurring."

Alexander and George (1981) emphasize the need for activities at the middle level:

> Friendliness is a needed element in the school climate, [and] a variety of learning experiences should be provided . . . to permit students to pursue their curiosity and grow intellectually. Several middle school authorities have emphasized the need for making the middle school curriculum an ongoing set of activities for continued learning and organized knowledge.

As Alexander and George explain, middle and junior high school teachers should learn how to plan curricula that are chock-full of activities, each one leading to the next.

## A Middle-School Curriculum

Certain principles, based on developmental characteristics, should underpin the middle years' curriculum. Winn, Regan, and Gibson (1991, pp. 266,267) offer the following characteristics, which can be used to ensure the effectiveness of middle-level curricula:

1. The learner must be an active participant.
2. Strategies for learning should be taught, modeled, and retaught as necessary.
3. Oral language should be encouraged to allow sharing of the thought process.
4. Transfer of learning strategies should be taught.
5. Vocabulary should be taught orally through regular use of new words as well as activities to enlarge vocabulary.
6. Small learning groups should be a regular part of the classroom organization.
7. Teacher feedback should deal primarily with learning rather than discipline.
8. Learners need to have time to react and share their learning with interested listeners.
9. Learners need to hear excellent readers read.
10. Reading should be viewed as a means to an end, not the end in itself.
11. Learners need to produce their own reading materials.

## Curriculum Issues

By the middle of the twentieth century, the question of how content should be structured had become a hot issue. The Progressive Movement had blended the various disciplines in the belief that more understanding would result. For example, the "core curriculum" had become very popular: A core of common experiences was believed essential for all students, and some of these experiences were interdisciplinary. But interdisciplinary movements were criticized severely by educators such as Arthur E. Bestor (1953), who believed that they had weakened the curriculum. Bestor and others criticized schools severely for this "anti-intellectualism."

## Curricula That Promote Inquiry

In the 1950s, urged on by such critics as California's superintendent of education, Max Rafferty, and U.S. Navy Admiral Hyman Rickover, the American public reexamined its schools. There was a general attitude of disappointment, culminating in the Russians' launching of the world's first satellite in 1957. Harvard University's president, James B. Conant, had already been insisting that the secondary school curricula should be more rigorous. He especially urged that stronger minimum requirements be made of all students, even more for the academically gifted.

As a result, a special committee convened in Woods Hole, Massachusetts, in 1959 to design a better system for educating American youth. The 35 leaders in education, government, industry, and science concluded that education should be built around broad theories and concepts. The following year,

Woods Hole Conference committee member Jerome S. Bruner reported the general conclusions of the study in his book *The Process of Education* (p.33). One of his often-quoted statements in that book expresses the emphasis that the committee placed on structuring knowledge so that it could be more easily learned. Said Bruner: "Any subject can be taught effectively in some intellectually honest form to any child."

The 1960s saw a veritable alphabet soup of educational programs that often integrated two or more disciplines in an attempt to help students learn to inquire and discover relationships. Some of the more popular programs were the SMSG (Science-Mathematics-Study Group), ESCP (Earth Science Curriculum Project), BSCS (Biological Sciences Curriculum Study), PSSC (Physical Science Study Committee), and ISCS (Intermediate Science Curriculum Study). Another contribution was Benjamin Bloom's Taxonomy of Educational Objectives, which enabled teachers to build learning experiences on increasingly higher levels of the thought processes. With advances in technology came another reason for structuring learning experiences: Students needed to be stimulated to think through processes and to establish relationships themselves, not just to remember facts but to use those facts to solve problems.

## Curricula That Humanize

An important goal of today's schools is to humanize the school environment. The first schools were typically one-room buildings designed to accommodate at most a few dozen students, but during the early 1950s there was a national trend toward consolidation. This resulted in larger and larger schools, until today a school of 2000, 3000, or 4000 students is common. The advantage is that more diversity of subjects is possible; the disadvantage is the resulting impersonal, dehumanizing environment.

## Multicultural Curricula

Currently, members of the many different cultures represented in our schools are receiving attention. Researchers are trying to determine the most effective ways to teach in multicultural settings and to design curricula that promote an appreciation for diversity. The area of concern is expanding to include groups that have traditionally been ignored even when attention was given to other minority groups.

Effective management of multiculturalism will require each faculty and each faculty member to invent curriculum and instructional approaches to meet the needs of the unique student body at each school and the needs of each unique classroom. Student involvement in the development of multicultural curricula, individualization, and personalization is indispensable.

## Curricula That Individualize or Personalize

The 1960s saw much attention being placed on individualizing the curriculum, and some very good programs were developed. Individualized Guided Education (IGE), a program developed in Wisconsin, and Individually Prescribed Instruction (IPI), developed at the University of Pittsburgh, are two of the most successful. The competency-based movement of the 1970s introduced individualization into American schools at all levels, elementary through university. Competency-based programs have made significant contributions to individualizing education but, ironically and often justifiably, have been labeled *dehumanizing.* It is becoming increasingly obvious that mere individualization is not enough. Our huge contemporary schools with their complicated schedules (many running on double shifts) need more. They need ways of personalizing all aspects of the schooling process.

Technology offers new opportunities to personalize the curriculum. This may seem strange to those who consider technology impersonal, but it is not at all strange if you consider the advise of technology experts who tell us that the first and most important rule for effective educational technology is to start with the student and design the curriculum and technology to fit the student. Means and Olson (1994, p. 18) say "Technology plays an important role, but it is a supporting role. The students are the stars." It is also not strange to David Thornberg, the author of *Edutrends 2010* (1992), who says that "informational technology has become personalized (and) . . . students will be taking more control over their learning, taking control away from the educator." (Betts, 1994, p. 20) Teachers whose major concern is the development of their students should welcome this change and should design open-ended curricula to promote student independence.

One example of using technology to encourage minority students to stay in school is an English and journalism curriculum at San Diego's inner-city school, Memorial Academy. About 80 percent of the students in this program are minorities. Using HyperCard (Claris Works software for the Macintosh), the teacher, Linda Taggart (1994), tells students to discover all they can about their parents and their origin. They develop "stacks" (electronic flipbooks similar to index cards). Since the students began using the computer to write their program, Taggart reports that they have become more highly motivated and their stories are longer and more thoroughly revised (p. 34).

## The New Basics

How can anyone know what needs the future will bring and what goals future schools will have? The task is not as impossible as it sounds; in fact, there are some definite goals. Dr. Harold Shane, former professor of education at Indiana University, called them the "new basics" for our secondary schools. These goals include the need to (1) learn how to live with uncertainty, complexity, and change, (2) develop the ability to anticipate, (3) adapt to new structures, new constraints, and new situations without emotional drain and emotional collisions, (4) learn how to learn, that is, learn how to search out contradictions in one's values and understandings, (5) see relationships and be able to sort and weigh them, (6) understand the facts of life (realities) and become aware of alternatives; (7) learn to analyze the consequences of one's choices, (8) learn how to make choices, and (9) learn how to work together to get things done. For example, youth must learn how to reach compromises and how to accept compromises with honor.

## Seven Cardinal Principles

In 1972 the NEA assembled a committee of 50 of the world's most renowned educators, doctors, editors, philanthropists, national leaders of teachers' unions, and scientists to study the validity of the Seven Cardinal Principles of Secondary Education. Although this was not a research project, the predictions of a committee of this eminence are worthy of consideration. The committee reported that our society was moving through a "system's break," that is, experiencing irreversible changes in the universe, for example, changes in Americans' perceptions and attitudes toward the environment, material things, mistrust of institutions, and job alienation.

First, in support of its assertions the committee cautioned others to consider the decline of the "hydrocarbon age." The federal government estimates that if the United States were to stop importing petroleum, it would have only enough domestic petroleum to last for 12 years. Second, North Americans must learn to live less extravagantly. Third, U.S. citizens are living in an "era of entitlement" when people believe that the world owes them a living. Fourth, the U.S. may have to set a growth policy. As early as 1976 this country was importing 7 of the 13 basic ingredients of an industrial society. The nation is moving toward a more regulated society. If we continue to move toward guaranteed employment, guaranteed minimum wages, and guaranteed health care, we must regulate these programs to prevent freeloading. The United States is moving toward conservatism. We have about 20 years to learn to use and save wisely. Every 14 to 15 days the world grows by almost 3 million people, the population of the city of Miami or Houston. Every 3 or 4 days we add the population of South Dakota or Montana. It took all of human history until the time of the Civil War to grow to 1 billion people. The world population is going to expand by this amount in the next 9 years alone. The world can no longer feed its population; each year about 1 billion people starve. Food production increases 2 percent per year, and the population increases by 2 percent. In fact, we can't maintain our current starvation level. Because of spoilage and theft, the net increase of food production is greatly exceeded by the increase in birthrate.

As to the Seven Cardinal Principles, the committee predicted that they would remain relevant for future schools. In the same year as the NEA study

(1972), the U.S. Office of Education joined efforts with the National Association of Secondary School Principals to study the Seven Cardinal Principles. The USOE/NASSP Conference likewise accepted the Seven Cardinal Principles as being important goals of the future, to which they added improved consumerism, versatility, flexibility (a vital goal identified by the previous commission), and helping students learn to feel positive about themselves.

The USOE/NASSP Conference further agreed that the schools can not "do it all"; they must find new ways to share the responsibility of educating young people in an increasingly complex and often confusing society. As educational critic Lawrence A. Cremin (1961) reminds us, the school is only one of the many institutions in our society that are organized to educate our citizens. Others are churches, synagogues, families, libraries, museums, Boy Scouts, day care centers, factories, radio stations, and television networks.

In the *Seventy-fifth Yearbook* of the National Society for the Study of Education, the authors caution repeatedly that even with an awareness of the highly predictable changes discussed above, educational futurists must remember that no prediction is infallible and that in making predictions, futurists should keep open minds so as to avoid tunnel vision.

## Goals for 2000

The Goals for 2000, set by the President and the governors, have been well received by most people.

The public's opinions on these goals are shown in Table 3.3. The Goals for 2000 are as follows:

A. By the year 2000, all children in America will start school ready to learn [i.e., in good health, having been read to and otherwise prepared by parents, etc.].

B. By the year 2000, the high school graduation rate will increase to at least 90% [from the current rate of 74%].

C. By the year 2000, American students will leave grades 4, 8, and 12 having demonstrated competency in challenging subject matter, including English, mathematics, science, history, and geography. In addition, every school in America will insure that all students learn to use their minds, in order to prepare them for responsible citizenship, further learning, and productive employment in a modern economy.

D. By the year 2000, American students will be first in the world in mathematics and science achievement.

E. By the year 2000, every adult American will be literate and will possess the skills necessary to compete in a global economy and to exercise the rights and responsibilities of citizenship.

Table 3.3    The Public's Priorities for Goals for 2000

| Goal | Very High, % 1991 | Very High, % 1990 | High, % 1991 | High, % 1990 | Low, % 1991 | Low, % 1990 | Very Low,% 1991 | Very Low,% 1990 | Unknown, % 1991 | Unknown, % 1990 |
|------|------|------|------|------|------|------|------|------|------|------|
| A | 52 | 44 | 38 | 44 | 6 | 6 | 1 | 2 | 3 | 4 |
| B | 54 | 45 | 37 | 42 | 5 | 8 | 1 | 1 | 3 | 4 |
| C | 55 | 46 | 35 | 42 | 6 | 7 | 1 | 2 | 3 | 3 |
| D | 43 | 34 | 41 | 42 | 11 | 16 | 2 | 3 | 3 | 5 |
| E | 50 | 45 | 36 | 37 | 9 | 11 | 2 | 3 | 3 | 4 |
| F | 63 | 55 | 23 | 26 | 6 | 9 | 5 | 6 | 3 | 4 |

F. By the year 2000, every school in America will be free of drugs and violence and will offer a disciplined environment conducive to learning (National Education Goals Panel, 1991).

President Clinton signed the Goals for 2000: Educate America Act on March 31, 1994.

The public has some major concerns about the feasibility of these goals, as shown in Table 3.4. In summary, the public strongly supports these goals but is skeptical about the likelihood of their attainment.

## PHILOSOPHICAL FOUNDATIONS

Having reviewed the development of American schools, now let's examine the philosophical beliefs which undergird the curricula in these schools.

When Pythagoras (we are told) was asked what he meant when he called himself a *philosopher*, he replied as follows:

> Men enter their lives somewhat like the crowd meets at the festival. Some come to sell their merchandise, that is, to make money; some come to display their physical force in order to become famous; while there is a third group of men who only come to admire the beautiful works of art as well as the fine performances and speeches. In a similar way we meet each other in this life of ours; it is as if each of us were coming from afar, bringing along his own conception of life. Some desire nothing except money; some only strive for fame; while a few wish nothing except to watch or to contemplate the most beautiful things. But what are the most beautiful things? Certainly the universe as a whole and the order according to which the heavenly bodies move around are beautiful. But their beauty is merely a participation in the beauty of the first being which can only be reached by thought. Those who contemplate this first

Table 3.4    The Public's Assessment of Likelihood of
Attainment of Goals for 2000

| Goal | Very Likely, % | | Likely, % | | Unlikely, % | | Very Unlikely, % | | Unknown, % | |
|------|------|------|------|------|------|------|------|------|------|------|
| | 1991 | 1990 | 1991 | 1990 | 1991 | 1990 | 1991 | 1990 | 1991 | 1990 |
| A | 10 | 12 | 37 | 38 | 33 | 33 | 14 | 12 | 6 | 5 |
| B | 6 | 10 | 36 | 35 | 39 | 37 | 14 | 12 | 5 | 6 |
| C | 6 | 9 | 36 | 38 | 36 | 36 | 15 | 12 | 7 | 5 |
| D | 4 | 6 | 22 | 23 | 45 | 41 | 23 | 24 | 6 | 6 |
| E | 6 | 7 | 25 | 25 | 41 | 42 | 23 | 21 | 5 | 5 |
| F | 4 | 5 | 14 | 14 | 38 | 40 | 39 | 36 | 5 | 5 |

being [which Pythagoras seems to have described as the number and the pro-
portion constituting the nature of all things] are the philosophers, the "lovers
of wisdom." For wisdom is the knowledge of things beautiful, first, divine,
pure, and eternal. (Lobkowicz, 1967, pp. 5–6)

The Oxford English Dictionary defines philosophy as "the love, study,
and pursuit of wisdom, or of knowledge of things and their causes, whether
theoretical or practical." Regardless of the source of the definition, philosophy
always involves thinking and is not limited to any subject. It is usually concerned with asking questions which are general and difficult, such as: What is
the purpose of life? What is good? What is truth?

But philosophy can be applied to various disciplines or to specific areas of
thought. For example, natural philosophy is what we know as science.
Philosophy can also be applied to the study of education, thus the school of
educational philosophy or philosophy of education.

## Some Basic Philosophical Systems

For over 22 centuries, philosophers have grappled with many types of questions such as the ones above. These efforts have led to the formulation of several basic philosophical systems, including metaphysics, epistemology, logic,
idealism, realism, naturalism, pragmatism, essentialism, perrenialism, existentialism, progressivism, and reconstructionism.

Philosophies can be distinguished from one another according to the *major*
questions that each poses. *Major* is emphasized here because no question is
beyond the realm of philosophy. Examples of major questions are: What is

real? (metaphysics) What is true? What is the nature of knowledge? (epistemology) What is good? (axiology).

## Metaphysics

Metaphysics literally means "beyond nature." Metaphysics is the study of that which is beyond the natural. The word is used synonymously with *ontology*, the study of existence, or of what it means to be. Shakespeare posed the simple and yet exceedingly complex question "To be or not to be?" What do we mean when we say that we exist or when someone says, "I am"? Does this mean that we simply exist physically, or does it mean more? Does it imply that we also exist spiritually? Any answers to such questions that we might come up with could not be scientifically proved or disproved. Teachers who are able to discern arguable issues do not waste their time, energy, and emotions on matters that have a personal, perceptual base.

When developing curricula, teachers can maximize the results by having a clear concept of what they are striving to have their students become. Most people would agree that the role of philosophy in education is broader than just imparting knowledge; part of this role must be to lead students to become independent inquirers who value wisdom. As we saw earlier, not all educators agree on the role that inquiry should play in education.

Education must also go beyond the empirical sciences and include the study of the supernatural. An example of the need to include the study of existence is found in one of the curriculum models upon which this book is based: the study of concepts, the building blocks in any discipline.

## Epistemology

*Epistemology* is the branch of philosophy that seeks the truth about the nature of knowledge. Epistemologists ask specific questions about the nature of knowledge. For example, does each discipline have its own unique structure, and therefore should it be taught or explored in unique ways? A central purpose of the Woods Hole Conference, discussed in Chapter 1, was to identify the special structures of disciplines, particularly the sciences, mathematics, and foreign language.

Epistemologists might ask educators, "Is one method of learning better than another? Are teaching and learning methods situation-specific? Is the scientific method superior to others?" Educators who think so are likely to include more of the hard sciences in the curriculum; those who accept other learning processes are apt to include more of the humanities in the curriculum. Is giving students information inferior or superior to helping them discover? Is insight better than inquiry? Is knowing more or less important than learning? How teachers answer these questions inevitably affects the kinds of curricula they establish in their classrooms.

## Axiology

*Axiology* is the school of philosophy that deals with values and ethics, raising such questions as "What is good?" "What is valuable?" "What is right?" "What is wrong?" "Is pleasure seeking wrong?" Asking such axiological questions helps teachers understand the role of ethics and values in the curriculum. Chapter 1 mentioned the role that religion had in colonial curricula. Although the church has been legally separated from state-supported schools, some contemporary educators and citizens at large still believe that the role of religion is as important today as it was in colonial America—or even more important.

## Logic

Although teachers vary greatly in their beliefs in the roles of various philosophical constructs in our public schools, teachers unanimously agree that the ability of students to think logically should be a goal of all curricula. Logic is important to teachers because it helps them improve the accuracy of their own conclusions, it helps them more clearly understand the thought patterns of their students, and it helps both teachers and students test the accuracy of their own conclusions.

There are three types of logic: deductive, inductive, and dialectic. *Deductive reasoning* starts with the general and moves to specific. *Inductive reasoning* starts with specifics and makes generalizations about these specifics. *Dialectic reasoning* begins with a thesis, moves to antithesis, and ends with synthesis; then the cycle is repeated.

## Idealism

One of the oldest philosophical systems, *idealism* holds that reality is in ideas. Some say that this system could have well been called *ideaism,* but instead, *idealism* was chosen because the system strives toward perfection. Plato is considered to be the father of idealism. The idealists believe that there are universal truths and values, that the ultimate of human existence is the soul, and that God is the supreme source of absolute and eternal truth.

Educators who support this thought system believe that their role is to make students aware of the absolute ideals, the unanswered truths and values. Their curriculum is rich in the liberal arts, particularly philosophy, theology, and literature.

Some important contributors to idealism include Plato (427–347 B.C.), St. Augustine (354–430), René Descartes (1596–1650), Immanuel Kant (1724–1804), and G. W. F. Hegel (1770–1831).

An important contribution of idealism is in the emphasis that idealists place on thinking. At a time when schedules keep most people running at breakneck speed, proponents of idealism would say that never before have individuals had a greater need for a philosophy that reminds us that our role as educators is to teach students to stop and think.

Critics of idealism would say that today's pace—in school and out of school—does not provide time for thinking through all the issues that confront us. Some critics say that society would never progress if everyone just sat around thinking.

## Realism

Like the idealists, realists believe that human beings should seek the truth. Realists believe in rational explanations, and they believe that the scientific method should be used to discover the rationality of the universe. Formalized during the sixteenth and seventeenth centuries by the English philosopher Francis Bacon, the *scientific method* consists of the following steps:

1. Define the problem
2. Formulate a hypothesis
3. Gather data
4. Interpret the data
5. Use reason to draw a conclusion
6. Test your conclusion

To the realist, the truth is limited to that which can be tested and proved empirically (using the five senses). John Dewey (1939, p. 111) said that the "scientific method is the only authentic means at our command for getting at the significance of our everyday experiences of the world in which we live."

For the realist, the sciences and mathematics should dominate the curriculum. Students should be taught to use logic and the scientific method. The realists believe that the subjects should remain separate; that is, they do not support interdisciplinary programs. The realist searches for the natural order in all things, including content generalizations such as concepts, principles, axioms, and theorems.

Some important contributors to realism include Aristotle (384–322 B.C.), St. Thomas Aquinas (1225–1274), Francis Bacon (1561–1626), John Locke (1632–1704), Johann F. Herbert (1776–1841), and Alfred North Whitehead (1861–1947).

Proponents of realism would argue that our schools should build the curriculum around real-life problems. The current emphasis on integrated curriculum, conceptual themes, and problem solving reflect this philosophy. Critics would say that they just do not have the time to assign problems and wait for students to discover the answers. These teachers will say that they barely have time to cover the necessary content, even when using the most economical instructional strategies.

## Pragmatism

The philosophical structure called *pragmatism* had its origin in the sixteenth and seventeenth centuries. Its major contributors include the English philosopher Francis Bacon (1561–1626), and the German philosopher Immanuel Kant (1724–1804), who coined the term *pragmatism* which means "practical." Pragmatists ask the questions, What is it good for? How can it be applied? Although pragmatism began in Europe, its growth has been led by American philosophers such as Charles Pierce (1839–1914), William James (1842–1910), and John Dewey (1859–1952).

Unlike the idealists and the realists, the pragmatists do not seek universal truths. Rather, they view the world as a world of change. English poet John Wilmont expresses the pragmatist's view of the world: "Tis nature's way to change. Constancy alone is strange."

Since the world is ever-changing, human beings must constantly examine their own desires. Information which is useful to help people reach their desires is valuable.

To the pragmatist, the role of education is to help students learn how to discover themselves, and the best way to do this is through direct experience. So the curriculum should be learner-centered and experience-based, full of problem-solving activities, one type of curriculum that was described in Chapter 1 and that dominated the Progressive Education Era.

An example of pragmatism in today's schools is the American Studies program (see pages 130-136). Another example is the Montessori method. The curricula for all these programs are experiential, and all involve problem solving. Those in today's schools who oppose this philosophy would claim that the content essential to understanding is missing. In some communities today, a debate is raging over the reform policy that requires teachers to use a "framework" in lieu of content guides. Some reformers claim that the framework, presented in the form of interdisciplinary, thematic problems, is all that is needed; that is, the important content will be discovered naturally in the course of completing the problems. Those who resist want more assurance that the important content will be covered. They say that the major concepts required to understand each discipline should be identified. However, not all systems using the curriculum framework choose not to specify pertinent content. Those states and districts that identify the pertinent content to be taught generally receive more positive responses from teachers.

## Existentialism

One of the newest philosophical structures is *existentialism*. Existentialists believe that the only meaning of life is what each individual makes of it. What is important is the present, and therefore, individuals should be free to do what makes them happy (eat, drink, and be merry).

Educators who accept this structure design curricula with a lot of electives. The curriculum of the famous English school Summerhill reflects an
existentialist view. The school gave students almost total freedom. The only
rules were that students cannot hurt other people or the property of others. In
his book *Emile*, French philosopher Jean-Jacques Rousseau (1712–1778), generally considered a pragmatist, offered a curriculum that reflected existentialist
thinking. The subject of the book, a boy named Emile (who was modeled after
a tutee of Rousseau), was free to do as he pleased, but when he broke a window in his room, he suffered the consequences of his behavior—the cold wind
and rain blew in. Many famous, private, and permissive American schools
also reflect an existentialist perspective.

The complete devotion of existentialism to individuality limits the influence that this philosophical structure has had on schools. Some major contributors to existentialism are Sören Kierkegaard (1813–1855), Gabriel Marcel
(1889–1973), and Jean-Paul Sartre (1905–1980).

Critics of existentialism worry about society's becoming hedonistic. Many
people point to the increase in crime and the decline in morality in modern society. They say that they do not want role models like Rousseau, who gave all his
own children away to free himself to travel and "ponder life's sweet existence."

New forms of existentialism are found in today's schools. For example, the
distribution of condoms to students can be viewed as a reflection of the permissiveness that characterizes this philosophy.

Proponents of this philosophy argue that the curriculum should teach students to live for the moment. This, after all, is their perception of the purpose
of life.

## Essentialism

In rebuttal to the Progressive Education Movement, William Bagley organized
a new philosophical structure called *essentialism*. Bagley believed that the purpose of schools is to stabilize society by teaching that knowledge which is
essential. This would require mastery of subjects such as reading, writing,
arithmetic, history, and English, which are essential to prepare students for
productive lives. The teaching of these subjects should be organized from the
simple to the complex and from the concrete to the abstract.

Clearly, the curriculum for essentialists has no room for frills or individualizing or for nonessential, "popular" courses. Academic rigor must be the
standard for all if the essential intellectual and practical goals are to be reached.

## Perennialism

*Perennialism* emphasizes that knowledge which has endured through the years.
Americans Robert Hutchins and Mortimer Adler introduced perennialism during the twentieth century. Perennial subjects include classical literature, philosophy, science, history, and the fine arts. The goal of the perennialist is to develop
and challenge the intellect—to prepare students for life by teaching them to
think. The perennial curriculum emphasizes the humanities and the three R's.

Opponents of perennialism would argue that the purpose of schools is to teach students to think.The perennialists agree but believe that the best way to achieve this lofty goal is through studying a combination of classical subjects (including the humanities and the fine arts) and the basics.

Some critics of Perennialism argue that students cannot be prepared for the changing world by studying age-old subjects. For example, many parents believe that the main purpose of education is to prepare students to get good paying jobs. These parents will not settle for their children just gaining knowledge; this might be nice, but it isn't as important as knowing how to earn a living.

Herein lies a natural conflict between perennialist teachers and parents who hold a more conservative "earn a living" attitude. In college most teachers learn to appreciate the arts and literature. They may want more for their students than the parents want.

## Reconstructionism

Like pragmatism and perennialism, reconstructionism is considered an American structure. Reconstructionists believe that the schools should be "reconstructed" to remove from our society such cultural crises as poverty, racism, ignorance, and war.

Reconstructionists are quick to remind us that most teachers come from middle-class families and therefore have a propensity to protect the society they have always known. Reconstructionists say that because of their middle-class backgrounds, most teachers don't know about poverty and unemployment.

Reconstructionist-based curricula focus on the major problems of society and prepare students to make critical analyses. Emphasis is placed on the behavioral sciences, and students are taught to influence the community.

Some major contributors to reconstructionism include Plato (427–347 B.C.), Harold Rugg, St. Augustine (354–430), John Dewey (1859–1952), George Counts (1889–1974), and Theodore Brameld (1904-    ).

Reconstructionists believe that society has lost its way (Armstrong et al., 1993), and they believe that society has traveled too far down its misguided path to be corrected by tinkering; correcting its problems will require major reform. Reconstructionists believe that the role of the school is to empower citizens with the capacity to ensure that democratic principles will be followed, bringing equity to all areas of society.

Reconstructionists believe that a major responsibility of the schools is to teach students to analyze and question practices that they perceive as being unfair to individuals or groups, and that perhaps the schools' foremost responsibility is to motivate students to take action to correct inequities.

George S. Counts and Harold Rugg were major leaders in the development and growth of reconstructionism. In his book *Dare the Schools Build a New Social Order?* Counts (1932) answered his own question with a resounding yes.

Reconstructionists have always been concerned with the mission of the school's curriculum, which, to them, is clear: To redesign a society which has become inequitable. Modern reconstructionists are keenly focused on the Goals for 2000 and on the direction of educational reform programs. Some contemporary topics that concern reconstructionists are AIDS, pollution, immorality, inhumanity, world hunger, crime, and war. Reconstructionists believe that topics such as these should dominate the curriculum. These topics are especially important because they are universal; reconstructionists believe that the curriculum should address global problems.

Thus reconstructionists believe that the curriculum should enlighten students politically. Believing that they have a responsibility to improve society in every way, they would quickly recognize and take action to correct the failure of educators to promote the cause and value of education to the masses.

The reconstructionist philosophy, which is deeply concerned with the welfare of society and espouses action to improve the community and society, should not be confused with *revolutionism*, which holds that the only way to improve society is to destroy the existing system. The concept of reconstruction has appealed to a wide range of personalities and fostered a number of subphilosophies. For example, some educators and philosophers consider Francis Parker and John Dewey to be superb examplars of reconstructionism, whereas others, for example, Counts, perceived them and other progressives as failures. Viewing progressive educators as weak and ineffective, Counts (1932, p. 259) called on them to:

> . . . Face squarely and courageously every social issue, come to grips with life in all of its stark reality, establish an organic relation with the community, develop a realistic and comprehensive theory of welfare, fashion a compelling and challenging vision of human destiny, and become somewhat less frightened than it is today at the bogeys of imposition and indoctrination. In a word, Progressive Education cannot build its program out of the interests of children: it cannot place its trust in a child-centered school.

Obviously, Counts was more radical in his beliefs and the ways he communicated them than were the progressives.

## Application of Reconstructionism Today

In the 1990s every school in the United States is being affected by education reform. Indeed, in some ways and to varying degrees, most schools are contributing to the reform movement. Yet the nature of reform from one school to another differs immensely. Some faculties embrace reform, seeing it as an opportunity to improve education for the students; other see it as an imposition on their time and energy. Because reform is being forced rapidly by outside change agents, many highly professional, highly energetic, and highly dedicated teachers find it impossible to avoid feeling imposed upon by state and local reformers.

The nature of the cultures in the surrounding community partly explains the differences in the ways various faculties feel. The local school administration and its policies can also be strong forces shaping the ways faculties feel about and react to reform policies.

The above comments have described school faculties as though each is a living organism with a single mind-set; yet each faculty is made of individual personalities, each one of which can be described as either a reconstructionist or not. Each activist can be placed on a scale, some on the moderate side with Dewey and Parker, and others on the extreme side with Counts. As we think about the school with which we are most familiar, it is easy to identify the extremists but it is sometimes not so easy to pigeonhole the many individuals who do not openly express their philosophies.

Some individuals may question the value of studying philosophies in a curriculum course. Yet, if we think of philosophies not so much as dry statements in dusty books but rather as the people we know, and if we consider the tremendous influence some of our fellow teachers have in every meeting they attend, from meetings to plan for an accreditation visit to deciding how to use this year's in-service planning days, then perhaps we can see that our individual and collective philosophies determine how we behave toward all issues. Indeed, our philosophies even determine how we feel about issues and about other people. In no other philosophical structure is this more obvious than it is in reconstructionism.

## Some Influences of Philosophy on Education

### Assessment

The philosophy of education is concerned with abstract and difficult questions such as, "What are the purposes of education?" The philosophy of education helps in the establishment of long-range objectives.

An analogy may help to explain this major function of the philosophy of education. A traveler had been lost for several hours: After escaping from a series of traffic jams which had left him feeling quite exasperated, he finally found the open road. As he drove along happily and rapidly, a passenger inquired if he weren't still lost. "Well, yes," he replied, "as a matter of fact I am still lost, but we are making excellent time, aren't we?"

Educators can make good time and yet be lost and without any long-range goals. Curriculum developers must know what to teach and what effects they wish schooling to have on students. They must know what they would have students become. For these answers, curriculum developers must turn to the philosopher, for the philosopher will force them to formulate a system of values and decide which values are more important than others. Armed with a system of values, curriculum developers can then adjust teaching methodology and the curriculum in accordance with their ultimate educational objectives. As one philosopher, Herbert Spencer, said: "In determining a curriculum, our first step must be to classify, in order of their importance, the leading kinds of activity which constitute human life."

Since the value systems of no two people are the same, there will always be conflict. Our values are continually changing, and we must continually readjust our school programs to align them with our current value system.

## The Teacher's Influence

The second contribution philosophy makes to education is through the influence of the teacher. Thought inevitably leads to action; the way teachers think influences the way they act. Our values and our views of the totality of existence will affect our relationships with others. If the teacher has good rapport with students, the teacher's beliefs and value system will affect the pupils.

For example, consider two political points of view and how each might affect the teacher's classroom behavior. President Franklin D. Roosevelt once said: "The real safeguard of democracy is education. The importance of education is greater than the welfare of any political party." In marked contrast, it was Adolf Hitler's belief that education was not a means for protecting democracy but was a corroding poison which had the power to destroy it.

An American history or government teacher who possesses the first point of view, the democratic philosophy, will obviously approach classes differently than will a foreign teacher who holds the point of view held by Hitler. Certainly the teacher who holds an authoritarian point of view will resent being questioned by students. Democratic teachers would purposefully plan for their students to question their statements. As R. S. Peters (1966) said, teachers should not be interested in having the students accept their point of view or even in what point of view the pupil possesses; rather, the teacher should be concerned with whether the student's view, whatever it may be, is based on sound reasoning.

Teachers often find themselves in a seemingly impossible position when trying to teach about such controversial issues as abortion, drug use, and war. Students inevitably ask questions to learn their teachers' points of view. If teachers reveal their opinions, many students will accept them without questioning their validity. This is perhaps the worst thing that could happen because it prevents students from engaging in the process of reasoning. Ideally, the teacher's desire for students to engage in the reasoning process will eclipse the desire to have pupils accept the teacher's views. However, this does not suggest that teachers should have no influence on students. Rather, teachers have a particular type of influence: (1) fostering of the ability to think independently rather than to blindly accept the opinions of others and (2) simultaneously promoting the foundations upon which the United States Constitution is based.

## An Agent of Change

What role does the philosophy of education play in changing education? Some philosophers view philosophy as a theoretical activity which follows its own disciplinary rules and is not in itself practical or reforming. If you accept this point of view, you must believe that it is not the purpose of philosophy of education to change education. However, this philosopher points out that it is essential that the person who philosophizes about education care intensely about the practice and improvement of education. The word improvement implies change. This suggests that although philosophers are unlikely to suggest specific changes in our schools, they are likely to affect teachers so that the teachers will be stimulated to make changes, the need for which the philosopher may be quite unaware.

With regard to the role that philosophy of education plays in making changes, some things are clear: (1) The philosophy of education does contribute to change, but only when such change is needed, (2) the contribution may be more indirect than direct, and (3) the types of change caused by the philosopher deal with the important values of life and therefore, are likely to be monumental changes. Currently, there exists an urgent need for educators to look at the whole education process in totally new and different ways, to explore the subconscious part of behavior, and to consider the basic overall changes in people when designing school curricula. This seems to illustrate the type of change that the philosopher is likely to stimulate—major change brought about as an indirect result of the philosopher's help in sorting out the more valuable things in life.

## A Moral Guide

Should our curriculum teach ethics? If so, what role does philosophy play in moral education? If we believe that no knowledge exists merely for its own sake, and all knowledge must in some way affect conduct, the answer to these questions is that teachers cannot avoid teaching ethics. Another reason why teachers must be concerned with ethics is that, in any society, education serves to help initiate its young into its culture, and certainly moral beliefs are a large part of any culture.

But education must do more than just hand down the ethics of one generation to the next. As our culture changes, so do our moral standards. In ancient Greek, *heritage* meant "process"; later it meant "content." Now it means the whole intellectual, moral, and cultural setting into which we are born.

By *ethical and moral foundations* we mean how our society responds to the basic question Are there relationships that are right and any that are wrong? The answer is not clear. In the Western world there are two opposing positions: The Christian tradition, which possesses beliefs of absolute right and wrong, and the Greek view that human beings, through their own reasoning, make their own morals. This places teachers in a difficult position. How can they transmit such conflicting information to students?

As previously noted, some educators believe that education must strive to enable pupils to think for themselves and make up their own minds. Most modern educators would agree that the curriculum must respect students' intellectual integrity and promote their capacity for independent judgment.

With respect to the moral role of philosophy in education, we can say that (1) education has a moral responsibility to its pupils, (2) teachers should teach the morals of the society to their pupils, and (3) teachers must not impose their beliefs on their pupils but must encourage them to apply their own intellectual ability to reason out their own modes of behavior.

## A Clarifier

Philosophy has yet another role in education: To help clarify concepts such as *cause, self, mind,* and *good*. By doing this, philosophers will inevitably help to clarify the relationships of these abstractions to each other, which will lead to the criticizing of current educational theories.

## A Process

The preceding paragraphs have presented philosophy as a thinking process for answering the most abstract, the most general, and certainly the most difficult types of questions. Kant told his pupils: "You will not learn from me philosophy, but how to philosophize, not to repeat, but how to think. Think for yourselves, inquire for yourselves, stand on your own feet." An important role of educational philosophy is to make us aware of the need for asking questions.

## Some Changes Made by Philosophers

If the philosophy of education is a process, if it is more than just thinking for fun, if it has any practical meaning to education, then surely we should be able to look at a contemporary curriculum and see some evidence of the influence of the important philosophers of education. The next paragraphs deal with a few of the many important changes made by just a few of the many important philosophers who were interested in improving education.

### Rousseau

Jean-Jacques Rousseau is perhaps best known for his belief in the "innate goodness" of the child. He believed that there existed a pattern for perfection which would develop naturally within each child if it were not tampered with by adults. Therefore, he perceived the role of education as that of kindling the child's natural growth and development pattern. He cautioned teachers not to interfere with this natural process by imposing restrictions on the child and punishing the child. Exactly how would Rousseau have us educate our children?

In his book *Emile*, Rousseau described the type of education he advocated. The first 11 years of one's education should be nature's education or "negative" education. He believed that nature has set in us a natural speed for learning and that the child should be left alone to learn at his or her own speed. If this is done, the child will learn kindness and respect for genuine authority, law, and order. Rousseau suggested that, during these years, books, lectures, formality, and all forms of structure be avoided. Can this philosophy be seen in today's curricula and in today's classrooms? If so, at what levels? Is the curriculum less rigid than ever before? Are the activities more child-centered? Many current reform laws require performance evaluation and progress reporting in lieu of pencil and paper tests. Is Rousseau's philosophy reflected in these reform practices?

Rousseau would have social education begin at age 12. He believed that among adolescents shyness and other feelings and emotions are natural forces of control. During the earlier years, Rousseau would have us protect our children from others, but we must teach them to socialize as adolescents. Why? Because this is the strongest defense we can give them against their corrupt environment.

But, you may ask, is this reasonable? Can we teach the child in isolation from others? Is it practical today? Many people would object to such a point of view even if it were practical, because they do not believe, as Rousseau did, that society is naturally corrupt. Do you disagree with parts of Rousseau's philosophy?

Through today's curricula, teachers encourage students to ask questions. Frequently, unit projects are encouraged or required. To some degree, at least, students are involved in the selection of course content. Rousseau would be pleased that most daily lesson plans encourage at least some student participation. All these practices seem distinctly correlated with Rousseau's belief in the natural developmental process of the child.

The philosophy of Rousseau is seen vividly in many "experimental" schools. The famous English school Summerhill, whose practices approach the complete freedom which Rousseau advocated for children, has successfully existed for well over half a century.

## Pestalozzi

Johann Heinrich Pestalozzi (1746–1827) was influenced greatly by the works and ideas of Rousseau, yet he was more realistic than Rousseau. Pestalozzi attempted to implement Rousseau's ideas in his school and found them most impractical. Pestalozzi saw that *some* structure in schools is necessary. He viewed the school as a good home, the teacher as a good parent. He believed that the practice of education is concerned with living and that children learn most when they do what children naturally do.

A second major difference between the theories of Pestalozzi and those of Rousseau is that, instead of protecting children from society, Pestalozzi believed that the school should help develop the society. Pestalozzi would be pleased to see contemporary schools dealing with society's most controversial, most difficult, and most important problems. The authors of most of the educational reform reports clearly believe that the school is responsible for solving these problems. This belief was vivid at the time of *Sputnik* and it is equally so today.

### Montessori

Maria Montessori was undoubtedly influenced by the works of both Rousseau and Pestalozzi. This is clearly seen in the concern she showed for the freedom of the individual student. She not only believed that it was morally wrong to rob pupils of their individual freedom but that children could learn more when pursuing activities which interested them. This meant that the teacher should observe children and discover what kinds of activities they enjoy, and then design curricula accordingly. Knowing that children enjoy games, Montessori developed games to teach. These games were the forerunners of many learning games used in today's curricula.

### Dewey

Because philosophers deal with global ideas, they are frequently criticized. Many people find it disturbing that philosophers tell us how education should be and what it should do for students without telling us how it can be done. Perhaps the most common criticism of philosophy is that it is not practical.

This criticism could never be directed at John Dewey, who seemed to think that no idea about education was worthwhile unless it could be implemented in our schools. He also took that additional and so essential step—he suggested how to make education as it should be. Dewey's theory was that children "learn by doing." Students should be involved through the use of all their senses.

Dewey's philosophy is reflected in schools throughout this country and in the many experimental laboratory schools which he helped develop. He helped to make our schools pupil-centered instead of subject-centered and teacher-centered.

## Some Specific Influences of Philosophical Structures on School Curricula

Having reviewed some of the general ways that philosophy affects schools, now let's focus our attention on the specific philosophical structures discussed in this chapter and the specific ways that each of them is affecting our schools. For example, Sizer (1992) has made a plea for schools to empower students with greater independence. In fact, he has said that the schools, themselves, have contributed to students' high level of dependence. Suppose that some of your faculty supports essentialism, some support idealism, and others support existentialism. In what ways might adherents of each of these philosophical structures purposely or inadvertently pursue practices that contribute to your students' level of dependency?

For example, essentialists often insist on covering so much content at each grade level that teachers are left with no alternative but to lecture, adhering closely to the textbook if, indeed, they are to ensure that their students master the content essential to their success at the next grade level. Might this not prevent students from engaging in problem solving and meaningful dialogue? Or suppose that the idealist faction refuses to support a move by the rest of the faculty to increase the required field experiences, insisting that field experiences are a waste of time and maintaining that, if students are taught how to reason, they will be prepared to handle any situation they might encounter throughout their lives.

Or, suppose that your school is plagued with crime and violence. In an attempt to curb this problem, a series of faculty meetings is held to plan a strategy to deter students from participating in destructive behavior. The idealists might be the strongest support force for this campaign, but the existentialists might resist these efforts, insisting that students are being denied the pursuit of happiness by a group of zealots. Granted, such positions reflect the behavior of extremists; yet extremists are not uncommon nowadays.

Examining the positions that members of different philosophical structures might take on any controversial issues that affect your school can help you be better prepared to avoid or address these problems. For example, many communities today are plagued by left-wing and right-wing extremist groups whose intent is to drastically change the schools. Understanding how these individuals think can be a profitable first step in preparing a strategy to deal with them. A better understanding of the views of others can help us deal with them more rationally and more effectively. An absence of understanding can provoke emotional outbursts which can be as damaging and threatening as is the group we are trying to control or subdue.

## SUMMARY

Formal education in America began in the homes, where teaching of reading, Puritanism, and colonial law was required. In 1635 the forerunners of our current high schools appeared; similar to the English schools, they were designed to prepare the elite for the university. Because their curricula were dominated by classical Latin and Greek, they were called *Latin grammar schools.* They soon gave way to more practical curricula based on the Franklin Academy, founded in 1750. But these schools were private, and many people could not afford them. The first public high schools, called the *Boston English High Schools,* appeared in 1821. Most were very pragmatic, but some were just the opposite.

In 1918 the NEA appointed a commission to identify the goals of secondary schools. Many educators think that the results of the commission, called the *Seven Cardinal Principles of Secondary Education,* are as applicable today as they were then. The twentieth century brought the Progressive Education Movement, which emphasized the practical, child-centered curriculum for 50 years until it gave way to a subject-centered curriculum. This conservative, subject-centered curriculum yielded to a process-centered curriculum following the launching of *Sputnik* in 1957.

All teachers have philosophies, and their personal philosophies inevitably affect their teaching behavior. By examining their beliefs, teachers and other curriculum developers can use these beliefs to design curricula to achieve their overall aims. An awareness of all the major philosophical structures empowers teachers to use their preferred structures to design curricula.

Many philosophical structures have certain concepts in common; in other respects, they differ totally. The only structure universally accepted by educators is logic; almost everyone agrees that the schools should help students learn how to think logically.

## QUESTIONS

1. Why should the textbook be one of several curriculum determiners?
2. Why did the Latin grammar schools become obsolete?
3. Why did the Franklin Academy lose its popularity?
4. What is the significance of the dame schools?
5. What qualities of the Seven Cardinal Principles of Secondary Education have given these principles their endurance?
6. Why has the textbook been the single greatest curriculum determiner throughout the history of American schools?
7. What is the significance of such curricula as the Quincy System, the Gary Plan, the Dalton Plan, and the Winnetka Plan?
8. If the curricula of the Progressive Era were so successful, why did this era end?
9. How does the basis for the development of the junior high school differ from that of the middle school?
10. What is the significance of the Old Deluder Satan Act?
11. What relationships can you see between events in the history of American schools and the current education reform efforts in your district?
12. What is the relationship between the study of the history of our schools and efforts to determine what contemporary curricula should achieve?
13. Suppose that you could use only two of the philosophical structures described in this chapter to develop a curriculum. On which two structures would you base your curriculum? Why?
14. In your subjects, which is the more useful strategy, inductive logic or deductive logic? Why?

15. How does philosophy give direction without dictating directions? (Hint: At this moment, how is the author of this book influencing or directing your thinking?)

16. Why are philosophers always long on questions and short on answers?

17. Why must education work to stabilize society, and change society?

18. Why do teachers have no alternative but to affect the values and morals of their students?

19. Name three qualities in contemporary society that you believe are worth protecting and three qualities that you think should be abolished. Justify your choices.

20. What is your strongest philosophical belief? How can you use this conviction to contribute to your district school reform movement?

## SUGGESTED FURTHER ACTIVITIES

1. Name one goal or aim that you think is of utmost importance to today's schools. Explain how you can work toward achieving that aim or goal.

2. Make a list of the legislated education reforms in your district. This may require some interviews with some of your education professors and/or a visit to your library's reference room and government documents department.

3. Interview three teachers and ask each to identify strengths and weaknesses in local school reform. Make a chart showing the strengths and the weaknesses.

4. Interview one or more education professors and ask them what changes education reform has stimulated in the classes they teach.

5. Compare and contrast the Seven Cardinal Principles of Secondary Education and the Goals for 2000.

6. Make a list of the unique characteristics of transescence and, for each characteristic, describe one way the curriculum can be changed to meet the needs of students in this stage of development.

7. Examine the legislation described in this chapter and list one purpose for each law. Tell how effectively you think current school curricula meet the purpose of each law.

8. What precautions can you take to ensure that your own future curricula are not textbook-dominated?

9. Make a list of the major concepts presented in this chapter.

10. Describe one characteristic of modern classrooms (for example, physical, emotional, psychological) that resulted from the thrust of the Progressive Education Movement.

11. Explain and defend the statement "Curriculum development should take a philosophically eclectic approach." Then challenge the statement.

12. Research the topics of values and morality in education and write a report explaining the differences between values and morals.

13. For the school with which you are most familiar, describe features in the curriculum that reflect the various philosophical structures discussed in this chapter.

14. Read the book *Summerhill* by A. S. Neill and write a brief paper describing the philosophy upon which that school operates.

15. Interview three teachers, asking them what they perceive as the number one purpose of schools. Contrast these responses with the Goals for 2000 and with the Seven Cardinal Principles of Secondary Education listed in Chapter 3.

16. Read the book *Emile* by Jean-Jacques Rousseau and write a paper describing Rousseau's philosophy.

17. Examine your own philosophy of education and decide what you consider to be the three most important purposes of the schools. Then describe at least one student activity you might assign to achieve each purpose.

18. *Philosophy* is the love for the pursuit of wisdom. Describe a strategy for designing your curricula so that your students will be guided to love the pursuit of wisdom.

19. Review the philosophical structures discussed in this chapter and then examine the elements of school reform that are affecting your district. Describe any needs that you see for your reform efforts to use philosophy in designing future reform activities.

20. Disregarding physical attributes, identify your greatest personal strengths and your most important weaknesses. Explain how you can modify or shape your curricula to capitalize on your strengths and compensate for your weaknesses.

## BIBLIOGRAPHY

Alexander, Lamar (1986, November). Time for results: An overview. *Phi Delta Kappan, 68*, 202–204.

Alexander, W. M. and George, P. S. (1981). *The exemplary middle school*. New York: Holt, Rinehart and Winston.

Archambault, R. D. (1964). *John Dewey on education*. New York: Random House.

Armstrong, D. G., Henson, K. T., & Savage, T. V. (1993). *Education: An introduction* (4th ed.). New York: Macmillan.

Backbone (1991, April). Essential for survival on the troubled journey. *A Quarterly Information Resource on issues facing children, adolescents, and families, 7*(1), 1–3.

Betts, F. (1994). On the birth of the communication age: A conversation with David Thornburg. *Educational Leadership, 51* (7), 20–23.

Bonar, B. D. (1992, Fall). The role of laboratory schools in American education. *National Association of Laboratory Schools Journal,* 17(1), 42–53.

Brendtro, L. K., Brokenleg, M., & Van Bockern, S. (1990). *Reclaiming youth at risk, our hope for the future.* Bloomington, IN: National Education Service.

Bruner, J. S. (1960). *The process of education.* Cambridge: Harvard University Press.

Bruner, J. S. (1960). *Toward a theory of instruction.* Cambridge: Harvard University Press.

Campbell, J. K. (1967). *Colonel Francis Parker: The children's crusader.* New York: Columbia University Teachers College Press.

Carbone, P. F., Jr. (1991, Summer). The teacher as a philosopher. *Education Reform,* 55(4), 319–332.

Carroll, Lewis (1898). *Alice's adventures in Wonderland.* London: Oxford University Press.

Coles, R., & Geneve, L. (1990, March). The Moral life of America's school children. *Teacher Magazine.*

Counts, G. S. (1932). *Dare the schools build a new social order?* New York: John Day.

Cremin, L. A. (1961). *The transformation of the school: Progressivism in American education, 1876–1957.* New York: Knopf.

Cremin, L. A. (1976). *Public education.* New York: Basic Books.

Davis, O. L., Jr. (Ed.). (1976). *Perspectives on curriculum development 1776–1976.* Washington, DC: Association for Supervision and Curriculum Development.

Dewey, John (1939). *Experience and education.* New York: Macmillan.

Eichorn, D. H. (1980). The school. In M. Johnson (Ed.), *Toward adolescence.* 79th Yearbook of the National Society for the Study of Education. Chicago: University of Chicago Press.

Epstein, H. T. (1976). A bibliography based framework for intervention projects. *Mental Retardation, 14,* 26–27.

Hall, G. S. (1904). *Adolescence, its psychology, and its relations to physiology, anthropology, sociology, sex, crime, religion, and education.* (Vols. I and II.) New York: Appleton.

Henson, K. T. (1986, April). Middle schools: Paradoxes and promises. *The Clearing House, 59,* 345–347.

Henson, K. T. (1993). *Methods and strategies for teaching in secondary and middle schools* (2nd ed.). New York: Longman.

Holt, John (1971). *How children fail.* New York: Pitman.

Hudson, L. (1966). *Contrary imaginations: A psychological study of the English schoolboy.* Middlesex, England: Penguin.

Jones, V. (1991). Responding to students' behavior problems. *Beyond Behavior, 2*(1), 17–21.

Klingele, W. E. (1979). *Teaching in middle schools.* Boston: Allyn & Bacon.

Konopka, G. (1973). Requirements for healthy development of adolescent youth. *Adolescence, 8,* 2.

Lobkowicz, Nicholas (1967). *Theory into Practice.* Notre Dame, IN: University of Notre Dame Press. (Cicero, Tusc. v.3, 8–9; Jamblichus, DeVita Pyth.) 58–49.

Means, B. and Olson, K. (1994). "The link between technology and authentic learning." *Educational Leadership, 51*(7), 15-18.

Meyersohn, Maxwell (1950). *The wit and wisdom of Franklin D. Roosevelt.* Boston: Beacon Press.

National Education Association (1923). *Research Bulletin.*

National Education Goals Panel (1991). *Goals Report.* Washington, DC: U.S. Government Printing Office.

Neill, A. S. (1960). *Summerhill.* New York: Hart Publishing Co.

Neimark, E. (1975). In F. D. Horowitz (Ed.), *Review of child development research* (Vol. 4). Chicago: University of Chicago Press.

Nord, W. A. (1991). "Teaching and morality: The knowledge most worth having." In D. D. Dill et al (Eds.), *What teachers need to know.* San Francisco: Jossey-Boss.

Offer, D. (1969). *The psychological world of a teenager.* New York: Basic Books.

Onions, C. T. (1933). *The Shorter Oxford English Dictionary.* Oxford: Clarendon Press, p. 1488.

Perkins, D. (1994). Do students understand understanding? *Education Digest, 59*(5), 21–25.

Peters, R. S. (1966). *Ethics and education.* Atlanta: Scott, Foresman, p. 125.

Phenix, P. H. (1961). *Philosophy of education.* New York: John Wiley and Sons, p. 56.

Renner, J. W., Bibens, R. F., & Shepherd, G. D. (1972). *Guiding learning in the secondary school.* New York: Harper & Row.

Rousseau, J. J. (1979). *Emile.* (Alan Bloom, Trans.). New York: Basic Books.

Shannon, R. L., & Shannon, D. M. (1991, Fall). The British Infant School. *Educational Forum, 56*(1), 61–70.

Sizer, T. R. (1992). *Horace's compromise: The dilemma of the American high school.* Boston: Houghton Mifflin.

Smart M. S., & Smart, R. C. (1978). *Adolescence* (2nd ed.). New York: Macmillan.

Smith, F. R., & Cox, C. B. (1976). *Secondary schools in a changing society.* New York: Holt, Rinehart and Winston.

Smith, T. L. (1912). *The Montessori System.* New York: Harper and Brothers.

Snodgrass, D. M. (1991). The parent connection. *Adolescence, 26,* 83–87.

Spencer, Herbert. (1960). *Education: Intellectual, moral and physical.* New York: D. Appleton, pp. 17–18.

Standing, E. M. (1962). *The Montessori revolution in education.* New York: Shocken Books.

Steeves, F. L., & English, F. W. (1978). *Secondary curriculum for a changing world.* Columbus, OH: Charles E. Merrill.

Stefanich, G. P. (1990). Cycles of cognition. *Middle School Journal,* 22(2), 47–52.

Stinnett, T. M., & Henson, K. T. (1982). *America's public schools in transition: Future trends and issues.* New York: Columbia University Teachers College Press.

Swaim, J. H. (1991, March). Reform of teacher education: Implications for the middle level. *Middle School Journal,* 22(4), 47–51.

Taggert, L. (1994). "Student autobiographies with a twist of technology." *Educational Leadership,* 51(7) 34–35.

Thayer, V. T. (1965). *Formative ideas in American education.* New York: Dodd, Mead.

Thornburg, D. D. (1992). *Edutrends.* San Carlos, Ca.: Starsong Publications.

Van Til, William. (1978). *Secondary education: School and community.* Boston: Houghton Mifflin.

Walker, B. F. (1976). *Curriculum evolution as portrayed through old textbooks.* Terre Haute IN: Curriculum Research and Development Center, Indiana State University.

Winn, D. D., Regan, P., & Gibson, S. (1991, March–April). Teaching the middle years learner. *The Clearing House, 64,* 265–267.

Wynne, E. A., & Ryan, Kevin. (1993). *Reclaiming our schools: A handbook on teaching character, academics, and discipline.* New York: Macmillan.

Zirpoli, T. J., & Melloy, K. J. (1993). *Behavior management: Applications for teachers and parents.* New York: Macmillan.

# Chapter 4

# CONCEPTS, THEORIES, AND MODELS

*No man claiming to be practically versed in a science can disdain its theory without exposing himself as an ignoramus in his field.*

IMMANUEL KANT

## OBJECTIVES

This chapter should prepare you to:

• Describe the role that concepts play in learning.
• Contrast the roles of theories and models in curriculum development.
• Describe and correct two common misconceptions about theory.
• Describe students' relationships with theory.
• Criticize the strengths and weaknesses of six curriculum development models.

## A FUTURE TEACHER'S DILEMMA

Next semester I will be a senior; my grade point average is 3.73—and I feel as if I know nothing. In almost every class I attend, I get nothing but information. I've read that great minds discuss ideas, but my college classes are like petrified forests. Perhaps the ideas are there, but too long ago they were buried under the tons of information built up through the centuries. Long ago the simple-minded pleasure of giving precise answers to precise questions replaced the hard work of intellectual endeavor. It didn't happen overnight; it took a long time, and now, here we are—the petrified forest of education.

Why can't educators see that there is simply too much information to learn? It is important to use the mind. It is important to be able to deal with ideas. It is important to be aware of the changing world out there. Here is the frustration: We are constantly looking backward in order to invent the future. It is not that we don't need information, but must accumulating information be the be-all and end-all?

To me intellectual curiosity is the only constant in education. And unless that curiosity is awakened, no education will, or indeed can, take place. And this awakening does not come from information. Ideas awake the intellect. I realize that ideas is an abstract term. That is precisely why it is so important. Ideas are concepts. As you deal with them, as you try to bring them to concreteness, as you focus your mind on them, you are truly becoming educated. Again, I grant that information is a necessity, but it is gained throughout a lifetime. Unless educators see the difference between wisdom and knowledge and begin dealing with the mind rather than just with information, the classroom will continue to be a sea of mediocrity.

In trying to get an education, I feel like the nonswimmer who dived into the deep end of the pool. My instructors do not know how to swim either. They know all about the ways one should dive; they know all about the right strokes; they know all about the proper breathing procedures; but they have never been in the pool. It isn't that they don't want to help—they just don't know how. The best they can do is stand at the edge of the pool and throw me the empty container that used to hold the life preserver.

I hasten to say that I do not intend to criticize; rather, I am making a plea. For one day soon, I will be a teacher. What am I to do? I cannot go back, for I am already in the water. I cannot go forward, for I cannot swim. There is only one answer: I must learn to swim—even if only enough to stay afloat.

Unfortunately, this bored and disappointed student's description of education is quite typical. But "understanding is not a private possession to be protected from theft but, rather, a capacity developed through the free exchange of ideas" (Wiske, 1994, p. 19), and teachers can change this state of affairs. This chapter discusses ways that teachers and other curriculum developers can put meaning into education.

## INTRODUCTION

This chapter focuses on concepts, theories, and models. Constructivists emphasize the importance of using concepts to build the curriculum for each course. Theories are important because they expand upon concepts. Models are important because they provide examples that can be followed. Although it is not important to try to understand all the relationships between concepts, theories, and models, educators should understand that the main power of each is its *generalizability*, a quality that is important to all curriculum planning because it increases applicability while encouraging the creativity of the curriculum developer.

## THE ROLE OF RESEARCH

In defining *professionalism*, Kowalski and Reitzug (1993, p. 25) list several qualities of professionals and add: "Research is another characteristic commonly used to identify professions." Yet educational psychologists and other educators know that generally teachers do not use research to guide their teaching. Egbert (1984, p. 14) says, in reference to teachers' planning, "Teachers ignore research and overestimate the value of personal experience." Brown (1990) echoes this concern, saying that teachers usually do not base their planning on the factors that affect achievement. When Marshall (1991, p. 227) asked teachers why they used traditional methods, that is, students seated in rows, quiet classrooms, and teacher-dominant, textbook-oriented, pencil and paper instruction, the responses were:

- "It's the way I was taught."
- "It's the way I learned."
- "It's the easiest [most expedient] way to cover the material."

Bellon et al (1992, p. 3) acknowledge teachers' failure to know about and use research: "Many experienced teachers are not conversant with the research on teaching. . . . Teachers will adopt new approaches without understanding the underlying principles and assumptions. . . . Most teachers, however, are interested in the research and would like to make selected applications of research findings." Yet teachers have their own theories based on their personal experiences, and they are reluctant to give up their theories even when physical evidence contradicts them (Woods, 1994). Furthermore, students' theories are often very different from what their teachers think they are (Heckman, Confer, & Hakim, 1994).

## LACK OF RESEARCH BASE

Until recently, teachers had both an excuse and a reason for ignoring the research: Very little research on teaching was available. But during the second half of the twentieth century, research on teaching has been increasing. Good (1990, p. 17) explains:

> In the past twenty years, improved research and research methodology have increased dramatically our knowledge of teaching. This progress has been achieved despite inadequate funding. Notable progress also has been achieved in the understanding of learning, motivation, and management in complex social settings as well as in the understanding of human development with associated implications for instruction. Research linking teacher behavior to student achievement has thus made enormous strides. What was once a very limited collection of results of various studies that did not combine to form

easily interpretable patterns has become an increasingly integrated knowledge base that includes a sizable collection of replicated correlational findings, many of which have been validated experimentally.

According to Good, 20 years ago research on the curriculum and instruction was fragmented. The scattered studies were isolated, and they provided only microscopic glimpses of segments of the educational process. But with the newly acquired knowledge base, educators can more effectively use the data to make instruction-related decisions.

During the past two decades, we have learned a great deal about instruction in American schools. Sophisticated observational research has yielded more knowledge about schooling than had been obtained in the previous 85 years. There is now an extensive quantitative and qualitative database to aid educators in understanding classroom problems and in making decisions about instructional issues.

One promising development that has been pulling teachers back into the center of schoolwide curriculum development and that is giving teachers a renewed interest in curriculum research and development is their participation in action research projects (discussed further in Chapter 8).

The involvement of teachers in research ranges from micro (classroom level) projects to macro (schoolwide) restructuring projects. Action research projects usually involve more than one teacher, may or may not involve university staff members, and usually begin with a perception of a gap between the current state of affairs and a more desirable state (Bracey, 1991).

## SCIENCE VERSUS COMMON SENSE

Another reason teachers and others reject research is their reliance on common sense; but common sense isn't reliable. For example, when inexperienced drivers enter a fog area, they almost invariably put their lights on high beam. Common sense has told them that the high beams will help them see better. But they don't. In fact, because of increased reflection, the high beams can be blinding to the driver. Or, when a car skids, common sense tells the driver to turn the wheel in the direction opposite to the skidding. But doing this intensifies the problem.

Readers who have taken a physics or a general physical science course may remember the problem that involves simultaneously shooting a rifle horizontally and dropping a bullet vertically. The problem is to determine which bullet will hit the ground first. Common sense says that the dropped bullet will hit the ground first because the distance it travels is shorter. In fact, the two bullets land simultaneously. (Disregarding any wind resistance, free-falling bodies travel at a speed of 9.8 m per second per second, regardless of their horizontal speeds.)

Kerlinger (1973, pp. 3–5) uses the work of Whitehead (1911) and Conant (1951) to show that, although science can also be misleading, it differs significantly from common sense:

Whitehead has pointed out that in creative thought common sense is a bad master. "Its sole criterion for judgment is that the new ideas shall look like the old ones." This is well said. Common sense may often be a bad master for the evaluation of knowledge. But how are science and common sense alike and how are they different? From one viewpoint, science and common sense are alike. This view would say that science is a systematic and controlled extension of common sense, since common sense, as Conant points out, is a series of concepts and conceptual schemes satisfactory for the practical uses of mankind. But these concepts and conceptual schemes may be seriously misleading in modern science—and particularly in psychology and education. It was self-evident to many educators of the last century—it was only common sense—to use punishment as a basic tool of pedagogy. Now we have evidence that this older common sense view of motivation may be quite erroneous. Reward seems more effective than punishment in aiding learning.

Science and common sense differ sharply in five ways. These disagreements revolve around the words "systematic" and "controlled." First, the uses of conceptual schemes and theoretical structures are strikingly different. While the man in the street uses "theories" and concepts, he ordinarily does so in a loose fashion. He often blindly accepts fanciful explanations of natural and human phenomena. An illness, for instance, may be thought to be a punishment for sinfulness. . . . The scientist, on the other hand, systematically builds his theoretical structures, tests them for internal consistency, and subjects aspects of them to empirical test. Furthermore, he realizes that the concepts he is using are man-made terms that may or may not exhibit a close relation to reality. Second, the scientist systematically and empirically tests his theories and hypotheses. The man in the street tests his "hypotheses" too, but he tests them in what might be called a selective fashion. He often "selects" evidence simply because it is consistent with his hypothesis. . . . The sophisticated social scientist, knowing this "selection tendency" to be a common psychological phenomenon, carefully guards his research against his own preconceptions and predilections and against selective support of his hypotheses. For one thing, he is not content with armchair exploration of a relation; he must test the relation in the laboratory or in the field. He insists upon systematic, controlled, and empirical testing of these relations. A third difference lies in the notion of control. In scientific research, control means several things. For the present let it mean that the scientist tries systematically to rule out variables that are possible "causes" of the effects he is studying other than the variables that he has hypothesized to be the "causes." The layman seldom bothers to control his explanations of observed phenomena in a systematic manner. He ordinarily makes little effort to control extraneous sources of influence. He tends to accept those explanations that are in accord with his preconceptions and biases.

Another difference between science and common sense is perhaps not so sharp. It was said earlier that the scientist is constantly preoccupied with relations among phenomena. So is the layman who invokes common sense for his explanations of phenomena. But the scientist consciously and systematically pursues relations. The layman's preoccupation with relations is loose, unsystematic, uncontrolled. He often seizes, for example, on the fortuitous occurrence of two phenomena and immediately links them indissolubly as cause and effect.

A final difference between common sense and science lies in different explanations of observed phenomena. The scientist, when attempting to explain the relations among observed phenomena, carefully rules out what have been called "metaphysical explanations." A metaphysical explanation is simply a proposition that cannot be tested. To say, for example, that people are poor and starving because God wills it, that studying hard subjects improves the child's moral character, or that it is wrong to be authoritarian in the classroom is to talk metaphysically.

None of these propositions can be tested; thus they are metaphysical. As such, science is not concerned with them. This does not mean that a scientist would necessarily spurn such statements, rule them out of life, say they are not true, or claim they are meaningless. It simply means that as a scientist he is not concerned with them. In short, science is concerned with things that can be publicly observed and tested. If propositions or questions do not contain implications for such public observation and testing, they are not scientific questions.

So, a basic difference between the behavior of the layperson and the scientist is that the layperson lacks the objectivity that the scientist derives from using a systematic process. Teachers have historically treated information as have laypersons. Ozmon and Craver (1981, p. 238) have observed this quality of teacher behavior:

> Teachers constantly call for practical solutions to educational problems. But this concern with "practicality" is itself open to analytic inquiry: just what is the meaning of "practical" in this instance? Often, the "practical" teacher wants a technique, a gimmick, to apply to and solve his dilemma. It is reasonable, however, to observe that such "practical" solutions are often theoretical in the worst sense. Techniques are sometimes used indiscriminately. They are applied generally and universally in situations for which they were not designed; however, they are deemed "practical" because their mechanics are known and they are capable of being acted upon.

## WORD TRAPS

Chapter 1 contained some criticisms of current education reform practices. Criticism was directed toward the overreliance on achievement test scores and the careless use of terminology. This concern appeared again in Chapter 2, in reference to the awkward and careless way writers use such terms as *multicultural education* and *pluralistic education*. Ozmon and Craver (1981, p. 238) explain the danger in the overuse and misuse of the word *practical*:

"Achievement" is a rubric by which many educators swear, and the worth of any educational activity is judged upon students' achievement scores. "Achievement" in such instances is usually understood to be a "practical" outcome of one's education, but such emphasis may serve to retard one's education if the meaning of achievement is vague and unclear. Suppose one wants to learn how to play the piano, and the educator says that the "practical" approach is to proceed by achievement in learning to play scales. However, such a method may result in the student's learning to play scales but not in developing his ability to play the piano or in sustaining his interest. We may pose the question: how "practical" is this approach?

Criticism of theory is not new. Practitioners have always been critical, especially when the theory does not work when applied to practice. Two centuries ago Kant (1793, p. 41) had a good response for the critics of his day:

> Thus, when the theory did not work too well in practice, the fault lay, not in the theory, but rather in there not being enough theory which a man should have learned from experience.

Glaymour (1980, p. 3) speaks to the cumulative nature of theory:

> The scientist may make both his bread and his reputation by the subtlety, ingenuity, and plausibility with which he can relate the happenings in his laboratory to controversial hypothesis. . . . Much of the scientist's business is to construct arguments that aim to show that a particular piece of experiment or observation bears on a particular piece of history, and such arguments are among the most celebrated accomplishments in the history of our sciences. Kepler argued for elliptical orbits from a study of the motions of Mars, and for a relation between planetary distances and planetary periods from a study of Mars and other planets; Newton argued for his law of universal gravitation from Kepler's laws and experiments with pendulums, and using Newton's laws and the observations of planets, Leverrier argued for an anomaly in Mercury's motion. Einstein argued that displacement of the apparent positions of stars during an eclipse would give evidence of truth of general relativity, and Eddington argued that the phenomenon gave evidence for a particular part of that theory.

Ozmon and Craver's comments (1981, p. 238) are uncomfortably reminiscent of the recent education reform reports. The most common words in these reports are *rigor* and *excellence*, and the degree of attainment of "excellence" is to be measured by student achievement on standardized exams. But Ozmon and Craver show that these are word traps:

> It can be seen how our use of words is intimately connected with the presuppositions underlying their use. In the case above, what was believed to be practical was in fact not very practical at all. The proposition that one learns to play the piano by achievement in playing scales is itself theoretical and not always supported by factual circumstances (although playing the scales may help achieve the goal). Similar conditions exist with regard to numerous educational prescriptions.

Recall the student's plea at the beginning of this chapter. Too often, educators attend to the specifics while ignoring the meanings that these specifics would have if students were prepared to make generalizations and apply those generalizations to their own lives and to the world around them. Perkins (1994, p. 23) expresses this concern:

> Knowledge tends to get glued to the narrow circumstances of initial acquisition. But an understanding performance virtually by definition requires a modicum of transfer because it asks the learner to go beyond the information given, tackling some task that reaches further than the textbook or lecture.

Words seem to be a common trap for educators and students alike. Too often, the aim is "achievement," but when measured by pencil and paper tests, that achievement amounts to no more than memorizing words or facts. To get beyond the mere memorization of facts, teachers need three tools: (1) concepts, (2) theories, and (3) models.

# CONCEPTS

Tyson and Carroll (1970, p. 25) define *concept* as follows:

> A concept is an inference based upon the notation of recurrence in the context of variance which enables one to order and organize experience.

Unlike a fact, a concept has a recurring quality that gives it a very special power, called *generalizability*. The recurring quality may be a physical property, such as the four legs and flat surface that recur in tables, or the recurring quality could arise from other properties such as utility, which recurs in the case of all tools. Or the recurring quality can be an abstraction as reflected in such feelings as love, hate, doubt, or curiosity.

The power of the concept in learning must never be underestimated. Einstein (1951, p. 7) said that it is the very essence of all thinking:

> What precisely is "thinking"? When at the reception of sense-impressions, memory-pictures emerge, that is not yet "thinking." And when such pictures form series, each member of which calls forth another, this too is not yet "thinking." When, however, a certain picture turns up in many series, then—precisely through such return—it becomes an ordering element for such series, in that it connects series which in themselves are unconnected. Such an element becomes an instrument, a concept. I think that the transition from free association or "dreaming" to thinking is characterized by the more or less dominating role which the "concept" plays in it.

Ward (1969, p. 423) describes the concept's special power of generalization:

> You enter the old kitchen, in which there is a blazing hearthfire complete with bubbling, boiling teakettle. Oh, it's always there anyway; you've seen it before. Besides, your mind is on something else. Your quaint kitchen is pretty well

tuned out by you, or you only perceive it at the (blob) level. Wait, something focuses your attention on the event system that is the boiling kettle. You've noticed. Now you're beginning to operate. You've noticed something, and something is happening. The lid jumps up and down. You wonder why. Ah, cause, the why sets you to scrutinizing relationships. First you attend, focus, observe, isolate. Next, you want the cause of something. Establishing tentative cause gets you to infer a low-level generalization. "That lid will move because steam is pushing it up and down. If that particular kettle is put on that fire and it boils, then its lid will jump up and down" a relatively low level of abstraction because the particulars of the scene are still involved. The next level of abstraction, of generalization, will take you to a point of thinking, "When a kettle is placed on a fire, the water will boil and cause a loose lid to move."

This illustration shows how concepts can be discovered and formulated by students. The curriculum should be carefully designed to help students see the relationships among concepts. Stefanich (1990, p. 48) discusses this:

> Students tend to deal with concepts in isolation. They cannot effectively consider a number of isolated examples and apply these to general theory or principle. They cannot effectively apply a general principle to a number of instances or examples. They are unable to cognitively process variable time frames or situations which require simultaneous consideration of multiple characters or events.

Since students tend to deal with concepts in isolation, the teachers' job of getting their students to see the relationships among concepts may be made easier by explaining the tentative nature of concepts. The boundaries of all concepts are tentative. Even all disciplinary boundaries are tentative (Gardner and Boix-Mansilla, 1994).

## EXAMPLES OF CURRICULUM CONCEPTS

Some generalizations offered as axioms by Oliva (1992, p. 45) follow.

Axiom 1.   Change is both inevitable and necessary, for it is through change that life forms growth and development.

Axiom 2.   A school curriculum not only reflects but is part of its time.

Axiom 3.   Curriculum changes made at an earlier period of time can exist concurrently with newer curriculum changes at a later period of time.

Axiom 4.   Curriculum changes result from changes in people.

Axiom 5.   Curriculum change is effected as a result of cooperative endeavor on the part of groups.

Axiom 6.   Curriculum development is basically a decision-making process.

Axiom 7.   Curriculum development is a never-ending process.

Axiom 8.   Curriculum development is a comprehensive process.

Axiom 9.   Systematic curriculum development is more effective than trial and error.

Axiom 10.   The curriculum planner starts from where the curriculum is just as the teacher starts from where the students are.

These axioms are not offered so that the reader can memorize them. Rather, if the reader selects and focuses on one or more of the axioms that seem to make sense, they constitute excellent examples of generalizations which shape the thinking of curricularists. Obviously, these axioms were considered important by Oliva and also by the author, who has used some of them to assess curriculum development. Appendix E contains an abstract of an article which shows how these axioms guided the thinking of the director of a curriculum development team and how the director used them to evaluate the curriculum development process.

## THEORIES

Concepts can be assembled to form even more powerful mental tools—theories and models. Kerlinger (1973, p. 9) gives the following definition of *theory:*

> A theory is a set of interrelated constructs (concepts), definitions, and propositions that present a systematic view of phenomena by specifying relations among variables, with the purpose of explaining and predicting the phenomena.

Philosophy can help the educator use theories. One can begin by formulating a theory of education. Others have attempted to do this; most have been unsuccessful. But certainly this poor record should not preclude teachers from creating their own philosophies of education. On the contrary, curriculum coursework should prepare teachers to formulate their own theories and philosophies about education. In fact, Chapter 11 in this text encourages readers to do precisely that.

The relationship between philosophy and educational theory was explained by John Dewey in 1916. Ozmon and Craver (1981, p. 254) discuss Dewey's views:

> According to Dewey, it could be said that theory of education is a set of "generalizations" and "abstractions" about education. Abstraction has received a bad name in popular speech because it is thought to be remote from practical affairs. It can, however, serve a useful purpose for, as Dewey put it, abstraction is "an indispensable trait in the reflective direction of activity." In this sense, theoretical abstractions or generalized meanings have a connection with actual, practical affairs. Things are generalized so they may have broader application. A theory of education contains generalizations that are applicable to a number of situations. Theory becomes abstract in the remote or abstruse sense when it fails to make reference to practical applications. In the sense of useful theory, however, abstraction broadens it, in a public sense, to include any person or situation in like circumstances, and not just in a narrow sense of a solitary individual.

For many people, the term *theory* may evoke images of scientists working in laboratories. People also tend to believe that theories, when followed precisely, will lead to the correct answer. But these common views of theory have some basic problems. First, scientists are not the only people who theorize. Certainly at one time or another, all of us have theorized. As Ozmon and Craver (1981, p. 255) explain:

> Experienced teachers do this quite often. They exchange ideas and methods they have found fruitful in achieving certain educational goals. In this sense, they are theorizing or building theory, even though it may not be very sophisticated. One person tries another's approach, and afterward discusses it. They both find ways to redefine goals and vary, expand, or redirect the approaches for future use. The very "practical" matter of approaches and goals has been generalized to a degree, abstracted if you will. These approaches and goals have been tested and found successful, or they have been altered, improved, or found wanting. In this way theory and practice may build upon each other.

Second, theorizing occurs both inside and outside the laboratory. Each time we buy a new automobile or dishwasher, we theorize about its future performance and its durability. Finally, theories do not always produce correct answers; they do no tell us what we should do. The purpose of a theory is not to tell us what to do or what we should do. Although some theories have predictive powers and can tell us what will very likely happen if we do this or that, the decision to choose one alternative over another is ours. So the role of the theory is not to guide our behavior; rather, it is to help guide our thinking. More accurately, theory is one of several forces that work together to guide our thinking. For example, our emotions and our value systems also play important roles in our decisions to think—and act—in certain ways.

There is no sense of finality in theories. They are never final, for science is fluid in nature. The more we learn, the more we are able to learn. Learning is like stepping on a rock to see farther, and then stepping on another, larger rock, and then another. Or it is like the work of an astronomer. Each time a more powerful telescope is invented, our knowledge of the universe expands, and often our theories must be changed to accommodate new information.

Sometimes the best examples are the nonexamples. So let's look at what a theory is not. Often theory is criticized for being unrelated to practice. Beauchamp (1981, pp. 36–37) explains:

> The world of practicality is built around clusters of specific events. The world of theory derives from generalizations, laws, axioms, and theorems explaining specific events and the relationships among them. The fact that the worlds of theory and practice are different does not minimize the known interrelationships that exist between them. The operational vistas opened up and explained by theories increase the possible choices of behaving for the practitioner; the theories, however, do not tell him how to act. A theory may clarify relationships among any given set of events, but it does not and cannot direct the execution of that set of events. Newsome (1964) made this distinction clear when he noted that theory is not what is practiced. A person cannot practice a

set of logically related statements; he performs an activity. Theories of instruction, for example, might account for classroom discipline, grouping practices, lesson planning, and instructional materials as components of instruction, but the theories cannot tell teachers how to behave with respect to those functions.

Applied to curriculum development, theories cannot tell teachers and other curriculum developers to develop curricula a particular way. But theories can guide the curriculum developer's thinking and therefore indirectly improve curriculum design.

To be useful, an educational theory doesn't have to be proved. Some theories are used to predict; others are used to explain. Pratt (1971) explains:

> What theory provides is order and intelligibility out of miscellaneous and unrelated profusion of phenomena.

Theories need not be complicated, esoteric, and pedantic. Obviously, they cannot be of value if they are obscure. Ozmon and Craver (1981, p. 258) say:

> If a theory does not help us communicate in a better or more advantageous way, criticize our assumptions and actions, gain perspective, seek out new possibilities, order and direct practice, then we had better let it go or revise it in new directions.

## Sample Theories

Sample theories from the four major content areas are given below. This material is from *Conceptual Tools for Teaching in Secondary Schools* (Tyson & Carroll, 1970).

1. Science
   a. The total amount of energy is not affected by energy transformation. *Energy transformation is a common phenomenon. If you rub your hands, mechanical energy is converted to heat energy. If you burn a candle, chemical energy is converted to heat and light; and in a dry cell, chemical energy can be converted to electric energy. But whether one is concerned with burning oil in the home, gasoline in the automobile, glucose in the body, or the transfer of the energy of moving water into a flow of electrons in a conductor, the total amount of energy in any given system remains the same. This conceptual scheme is a primary concern in the discipline of physics.*
   b. A body at rest remains at rest, and a body in motion remains in uniform motion in a straight line unless acted upon by an external force.
2. English
   a. Effective writing is a function of clear, concise sentences.
   b. Monotony in written expression can be avoided by providing for variety in sentence structure.
   c. Each man's welfare is dependent upon every man's welfare.

*No man is an Island entire of itself; every man is a piece of the Continent, a part of the maine . . . any man's death diminishes me, because I am involved in Mankind; and therefore never send to know for whom the bell tolls, it tolls for thee (John Donne).*

3. Social Studies
   a. Attitudes are a function of group affiliation.
   b. An increase in an individual's economic power is an increase in his liberty.
   c. Freedom of association increases the liberty of man.
   d. Religious freedom is dependent upon the separation of Church and State.
   e. Civilization is the victory of persuasion over force.
4. Mathematics
   a. In a right angle the square of the hypotenuse is equal to the sum of the squares of the other two sides.
   b. The equality of congruence of two or more objects is dependent upon the equality of corresponding parts of the objects.
      (1) If two angles and the included side of one triangle are equal to two angles and the included side of another triangle, the triangles are congruent.
      (2) If two angles and the side not included of one triangle are equal to the corresponding parts of another triangle, the triangles are congruent.
      (3) If the hypotenuse and an acute angle of one right triangle are equal to the hypotenuse and an acute angle of another right triangle, the triangles are congruent.

Some of these theories are familiar because we memorized them in high school. We still use some of them but only on special occasions (e.g., the Pythagorean theorem). Other theories guide our daily thinking (e.g., the freedom theory and the economics theory). So, using a theory requires awareness and understanding, not memorization. As you continue through this book, your goal should be to understand and recall the relationships between the curriculum development theories.

## MODELS

The third special tool that teachers need is models. Rivett (1972) has defined *model* as "a set of logical relationships, either qualitative or quantitative, which will link together the relevant features of the reality with which we are concerned."

Compare Rivett's definition with Beauchamp's (1981, p. 27) description of the role of the model:

Functionally, models are used to represent events and event interactions in a highly compact and illustrative manner.

It should be noted that a model is not reality. Rather, like a painting or a story, it is a visual or written description of someone's perception of reality. It is told that, during an exhibition of Matisse's works, a woman criticized one of the drawings, saying, "The hand doesn't look like a hand." Matisse replied, "It's not, madam. It's a drawing of a hand." Like theories, models help explain various related concepts and the relationships between the various parts of the models. Puryear (Hill, 1986, p. 57) addresses the purpose of models:

> The purposes of a model are to help us organize what we already know, to help us see new relationships, and to keep us from being dazzled by the full-blown complexity of the subject. A model is not intended to be a picture of reality but a tool for thinking.

Like theories, models are imperfect. As more knowledge is gained about what a model portrays, the model becomes weaker; its image grows blurry. Because of the self-eroding nature of models, modifying them from time to time is required. Currently, there is no adequate theory of education. It follows, then, that since curriculum theory is a subtheory of educational theory and since curriculum models represent curriculum theory, neither curriculum theory nor any curriculum model can be "perfect" until a satisfactory theory of education has been developed. Meanwhile, teachers and other curriculum workers will still benefit from learning all they can about different curriculum models. Models possessing a variety of qualities are described in the following paragraphs.

## The AIM Model

The simple nature of the visual representation of the AIM program shown in Fig. 4.1 should not be interpreted as shallow. On the contrary, a distinguishing quality of the AIM Program is its comprehensiveness. This program required every school teacher in the state to gather with other teachers and develop a written curriculum plan that addressed desired outcomes (educational objectives), student behavior, and teacher behavior for every lesson throughout the year. Teachers were required to identify and list materials and other resources, including human resources (consultants), needed to achieve the objectives. Rounding out this program, teachers were required to write test items for every class period throughout the year. When the products of all of the committees were assembled, the result was a curriculum plan that covered every hour of a student's schooling from the first day of the first grade through high school graduation. It is simple and clear. It begins with objectives and moves in the direction shown by the arrows. Both student activities and teacher activities are included, but no foundation elements and no philosophy statement are offered.

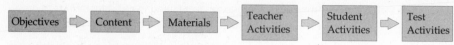

**Figure 4.1**  The AIM curriculum model.

## Taba's Inverted Model

Hilda Taba's approach to curriculum development is referred to as the *inverted model* because it begins in the classroom with the teacher, as contrasted with other models, which begin in district, state, or federal offices. The model has eight steps, as follows:

### Step 1: Diagnosing Needs

Taba believed that curriculum development should begin with the available information on the community and its schools. Any additional data that were needed would be gathered by using a needs assessment. The new data would be combined with the existing data to form a comprehensive view of local needs.

### Step 2: Formulating Specific Objectives

The combined data from Step 1 would inform teachers of needed objectives. Taba recommended that the objectives be:

1. Concepts to be learned
2. Attitudes to be learned
3. Ways of thinking to be reinforced
4. Habits and skills to be mastered

The objectives would be the basis of a new teaching unit. Taba recognized that the knowledge available at this point was incomplete and believed that, as more knowledge was gained, the objectives could be clarified. Taba recommended that schools avoid spending months formulating objectives and, instead, get on with the development of the unit.

### Step 3: Selecting Content

With this model, content selection begins by choosing topics carefully. The dimensions of each topic must be specified. The logic of the subject matter chosen dictates the dimensions. Thus each choice must be supported by a rationale. What levels can students of this age master? What topics do they find stimulating? Those questions are essential to all curriculum planning. To answer them, curricularists may turn to the work of Jean Piaget.

Table 4.1 shows the psychological stages in Jean Piaget's developmental hierarchy reached by the majority of students at each age. Teachers should be

Table 4.1 Percentage of Individuals in Piagetian Stages

| Age (Years) | Preoperational | Concrete Onset | Concrete Mature | Formal Onset | Formal Mature |
|---|---|---|---|---|---|
| 7 | 35 | 55 | 10 | | |
| 8 | 25 | 55 | 20 | | |
| 9 | 15 | 55 | 30 | | |
| 10 | 12 | 52 | 35 | 1 | |
| 11 | 6 | 49 | 40 | 5 | |
| 12 | 5 | 32 | 51 | 12 | |
| 13 | 2 | 34 | 44 | 14 | 6 |
| 14 | 1 | 32 | 43 | 15 | 9 |
| 15 | 1 | 14 | 53 | 19 | 13 |
| 16 | 1 | 15 | 54 | 17 | 13 |
| 17 | 3 | 19 | 47 | 19 | 12 |
| 18 | 1 | 15 | 50 | 15 | 19 |

SOURCE: G. P. Stefanich (1990, November), Cycles of cognition. Middle School Journal, 22(2), p. 49. Used with permission from G. P. Stefanich and Middle School Journal. Originally taken from H. T. Epstein, "Brain growth and cognitive learning." Colorado Journal of Educational Research, 3, 1979.

careful to select content and activities that parallel students' developmental levels using the developmental stages as general guidelines and never as rigid lines of demarcation. Perkins (1994, p. 23) cautions, "Teachers teaching for understanding do well to bear in mind factors like complexity, but without rigid conceptions of what students can and cannot learn at certain ages."

## Step 4: Organizing Content

Content organization should begin with simple topics which are then explored in greater depth. Each idea should be a little more difficult to comprehend. Content organization will be more successful if the developer anticipates what learner activities will be needed and what generalizations should be developed (handing generalizations to students should be avoided).

## Step 5 and 6: Selecting and Organizing Activities

Content mastery is only one goal of instruction, and some objectives cannot be met through outcomes. Thus all objectives except the lowest level (recall) need accompanying objectives. Each activity must have a definite function. At this time the developmental level of the students should be reconsidered. What kinds of activities does this age group need in order to develop the understandings sought?

Some activities are multipurpose; that is, they can help students achieve more than one objective. Variety in activities and obtaining suggestions from other teachers is essential. The activities must follow a sequence which makes continuous and accumulative learning possible. Each activity must be introduced, discovered by the student, and then be connected by the student to previous experiences. An important goal is to help students understand why they hold the particular perceptions they have. Woods (1994, p. 35) says that she attempts to select activities that achieve this goal in all her classes: "Helping them understand the basis of their own reasoning and test it against the real world has become for me a fundamental curriculum practice."

### Step 7: Evaluating

Ideally, a unit should be evaluated continuously. As the coverage of units progresses, the material in the early units should be reevaluated and revised as needed. The evaluation can conclude with an appraisal of the progress of the students and can also include the students' preferences.

### Step 8: Checking for Balance and Sequence

Now it is time to see whether the content outline matches the logic of the core ideas. Do the activities provide opportunities to learn how to generalize? Does the content sequence flow? Is there balance between written and oral work, research and analysis, and different forms of expression? Is the organization flexible? Do students feel free to open up and talk? Does the unit fit the school's climate? (For example, are the necessary materials available? Do the teachers have the necessary expertise?)

### Summary of the Taba Model

Taba's model has several unique strengths. Its inverted dimension involves teachers in its development. This gives teachers a level of commitment and ownership not common to other models and prepares them to implement the model. Its unit base ties curriculum to instruction. Since *curriculum* is often interpreted to mean a document, as separate from instruction, too often curriculum development is thought of as disconnected from teaching. By bringing together curriculum and instruction, the model ties theory to practice.

## Tyler's Ends-Means Model

Tyler's ends-means model introduced a revolutionary idea to curriculum planning. He said that the curriculum developer should start by deciding what purposes the curriculum is to have and then plan accordingly. Today, this approach seems embarrassingly simple, but it was revolutionary at the time since no curriculum developer had ever presented such a model. Figure 4.2 summarizes Tyler's model.

Tyler suggested that several ends, which he called *goals, educational objectives,* and *purposes,* be identified by examining three elements: the learners, life in the community, and subject matter.

## The Student as a Source

Tyler believed that a broad and comprehensive analysis of the student should be made. The curriculum developer should determine the learner's needs and wants. Taking account of the learner's needs and wants is important in motivating the student to learn. The students' abilities must also be considered.

## Society as a Source

Tyler believed that the process of generalizing is central to all learning. Since the learner needs to understand the environment, interacting with others is essential. This makes the local community and society at large the students' learning laboratory. By studying the community and the society, the student can find problems to solve and ways of solving them.

## Subject Matter

Tyler was heavily influenced by John Dewey, who stressed learning by doing. He was also influenced by Jerome Bruner (1966), who wrote about the structure of knowledge. They said (and Tyler agreed) that, to master a subject, one must understand its underlying structure.

## Philosophy

According to Tyler, sound curriculum development begins with sound thinking and that sound thinking begins by formulating a philosophy. He believed that it is necessary to define a school's philosophy. If Tyler were to lead others in curriculum development, he would insist that teachers spell out their own individual philosophy and also that of their school. In this respect, Tyler's model reflects the axiom "To understand others, you must first understand yourself. To serve others you must understand both the serving agency [the school] and yourself."

Figure 4.2  Tyler's ends-means model.

## Psychology

In Tyler's model, effective curriculum development requires an understanding of the learner's levels of development and the nature of the learning process. This understanding helps to refine the list of objectives. According to Oliva (1992), Tyler would have curriculum workers use philosophy and psychology as "screens," filtering out objectives which are beyond the student's capacity to attain and objectives which run counter to the faculty's philosophy.

## The Oliva Model

Peter Oliva first introduced a curriculum development model in 1976 (see Figure 4.3). In 1992 he expanded the model as shown in Figure 4.4. He explains them as follows:

> Some years ago I set out to chart a model for curriculum development that met three criteria: the model had to be simple, comprehensive, and systematic. . . . Although this model represents the most essential components, it can be readily expanded into an extended model that provides additional detail and shows some processes that the simplified model assumes.

## The 12 Components

Figure 4.4 shows a comprehensive, step-by-step process that takes the curriculum planner from the sources of the curriculum to evaluation.

In the figure, the squares represent planning phases; the circles, operational phases. The process starts with component I, at which time the curriculum developers state the aims of education and their philosophical and psychological principles. The aims are based on beliefs about the needs of our society and the needs of individuals living in our society. This component incorporates concepts similar to Tyler's use of philosophy and psychology as "screens."

Component II requires an analysis of the needs of the community in which the school is located, the needs of students served in that community, and the exigencies of the subject matter that will be taught in the given school. Sources of the curriculum are seen as cutting across components I and II. Whereas component I treats the needs of students and society in a more gener-

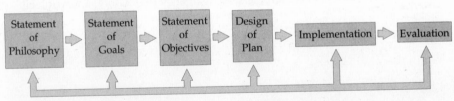

**Figure 4.3** Oliva's 1976 Model for curriculum development. Reproduced by permission of Longman.

I–IV and VI–IX:  Planning Phases
V:  Planning and Operational Phase
X–XIII:  Operational Phases

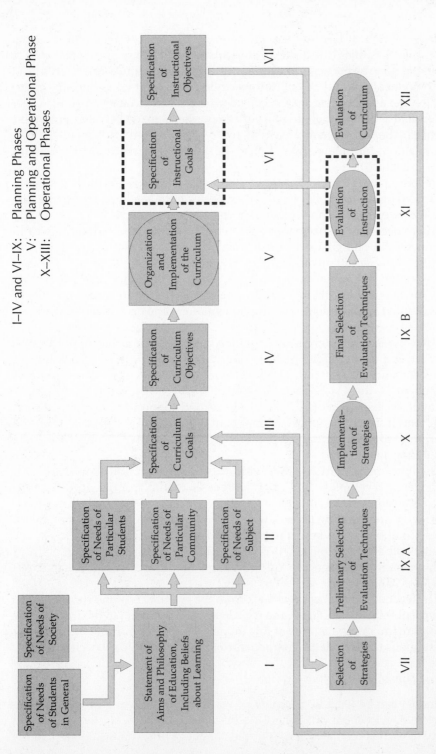

**Figure 4.4** Oliva's 1992 model for curriculum development.

al sense, component II introduces the concepts of needs of particular students in particular localities (the needs of students in particular communities are not always the same as the general needs of students throughout our society).

Components III and IV call for specifying curricular goals and objectives based on the aims, beliefs, and needs specified in components I and II. A distinction that will be clarified later with examples is made between goals and objectives. The tasks of component V are to organize and implement the curriculum and to formulate and establish the structure by which the curriculum will be organized.

In components VI and VII an increasing level of specification is sought. Instructional goals and objectives are stated for each level and subject. A distinction between goals and objectives is visually portrayed.

After specifying instructional objectives, the curriculum worker moves to component VIII and chooses instructional strategies for use with students in the classroom. Simultaneously, the curriculum worker initiates the preliminary selection of evaluation techniques, phase A of component IX. At this stage, the curriculum planner thinks ahead and begins to consider ways to assess student achievement. The implementation of instructional strategies—component X—follows.

After the students have been provided with the appropriate opportunities to learn (component X), the planner returns to the problem of selecting techniques for evaluating student achievement and instructor effectiveness. Component IX, then, is divided into two phases: The first precedes the implementation of instruction (IX A), and the second follows the implementation (IX B). The instructional phase (component X) provides the planner with the opportunity to refine, add to, and complete the selection of means to evaluate pupil performance.

During component XI, the evaluation of instruction is carried out. Component XII completes the cycle, with evaluation not of the student or the teacher but rather of the curricular program. In this model, components I to IV and VI to IX are planning phases, whereas components X to XI are operational phases. Component V is both a planning and an operational phase.

Like some other models, this one combines a scheme for curriculum development (components I to V and XII) and a design for instruction (components VI to XI).

The feedback lines that cycle back from the evaluation of the curriculum to the curriculum goals and from the evaluation of instruction to the instructional goals are important features of this model. These lines indicate the necessity of continuous revision of the components of their respective subcycles.

## Use of the Model

The model can be used in a variety of ways. First, it offers a process for the complete development of a school's curriculum. By following the model, the faculty of each special area, for example, language arts, can fashion a plan for the curriculum of that area and design ways in which it will be carried out through instruction. Or the faculty can develop schoolwide, interdisciplinary programs that cut across areas of specialization such as career education, guidance, and extraclass activities.

Second, a faculty can focus on the curricular components of the model (components I to V and XII) to make programmatic decisions. Third, a faculty can concentrate on the instructional components (VI to XI).

## *Summary of the Oliva Model*

A particular strength of the Oliva model is its inclusion of foundations. The original model requires a statement of philosophy, which is extremely important and, unfortunately, is not common among curriculum documents. The revised model includes societal and student needs, which are also invaluable parts of curriculum models.

## Saylor-Alexander Model

In 1966, Saylor and Alexander (1966) introduced a curriculum model which has very strong foundations (see Figure 4.5). This model was designed to suggest a process for selecting learner activities. A special strength of the model is its comprehensiveness. In a sense, it connects the curriculum with instruction by showing that teaching methods and strategies result from the curriculum plan. Another major strength of the model is that all steps in its suggested curriculum development process are grounded in social, philosophical, and psychological foundations.

## Macdonald's Model

James B. Macdonald perceived *teaching* as a personality system acting in a professional role, and *learning* as a personality system (the student) performing task-related (learning) behaviors. He defined *instruction* as the social system within which formal teaching and learning take place, and *curriculum* as the social system which eventuates in a plan of instruction. Macdonald used a Venn diagram (see Figure 4.6) to illustrate his model and to show the relationships of its elements. He defined the intersecting parts of the diagram as follows:

   V. Concomitant learning
   VI. Modification of behavior through teacher feedback
  VII. In-service experiences
 VIII. Supervision experiences
   IX. Pupil-teacher planning experiences
    X. Pupil-teacher planning experiences

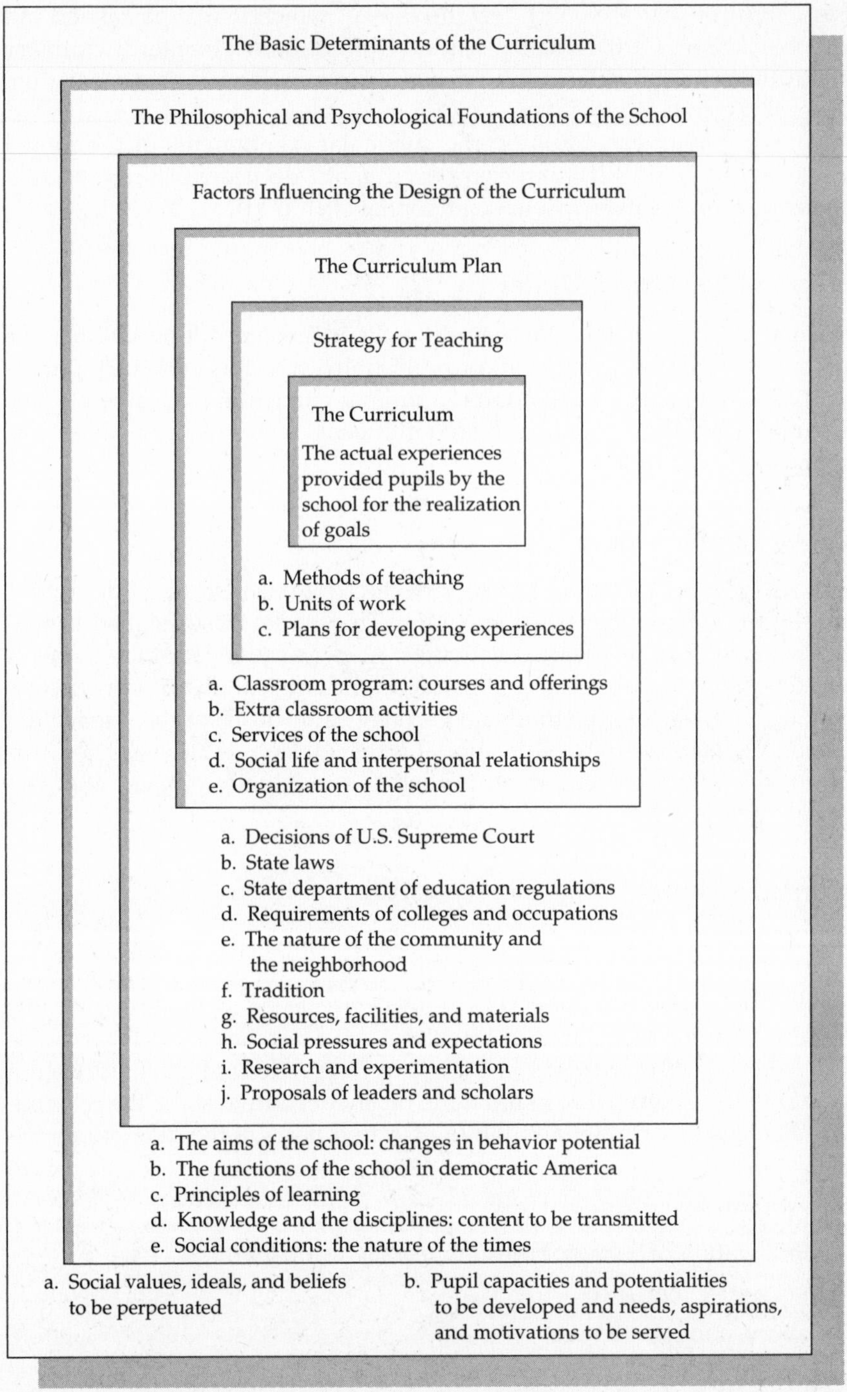

The Basic Determinants of the Curriculum

The Philosophical and Psychological Foundations of the School

Factors Influencing the Design of the Curriculum

The Curriculum Plan

Strategy for Teaching

The Curriculum

The actual experiences provided pupils by the school for the realization of goals

a. Methods of teaching
b. Units of work
c. Plans for developing experiences

a. Classroom program: courses and offerings
b. Extra classroom activities
c. Services of the school
d. Social life and interpersonal relationships
e. Organization of the school

a. Decisions of U.S. Supreme Court
b. State laws
c. State department of education regulations
d. Requirements of colleges and occupations
e. The nature of the community and
   the neighborhood
f. Tradition
g. Resources, facilities, and materials
h. Social pressures and expectations
i. Research and experimentation
j. Proposals of leaders and scholars

a. The aims of the school: changes in behavior potential
b. The functions of the school in democratic America
c. Principles of learning
d. Knowledge and the disciplines: content to be transmitted
e. Social conditions: the nature of the times

a. Social values, ideals, and beliefs to be perpetuated

b. Pupil capacities and potentialities to be developed and needs, aspirations, and motivations to be served

**Figure 4.5** The Saylor-Alexander curriculum model.

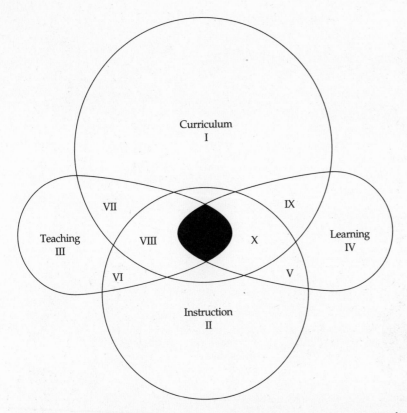

**Figure 4.6**  Macdonald's curriculum model. [Reproduced by permission from James B. Macdonald (1976). Educational models for instruction. In James B. Macdonald and Robert R. Leeper (Eds.), *Theories of Instruction*. Alexandria, VA: Association for Supervision and Curriculum Development.]

A strength of Macdonald's model is in its presentation of the relationships among the model's various elements. Such relationships are essential if a curriculum is a structured series of intended learning outcomes, as he perceived.

## The Zais Eclectic Model

Figure 4.7 is a simple eclectic model developed by Robert S. Zais that attempts to portray in static terms the components of the curriculum and the principle forces that affect its substance and design. The model is not concerned with processes—of curriculum construction, development, or implementation—or even with design per se. Its purpose is to portray graphically the principle variables, and their relationships, that planners need to consider in curriculum construction.

## THE CURRICULUM

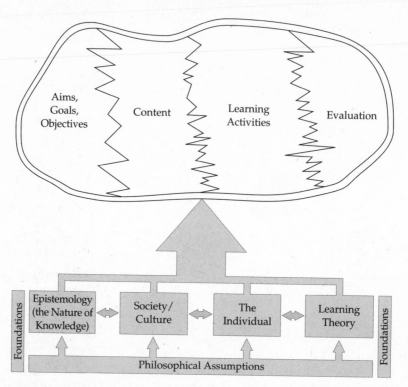

**Figure 4.7** The Zais model of the curriculum and its foundations. Reproduced by permission of HarperCollins.

The curriculum is shown in the model as a somewhat formless entity girdled by a double line. This indicates that, although the boundaries of the curriculum (as we currently understand them) are somewhat ill-defined, it is essentially an integrated entity. Within the double line the components that make up the curriculum (aims, goals, objectives, content, learning activities, and evaluation) are separated by jagged lines. This is meant to emphasize the relatedness of each component to all the others and to suggest that, as in a jigsaw puzzle, all the pieces should fit precisely to produce a coherent picture.

The large shaded arrowhead that joins the four foundation blocks to the curriculum indicates the influence of curriculum foundations on the content and organization of curriculum components (i.e., the curriculum design). In other words, we might say that the foundation blocks represent the soil and climate which determine the nature of the curriculum "plant." Each foundation block is joined to the others by double-headed arrows, suggesting the interrelatedness of all the areas. Although intimately connected, however, the foundation blocks do not, as do the curriculum components, form a unified whole. Undergirding the four foundation blocks is the broad area of philosophical assumptions. This aspect of the model indicates that, consciously or unconsciously, basic philosophical assumptions influence value judgments made about the foundations.

## Summary of the Zais Eclectic Model

The Zais eclectic model, dealing only with the static nature of a portion of the curriculum enterprise, is quite modest. Yet it is highly significant because it addresses probably the most crucial curriculum issues: the nature of the curriculum and the forces that determine its content and organization. It is interesting to note in this regard that far more attention has been paid in the literature to prescribing processes of curriculum development and change than to developing an understanding of the bases and nature of the curriculum itself. This typically American emphasis on activity and "how to do it," however, does not seem to have borne much fruit. Experience shows that in spite of a surplus of instruction and of activity in the processes of curriculum improvement and change, the curriculum remains controlled for the most part by the forces and events of historical accident, to say nothing of the influences of fashion and fad. In short, superficial understanding has apparently generated superficial strategies that get superficial results.

## Cornett's Personal Practical Theories Model

In 1990, Jeffrey Cornett introduced a curriculum model which he uses in his graduate curriculum classes to engage students in action research. He defines *personal practical theories* (ppt's) as "those systematic theories or beliefs held by each teacher that are based upon personal experiences derived from non-teaching activities (such as student and parent and practical experiences that occur as a result of designing and implementing the curriculum through instruction)."

As shown in Figure 4.8, the role of professor or teacher is central to the evolvement of ppt's. The professor or teacher observes the students and adjusts instruction according to their needs (theory A).

Theory B, on the importance of subject matter constructs, guides content selection and emphasis. Subject matter constructs include such concerns as forming a personal definition of *curriculum* from conflicting definitions, the hidden curriculum, teacher thinking research, and action research and its potential for enhancing teacher understanding of curriculum and change theory. These concepts are presented through a variety of instructional strategies.

Theory C acknowledges the importance of students' *perceptions* of personal and practical experiences. Concepts are introduced, and small group discussions are used to permit students to discuss their classroom and personal

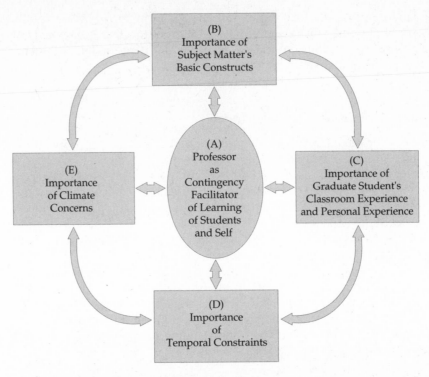

**Figure 4.8** Cornett's personal practical theories (ppt's) model of the curriculum. Used with the author's permission and with permission from *Theory Into Practice.*

experiences. Students are invited to give examples and to discuss their experiences in the light of information presented in class.

Theory D, on the importance of temporal factors, considers the time available for subject matter concepts, students' experiences, and the blending of the two.

Theory E, on the importance of climate factors, emphasizes such values as mutual respect, trust, caring, opportunities for involvement, and academic social growth.

Throughout, this model requires professors or teachers to reflect on their behavior and the bases on which this behavior is selected. An action research project promotes similar reflection among students and is also aimed at encouraging students to comment on the practices of other students, other teachers, administrators, and university researchers.

Cornett's model challenges students to examine their perceptions, beliefs, and values and in doing so invites students to make learning personal. Following are two curriculum projects that thrust the student into the center of learning, making their curriculum a personal experience.

# PROJECT ESCAPE

Although educators at all levels disagree widely on the pros and cons of education reform, most agree that there is always room for improving school programs. Constant improvement depends on a constant flow of credible ideas and innovations. Since part of the responsibility for introducing effective innovations must be borne by teacher education programs, a continuous flow of elementary and secondary school curriculum innovations requires a continuous flow of innovations among teacher education programs. In other words, our teacher education institutions must be wellsprings of curriculum improvement. A program that reflects much of the current thinking among both educators and critics among laypeople is described below.

With its origins as a normal school, the School of Education at Indiana State University has a history of developing innovative programs and offering them as models to other teacher preparation programs throughout the nation. One such program is called *Project ESCAPE*, (from *Elementary and Secondary Cooperative Approach to Performance Education*). It was created to provide an alternative to education students who prefer classroom-based programs over traditional university-based programs.

A major difference between this program and traditional teacher education programs is its competency base, but perhaps its most profound difference is that all the competencies are developed in elementary and secondary classrooms, instead of in traditional teacher education courses.

The program began with the identification of 25 elementary master teachers and 25 secondary master teachers, selected by their principals. These teachers examined their own classes and identified the one major area of teacher skills that would profit most from improvement. Then the teacher was given the sample learning module shown in Table 4.2 and was asked to develop a module for class. The only restrictions were that the module be highly tactile, visual, and activity-based and not require extensive reading.

Once the module was developed, it was assessed to determine the approximate number of hours required to complete it. This number was divided by 15 to arrive at a number of credit hours. For example, a module that required 45 hours to complete was assigned 3 credit hours. The lengths of the 48 ESCAPE modules ranged from 0.5 to 3.5 credit hours.

Each module was supported by a rationale designed to inform students of the benefits it offered to encourage students to choose the module. Table 4.3 is a sample rationale statement.

Each module is accompanied by a flowchart (See Figure 4.9) to help guide the student. Each module has a self-evaluation and a preassessment (which is equivalent to the postassessment). If a student passes the preassessment, the student receives credit and is not required to complete the module. Refer to Table 4.2, where preassessment and postassessment examples are given.

**Table 4.2  Sample Learning Module: Spelling Words with *ie* and *ei***

## OBJECTIVES

The purpose of this module is to focus attention on commonly misspelled ie/ei words. Completion of the following specific objective is required for satisfactory demonstrations of this competency.

Spell correctly 100 percent of the words in the list containing the *ie/ei* element.

## RATIONALE

To be considered an educated person, a student must spell correctly. This judgment may be illogical, but it is inescapable. Of course, spelling is of itself essential to good writing.

## MODULE GUIDE

1. Read the objectives and the rationale.
2. Take the preassessment. If you score 100 percent, you have completed the module.
3. Do the instructional activities.
4. Take the postassessment.

## PREASSESSMENT

Ask someone to dictate to you the words listed in the postassessment. Try to write them correctly. If you score 100 percent, you have completed the module.

## INSTRUCTIONAL ACTIVITIES

1. Memorize the following rhyme:
   I before e except after c
   or when sounded like a
   as in neighbor or weigh
2. Memorize the following exceptions to the rhyme:
   a. Leisure    c. Seize    e. Their
   b. Neither    d. Weird

## POSTASSESSMENT

Have someone dictate the following list to you. Try to spell the words correctly. A score of 100 percent is required for completion of the module.

|   |   |   |   |
|---|---|---|---|
| a. achieve | e. ceiling | i. freight | m. seize |
| b. apiece | f. conceited | j. heinous | n. their |
| c. belief | g. deceived | k. neighbor | o. veil |
| d. neither | h. received | l. reign | p. weigh |

## REMEDIATION

If you have scored less than 100 percent on the Postassessment, repeat the Instructional Activities with the help of your module resource person.

**Table 4.3   Sample Rationale Statement**

When teachers begin to plan for the learning activities of their pupils, they assume roles of decision makers as to what and how curriculum content is to be taught, as well as to what activities and behaviors will be engaged in by the pupils and teachers. These decisions cannot be guided alone by their preferences. There are certain rules and regulations that are imposed by the state, the school corporation, and the local school that limit their complete autonomy in these matters. To ensure secure legal positions in their classrooms, the teachers must have a knowledge of these rules and regulations and must work within the framework imposed by these regulations.

Today, teachers are being held accountable for the educational decisions that they make. More and more teachers are having to defend their actions in court. There are at least three reasons why this is true: the decline in reliance on the doctrine of "sovereign immunity" of school districts, students' increasing knowledge of these legal rights coupled with changing attitudes toward teachers and schools, and the decline of the acceptance of *in loco parentis* as a legal theory.

It is well worth noting that much court litigation that resulted in severe penalties for the teacher might have been avoided had the teacher had knowledge of the law. He claimed that the teachers generally are not aware of their legal responsibilities and limitations. Teachers are presumed to know the statutory laws of individual states that may require or prohibit certain behavior or acts and to know the rules and regulations established by their local boards of education. Yet, Hill (1973) conducted a study in which he compared teachers' knowledge of the law with that of people in other professions. He found that teachers ranked last in their knowledge about pertinent legislation that was passed. He noted that teachers make decisions in education as if legislation does not exist. Since ignorance of the law is not a valid defense, knowledge of rules and regulations that limit teacher decisions is necessary for all teachers.

SOURCE: *A module on modules*. Elementary and Secondary Education Act of 1965. Terre Haute, IN: Vigo County School System/Indiana State University.

A list of the 48 ESCAPE modules is given in Table 4.4. Some modules focus on skills and content that are considered to be indispensable for all teachers; these modules are required of all students. Other modules are optional, and each student must choose from among the optional modules to have enough credits to fulfill the teacher certification requirements of the state.

All ESCAPE program graduates are given computer printouts showing the competencies they have completed. The printouts begin with personalized statements (see Table 4.5). Following this statement is a list of the competencies the student has mastered as attested to by the program director. The intention is to provide a competency-based testimony to prospective employers.

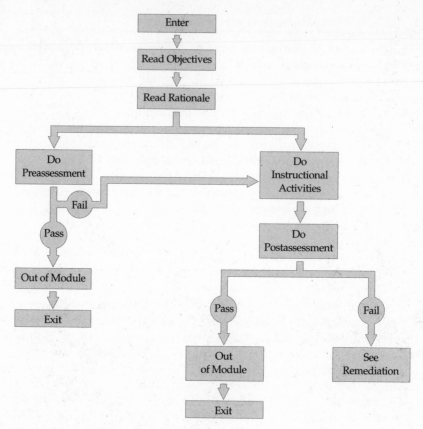

**Figure 4.9**  Module guide for students.

A final note of interest to curriculum workers is the module evaluation instrument (see Table 4.6). Particular attention should be paid to the fact that this instrument is not designed to measure student performance but, rather, to provide ongoing quality control for the module.

## AMERICAN STUDIES PROGRAM

One of the most promising and yet underused types of curriculum which is attractive to all subject areas and all grade levels is the *experiential curriculum*. Students enjoy experiential programs because of the opportunities they give students to be involved in "real-life" activities; teachers appreciate experiential programs for their power to motivate students. A description of a successful experientially based program follows.

**Table 4.4   ESCAPE Modules**

I. Organizing and Teaching Subject Matter

 A. Planning
  101—**Curriculum**—fitting the curriculum of a subject or grade level into the total academic program
  102—**Planning and Teaching a Unit**—developing, executing, and evaluating plans with a central theme
  103—**A Daily Lesson Plan**—developing, executing, and evaluating a daily lesson plan
  104—**Conference Planning**—familiarizing the student (teacher) with procedures and organization of conference planning for an entire class
 B. Techniques for Teaching Subject Matter
  111—**Principles of Reinforcement**—identifying and applying various reinforcement methods in the classroom
  112—**Asking Questions**—asking higher order questions
  113—**A Module on Modules**—identifying parts of a module

II. Human Dynamics of Teaching

 A. Teacher-Pupil Interaction
  201—**Motivation**—using Maslow's Hierarchy of Human Basic Needs to assist motivational learning activities
  202—**Consistency**—demonstrating using consistency with pupils in and out of the classroom
  203—**Classroom Management**—demonstrating skills and techniques utilizing the democratic process in the classroom
  204—**Reinforcement Techniques in Written Work**—using written reinforcement techniques on written work
  205—**Handling Discipline Problems Objectively**—recognizing and handling discipline problems
  206—**Humor in Education**—demonstrating a sense of humor in the classroom
 B. Diagnosing Classroom Climate
  211—**The Sociogram: Social Isolates**—using the sociogram to identify social isolates and prescribing a suitable remedy
  212—**Learning Difficulties**—diagnosing learning difficulties and prescribing appropriate teaching-learning strategies
  213—**Children's Misbehavior Goals**—identifying and dealing with children's misbehavior goals as described by Adler
 C. Teacher-Pupil Relationships
  221—**Empathetic Responses**—aiding in developing empathetic responses
  222—**Group Structure and Dynamics**—reviewing group processes and their effects upon dynamics and task achievement
  223—**Attitude Feedback**—measuring and finding a means to a positive attitude
  224—**Value Clarification**—defining values and related behavioral problems
  225—**Recognizing Enthusiasm**—identifying verbal and nonverbal behaviors which demonstrate enthusiastic teaching and assessing the consequences of those behaviors

III. Developing Teaching Skills

 A. Technical Skills of Teaching
  301—**Handwriting**—demonstrating the ability to form letters according to the curriculum guide of the student's (teacher's) school
  302—**Use of Instructional Media**—developing and executing an instructional presentation demonstrating the proper operational techniques of audio-visual media

**Table 4.4    ESCAPE Modules    (continued)**

303—**Plan Book-Grade Book: Development and Utilization**—developing and using a plan book and a grade book to meet the needs of a student's (teacher's) teaching situation

304—**Utilizing and Supplementing Cumulative Records**—familiarizing the student (teacher) with ten pupils through cumulative records, observations, and interviews

305—**Parent Conferences**—conducting a parent-teacher conference

306—**Field Trips**—planning and/or executing a field trip

B. Varied Approaches to Teaching

311—**Individualizing Instruction**—demonstrating techniques of individualizing instruction

312—**Guided Discovery**—using the guided discovery technique

313—**Problem Solving**—using the problem-solving technique

314—**Performance-Based Education in the Classroom**—preparing and implementing a performance-based lesson plan identifying specified skills or competencies

315—**Creativity**—describing and demonstrating the humanistic teaching technique of creativity

316—**Individual Needs**—using activities for meeting individual performance levels

C. Verbal Communication in Teaching

321—**Enunciation**—focusing attention on and corrective measures for commonly mispronounced words

322—**Communicating on the Pupil's Level**—restating a school directive at the pupil's level of understanding

323—**Voice Simulation**—using voice simulations in story telling, story reading, and role playing

324—**Listening Skills**—using listening variables and reacting to pupil comments to facilitate better pupil understanding

325—**Lecture and Demonstration**—describing and practicing lecture and demonstration techniques

IV. Professional Responsibilities

A. Policies and Regulations for the Classroom

401—**Rules and Regulations**—familiarizing the student (teacher) with state and local regulations, requirements, and curriculum policies

402—**Emergency Preparedness**—demonstrating knowledge of and developing a plan for federal, state, and local Emergency Preparedness Plans

403—**School Policy**—demonstrating knowledge of local policies and procedures as presented in policy handbooks

404—**Good Health**—demonstrating the importance of a working knowledge of health factors in education

B. Professional Contributions of the Classroom Teacher

411—**Professional Organizations**—learning about professional educational organizations

412—**Code of Ethics**—demonstrating a knowledge of ethical behavior

413—**Legal Responsibility of the Teacher**—demonstrating legal responsibility

414—**School Communication and the Community**—demonstrating the ability to communicate with the community through various media

415—**Co-Curricular Activities**—identifying common problems of and participating in activities not part of the regular academic program

416—**Professional Growth**—demonstrating a knowledge of professionalism, an awareness of impedances to it, opportunities and resources for growth, and professional responsibilities

**Table 4.5  Competencies Printout used in Interviews**

---

The purpose of this printout is to attest to the fact that [name of student] has demonstrated a mastery level of competence in the following teaching behaviors:

In the area of PLANNING, [name of student] has demonstrated a mastery level of expertise in [for students who completed Module 101] fitting the curriculum of a subject or grade level into the total academic program; [for students who completed Module 102] developing, executing, and evaluating plans with a central theme; [for students who completed Module 103] developing, executing, and evaluating a daily lesson plan; and [for students who completed Module 104] planning and organizing a conference planning session for an entire class.

In the area of TEACHING STRATEGIES, [name of student] has demonstrated a high level of competence in. . . .

---

What can a school do to generate enthusiasm among students for nonbasic courses? In the American Studies Program at Central High School in Tuscaloosa, Alabama, students look forward to going to jail.[1]

The American Studies Program was conceived in response to a federal court ruling that achieved racial desegregation by pairing two recently built segregated high schools. Although this measure eliminated segregation in the schools, many people felt that it did so at the expense of the students' community identity. And many students did indeed respond negatively to the ruling. The level of participation in school activities decreased, and absenteeism soared.

A committee of teachers, administrators, and faculty members from the University of Alabama concluded that participation in community life would diminish feelings of alienation among the students. The American Studies Program they designed is housed in the Old Jail, which is located in Tuscaloosa's historical district. The program provides students with a sense of community, gives them a reason to explore their different heritages, involves them in the preservation of the area's history, and requires them to participate in the political life of the city.

The program began in 1980 with 145 juniors and seniors and has continued to grow. The staff consists of a director and three teachers who team-teach

---

[1]This program description first appeared as a *Phi Delta Kappan* article written by Jane Ingram, Kenneth T. Henson, and Adolph B. Crew.

**Table 4.6    Module Evaluation Instrument**

|  | Unsatisfactory (0 points) | Satisfactory (1 point) | Very Satisfactory (2 points) | Not Applicable |
|---|---|---|---|---|
| 1. Was the format easily read? | _____ | _____ | _____ | _____ |
| 2. Were the Objectives stated in behavioral terms? | _____ | _____ | _____ | _____ |
| 3. During the initial introduction of the lesson, was adequate attention given to the review of facts and concepts learned in the previous lesson? | _____ | _____ | _____ | _____ |
| 4. Were key questions listed in order to determine the pupil's comprehension and application of the concept reviewed? | _____ | _____ | _____ | _____ |
| 5. Were the concepts, facts, or examples relating to the achievement of the objectives listed? | _____ | _____ | _____ | _____ |
| 6. Was the step-by-step-development of the lesson clearly outlined? | _____ | _____ | _____ | _____ |
| 7. Was a variety of activities provided to meet individual differences in needs, interests, and abilities of the pupils? | _____ | _____ | _____ | _____ |
| 8. Were the pupils' learning activities meaningful enough to be conducive to achieving the objectives. | _____ | _____ | _____ | _____ |
| 9. Was the summary complete enough to ensure a basis for the next lesson? | _____ | _____ | _____ | _____ |
| 10. Were provisions made for flexibility? | _____ | _____ | _____ | _____ |

in a four-hour block each morning. The students return to the main campus for classes each afternoon.

Flexible scheduling allows students to attend town meetings, seminars, and labs and to participate in extended field trips. Films, lectures, and performances in the program are followed by seminars attended by 25 to 30 students. The labs are designed to focus on the skills in reading, writing, speaking, and problem solving that are required for specific tasks.

The courses for juniors—American history, American literature, writing, and environmental science—emphasize historical preservation. The students are encouraged to become familiar with the many resources available through the University of Alabama and the local junior college and from the citizens of Tuscaloosa. Some students research local history, using genealogies, oral histories, and data from their own archeological survey. Another group is the staff of *Timepiece,* a student publication that features project-related articles, interviews, family stories, and local tall tales.

Students also visit Tanglewood, a 480-acre plantation donated to the university in 1949. The mansion, built in 1858, contains documents dating back as far as 1819 that provide fascinating insights into the history of a southern family. The original land grant, signed by President Martin Van Buren, hangs on one wall beside two original bills of sale for slaves. Students camp out on the grounds of the estate, using only equipment that would have been available in the mid-nineteenth century. Such activities encourage cooperation and a sense of community among the students.

The seniors' course of study is broader. It revolves around participation in the national political process. Students form their own government and explore such themes as the struggle to survive (frontier and wilderness), the struggle to cooperate (the formation of government, with emphasis on the executive branch), the struggle to create (the legislative branch), and the struggle to justify (the judicial branch).

Significant contemporary events are used as peak experiences in the curriculum. Local, state, and national elections provide students with a variety of opportunities through which they can investigate the American political process. Some students volunteer to work in the campaign headquarters of a political party or candidate of their choice. Candidates and their campaign organizers visit the classroom and describe the electoral process to the seniors. Appropriate literature, such as Robert Penn Warren's *All the King's Men,* helps to relate classroom work to field study.

The seniors also study and employ propaganda techniques in a mock debate and election. They learn to analyze the arguments offered on opposing sides of controversial issues and to write position papers on the issues. As a community service, on the day after an election, students collect every visible campaign poster within the city limits. The culminating experience of the senior semester is an extended field trip to Washington, D.C.

There are many important advantages to the American Studies Program. Perhaps the most important is that it provides an opportunity for personal growth. Students learn to look at experience as multifaceted, to make judgments from a broader base, and to bring their own heritage into clearer focus. For many, this method of perceiving experience and making judgments will become a habit. The experiential nature of the program necessitates firsthand learning by the students. Because they are given tasks that require cooperation, they have developed a sense of community by the end of the semester. At the same time, students' personal investment in these tasks motivates them to improve their basic skills in reading, writing, speaking, and problem solving.

Thanks to its popularity and record of success, the American Studies Program has become a permanent part of the Tuscaloosa curriculum. An officer of the Southeastern American Studies Association described Tuscaloosa's program as "the most extensive and challenging application of American Studies in the high school that has ever been attempted anywhere in the country." The team of American Studies teachers at Central High School has found the experience both time- and energy-consuming but professionally fulfilling. The students, too, have found that the program requires extra time and effort. But there is general agreement among all the participants that the quality of the experience makes it worthwhile.

## ALVERNO COLLEGE

Another innovative teacher education program is located in Milwaukee, Wisconsin. Like Project ESCAPE, the Alverno College program is outcomes-based and performance-based. Figure 4.10 shows the abilities required of Alverno students and their levels of mastery.

Many contemporary K–12 education reform programs require students to assess their own progress; continuous self-assessment is an important feature of the Alverno program.

Another important feature is the recognition that students can achieve at various levels of mastery. As Alverno students increase their levels of mastery, they earn more units of credits. All students are required to earn high levels of mastery in some areas of performance.

The Alverno program is a highly personalized program. As seen in earlier chapters, there is currently a strong perceived need to personalize curricula. Consider the effects that performance-based programs such as Project ESCAPE and the Alverno program have on personalizing or depersonalizing student experiences. For further discussion on this issue, see Appendix D.

## SUMMARY

According to the literature (Egbert, 1984; Brown, 1990; Marshall, 1991), most teachers teach the way they were taught, ignoring the research. But during the past two decades, a strong knowledge base on teaching has been developed.

Teachers rely on common sense, but common sense is not reliable. Science has given us a much more reliable system that includes concepts, theories, and models.

Currently, there is no good theory of education, but there are opportunities to contribute to the development of such a theory.

Teachers often criticize theory, saying that it is unrelated to practice. Actually, theory is not supposed to dictate practice; the role of theory is to guide our thinking. Thus, theory, plus several other factors including our emotions and our value systems, determines our behavior.

There are two types of models: descriptive and predictive. Descriptive models explain the relationships between their parts. Predictive models help us predict future consequences. Two of the most influential curriculum models

ALVERNO COLLEGE
Milwaukee, Wisconsin

ABILITY-BASED
LEARNING PROGRAM

**Abilities that**
- **involve the whole person**
- **are teachable**
- **can be assessed**
- **transfer across settings**
- **are continually re-evaluated and re-defined**

The curriculum is an ability-based, outcome-oriented approach to liberal arts/professional education. To earn a degree at Alverno College a student demonstrates the eight broad abilities listed below, at increasingly complex levels, in general education and in her areas of specialty.

These abilities constitute liberal education at the college and undergird and infuse advanced study in the disciplines and professions. Within the curriculum of a given major, the student develops the abilities according to the distinctive requirements of the disciplines and professions.

Throughout her course of studies, the student participates in performance-based assessments and learns to assess herself. Her progression toward a degree is based upon these assessments, both internal and external.

With demonstrated achievement at each level the student receives one level unit. For a Bachelor's degree, in addition to 32 units awarded when she has demonstrated the first four levels of each of the eight abilities, the student must achieve another 8 units, at least one of them at level 6. Advanced levels of any given ability require more time and effort to achieve than lower ones. For an Associate of Arts in General Studies, a student demonstrates her ability at the first four levels in each of the eight areas.

### Abilities and Developmental Levels

1. **Develop communication ability (effectively send and respond to communications for varied audiences and purposes)**

   Level 1—Identify own strengths and weaknesses as communicator
   Level 2—Show analytic approach to effective communicating
   Level 3—Communicate effectively
   Level 4—Communicate effectively making relationships out of explicit
        frameworks from at least three major areas of knowledge
   In majors and areas of specialization:
   Level 5—Communicate effectively, with application of communications theory
   Level 6—Communicate with habitual effectiveness and application of theory,
        through coordinated use of different media that represent
        contemporary technological advancement in the communications field

   IN WRITING, READING, SPEAKING, LISTENING, USING MEDIA, QUANTIFIED DATA, AND THE COMPUTER

2. **Develop analytical capabilities**

   Level 1—Show observational skills
   Level 2—Draw reasonable inferences from observations
   Level 3—Perceive and make relationships
   Level 4—Analyze structure and organization
   In majors and areas of specialization:
   Level 5—Establish ability to employ frameworks from area of concentration or support area discipline
        in order to analyze

**Figure 4.10**

Level 6—Master ability to employ independently the frameworks from area of concentration or support area discipline in order to analyze

### 3. Develop workable problem-solving skill

Level 1—Articulate and evaluate own problem-solving process
Level 2—Define problems or design strategies to solve problems using discipline-related frameworks
Level 3—Select or design appropriate frameworks and strategies to solve problems
Level 4—Implement a solution and evaluate the problem-solving process used

In majors and areas of specialization

Level 5—Design and implement a process for resolving a problem which requires collaboration with others
Level 6—Demonstrate facility in solving problems in a variety of situations

### 4. Develop facility in making value judgments and independent decisions

Level 1—Identify own values
Level 2—Infer and analyze values in artistic and humanistic works
Level 3—Relate values to scientific and technological developments
Level 4—Engage in valuing in decision-making in multiple contexts

In majors and areas of specialization:

Level 5—Analyze and formulate the value foundation/framework of a specific area of knowledge, in its theory and practice
Level 6—Apply own theory of value and the value foundation of an area of knowledge in a professional context

### 5. Develop facility for social interaction

Level 1—Identify own interaction behaviors utilized in a group problem-solving situation
Level 2—Analyze behavior of others within two theoretical frameworks
Level 3—Evaluate behavior of self within two theoretical frameworks
Level 4—Demonstrate effective social interaction behavior in a variety of situations and circumstances

In majors and areas of specialization:

Level 5—Demonstrate effective interpersonal and intergroup behaviors in cross-cultural interactions
Level 6—Facilitate effective interpersonal in intergroup relationships in one's professional situation

### 6. Develop global perspectives

Level 1—Assess own knowledge and skills to think about and act on global concerns
Level 2—Analyze global issues from multiple perspectives
Level 3—Articulate understanding of interconnected local and global issues
Level 4—Apply frameworks in formulating a response to global concerns and local issues

In majors and areas of specialization.

Level 5—Generate theoretical and pragmatic approaches to global problems, within a disciplinary or professional context
Level 6—Develop responsibility toward the global environment in others

**Figure 4.10   (continued)**

7. **Develop effective citizenship**

Level 1—Assess own knowledge and skills in thinking about and acting on local issues
Level 2—Analyze community issues and develop strategies for informed response
Level 3—Evaluate personal and organizational characteristics, skills and strategies that facilitate accomplishment of mutual goals
Level 4—Apply her developing citizenship skills in a community setting

8. **In a majors and areas of specialization:**

Level 5–Show ability to plan for effective change in social or professional areas
Level 6—Exercise leadership in addressing social or professional issues

9. **Develop aesthetic responsiveness: involvement with the arts**

Level 1—Articulate a personal response to various works of art
Level 2—Explain how personal and formal factors shape own responses to works of art
Level 3—Connect art and own responses to art to broader contexts
Level 4—Take a position on the merits of specific artistic works and reconsider own judgments about specific works as knowledge and experience change

In majors and areas of specialization:

Level 5—Choose and discuss artistic works which reflect personal vision of what it means to be human
Level 6—Demonstrate the impact of the arts on your own life to this point and project their role in personal future

---

**Figure 4.10   (continued)**

are Tyler's ends-means model and Taba's inverted model. Tyler's model proposes that we begin curriculum development by identifying desired outcomes and design the curriculum accordingly. Taba's model is called an *inverted model* because, unlike traditional models which were developed at the district, state, and federal levels, it begins in the classroom with teachers. Because of this, teachers are effective in implementing the new curriculum.

The value of any model or theory hinges on the degree to which its users understand the purpose of models and theories and on the willingness of the users to revise a model or theory as their local community, school, and students change. Confidence in models and theories and the skills required to use them effectively require a climate which makes teachers feel comfortable enough to put aside their dependence on the security they have when their only purpose is to help students remember facts. Put simply, effective use of theories and models requires a climate that encourages experimentation and tolerates errors.

## QUESTIONS

1. Why is teaching concepts inadequate?
2. What is the purpose of models?
3. What is the relationship between concepts and theories? Between theories and models?
4. Why is the scientific method superior to common sense?
5. What evidence can you offer to show that current education reform has used research? Has ignored research?

## SUGGESTED FURTHER ACTIVITIES

1. Select two curriculum models and contrast them.
2. Explain why all curriculum developers need to begin by stating their educational philosophy.
3. Contrast the three models discussed in this chapter. Give at least two unique strengths of each model.
4. Explain the uniqueness of the Tyler Ends-Means model.
5. Describe your strongest-held belief about (*a*) the nature of youth, (*b*) the role of the school in social development, and (*c*) the nature of learning.
6. Design a curriculum model which represents your own philosophical, social, and psychological beliefs.
7. Describe the biggest change that has occurred in society during your lifetime and explain how that change has or should have influenced school curricula.

## QUESTIONS ON THE FUTURE TEACHER'S DILEMMA

This chapter began with a monologue describing a student's pessimism and anxieties about going forward with a career in teaching. Much of the content in this chapter is about the role that generalizing plays in learning. The following questions are intended to help you make some generalizations about the important relationships between the student's statements and the content of this chapter.

1. The students plea for meaning that goes beyond the mere accumulation of disjointed facts contains a powerful sentence: *To me, intellectual curiosity is the only constant in education.* What does this sentence mean?

2. What is the real difference between wisdom and knowledge?

3. What can teachers and other curriculum developers do to respond to the growing body of information?

4. What is the student making a plea for?

5. What effect, if any, is contemporary education having on the student's concern?

6. How can teachers help students focus on ideas as opposed to facts?

7. How can the student's claim that educators look at the past to "invent the future" be applied to our schools' failure to address growing social problems such as the needs of minority students?

## BIBLIOGRAPHY

Beauchamp, G. A. (1981). *Curriculum theory* (4th ed.). Itasca, IL: Peacock Publishers.

Bellon, J. J., Bellon, E. C., & Bank, M. A. (1992). *Teaching from a research knowledge base.* Columbus, OH: Merrill.

Black, J. H., Efthim, H. E., & Burns, R. B. (1989). *Building effective mastery learning schools.* New York: Longman.

Bracey, G. W. (1991). Teachers as researchers. *Phi Delta Kappan, 72*(5), 404–405.

Brandweian, P. F. (1966). *Concepts in science.* New York: Harcourt, Brace, & World, p. 12.

Brown, D. S. (1990). Middle level teachers' perceptions of action research. *Middle School Journal,* pp. 30–32.

Bruner, J. S., Goodnow, J. J., & Austin, G. (1965). *A study of thinking.* New York: Science Editions, p. 45.

Bruner, J. S. (1966). *Toward a theory of instruction.* Cambridge: Harvard University Press, p. 78.

Carson, Terry (1990). What kind of knowing is critical action research? *Theory into Practice, 29*(3), 67–173.

Conant, J. (1951). *Science and common sense.* New Haven: Yale University Press.

Cooper, L. R. (1991). Teachers as researchers. *Kappa Delta Pi Record, 27*(4), 115–117.

Cornett, J. W. (1990). Utilizing action research in graduate curriculum courses. *Theory into Practice, 29*(3), 185–193.

Dewey, J. (1916). *Democracy in Education.* New York: Macmillan.

Dill, D. (1990). *What teachers need to know.* San Francisco: Jossey-Bass.

Egbert, R. L. (1984). The role of research in teacher education. In R. L. Egbert & M. M. Kluender (Eds.), *Using research to improve teacher education.* Lincoln, NE: American Association of College for Teacher Education.

Einstein, Albert (1951). Autobiographical notes, (Paul Arthur Schilpp, Trans.). In Paul Arthur Schilpp (Ed.), *Albert Einstein: Philosopher-Scientist,* (p. 7). The Library of Living Philosophers, (Vol. VII). New York: Tudor.

Gardner, H. & Boix-Mansilla, V. (1994). Teaching for understanding: Within and across the disciplines. *Educational Leadership, 51*(5), 14-18.

Glaymour, Clark (1980). *Theory and evidence.* Princeton: Princeton University Press.

Good, Tom (1990). Building the knowledge base of teaching. In D. D. Dill (Ed.), *What teachers need to know.* San Francisco: Jossey-Bass.

Heckman, P. E., Confer, C. B., & Hakim, D. (1994). Planting seeds: Understanding through investigation. *Educational Leadership, 51*(5), 36–39.

Hill, J. C. (1986). *Curriculum evaluation for school improvement.* Springfield, IL: Charles C. Thomas.

Hurlocke, E. (1925). An evaluation of certain incentives used in schoolwork. *Journal of Educational Psychology, 16,* 145–159.

Ingram, J., Henson, K. T., Crew, A. B. (1984). *Phi Delta Kappan, 66,*(4) 296–297.

Kant, Immanuel (1793). (E. B. Ashton, Trans.) *On the old saw: That may be right in theory but it won't work in practice.* Philadelphia: University of Pennsylvania Press.

Kerlinger, F. (1973). *Foundations of behavioral research* (2nd ed.). New York: Holt, Rinehart, & Winston.

Kowalski, T. J. and U. C. Reitzug (1993). *Contemporary school administration: An introduction.* New York: Longman.

Macdonald, J. B. (1965). Educational models of instruction. In J. B. Macdonald and R. R. Leeper (Eds.). *Theories of instruction.* Washington, DC: *Association for Supervision and Curriculum Development.*

Marshall, Carol (1991 March–April). Teachers' learning styles: How they affect student learning. *The Clearing House, 64*(4), 225–227.

McElroy, Lon (1990). Becoming real: An ethic at the heart of action research. *Theory Into Practice, 29*(3), 209–213.

Newsome, G. L. (1964). In what sense is theory a guide to practice in education? *Educational Theory, 14,* 36.

Oliva, P. F. (1976). *Supervision of today's school.* New York: Harper & Row, p. 232.

Oliva, P. F. (1992). *Developing the curriculum* (3rd ed.). New York: HarperCollins.

Ozmon, H. O. & Craver, S. M. (1981). *Philosophical foundations of education* (2nd ed.). Columbus, OH: Merrill.

Perkins, D. (1994). Do students understand understanding? *Education Digest, 59*(5), 21–25.

Pratt, Richard (1971). *Contemporary theories of education.* Scranton, PA: International Textbook.

Rivett, Patrick (1972). *Principles of model building.* New York: John Wiley.

Sanger, Jack (1990). Awakening a scream of consciousness: The critical group in action research. *Theory Into Practice, 29*(3), 174–178.

Saylor, J. G. & Alexander, W. M. (1966). *Curriculum planning for modern schools.* New York: Holt, Rinehart, & Winston.

Stefanich, G. P. (1990). Cycles of cognition. *Middle School Journal, 22*(2), 47–52.

Taba, Hilda (1962). *Curriculum development: Theory and practice.* New York: Harcourt, Brace, Jovanovich.

Tripp, D. H. (1990). Socially critical action research. *Theory Into Practice, 29*(3), 158–166.

Tyson, J. C. & Carroll, M. A. (1970). *Conceptual tools for teaching in secondary schools.* Boston: Houghton-Mifflin.

Ward, M. W. (1969). Learning to generalize. *Science Education, 53*, 423–424.

Whitehead, A. N. (1911). *An introduction to mathematics.* New York: Holt, Rinehart, & Winston. p. 157.

Wiske, M. S. (1994). How teaching for understanding changes the rules in the classroom. *Educational Leadership, 51*(5), 19–21.

Woods, R. K. (1994). A close-up look at how children learn science. *Educational Leadership, 51*(5), 33–35.

Zais, R. S. (1976). *Curriculum principles and foundations.* New York: Harper & Row.

# Chapter 5

# DESIGNING AND ORGANIZING CURRICULA

## OBJECTIVES

This chapter should prepare you to:

• Give two reasons why the traditional 6–3–3 school grade pattern changed.
• Describe three effects that *Sputnik* had on curricula in American schools and compare the impact of Sputnik to the impact of current education reform.
• Discuss the strengths and weaknesses of the subject-centered curriculum.
• Choose a curriculum design, and then express it in the form of a diagram and criticize it.
• Contrast the Trump Plan with the core curriculum.
• Discuss mastery learning research and give three unique qualities of mastery learning.
• Use curriculum design elements to critique those reform practices with which you are familiar.
• Discuss the need for local reform.

## THE LITTLE SCHOOL THAT GREW: REFORM VISITS A SCHOOL[1]

Once upon a time, in a land not too far away, a few townspeople got together and decided that the time had come to develop a system to educate their children. Every parent in town pitched in to build a schoolhouse; many rural people even walked into town to assist. Once the building was completed, a teacher was appointed to take charge. This teacher was a real leader of children because he got close to the children. They knew he was really interested in them. Being a real human being, he was especially aware of the things which mean the most to

---

[1]Taken from the author's article "The Little School That Grew," which appeared in the *Journal of Teacher Education*, Spring 1975, 26(1), 55-59.

children because he knew that these were the things which could help or hurt them most.

To complete the program, a second group got together to develop a curriculum. Since the parents were busy providing for their families, only the people without children could spare time to develop the new school's curriculum. So a few merchants, a few craftsmen, and a very few of the elite well-to-do fathers in town were there to comprise the first curriculum committee. (This practice of putting businesspeople in charge of education may have given rise to the current practice in current school reform.)

The meeting began with a decision on what courses should be included in the curriculum. The merchants made certain that mathematics was included. The well-to-do felt the subject a little too practical but after a brief dispute gave in to the suggestion. After all, people should know how to count their money and compute interest.

The craftsmen felt a real need for a vocational program to teach adolescents a trade so that the common eight-year apprenticeship would not be necessary. But for the representatives of the well-to-do group, this was really going too far. How could our schools carry on such practical nonsense? How could ivy grow on the premises where physical labor would be found? The only way the dispute was finally settled was through a rigid bargaining process. The well-to-doers gave in to the inclusion of a vocational course only because, in turn, they were promised a complete fine arts program of painting, sculpture, and music. At the end of the session, everyone was quite pleased with the curriculum. Even the teacher was happy, although he had no voting power on curriculum decisions (this was before teacher unions and site-based councils).

With the problem of content solved, the next problem to be faced concerned organizational details of the curriculum. The problem was a minor one relating to such matters as how chairs should be placed—the direction they would face, the number per row, and so forth. With only one room and barely enough chairs, the problem was soon solved.

The final problem was to determine time blocks allowed for each subject and length of the school day. The absence of a bell simplified this problem. Children came to school soon after sunup and were dismissed in time for the rural children to walk home and complete farm chores before nightfall. The only interruptions in between were a snack recess which began about midmorning, when some of the smaller kids would become hungry, and a lunch period which lasted until they became restless from being inactive. With the final task complete, school was ready to begin.

## The Little School Begins

The first day of school proved to be typical of many of the following days. Since the schoolhouse had only one room, the older children helped the younger ones with their lessons. The older children seemed to profit from helping the younger children. The teacher understood that self-fulfillment comes most easily through helping others. Perhaps the ease with which these youngsters got along with each other—ignoring differences in age and ethnic backgrounds—could be attributed to the teacher, who seemed to care so much for each child and who was able to see the person—the heart and soul of each individual.

At the back of the room on a large table were glasses of watercolors, a large pork and beans can full of brushes, and a stack of white paper. This was the art "room". No class hour was set aside for art. As the children finished their lessons, they were free to go to the back of the room and try out their skills. In fact, there was no planned instruction in art. The teacher was available when a child asked for help, but even then, little instruction was provided; mostly encouragement. The room was encircled with paintings attached to a line by clothes pins. On any day a production from each child of all the children was displayed, with as many subjects as there were students.

On another table were boxes of Tinkertoys and several pounds of modeling clay. How did the kids avoid getting clay on the Tinkertoys? They didn't. But why should they worry? The teacher didn't; nor did he complain when the earthy, rubbery smell lingered for hours after a piece of clay was dropped on the school's heating system, the wood stove.

At the front of the room was a large table surrounded by chairs. On this large table were piles of dominoes. There were no written instructions—only a set of house rules with plenty of keepers to enforce them. This was the nearest thing the school had to a math lab—unless one's concept of *curriculum* extends to the playground outside, where during any play period a number of marble games were going on simultaneously. There were two types: "for fun," or Introductory Marbles I for the learners, and "for keeps," or Advanced Marbles II for those who could hold their own in the competitive world. Some of the less physically agile (but quite adept mentally), students devised cigar boxes with holes through which a marble could barely pass and wagered any prospect a marble that he or she could not get the marble through the hole after dropping it from nose height. Even those who seemed a little slow at learning the three R's developed their own elaborate system of rules, altering them until they became workable.

As you might have expected, the physical education program was not well organized. When the time came each day for physical education, the kids left the building in groups. Some went to the ball field for a game of shove-up. The teacher was happy that the game was popular, for shove-up is a remarkable game. No choosing of sides is necessary. This is good for those who would always be chosen last, and it is good for the natural leaders, for it teaches them to get along with their less assertive peers. Once the game began, each player had an equal opportunity to play each position—even the pitching, which in other ball games is enjoyed by only one or two players with all the others left out. Finally, shove-up let each child experience success and failure without disappointing teammates, for when someone struck out, only that one child was out. This vigorous game was always enjoyed by all.

A second group rushed madly for the pine grove nearby to act out Robin Hood stories. Others congregated in an area known for less rigorous activities where furniture was made with sticks and beds were padded with straw. Some kids chose to spend their playtime hunting for bird nests, wading in a small pond, and seining for small fish and tadpoles.

The noon hour was a daily highlight. Paper sacks blossomed to give forth smells of sandwiches made from home-cured ham or sausage. Exchanges of sandwiches were common, since most kids brought two identical sandwiches and welcomed the variety. But taste was not as important as the opportunity to enjoy the food and the socializing. Some children sat under a large oak tree (some had favorite seats up in the tree where they enjoyed their noon meal). On hot days, the cool, shady cement doorsteps always attracted a few diners.

For many years, the little school continued to offer these uniquely human activities, and everyone assumed that the school's first teacher was doing a fine job and that it was a fine little school . . . until a certain event changed their minds.

## Change Comes to the Little School

While visiting the adjacent community, a school board member found a larger, more sophisticated school which had many fine qualities that were not to be found in the little school. When the board member returned, a meeting of the board was immediately called and the other members were informed of the many good qualities of the newer, larger school. When it was mentioned that School X had a lunchroom, someone asked, "Why can't our school have a lunchroom?" When the board was informed that the uniformity and structure in School X's curriculum were made possible by a multiplicity of classrooms and a bell system, someone asked, "Why can't our school have separate classrooms and a bell system?" Each time an advantage at School X was mentioned, the question "Why can't our school have that?" followed.

Since the school board at our little school was of the doing sort, immediate plans were begun to implement some of the innovations. A larger, two-story schoolhouse was constructed, and an electric bell system was installed. This made possible the dividing of the curriculum into many subject units and facilitated the next obviously needed change—the development of grades and grade levels. Additional teachers who were specialists in each subject were sought. The new building and the persuasive board members attracted the best of teachers, who were eager to implement the many innovations.

No one was more enthusiastic or more willing to experiment with the new program than the students. Like most young people, they readily accepted ideas of change. To the students, change meant freshness—a way to escape the existing school program. From listening to their parents, they learned that their school curriculum had gradually become dull, routine, and traditional.

The first year of the new curriculum brought some frustrations but, in general, was judged an overwhelming success. The students were getting expert instruction and were motivated in and outside the classroom by a real sense of competition. Classes were regulated by the bell system, and each child had learned to go to each designated place, and on time. A new lunchroom was providing a hot lunch for each student.

But as time went by, these innovations introduced some unforeseeable changes. After having been categorized and grouped according to age, grade, and ability level, the more capable students developed an attitude of superiority, and during the study periods—the only time of the day when all students came together—it became obvious that "superior" students had little tolerance for slower learners. In fact, competition had become so keen that they no longer continued to help each other. No one seemed to wish to help others, and no one needing help seemed to trust anyone enough to ask for help.

In the study halls, the slower students automatically bunched together into small groups. Some expressed their resentment toward the superior students by constantly flouting the rules of discipline. Others became passive and withdrawn. And even those who seldom understood their assignments knew that they had been singled out as "average" (meaning "below average") or low achievers. In other words, they had been labeled "failures."

A real difference could be seen in the way students moved about. Children who had once gaily skipped off to recess or leisurely wandered to the back of the room to assemble Tinkertoys were now literally running from room to room. When the bell system was originally installed, five minutes was allotted between periods. Later this was decreased to three minutes, then two.

Thirty minutes was provided for lunch. The lunch period bell sent each student running at top speed. The lucky few who captured positions at the head of the line were too excited to eat; the slower runners found themselves with only five to ten minutes to bolt down their food. The time of day which had once meant complete relaxation had now disappeared.

Some of the most dramatic changes occurred inside the classrooms. The new teachers presented eloquent lectures and held all students accountable for attaining set objectives, each having a minimum acceptable level of performance and specific conditions according to which it was to be demonstrated. Credit for the students' becoming much more disciplined cannot be given entirely to the new system—some credit must be reserved for the teachers. In art class, each student was carefully instructed on such matters as brush selection and the techniques of making strokes, for the designers of this progressive program understood that children should not waste time dabbling in water paints—creating meaningless paintings which are often crude and ugly. Rather, they should be told exactly what to do and how to do it well.

The foolishness which had once gone on in the playgrounds was now replaced with a highly structured and competitive program. Only those who excelled in physical skills and endurance participated, while the rest of the class engaged in other activities. The overweight kids could be found playing checkers and snacking. The handicapped kids were given plenty of time to think about their limitations. A couple of ethnic clubs removed the minority children from the relaxed midmorning games which had once contributed to the children's social skills. Some students enjoyed table tennis very much, but it had become obsolete, since no one ever won a letter in Ping-Pong. At least something was offered to all students who did not qualify for the ball teams: Time was provided for them to smoke and tell jokes. (This may have been the best the new physical education system had to offer.)

The little school had come a long way. Its administrators and faculty were proud. Parents knew from hearing teachers' comments that it must be one of the most progressive and innovative schools because its curriculum had been completely restructured to meet the demands of the times. Student complaints reinforced the faith in the new curriculum, because everyone knows that kids never like anything that is good for them.

## Curriculum Is Coming to the Little School

Ron McLean listened carefully as the little school's principal proudly recounted the recent restructuring of its programs. Ron's new role as the school's first counselor would include providing leadership for future curriculum change. He wanted to keep the curriculum current, and he knew that the job would require daily adjustments in design and organization.

"So, as you can see," the principal concluded, "We've worked awfully hard to bring our academic programs and our extracurricular programs up to date. With the pending educational reform legislation, and the recent research which says that the only way to significantly improve an entire curriculum is by restructuring, our timing could not have been better. Certainly, the changes will enable us to be more accountable for student progress on the new achievement exams. What do you think?"

Ron's first thoughts were, "I'd better not say all that I'm thinking." He wondered whether all schools had to make the hard choices that seemed to be between what students need and what the public wants. But he was much too politically astute to say so.

"I'm impressed with all the efforts that have been applied to this self-reforming process, and especially with its broad-based approach. It is comforting to know that a school can still have such strong support from the community. I am looking forward to next Wednesday night and my first opportunity to speak to the parent-teacher association."

Ron was being truthful. He really did admire this level of commitment from the teachers and parents. He felt fortunate to have this level of support at the school where he had just accepted a position. But Ron's mind ran beyond the pleasantries that are commonly shared during initial meetings with new employers; he knew that the thinking that prevailed at this school had some very basic flaws. He honestly did not believe in change for the sake of change. Ron thought that change should come only after much investigation. He thought that such major changes as the ones he had just heard described should be supported by research, or at least by a needs assessment or something that showed that such changes were needed.

Ron viewed his role not as that of actually introducing specific changes but as making the teachers and parents sensitive to needed changes and earning their commitment to those changes. "After all," he thought, "the teachers must be the true curriculum developers at any school, and they must learn how to rally their colleagues' support for needed change."

But Wednesday night was only two days away. He had to work fast. How could he best enlighten these teachers and parents on the need to base future curriculum changes on accumulated data that would support the need for change and would ensure that the changes selected would lead to overall improvement, not just to the satisfaction of the board members, but improvement for the students?

He had a problem, all right. It was a problem bigger than just planning for a PTA meeting. It was a problem of how to plan to get colleagues to critically examine the need for change.

As you continue reading this chapter, remember that curriculum changes are made every day and that teachers are involved in the decisions to change and how to change. This chapter will review some of the basic curriculum designs that have become standard over the years, and it will also introduce curriculum dimensions that provide ways of examining the curriculum, such as scope, sequence, articulation, and balance. Think critically about your own philosophy of education, the major purposes of schools, and the major flaws and shortcomings in today's curricula. As a curriculum planner who will be involved in schoolwide planning, you can significantly influence the quality of your school. This chapter will provide some of the concepts that you will need to achieve this goal.

## INTRODUCTION

Through the years, curricula have been tailored, modified, and shaped to fit the needs of a changing society. The curriculum for the first American schools was simple and straightforward because the purpose of the first schools was simple and straightforward—to prepare students for admission to Harvard College, a school of divinity.

But during the almost 400 years since then different demands have been placed on the schools. Each new and added purpose has required an adjustment in the curriculum. John Dewey (1916, 409) expressed the need for continuous curriculum design when he said,

> Democracy has to be born anew in each generation, and education is its midwife.

Almost a century has passed since Dewey made this statement, and educators are still worried that "A good deal of the typical curriculum does not connect—not to practical applications, personal insights, or much of anything. It's not the kind of knowledge that would connect, or it is not taught in a way that would help learners make connections" (Dewey, 1916, p. 24).

This chapter chronicles some of the most important curriculum designs. These designs are grouped according to the age level of the students they serve (elementary, junior high, middle level, and high school) and according to patterns that recur among them. Within each level, the major curriculum designs are discussed. (See Figure 5.1). For certain, many of these divisions are not as distinct and separate as Figure 5.1 might suggest. For example, it is common for a school at any level to have a combination of several designs. But separating the designs enables us to discuss and understand the unique characteristics of each design.

Since school systems typically start at kindergarten and go through grade 12, several patterns are common. Originally, the schools were designed for age 6 through about age 15. Later, as the school curriculum was extended to grade 12, the schools were divided into two areas: elementary (grades 1–6) and secondary (grades 7–12). But, at the secondary level the development range was too broad. Some students hadn't reached puberty; others were young adults.

| Level | Common Curriculum Designs |
|---|---|
| Elementary | Graded<br>Open education<br>Nongraded<br>Cooperative learning<br>Integrated |
| Junior high | Graded<br>Core curriculum<br>Open education<br>Cooperative learning<br>Integrated |
| Middle school | Graded<br>Nongraded<br>Open education<br>Cooperative learning<br>Integrated |
| High school | Graded<br>Subject matter<br>Broad fields<br>Alternative<br>Cooperative learning<br>Integrated |

**Figure 5.1** Common curriculum designs at various grade levels.

For this reason and for administrative convenience, the junior high school was formed. This was the origin of the 6–3–3 curriculum design.

As more knowledge about the effects of maturity on student behavior became available, it became apparent that the preadolescent or transescent age-group was very different from the younger and older students. Educators also learned that American youth were developing socially more rapidly than their predecessors had. It was decided that a special school was needed for this age-group; it became known as the *middle school*. The ages represented in middle schools vary; the most common ages are 11 to 14 and 11 to 15. The curricula for the systems which have these schools are 5–3–4 or 5–4–4. Since the kindergarten is common among curricula today, the patterns are often by K–5–3–4 or K–5–5–4. Figure 5.2 shows the changes in grade groupings through the years.

Although the number of curriculum designs that can be used at each level is almost unlimited, each design is associated more with some levels than with others.

Some of the more popular curriculum designs that have had an impact on the schools at various times include subject-centered, broad-fields, core, Trump Plan, spiral, mastery learning, open education, and problem solving.

## THE SUBJECT-CENTERED CURRICULUM

The first curricula of the Latin grammar schools were composed of religion, Latin, and Greek. Thus, the first American curriculum was subject-centered. *Subject-centered* implies that the curriculum is built around one or more subjects, but that isn't all. Throughout our schools' history, subject-centered curricula have been complemented by a particular teaching style, the lecture. The objective of subject-centered curricula is for the students to learn the subject, that is, the content.

| Years | Grade Levels Represented | | |
|---|---|---|---|
| 1835–1847 | Nongraded | | |
| 1848–1909 | 1–12 | | |
| 1910–1950 | 1–6–6 | | |
| 1951–Present | K–6, | 7–9, | 10–12 |
| | K–5, | 6–8, | 9–12 |
| | K–5, | 6–9, | 10–12 |
| | K–4, | 5–8, | 9–12 |

**Figure 5.2** Changes in grade groupings.

The subject-centered curriculum is the oldest curriculum design in the world. It isn't surprising to learn that subject-centered curricula are surrounded by tradition. In fact, the subject-centered content itself is traditional content, that is, content which over the years has been accepted.

As mentioned earlier, the major delivery system for subject-centered curricula is the lecture, itself the most traditional teaching method. Even the objective of subject-centered curricula is the traditionally accepted goal of accumulation of information.

## Strengths

The subject-centered curriculum design has several features that cause proponents to favor it. The continued use of this design through the years means that people are familiar with it and comfortable using it. Furthermore, its long use gives a sense of "tried and proven." or, "It was good enough for me; therefore, I trust it for my children."

A more tangible quality of the subject-centered curriculum is its tight organization. The content is rigidly sequenced. When using this design, teachers can, and almost always do, follow the sequence of the textbook. This makes the task of keeping track of where each lesson ends and where the next one begins easy. This tight organization also helps the teacher avoid accidental duplication of content and makes the testing simple. Easy design of tests was mentioned earlier as a strength of the textbook. Since the subject-centered design is characterized by use of textbooks, it benefits from the strengths and suffers from the weaknesses of textbooks.

The tightly organized subject-centered curriculum is easy to implement. Courses can be added to or eliminated from a school's program (or even added to or deleted from a student's individual curriculum). Thus transferring from one school to another, and even from one state to another, is easy. This advantage is realized by high school students who go on to colleges out of state.

Still another advantage of the subject-centered curriculum design is its efficiency. The well-organized, compact curriculum enables students to cover a lot of content in a short time. This advantage becomes clear when the design is contrasted with an inquiry curriculum (which requires students to discover relationships for themselves before they learn them), with case studies (which require students to sift relevant information from irrelevant information), with simulations and games (which are student-paced), with mastery learning (which permits students to remediate and recycle), or with the discussion method (which requires a lot of time to cover the material).

## Weaknesses

Among the limitations of the subject-centered curriculum are its failure to consider the unique needs and interests of students and its detachment from contemporary events in the world.

Perhaps the most severe criticism leveled against the subject-centered curriculum is the effect it has on learners. Although it is satisfying to the teacher, the subject-centered design is a poor motivator for students. Interestingly, the lecture is favored by poorer students because it places less classroom responsibility on learners. Too often, the goal is to be able to recall information rather than to attempt to understand it. Audrey Cohen (1993, p. 792) explains:

> Subject-oriented learning has combined with the increasing fragmentation of knowledge to create an information mania in our schools that makes simply digesting facts a priority and eliminates consideration of the goals to which facts and ideas might be applied.

Success in reaching the underachievers requires special effort from the teacher. O'Neal, Earley, and Snider (1991, p. 122) explain:

> Research indicates that while many underachieving students have poorer auditory and visual skills, their kinesthetic and tactile capabilities are high. Implications are that teachers may need to use a greater variety of instructional methods.

Geisert and Dunn (1991, p. 223) say that "difficult material needs to be introduced through each student's strongest perceptual modality (preferred learning style) and then reinforced through supplementary modalities." Obviously, the subject-centered curriculum design makes comparatively little use of such necessary reinforcement.

The subject-centered curriculum can be effective when used by teachers who are willing to alter their teaching styles and lower the level of instruction to the point at which the student can become a successful learner. But to assume that teachers will make this change is perhaps a mistake. Marshall (1991, p. 226) explains teachers' reluctance to leave the security of the subject-centered curriculum:

> Consequently, for teachers to change their teaching styles, to understand and risk planning instruction on the basis of learning style patterns of students—and, therefore, to teach successfully a wider range of learners—they must come to recognize, respect, and support the learning differences of students. If students do not learn the way we teach them, then we must teach them the way they learn.

## THE BROAD-FIELDS CURRICULUM

Realizing that the neat containers called *subjects* that had been designed to hold and dispense knowledge had limitations, educators decided to enlarge the containers. The results became known as the *broad-fields curriculum*.

An important goal of this design, devised around the turn of the century, was to reduce the propensity that students in subject-centered curricula had for memorizing fragmented facts. The broad-fields curriculum would solve this problem by broadening such subjects as history, geography, and civics into a curriculum category—social studies. Instead of studying reading, writing, literature, and speech, students would study language arts. Instead of taking physics and chemistry, students would take physical science. Instead of taking geology, physical geography, oceanography, mineralogy, paleontology, meteorology, and space science, students would take earth science. Instead of taking botany, anatomy, physiology, and zoology or biology, students would take biological science. In fact, larger categories such as biological science, earth science, and physical science were expanded to form general science.

Unfortunately, the broad-fields curriculum design has not always been effective. A major cause for its shortcomings is the way the curriculum has been delivered. For example, some teachers ignored the broad content generalizations that the creators of this design sought to help students develop. Other teachers taught the generalizations but as facts to be memorized; and as Harrison (1990, p. 503) cautions, this won't achieve the goal of having students understand the generalizations.

> Instruction must focus on the use of the concepts (content generalizations) and the context in which they occur in order to ascertain their practical connections.

Furthermore, success with this curriculum requires good note taking, and under the best conditions only 52 percent of the major ideas are captured in students' notes (Maddox & Hoole, 1975). When recording lectures, students focus more on less important points while missing the more important general understandings. King (1990, p. 131) reports:

> Researchers have found that when students take notes during a lecture they are far more likely to record bits and pieces of the lecture verbatim or simply paraphrase information rather than organize the lecture material into some sort of conceptual framework or relate the new information to what they already know.

Because the lecture affords teachers the opportunity to demonstrate their expertise, many teachers go on an ego trip, leaving the confused students behind. Stefanich (1990) says that this practice leads to failure: "In order to be successful teachers, we must be prepared to lower the level of instruction to the point where each student becomes a successful learner."

The broad-fields curriculum was an attempt to use an integration of traditional subjects to help students develop broad understanding in all areas. The curriculum has survived for over half a century: the approach enjoyed a resurgence during the early 1960s, stimulated by *Sputnik* and the Woods Hole Conference. Fortunately, the revival addressed the delivery system which had caused much failure when the broad-fields design was first implemented. Content generalizations such as concepts, principles, and themes were the organizing elements that were coupled with inquiry and discovery learning methods in the 1960 designs. The dependence of this curriculum design on its delivery system for success reflects the inextricable and interdependent relationship that exists between curriculum and instruction in general. The dependence on the teacher for the success of this curriculum can be generalized to all curricula. Eisner (1985, p. 195) explains:

> When the curriculum development movement got underway in the early 1960s, there was talk about the desirability of creating "teacher proof" curricula. That aspiration has, through the years, given way to the more realistic view that teachers are not mere tubes for curriculum developers. Teachers cannot and should not be bypassed.

## THE CORE CURRICULUM

Near the turn of the century, some innovative curriculum directors, such as Francis Parker, who was described in Chapter 3, began searching for a way to escape the fragmentation that characterized the traditional (subject-centered) curricula. The result was a design called the *core curriculum*. The theory behind the development of this approach begins with the realization that some content is indispensable for all students. This content would become the core. As can be seen in Figure 5.3, the core can be illustrated graphically.

Around the core are a number of spokes. These different spokes represent academic discipline courses (D), preprofessional courses (P), special-interest courses (S), and vocational courses (V).

The core curriculum has a dimension of versatility that makes it attractive to advocates of a variety of philosophies. For example, the essentialists can use the core to ensure coverage of the essential subjects. At the other extreme, the progressive educator can assign both content and activities to ensure that individual students' needs are met. In between, the pragmatists can use the core to ensure the coverage of practical curricula.

Zais (1976, p. 423) identified six types of curricula as core curricula: (1) the separate subjects core, (2) the correlated core, (3) the fused core, (4) the activity/experiences core, (5) the areas-of-living core, and (6) the social problems core.

The core curriculum represented the second attempt to integrate learning. Contemporary, real-life problems were used for organizing the curricula. Typically, core programs are organized into blocks of time, often two or three successive periods, during which the teacher or a team of teachers integrates two or more subjects or disciplines. Oliva (1992, p. 305) lists six characteristics of core curricula:

1. They constitute a portion of the curriculum that is required of all students.

2. They unify or fuse subject matter, usually English and social studies.

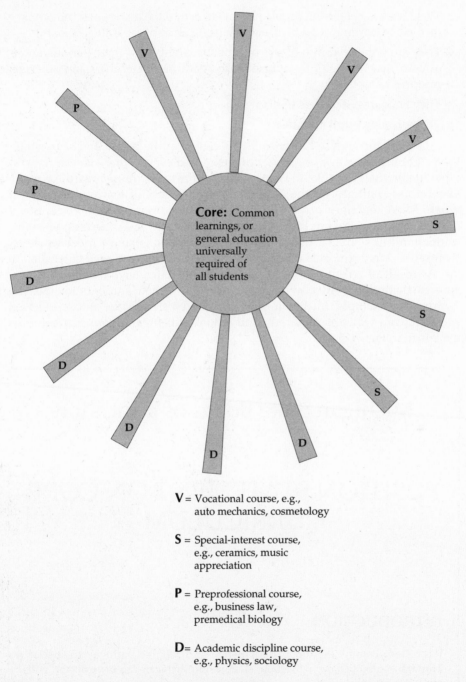

V = Vocational course, e.g.,
    auto mechanics, cosmetology

S = Special-interest course,
    e.g., ceramics, music
    appreciation

P = Preprofessional course,
    e.g., business law,
    premedical biology

D= Academic discipline course,
    e.g., physics, sociology

**Figure 5.3** Structure of the core curriculum design.

3. Their content centers on problems that cut across the disciplines; the primary method of learning is problem solving using all applicable subject matter.

4. They are organized into blocks of time, usually two to three periods under a "core" teacher (with the possible use of additional teachers and others as resource persons).

5. They encourage teachers to plan with students.

6. They provide pupil guidance.

The core curriculum has been best received at the junior and senior high levels, but it has never been universally accepted even at these levels. As with other innovative curricula, the success of the core curriculum, regardless of the version used, hinges on the ability and willingness of teachers to make it work. Most teachers are ill-prepared to implement problem-centered approaches or to integrate subjects and activities to achieve the comprehensive understandings sought by the core curricularists, because most teachers, themselves, were educated in textbook-oriented, subject-centered curricula.

As result of recent reform legislation many states have mandated a new core curriculum specifically designed to prepare their students for the 21st century. For example, Michigan has established a state-wide, outcomes based pre K–12 core which is required of all schools. Michigan's core curriculum is explained in Figure 5.4.

# Michigan State Board of Education

# POSITION STATEMENT ON CORE CURRICULUM

## INTRODUCTION

Education remains the most fundamental and reliable pathway to success. Through comprehensive education, students in Michigan can develop the skills needed to function effectively in a rapidly developing society.

Figure 5.4

Michigan has had a long tradition of providing quality education to all citizens. However, recent studies on the status of education in the State indicate that the knowledge and skills students receive in the course of elementary and secondary schooling needs to be strengthened to meet the demands today's graduates face in the changing workplace. Greater demands exist to prepare students for a changing economic and technological society in the twenty-first century. State and local educational agencies must play a critical role in improving and revitalizing K-12 school curriculum.

The State Board of Education Model Core Curriculum Outcomes are intended to provide a framework within which schools may examine the adequacy and relevance of their educational programs. The core curriculum outcomes provide expectations for all students to attain the necessary educational outcomes which will prepare them for effective adult living.

## EXPECTATIONS

Specifically, the core curriculum should:

1. Provide a clear framework within which curriculum planning can be conducted;

2. Enable teachers, students, parents, and the community to be clear about what is expected of each student;

3. Enable students to make identifiable progress through the various learning stages;

4. Specify essential educational outcomes which all students must achieve. Local districts are encouraged to go beyond the core curriculum to meet the individual educational needs of their students;

5. Encourage innovative approaches in the formulation and delivery of instruction; allowing local districts freedom in the way in which they select and use instructional materials; and

6. Support existing good practices. The new Model Core Curriculum Outcomes are far from totally new. Most are familiar to educators, and are built firmly upon present good practice which is supported by existing research, materials, books, and resources.

The core curriculum should stimulate critical thinking, discussion, problem-solving and engage students in active, rather than passive learning. At-risk children should learn from just as challenging a curriculum as other students; indeed special efforts should be expended to make the curriculum rich enough to compensate for their lack of access to context-broadening experiences in their homes and communities.

Figure 5.4 (Continued)

## PURPOSE

The purpose of the Michigan State Board of Education's Position Statement on the Core Curriculum is to bring Michigan policy for curriculum and learning in line with current research on effective schools and how students learn. This is begun by establishing a foundation of essential subject matter for achievement by all students, in conjunction with continuing concerns for the students learning styles, study skills and thinking skills that are embodied within the subject areas. Learning to learn is one of the paramount skills students need to acquire and build upon. Understanding and achieving of the core curriculum learning outcomes is the starting point for more advanced learning during the schooling process and throughout their adult lives. The interest in curriculum integration has expanded due to the explosive growth of knowledge and the desire for making the curriculum relevant to the lives of the students. Core Curriculum competencies, which transcend traditional curriculum boundaries, are identified to encourage a variety of approaches to curriculum construction and optional instructional delivery.

It is recognized that each and every person requires a firm educational foundation. Such a foundation is not only rooted in the basics of reading, comprehending, writing, computing, solving, learning and relating interpersonally, but it develops individuals' aesthetic appreciation, makes them technologically literate, develops their personal management skills, their team workskills, makes them career ready, fosters self worth and social/personal values. The Core Curriculum will provide that foundation.

The Core Curriculum is a means of promoting a schooling posture and firm position that all students are given ample opportunity to achieve the Broad Student Outcomes. These outcomes will provide all students with a solid foundation of skills, knowledge and understandings which are necessary for continual growth and success throughout their lives.

## POLICY AND GOAL

It is the policy of the State Board of Education that local school districts shall develop curriculum and deliver instruction to all students based upon a model core curriculum. The Model Core Curriculum Outcomes shall articulate the broad outcomes to be achieved by all students as a result of their school experiences as well as the educational outcomes in the various curricular areas that will enable achievement of the broad outcomes.

The major goal of delineating desirable educational outcomes is to "describe the spectrum of knowledge, skills, and attitudes which students should achieve by the conclusion of secondary school. These are desirable learnings which students will need in order to select and effectively function in their life-career roles of workers, family members, citizens, students, and self-fulfilled individuals. An

Figure 5.4 (Continued)

underlying assumption here is that the ultimate purpose of education is to permit each individual student to reach his or her optimum potential, so as to lead productive and satisfying lives". (The Common Goals of Michigan Education, 1980)

The Model Core Curriculum Outcomes provide the basis for building the school district's core curriculum. In addition to achieving the core curriculum outcomes, students should have other curricular opportunities for growth, based on individual needs, interests, and desires for specialization. Through the local curriculum development process, schools should ensure that the core curriculum program is an integral part of a sound, comprehensive curriculum that provide elective training and specialized learning opportunities for all students. A sound core curriculum should enable high school graduates to pursue further educational opportunities in an effective and efficient manner and without the need for remedial-level training or courses.

## BROAD STUDENT OUTCOMES

A clearly defined Core Curriculum will provide local school districts with direction and a solid foundation upon which their local curricula and instructional strategies can be structured. As a result of a K-12 education based on a well defined Core Curriculum, a Michigan student will be:

### A person who values and is capable of learning over a lifetime.

Examples: Seek new educational opportunities; select, initiate and demonstrate learning strategies appropriate from different life roles and situations; value learning and be motivated to continue learning; plan, monitor and evaluate his/her own learning; set goals, evaluate progress toward meeting them and revise as necessary; seek answers to questions in everyday work; and initiate formal and informal learning activities.

### A person capable of applying knowledge in diverse situations.

Examples: Identify problems; analyze situations/ problems; think critically and creatively; identify, access, integrate and apply a variety of resources; find and integrate information, probe for solutions; work cooperatively in varying contexts; recognize and use analogies and metaphors as tools for communicating; use available information to reason, make decisions and solve complex problems; identify, address and solve problems with a systematic process; and transfer models to real life situations.

### A person who makes and implement decisions and plans for successful living.

Examples: Describe him/herself as a decision maker; formulate positive core values in order to create a vision for the future; set priorities and goals;

Figure 5.4 (Continued)

evaluate options and take action toward accomplishing goals; have a vision for future options; and recognize and appreciate the values of others.

### A caring, sensitive and flexible human being.

Examples: Be open to new ideas; contribute time, energy and talents to improve the welfare of others; think globally and act within his/her local environment; know the benefits (strengths) of diversity; participate as an interdependent member of a diverse community and a global society; act in ways that will develop and foster a just society where all groups experience cultural democracy and improvement; tolerate ambiguity; and develop a knowledge of and value aesthetics.

### A creative and innovative person.

Examples: Recognize different perspectives; apply knowledge in diverse situations; create original products; express him/herself in a creative manner; demonstrate flexibility; express ideas in a new way; operationalize new ideas; be aware of and use creative talents; apply old ideas in new ways; generate new ideas; and accept and learn from error.

### A person able to communicate effectively in written, visual and spoken language.

Examples: Understand and make him/herself understood within the context in which he/she is operating; convey information clearly and concisely; select the mode of communication most appropriate within various contexts; express his/her needs, desires and opinions; operate as both the sender and receiver of messages; and access tools and strategies for gaining clarification.

### A competent and productive participant in society.

Examples: Function in a technological culture; apply mathematical/scientific/social/political concepts; understand the structure/functions/maintenance of the elements within his/her environment and his/her relationship to these; participate as a team member; manage personal daily living skills; and understand and recognize roles and responsibilities within various spheres of living.

These statements represent the desire of the State Board of Education and other citizens on behalf of every student. The intent of the state educational enterprise is to provide meaningful and clear direction; it is the responsibility of the local educational systems to provide effective delivery of instruction, with a core cur-

Figure 5.4 (Continued)

riculum as the nucleus, so that all students realize the attainment of these stated qualities.

## PRINCIPLES

A core curriculum shall be based on the following underlying principles that address content, instruction, assessment and school improvement. The Michigan State Board of Education Model Core Curriculum will:

## Curricular

Expand the academic preparation of each student.

> The core curriculum will promote the depth of educational development in all areas of learning and experience which are important to meet the future needs of the individual and our society in a global world.

Be developmentally and sequentially based and articulated through all learning levels.

> A core curriculum cannot be put in place at one point but rather must begin at the Pre-K level and move sequentially toward achieving the identified outcomes by taking into account the developmental growth of the individual. This developmental approach should lead to a sequential, relevant and articulated presentation of the curriculum.

Take into consideration the differences in a student's environment, experiences and changes in student populations patterns.

> A student comes to the school with the culture of both the family and community in which they live. The core curriculum must take these factors into account and build upon existing cultural strengths to provide the student with the optimal structure for learning to achieve the desired outcomes.

Relate to Michigan's Standards of Quality, Goals and Objectives, and Student Outcomes.

> The Michigan K-12 Program Standards of Quality document formed the basis for the development of the Model Core Curriculum Outcomes. The Essential Goals and Objectives in the various subject areas provide further clarification and elaboration of the educational outcomes.

Figure 5.4 (Continued)

## Instructional

### Be structured in a variety of approaches including inter-disciplinary and disciplinary.

Core curriculum should be guided by a conceptual framework. This conceptual framework must lead to assuring that all students will have significant options and opportunities to achieve desired outcomes using a variety of settings and approaches commensurate with local needs and resources.

### Assure access and opportunity for all students and attend to traditionally under represented students in various fields.

Equal educational opportunity is central in the implementation of the core curriculum. Provision must be made for the individual needs of students through the use of a variety of learning styles and pedagogical practices, different time allotments and additional time so that all students have ample opportunity to achieve the desired outcomes.

### Attend to the instructional practices and instructional materials and technology used to deliver the curriculum.

Optimum use of school time, resources and staff are key considerations in implementing the core curriculum. Instructional practices are influenced by curriculum and must be reviewed and changed as necessary when curriculum is revised. Effective instructional practices must engage learners as active participants in the curriculum. This is important to most current conceptions of how subject matter should be used in the delivery of instruction.

## Assessment

### Measure student attainment of the educational outcomes at the state, district and building levels.

Appropriate assessment techniques should be used to accurately measure student attainment of the various content, process, and skill outcomes. Assessment results should be used to upgrade student learning levels by improving curriculum content and instructional delivery methods.

## School improvement

### Be implemented within a long-range school improvement planning process.

Figure 5.4 (Continued)

A dynamic, future-oriented curriculum is a foundation of an effective school. The curriculum must take into account changing economic, social and political conditions in our country and in relationship to the global community. Provision should be made for its continuing update within the overall long-range school improvement plan.

## CORE CURRICULUM AREAS

The outcomes found in both the content and process areas, are derived from the Michigan K-12 Program Standards of Quality and the Essential Goals and Objectives documents approved by the State Board of Education. The outcomes are defined in the following curricular areas:

### World Studies Education

To include history, civics, economics, geography, and the study of foreign language, as well as the promotion of values such as personal and social responsibility, the dignity of work, sensitivity to our multicultural society, and the responsibilities of democracy that will engage learners in understanding of national and global economic, political and social conditions.

### Technological Competencies

To engage learners in the understanding of the use of technology and technological literacy that is required for successful living in contemporary society.

### Physical and Health Education

To include the development of the student's knowledge, skills, and abilities to make successful decisions that lead to a healthy life-style physically, mentally and emotionally.

### Mathematics and Science Education

To include quantitative and analytic reasoning and problem solving, scientific literacy, and technology, with an emphasis on content that will actively engage learners in applying knowledge to everyday experiences.

Figure 5.4 (Continued)

## Life Management Skills

To engage learners in the application of successful and ethical personal decision making processes and personal growth, responsible producer and consumer behavior, essential health, family roles and relationships, parenthood and nurturing, social factors and change, and civic and social responsibilities.

## Language Arts Education

To include reading, writing, speaking, listening, and literature, with emphasis on using language arts as part of the whole curriculum. Students should learn to apply effective reading, writing and speaking strategies to fit a situation and to use knowledge both flexibly and critically.

## Cultural and Aesthetic Awareness

To engage learners in uses of leisure time, verbal and non-verbal communications, inter-personal skills, use of community resources and appreciation of the relationship between individual freedom and responsibility.

## Career and Employability Skills

To engage learners in the acquisition and application of knowledge, skills and behaviors which focus upon academic skills, personal management skills and teamwork skills that are necessary for a person to obtain, maintain and progress on a job.

## Arts Education

Including music, visual and performing arts, will advance young people's appreciation from a historical and multicultural perspective of the arts, develop their creative and critical abilities, and provide them with an understanding of the relationships between the arts and other content areas and community resources.

The core curriculum should encompass the academic, citizenship, employability and personal knowledge and skills necessary to prepare students to become competent, problem solving citizens in our democratic society and in

Figure 5.4 (Continued)

## Figure A

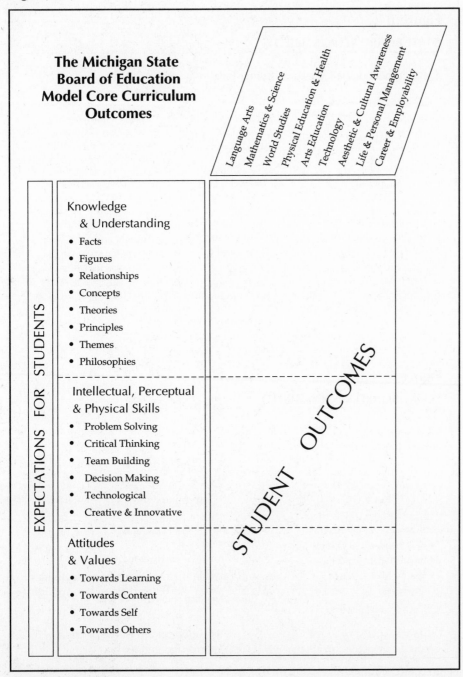

The Michigan State Board of Education Model Core Curriculum Outcomes

Language Arts
Mathematics & Science
World Studies
Physical Education & Health
Arts Education
Technology
Aesthetic & Cultural Awareness
Life & Personal Management
Career & Employability

EXPECTATIONS FOR STUDENTS

Knowledge & Understanding
- Facts
- Figures
- Relationships
- Concepts
- Theories
- Principles
- Themes
- Philosophies

Intellectual, Perceptual & Physical Skills
- Problem Solving
- Critical Thinking
- Team Building
- Decision Making
- Technological
- Creative & Innovative

Attitudes & Values
- Towards Learning
- Towards Content
- Towards Self
- Towards Others

STUDENT OUTCOMES

Figure 5.4 (Continued)

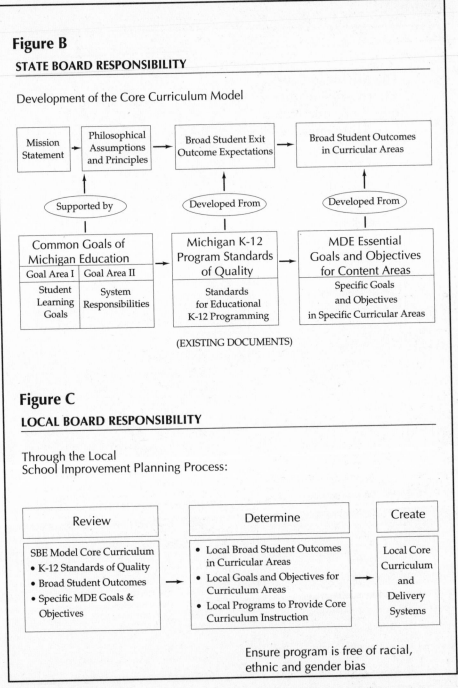

**Figure B**

**STATE BOARD RESPONSIBILITY**

Development of the Core Curriculum Model

| Mission Statement | Philosophical Assumptions and Principles | | Broad Student Exit Outcome Expectations | | Broad Student Outcomes in Curricular Areas |

Supported by

Developed From

Developed From

| Common Goals of Michigan Education | | Michigan K-12 Program Standards of Quality | MDE Essential Goals and Objectives for Content Areas |
| Goal Area I | Goal Area II | | |
| Student Learning Goals | System Responsibilities | Standards for Educational K-12 Programming | Specific Goals and Objectives in Specific Curricular Areas |

(EXISTING DOCUMENTS)

**Figure C**

**LOCAL BOARD RESPONSIBILITY**

Through the Local
School Improvement Planning Process:

| Review | Determine | Create |
| --- | --- | --- |
| SBE Model Core Curriculum<br>• K-12 Standards of Quality<br>• Broad Student Outcomes<br>• Specific MDE Goals & Objectives | • Local Broad Student Outcomes in Curricular Areas<br>• Local Goals and Objectives for Curriculum Areas<br>• Local Programs to Provide Core Curriculum Instruction | Local Core Curriculum and Delivery Systems |

Ensure program is free of racial,
ethnic and gender bias

Figure 5.4  (Continued)

our rapidly changing, interconnected and multi-cultural and multi-ethnic world. As such, the core curriculum should be gender fair and supportive of our multi-racial, multi-ethnic society. As a result of their total school experiences, students should be able to engage in everyday and specialized modes of inquiring, analyzing, explaining, communicating, coping, achieving, appreciating, and team building.

## MATRIX OF OUTCOMES

The State Model Core Curriculum is a set of student outcomes, not courses or programs. The learner outcomes are a set of expectations for what a student should know, be able to do, and develop as attitudes and values as a result of a K-12 public education in the State of Michigan. Each of the nine core curricular areas has provided a summary of the outcomes in the model document and each area is supported by more specific expectations as found in the various Departmental goals and objective documents. Figure A shows the need to have expectations in each core curriculum area for the formation of useful attitudes and values as well as the acquisition of content specific skills and formal knowledge about each content area. In addition to the content specific outcomes, the matrix also suggests that all areas should integrate a concern for process skills such as problem solving, critical thinking, decision making, and the nurturing of creative and innovative thinking.

## FRAMEWORK FOR DEVELOPMENT

The Michigan Core Curriculum Model is based on existing State Board of Education documents. Figure B shows the developmental process used by the Department of Education. The educational outcomes provide the student with the educational foundation to achieve the desired Broad Student Outcomes.

Based on the model core curriculum provided by the State Board of Education, local boards of education will determine the manner in which the core curriculum is delivered. The locally determined core curriculum will include the learning areas, specific studies, the sequence, the instructional strategies, and the learning level clusters in which the core curriculum will be taught. This should be done as part of the larger school improvement planning process, which includes the districts curriculum development process undertaken by each local schoolboard. Figure C on the preceding page suggests the localboard's task. Translating core curriculum outcomes into instructional programs is a local responsibility and can be best achieved through the local curriculum development and alignment planning and the district school improvement process.

Figure 5.4 (Continued)

Once the local core curriculum is in place, provision should be made to continuously update the core curriculum within the overall 3-to-5 year school improvement planning process.

The State Board of Education, in consultation with representatives of local educators, will develop a set of indicators and/or criteria to determine if a school district is in compliance with the desired core curriculum. The set of indicators will be used by the Department of Education and intermediate and local school districts to determine whether or not the core curriculum is being implemented.

The core curriculum areas will be considered in place when it can be verified by evidence of the following educational attributes: time allocation, instructional materials, curriculum scope and sequence, units and courses of study, syllabi, staff development, and appropriate assessment strategies. The Department of Education staff, in cooperation with educators from throughout the state, will also provide technical assistance to districts not meeting the criteria, as well as recognize those districts that meet or exceed the model core curriculum.

## CONCLUSION

The Michigan State Board of Education is committed to insuring that effective, high quality education and services are provided equitably to the people of Michigan and that every student from our public education is prepared to function as a competent, caring, productive, and responsible citizen in our multifaceted and increasingly complex and global society.

To achieve the above commitment, it is essential to identify a widely shared statement of what is expected of our students and to give shape to our vision of a well educated individual. Educational goals and outcomes help define basic direction of educational programs at all levels. The educational goals and outcomes should reflect standards that are high, clear and practical. They should define targets that are serious, specific and worth reaching. Goals that drive action result from the widest possible collaboration among members of public, local educators, and state policy leaders. The educational goals and outcomes proposed by the Model Core Curriculum Outcomes, clearly state that Michigan wants to become an education community that achieves high standards of quality. The children of Michigan will be able to take their places in the nation as workers, family members and effective participants in our democratic society.

Figure 5.4 (Continued)

## DISCUSSION

One of the outstanding features of the Michigan Core Curriculum is that it begins by identifying desired outcomes. An expression of these outcomes becomes the basis for selecting content and activities. This change reflects the general change in emphasis in programs nationwide from courses or programs to emphasis on expectations. These expectations include specific content mastery plus certain process skills such as problem solving, creative thinking, and critical thinking.

Another important feature of the Michigan Core Curriculum is its method of implementation. Local school boards are charged with determining the manner in which the core curriculum will be delivered. Furthermore, local educators will join the State Board of Education in developing an evaluation system to determine whether their district has met the state requirements.

## THE TRUMP PLAN

Throughout the twentieth century, grouping of students has been a topic of study and debate among educators and researchers. The results of such studies have been mixed. For example, Good, Reys, Grouws, and Mulryan (1990–1991) report that, in groups with a wide range of ability, the better students dominate the others. Yet Calfee and Brown (1979) say that when grouped homogeneously, low-ability students perform even less well. Centra and Potter (1980) found that the amount of time students spend in direct instruction is directly related to their level of achievement. Yet Julik (1981) reviewed more than 40 studies and reported that grouping had a strong motivating effect on students.

Proponents of the *Trump Plan*, which was developed in the late 1950s and introduced in the early 1960s, recommended arranging students in small groups (15 or fewer students) and in large groups of 100 to 300 students. Students would spend part of each day in small groups and part of each day in large groups. They would spend the remainder of the day studying alone or in small groups according to their preference. As shown in Figure 5.5, Trump had definite ideas about how much time should be allotted to these arrangements.

A strength of the Trump Plan was its variety: something for everyone. Furthermore, this plan specified a variety of teacher or discussion leader activities and a variety of media for the large groups. Small-group work provided a variety of activities involving all students. Independent study time also afforded students a high level of involvement: laboratory experiments, problem solving, reading, listening to tapes, or pursuing a variety of creative activities.

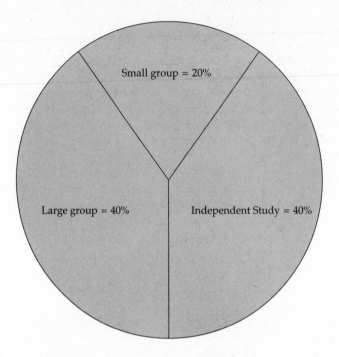

**Figure 5.5** The Trump Plan.

One feature of the Trump Plan is variable scheduling not only during the school day but throughout the year. Another feature, year-round instruction has had an important impact: On January 23, 1993, the *Richmond Register*, a daily newspaper in Kentucky carried an article headed "Ft. Knox pupils begin year-round school." The article explained that "year-round school is practiced in over 2000 school districts in the United States and it's growing rapidly".

## THE SPIRAL CURRICULUM

Throughout the twentieth century, connectionist psychologists have insisted that, when learning occurs, it occurs in steps, each part building on simpler content learned earlier. Constructivists agree that each part of the content should be tied to prior learning. Markle, Johnston, Geer, and Meichtry (1990, p. 53) explain:

> Constructivists describe learning in terms of building connections between prior knowledge and new ideas and claim that effective teachings help students construct an organized set of concepts that relates new and old ideas.

The *spiral curriculum* takes connectionism one step further, recommending that the same topics be returned to the curriculum at a later date, sometimes at a higher grade level. Having gained in maturity and in the accumulation of prerequisite knowledge, students will be able to develop understandings that were beyond their capacity when simpler elements of a topic were introduced earlier. The Spiral curriculum has been prevalent for several decades and the Spiral curriculum concept can be found in curricula today at all grade levels.

Curriculum planners should understand that the repetitive quality of the spiral curriculum has some disadvantage. For example, if students know that they will have multiple opportunities to learn a concept then they may take a casual attitude toward the topic. Dr. Joe Crosswhite, former president of the National Council of Teachers of Mathematics said that a major national weakness in our mathematics curricula is our failure to have a single designated grade level for each concept.

## MASTERY LEARNING

In 1963 an article in the *Teachers College Record* (Carroll, 1963) described a curriculum designed to ensure that all students could succeed. Rejecting the work of A. H. Thorndike, which correlated students' success with their IQ, Carroll said that all students could learn if certain curriculum and instructional adjustments were made.

First, this new program, called *mastery learning*, would incorporate flexible time, as much as each individual needed. Second, students who failed to master the content and objectives on the first attempt could recycle without penalty. Remediation using a variety of different learning styles would be provided between testing cycles. Formative evaluation, not the traditional summative evaluation, would dominate. *Formative evaluation* is given in small steps throughout the teaching unit. Its purpose is to promote learning by using test scores to improve both instruction and the curriculum. Formative test scores are never used to determine grades.

As to letter grades, which most schools require, mastery learning typically uses A's, B's, and I's; there are no C's, D's, or F's. Students who score below the level set for mastery (usually 80 percent) must remediate and recycle.

Like all other curriculum designs, mastery learning succeeds or fails depending on its application. Cunningham (1991, p. 84) explains:

> There are two essential elements of the mastery learning process. The first is an extremely close congruence between the material being taught, the teaching strategies employed, and the content measured. The second essential element is the provision of formative assessment, opportunities for students followed by feedback, corrective and enrichment activities.

There are basically two types of mastery learning: (1) teacher-paced and group-based, and (2) student-paced and individual-based (Block & Henson,

1986). Most mastery learning programs are student-paced; that is, the students set their own pace (Guskey & Gates, 1986). Most are individual-based; that is, individual students pursue the content independently. Though mixed, the results of studies on mastery learning programs are encouraging. The first studies (Bloom, Hastings, & Madaus, 1981) found that at least 95 percent of all high school students could master all school objectives. Burns (1979) reviewed 157 such studies. Although, in one-third of the studies (47) no differences in achievement were found, in two-thirds of the studies (107) mastery learning students significantly outscored their traditionally taught counterparts. In only 3 of the 157 studies did mastery learning students achieve less than their counterparts. The review by Burns covered 3000 schools and spanned over 15 years.

Guskey and Gates (1986) reviewed 25 studies of group-based and teacher-paced mastery learning programs in elementary schools and secondary schools. In all 25 studies, the students in mastery learning groups outlearned their counterparts.

But mastery learning is not without critics. Arlin (1984) describes mastery learning as a "psychological trap," lacking a proper conceptual basis. Slavin (1989, p. 79) says:

> If school districts expect that by introducing group-based mastery learning or . . . they can measurably increase their students' achievement, there is little evidence to support them.

## OPEN EDUCATION

The term *open education* is often used interchangeably with *open space* and *open classroom*. Of the three terms, *open space* is the clearest since it applies to physical space. Sometimes *open classroom* refers to open space, but usually it refers to *open education*, which is a much more philosophical concept. This book makes a distinction between open education and the open classroom.

Open education refers to a curriculum design which ties a unique educational process to a strong philosophical basis. It was developed and popularized in the renowned British infant schools. Perhaps the best way (at the least, an effective way) to understand open education is to understand the British infant school. The following is a true story:

> St. Barnabas and St. Philip's School in London's borough of Kensington was not what most Americans would expect to see when visiting an open education curriculum. From the outside it looked like any two-story, nineteenth-century brick building. Inside, some of the walls had been removed.
> What struck one immediately was the fact that each wall was covered with a vast array of charts, games, paintings, maps, and pictures—all very colorful. In one room, a tape recorder was playing. Pupils were huddled close to it lis-

tening to a story that was being told with the voice inflection and enthusiasm fitting for the age-group of the listeners.

The voice on the tape paused at regular intervals, during which a teacher used exaggerated expressions to lead the pupils to respond. After the tape was finished, the teacher supervised the pupils while they acted out the story they had heard.

In the courtyard, some children were feeding a pet turtle. A couple of other children were playing in a sandbox, pretending to be on the beach. The teacher promised to help them build sand castles later in the morning.

There was activity everywhere. Children were busy. Remarkably, they seemed to know exactly what they were doing, even though there were so many of them and they were engaged in so many types of activities. Some children seemed to be working in groups, and others appeared to be pursuing individual activities.

I made my way to the headmaster's office. He knew all the children. From having worked in a dozen such schools, I was not surprised. I knew that the headmaster or headmistress taught the lowest form (grade) and therefore knew all the students. Thus, the only students the headmaster or headmistress had to get acquainted with were the transfers. It made a lot of sense, and it also enabled the head to relate well to the young pupils.

Discussions with the headmaster and the teachers clearly revealed that each of these teachers was truly a curriculum developer. The teachers had made the most of the bright visuals that covered the walls. Even the tape recording, which was made by one of the teachers, revealed an enthusiasm and a satisfaction equaled only by their level of dedication to their teaching.

As a former science teacher, I was impressed with the amount of experimentation that was going on. These teachers were not afraid to fail, and this attitude was manifested in the pupils. But this was only one dimension in the philosophy of these teachers and others who teach in British infant schools. Like their fellow teachers, these teachers were operating according to the following common beliefs which the experts say are the essential elements of open education.

- Students are active agents in their own learning
- One student may learn differently from all others
- The teacher is responsible for helping all students discern how they learn best
- A major purpose of the school is to encourage exploration
- Students have rights as well as obligations
- Teachers are trained observers, diagnosticians of individual needs

Not everyone was bubbling with excitement. Permit me to share one additional experience. One child was very disagreeable. He made a loud fuss over everything his classmates did. A teacher was quietly observing this child. After a while, she explained to the other children that Tommy was having a rough day, and she said that she and the other children should help Tommy get over this rough spot. Whereupon, the teacher walked over to Tommy, and instead of scolding him, picked him up and carried him around for several minutes until his emotional state passed.

This visit to an open education school brought to mind the following words by Abraham Maslow (1973, p. 159):

> As I go back in my own life, I find my greatest education experiences, the ones I value most in retrospect were highly personal, highly subjective, very poignant combinations of the emotional and the cognitive. Some insight was accompanied by all sorts of autonomic nervous system fireworks that felt very good at the time and which left as a residue the insight that has remained with me forever.

In summary, open education is more than an architectural design. It is a curriculum design of structural content delivered mainly through student activities. Open education is founded on a set of beliefs about the nature of young people and the nature of learning. Success with open education requires understanding its philosophical and theoretical bases. As a final note, I have visited many open classrooms in the United States which exhibited all the characteristics just described, and I have visited some open classrooms in the United States that did not exhibit any of these features. For observations on why our open classrooms often fail, see Appendix *B*.

## PROBLEM SOLVING

The problem-solving curriculum became popular during the Progressive Education Era (from about 1925 to 1945) because of the emphasis during that time on learner-centered curricula. What better way to involve students than to give them problems to solve? Problem solving experienced a rebirth in the 1960s, when the post-*Sputnik* scare was at its peak. Realizing that American students were long on facts and short on the ability to apply these facts, curriculum designers cast the new interdisciplinary curricula in the form of problems.

These new programs were identified by titles and acronyms, that often reflected their developers. For example, Harvard had its Project Physics, and Boulder, Colorado, had its Earth Science Curriculum Project (ESCP). There was a Science-Mathematics-Study Group (SMSG). These curricula were three-dimensional, in that they came packaged in boxes with the apparatus needed to conduct hands-on investigations.

Typical of laboratory schools and other innovative schools during this era, the P. K. Young Laboratory School at the University of Florida was equipped with many objects including a set of scales, tension springs, a toy truck, and an inclined plane, to mention just a few of the dozens of gadgets. This was the hardware required to implement one of the problem-solving curricula. By requiring students to use this hands-on equipment to solve problems, these curricula forced students to apply their acquired knowledge.

Problem solving is still a valued curriculum design because many people maintain that this skill is a necessity for coping in the future. A special panel reporting to the National Center for Educational Statistics: (1991, p. 65), said that people will need the ability to integrate information from all disciplines and use integrative reasoning to solve problems:

> Integrative reasoning is essential in modern life and today's workplace. It represents not the ability to recall bits and pieces of information, but the "things" one can demonstrate one can do. These include communication, using technology and information effectively, and proficiency in working in a problem-solving capacity either alone or in teams

## SELECTING CURRICULUM DESIGNS

Since each curriculum design has a unique combination of strengths and weaknesses, curriculum developers who are informed about these designs can match them with the needs of their schools. For example, the many schools that are now being required by reform practices to implement integrated thematic units can benefit from the broad-fields design. Schools seeking ways to improve educational opportunities for minority students may choose to implement mastery learning because it gives students the time they need to master each concept and because it provides students with opportunities to remediate and recycle without penalty. Multicultural classes may choose the Trump Plan or problem-solving curricula because they provide students with opportunities to participate in cooperative group projects.

Education reform programs in many states are requiring their primary teachers to abolish the early grade levels. Teachers who have taught in open classrooms will have developed many prerequisite skills such as team teaching and continuous progress record keeping. Teachers wishing to increase the level of understanding in their classes or wishing to ensure that concepts are

| Curriculum A | Curriculum B | Curriculum C |
|---|---|---|
| H | H | H |
| G | G | G |
| F |   | F |
| E | E | E |
| D | D | C |
| C |   | D |
| B | B | B |
| A | A | A |

**Figure 5.6** Sequence versus continuity.

remembered in higher grades may choose the spiral curriculum. Teachers who are sensitive to the need for a solid set of content and experiences for all students while providing different tracks to meet their students' varying vocational ambitions may vote for the core curriculum.

## CURRICULUM DESIGN QUALITIES

No curriculum design is really unique. Rather, all designs have some qualities in common with other designs. It is the *combination* of features that makes each design unique. Examples of features are: scope, sequence, continuity, articulation, and balance.

### Scope

*Curriculum scope* refers to the breadth of the curriculum at any level or at any given time. For example, the scope of eighth-grade science refers to the variety of science topics covered during the eighth grade. Because scope concerns only one point in time, it is called a *horizontal dimension*.

### Sequence

*Curriculum sequence* is concerned with the order of topics over time. For example, in biology, students might study the cell and then tissue, organs, and systems. Because it concerns a period of time, curriculum sequence is called a *vertical dimension*.

### Continuity

*Continuity* refers to "smoothness" or absence of disruption in the curriculum over time. A curriculum might have good sequence but might also have disruptions. That curriculum would lack continuity. For example, as shown in Figure 5.6, curriculum A has good sequence and good continuity. Curriculum B has good sequence but lacks continuity. Curriculum C has poor sequence. Also, even though no topics are missing, the lack of order creates disruptions; therefore, curriculum C lacks continuity. So, sequence without continuity is possible, but continuity without sequence is not.

### Articulation

*Articulation* refers to the smooth flow of the curriculum on both dimensions, vertical and horizontal. Vertical articulation is called *continuity*. Its horizontal counterpart has no name.

## Balance

Another important curriculum feature is *balance*. Frequently, the layperson speaks of a "well-rounded education," implying that an individual is getting, or a school program is offering, a curriculum with balance between the arts and sciences, with balance between college prep subjects and vocational subjects, and so forth.

## A FINAL NOTE

Some of these programs are more student focused than others. A focus on students is important and should be a goal of all curriculum designs. Kowal (1991, p. 269) reminds curriculum designers that making the student the center of attention does not imply that students should always get what they want. Student wants and student needs may be two entirely different things:

> The task is not to design a . . . program based on who yells the loudest or the longest or to use compromise as a rationale for curriculum design. The basis of an appropriate rationale is centered on the student; how students can be best prepared for a future, which is at any given time unknown.

Designing curricula to meet the current and future needs of students is an ongoing challenge that educators must meet.

Most schools use modifications of several of these curriculum designs. In fact, because of the effect of the culture of the school and the culture of the local community, all curriculum designs have to be modified so that they fit the unique characteristics and needs of each school.

## SUMMARY

The subject-centered curriculum is the oldest curriculum design. Teachers like it because it employs the textbook and the lecture method. The textbook provides specific, tightly organized content, enabling teachers to show off their expertise. Students like subject-centered curricula because of the specific content and tight organization and because they can remain passive while in the classroom.

But near the turn of the twentieth century, educators became concerned that the subject-centered curricula led only to the memorization of disjointed facts and bits of information. So, the subject-centered curriculum was replaced in many schools by broad-fields curricula, which integrated the subjects to produce broader understanding.

At the time of the Progressive era (1920s), educators wanted curricula that would enable them to serve each individual student's needs. The core curriculum was devised to achieve this goal. The many variations of core curricula had two things in common: (1) a core of content required of everyone, and (2) a combination of content and activities used to meet particular goals.

During the late 1950s, the Trump Plan was developed. This design was different from existing designs because it focused on grouping. Students were required to spend 40 percent of their time in large groups, 20 percent in small groups, and the remaining 40 percent in independent study or in small groups if they preferred.

Like the core curriculum, the Trump Plan had strength in its variety. The Trump Plan included variation in methods, materials, and even in the length of the school day and the school year, including year-round curricula.

The spiral curriculum is built on two psychological foundations: connectionism and constructivism. It also employs developmentalism, recognizing that students are not ready to study certain concepts until they reach the required level of development and until they have had the necessary experiences.

Mastery learning is a curriculum design that purports to offer an opportunity for all students to succeed by giving individual students all the time they need to master the objectives, by affording them opportunities to remediate and recycle without penalty, and by using formative evaluation which is given during instruction, not with the purpose of assigning grades but in order to improve learning by changing the curriculum and instruction.

Open education, developed in England, has caused much confusion in the United States. Often called the *open classroom*, or *open space*, this curriculum design incorporates open space, but it is much more. It is built on a strong philosophical foundation encompassing such ideas as these: Students should be free to move and do, and they should be free to discover important knowledge; teachers should be the major curriculum developers, and they should be supportive; the administrators should be head teachers and should know all students.

Open education has been used extensively and with widely varying success in American schools. In all the successful schools, the teachers and administrators have understood the philosophical basis which undergirds this design.

The problem-solving curriculum has long been a favorite design for educators who espouse learner-centered education. The launching of *Sputnik* gave problem-centered curricula a boost. It was hoped that, by discovering the answers to problems, students would more thoroughly understand the broader content generalizations required to master a discipline.

These curriculum designs are all different, but they all have certain features in common: scope (breadth), sequence, continuity, articulation, and balance. Success with any of them depends on teachers understanding the underpinning philosophies and on the quality of instruction.

## QUESTIONS

1. What are your favorite qualities in the Little School That Grew?

2. Can you identify any practices in contemporary education reform that parallel the forces that caused the Little School to lose some of its valuable qualities?

3. What curriculum designs were reflected in the curriculum of the Little School before and after its changes?

4. Can you think of ways to make the changes the Little School made and yet avoid the losses it suffered?

5. Which curriculum design presented in this chapter do you see evidenced most in your own school? Why do you think this design dominates at your school?

6. To what extent is formative evaluation (compared to summative evaluation) used in your school? Why?

7. What kinds of balance do you think your own college curriculum should strive to maintain? Examples: humanities versus sciences, general studies versus major subject.

8. Do you believe that it is important for teachers to understand a program's underlying philosophy? Why or why not?

9. Do you think that American culture has any qualities which cause teachers to implement practices without fully understanding their philosophies? Name some of these qualities.

10. Which is worse in curriculum design, poor sequence or poor continuity? Why?

11. Do the current education reform practices in your school have sound philosophical and theoretical bases? Explain.

## SUGGESTED FURTHER ACTIVITIES

1. Select a curriculum design from this chapter and research its (*a*) philosophical and psychological bases, and (*b*) its degree of success as reported in the research and other literature.

2. Examine your own school (or visit a local school) and identify what evidence you can find for each of these designs. Don't be surprised if you learn that the school uses a combination of several designs rather than a single "pure" design.

3. Get a copy of your state's curriculum guide from your library or from a local school counselor. Choose a discipline and grade level. For your chosen discipline and a grade level, describe the program in your state's cur-

riculum guide in terms of (*a*) how the content is sequenced, (*b*) the scope of content, and (*c*) the balance between the sciences and the arts and between required subjects and electives.

4. The success of any curriculum design depends on the teacher's ability to implement the design. Select a design and describe how you could help teachers prepare to use it successfully.

5. Make a list of the reform elements under way in your district. Now compare the curriculum designs in this chapter with the items in your list. What designs offer the best opportunities to meet some of the local reform goals?

## BIBLIOGRAPHY

Arlin, M. (1984, Spring). Time, equality, and mastery of learning. *Review of Educational Research, 54*, 71–72.

Bestor, A. (1953). *Educational Wastelands: The retreat from learning in our public schools.* Urbana, IL: University of Illinois Press.

Block, J. H., Efthim, H. E., & Burns, R. B. (1989). *Building effective mastery learning schools.* New York: Longman.

Block, J. H. & Henson, K. T. (1986, Spring). Mastery learning and middle school instruction. *American Middle School Education, 9*(2), 21–29.

Bloom, B. S., Hastings, J. T., & Madaus, G. F. (1981). *Evaluation to improve learning.* New York: McGraw-Hill.

Burns, R. B. (1979). Mastery learning: Does it "work"? *Educational Leadership, 37*, 110–113.

Calfee, R., & Brown, R. (1979). Grouping students for instruction. *Yearbook of the National Society for the Study of Education 78*(P. II), 144–148.

Carroll, J. B. (1963). A model of school learning. *Teachers College Record, 64*, 723–733.

Centra, J., & Potter, D. (1980). School and teacher effects: An interrelational model. *Review of Educational Research, 50*, 273–291.

Cohen, A. (1993). A new educational paradigm. *Phi Delta Kappan, 74*(10), 791–795.

Cunningham, R. D., Jr., (1991, September). Modeling mastery teaching through supervision. *NASSP Bulletin, 75*(536), 83–87.

Darling-Hammond, L. (1993). Reforming the school reform agenda. *Phi Delta Kappan, 74*(10), 756–761.

Dewey, John (1916). The need of an industrial education in an industrial democracy. *Manual Training and Vocational Education, 16*, 409–414.

Eisner, E. W. (1985). *The educational imagination* (2nd ed.) New York: Macmillan.

Geisert, G., & Dunn, Rita (1991, March). Effective use of computers: Assignments based on individual learning style. *The Clearing House, 4*(4), 219–223.

Good, T. L., Reys, B. S., Grouws, D. A., & Mulryan, C. M. (1990–1991). Using work groups in mathematics instruction. *Educational Leadership, 47*(4), 56–62.

Guskey, T. R., & Gates, S. L. (1986). Synthesis of research on the effects of mastery learning in elementary and secondary classrooms. *Educational Leadership, 45*(8), 73–80.

Harrison, C. J. (1990). Concepts, operational definitions, and case studies in instruction. *Education, 110*(4), 502–505.

Henson, K. T. (1975). "The little school that grew." *Journal of Teacher Education, 26*(1), 55—59

Henson, K. T. (1979, Winter). Why our open classrooms fail. *Educational Horizons, 35,* 82–85.

Julik, J. A. (1981, April). The effect of ability grouping on secondary school students. Paper presented at the American Educational Research Association, Los Angeles.

King, A. (1990, November–December). Reciprocal questioning: A strategy for teaching students how to learn from lectures. *The Clearing House, 64,*(2), 131–135.

Kowal, J. (1991). Science, technology, and human values: A curricular approach. *Theory Into Practice, 30*(4), 267–272.

Maddox, H. & Hoole, E. (1975). Performance decrement in the lecture. *Educational Review, 28,* 17–30.

Markle, Glenn, Johnston, J. H., Geer, Cynthia, & Meichtry, Yvonne (1990, November). Teaching for understanding. *Middle School Journal, 22*(2), 53–57.

Marshall, Carol (1991, March–April). Teachers' learning styles: How do they affect student learning? *The Clearing House, 64*(4), 225–227.

Maslow, A. (1973). What is a taoistic teacher? In L. J. Rubin (Ed.), *Facts and feelings in the classroom.* (pp. 149–170). New York: Walker.

National Center for Educational Statistics (1991, September). *Education Counts.* Special Study Panel on Education Indicators to the Acting Commission of Education Statistics. Washington, DC: U.S. Department of Education.

Oliva, P. F. (1992). *Developing the curriculum* (3rd ed.). New York: Harper-Collins.

O'Neal, M., Earley, B., & Snider, Marge (1991). Addressing the needs of at-risk students: A local school program that works. In R. C. Morris (Ed.), *Youth at risk* (pp. 122-125). Lancaster, PA: Technomic Publishing.

Perkins, D. (1994). Do students understand understanding? *Education Digest, 59*(5), 21–25.

Rathbone, C. H. (1971, September). The open classroom: Underlying premises. *Urban Review*, 4–10.

Rubin, Louis (1977). Open education: A short critique. In Louis Rubin (Ed.), *Curriculum handbook: The disciplines, current moments, and instructional methodology*. Boston: Allyn & Bacon, p. 375.

Slavin, R. E. (1989, April). On mastery learning and mastery teaching. *Review of Educational Research, 50,* 77–79.

Stefanich, G. P. (1990, November). Cycles of cognition. *Middle School Journal, 22*(2), 47–52.

Trump, J. L. & Baynham, Dorsey (1961). *Focus on change: Guide to better schools*. Chicago: Rand McNally.

Zais, R. S. (1976). *Curriculum: Principles and foundations*. New York: Harper & Row.

# Chapter 6

# AIMS, GOALS, AND OBJECTIVES

## OBJECTIVES

This chapter should prepare you to:

- Differentiate between the uses of educational aims, goals, and objectives.
- Write an objective for each level of the three domains.
- Explain how objectives fit into the total curriculum.
- List three ways to involve students in curriculum planning.
- Tell what the teacher can do to use objectives in a positive way to support education reform.

## SAN SONA ELEMENTARY REQUIRES PERFORMANCE OBJECTIVES

San Sona Elementary School has the reputation of being one of the most innovative, experimental, and advanced schools in its district. The many oil wells in the area make financing one of the least of the principal's worries. The state's education reform program has been pressing all schools to increase the level of achievement of their students.

When Sondra Bell became principal last year, she promised the board members that, with their support, she would lead the school to even greater heights.

As Sondra planned her annual report, she realized that the members of the board had lived up to their part of the bargain, but she wondered whether they felt as positive about her. The report was to contain two parts, "In Retrospect" and "In Prospect." Because she thought that the first part was a little weak, Sondra decided to compensate by planning an impressive In Prospect section.

She began by spelling out her objectives for the coming year. Could she impress the board by planning everything for the coming year around the performance objectives that she would set for the students? It seemed logical to use this approach, so she pulled out a taxonomy of educational objectives from the notes she had taken in her curriculum course. For each daily lesson, she wrote an objective at each level of the cognitive domain. But when she began writing objectives for all levels of the affective domain, her task became more difficult. Although she had initially planned to write objectives that represented all levels of all three domains, Sondra gave up in despair long before the task was completed.

Rather than admit failure, Sondra appointed a committee consisting of the department heads and one or two members of each department. She assigned them exactly the same task—to write sample objectives at all levels in all domains for each subject in the entire school curriculum. The faculty was not at all happy with this request. Most teachers were already using objectives in planning their lessons, but they thought this was going too far.

Sondra heard some of their complaints so often that she almost suspected a conspiracy. Most teachers insisted that the implementation of the education reform practices had already made their workload almost impossible. Sondra supposed that they were telling the truth, because a new performance evaluation system required all teachers to develop portfolios for all their students and forbade the use of paper tests. In addition, soon all tests would have to be aligned with the state's 150 new valued outcomes. As Sondra reflected, she realized that, indeed, the new education reform requirements were truly overloading her faculty.

Another complaint that was voiced daily questioned the value of stating everything in terms of objectives. Some teachers speculated that it was just another policy imposed upon them from the outside and written by nonteachers who had little or no experience in writing objectives for classroom use. Other teachers said that they thought that trying to write everything in terms of objectives would restrict activities and make lessons seem overstructured or prefabricated. Some said that the use of objectives would lead to totally depersonalized teaching.

As Sondra considered these complaints, she wondered whether there might be a more acceptable way to convince the faculty to use objectives with all lessons.

## INTRODUCTION

Curriculum developers at all levels have some roles in common. Today, as never before, reform programs hold teachers, instructional supervisors, administrators, and curriculum specialists responsible for student achievement. Although most of the reform reports speak of quality, an amorphous term, former deputy secretary of the U.S. Department of Education David Kearns (1994, p. x) says, "Quality is not the ends—it is the means." Siegel and Byrne (1994, p. 2), both officers of the National Alliance of Business, are clear about their perception of the school's role:

> The primary objective of the current education restructuring movement is to improve learning.

Each reform movement has its distinguishing characteristics. Some of these qualities are not new, yet invariably as some of them are recycled they are modified and relabeled to a degree that makes them unrecognizable to many. Outcome-based education is a good example. A full half-century ago Ralph Tyler introduced his Ends-Means curriculum model, a simple model with a practical message: Curriculum planning should begin by determining the desired end results and the curriculum should be designed accordingly. A decade later, competency-based education began to raise its head. At the university level, competency-based proponents proclaimed that teacher education should also become competency-based.

The competency-based movement took Tyler's ideas to the implementation stage. At the public school level, instruction was broken down into student performance tasks. At the university level, teaching competencies were identified. At each respective level the performer became the center of the process. By the mid-1960s mastery-learning developed, taking this learner-centered competency approach even further. New features were added giving a new configuration to the curriculum. These were not just minor add-ons but included some bold changes such as variable time, recycling without penalty, multiple instructional strategies, and a new criterion-referenced grading system.

Outcome-based education of the 1990s is an extension of this metamorphic process, focusing even more on instruction. The 1990s reform movement's underlying premise that all students can learn has added an increased level of accountability to outcome-based education. That this movement has its critics is understandable. Perhaps the greatest criticism in the professional community is an expressed concern that the program may not encourage the best students to do their best. Towers (1994) expresses this concern for outcome-based teacher education,

> To a degree, one may be allowing our best and brightest future teachers to go unchallenged, drifting aimlessly from one undemanding task to the next (p. 627).

As with many reform practices, this criticism has an unmistakable ring of familiarity. The use of objectives and, in particular, stating minimal levels of performance required to reach an acceptable level have always produced concern (real or otherwise) that students will aim their performance at the floor level rather than the ceiling.

## CALIFORNIA'S EFFORT TO HELP LIMITED-ENGLISH-PROFICIENT STUDENTS

During the 1990s, California's Commission on Teacher Credentialing has taken several actions to improve instruction for limited-English-proficient (LEP) students. The Commission began by recognizing that these students have the two kinds of needs mentioned earlier: (1) they need to improve their English skills but they cannot afford to put their other learning on hold while they study English; and (2) they need immediate access to the core curriculum. Whenever possible, California provides LEP students core content instruction in their primary language, consistent with the state and national laws. The strategy calls for first teaching these students those subjects such as mathematics and science which are less language dependent. As the LEP students develop English proficiency they can begin receiving instruction using simple words, visual aids, and nonverbal language. Such instructional approach is called "sheltered subject-mater instruction."

California teachers who wish to provide maximum assistance to limited-English-proficient students—whether planning to teach a single subject or multiple subjects—may choose a Cross-cultural, Language and Academic Development Emphasis (CLAD) or they may choose a Bilingual, Cross-cultural, Language and Academic Development (BCLAD) emphasis. California's Limited-English-Proficiency program has the following goals:

- The new system of teacher preparation and credentialing should equally serve the needs of students from all language groups.

- The new system should be demographically responsive, that is, it should be able to react quickly and efficiently when changing demographics require modifications.

- The new system should alleviate rather than exacerbate the shortage of teachers trained and certified to teach LEP students.

- The new system should be clear, equitable, and internally consistent, allowing candidates access to credentials through a variety of comparable routes, and providing school personnel with clear information about the authorizations associated with each credential.

- The new system should encompass both: (a) teacher training programs for preservice teachers and (b) examinations for already credentialed teachers. Because both routes lead to the same authorizations, the scope and content of the programs should be as congruent as possible with the scope and content of the exams.

California has made certification for teaching LEP students available to both preservice teachers and in-service teachers. The bilingual, cross cultural, language and academic development program and the cross cultural and academic development program share a common multitiered knowledge and skills base which represents the following six domains:

*Domain 1: Language Structure and First- and Second-Language Development.* Domain 1 includes two primary areas. The first is language structure and use, including universals and differences among languages and the structure of English. The second area includes theories and models of language development as well as psychological, social-cultural, political, and pedagogical factors affecting first-and second-language development.

*Domain 2: Methodology of Bilingual, English Language Development, and Content Instruction.* Three areas are included in Domain 2. The first covers theories and models of bilingual education, at a level needed by all teachers of LEP students (not just bilingual teachers). This area includes the foundation of bilingual education, organizational models, and instructional strategies. The second area covers theories and methods for instruction in and through English, including approaches with a focus on English language development, approaches with a focus on content area instruction, and working with paraprofessionals. The third area in this domain consists of the knowledge and skills needed to appropriately assess students' language abilities and subject-matter achievement.

*Domain 3: Culture and Cultural Diversity.* Domain 3 includes the nature of culture, aspects of culture that teachers should learn about their students, ways that teachers can learn about their students' cultures, ways teachers can use cultural knowledge, issues and concepts related to cultural contact, and the nature of cultural diversity in California and the United States, including demographics and immigration. It will not focus on any specific cultural group but on culture in general and its impact on education.

*Domain 4: Methodology for Primary Language Instruction.* Domain 4 includes the characteristics of bilingual programs, instructional delivery in bilingual classrooms (which includes organizational strategies, the use of English and the primary language, and working with paraprofessionals), and factors to consider in the selection and use of primary language materials.

*Domain 5: The Culture of Emphasis.* Domain 5 consists of the knowledge and skills related to the culture associated with a bilingual teacher's language of emphasis. It includes the origins and characteristics of the culture of emphasis and the major historical periods and events, demography, migration and immigration, and contributions of the culture of emphasis in California and the United States.

*Domain 6: The Language of Emphasis.* Domain 6 includes proficiency in the language in which the teacher wishes to be authorized to provide primary language instruction. Language proficiency will be required in the areas of speaking, listening, reading, and writing.

These six domains of knowledge and skill are the heart of the new CLAD/BCLAD system. The requirements for each of the credentials or authorizations in the system are based on these domains.

Terms such as *performance evaluation, alternative assessment,* and *valued outcomes* reflect the determination of the states to hold educators responsible for ensuring that their students are making satisfactory academic progress.

*Curriculum alignment* is another popular term of the 1990s that reminds educators of their special responsibility for ensuring the academic success of their students. Haberman (1992, p. 11) says, "All schools offer four curricula:

What's in the textbooks, what the teachers actually teach, what the students learn, and what is included on tests." Curriculum alignment means adjusting the planned curriculum so that the taught curriculum will parallel the tested curriculum (English, 1992).

Bill Zlatos (1994, pp. 26–28) says that *outcome-based education (OBE)*, which he defines as stating clearly what students are to learn (desired outcomes), measuring their progress on actual achievement, meeting their needs through various teaching strategies, and giving them enough time and help to meet their potential, is the fastest-growing educational reform of the 1990s. Although critics challenge the effectiveness of OBE, Connecticut, the first state to adopt statewide goals using OBE, has had increases in graduation rate, in percentage of students going on to college, and in average reading and math scores. Unfortunately, as discussed elsewhere in this book, the concept evokes resentment among many people. Zlatos has concluded that, "Up to now, the consensus is that opponents have been winning the skirmishes on OBE."

Ideally, curriculum development should begin by examining the desired outcomes. Such "formative" assessment will be discussed in Chapter 9. The purpose is simply to know what the curriculum, and hence the instruction that follows, is trying to achieve. Many states are developing tests which all schools must administer periodically to their students. Obviously, curriculum developers should examine these desired outcomes and design the curriculum accordingly.

Increased accountability requires a cooperative approach to curriculum development. As expressed by Essex (1992, p. 231), subject matter teachers should meet at regular intervals to discuss and plan curriculum and to develop sound strategies designed to achieve quality standards. In an interview, Anderson (see Dagenais, 1994, p. 53) expressed concern for teachers' failure to interact with other teachers:

> I think that the most disabling tradition in America and, in fact, world education is the self-contained classroom. Teachers work by themselves and are insulated from intervention by the four walls of their room and the tradition of being fully in charge.

Earlier, we used the word *ideally*, but, as practitioners know very well, most curriculum development doesn't occur under ideal conditions. Although the "ideal" is helpful in understanding the curriculum development process, most curriculum developers must deal with something short of the ideal: Instead of developing new curricula, they find themselves revising (or "patching up") existing curricula. As Essex (1992, p. 231) has mentioned:

> They [teachers] also should seek appropriate opportunities to revise curricula and modify instructional strategies as the need arises.

Teachers must also involve students and parents in reshaping the curriculum. Current reform seems to demand a holistic approach. Siegel and Byrne (1994, p. 2) explain:

The key relationships in restructuring education are the ones between students and those with whom they interact most closely: their teachers, parents, and peers. Seen in this light, learning is a shared responsibility and is the chief product of these relationships.

*Teacher empowerment* is another term associated with education reform. Haberman (1992, p. 11) says, "I believe that classrooms, by controlling their teaching behavior, still retain the most powerful influence on students' learning and can serve as curriculum leaders." Whether the curriculum developer is a teacher, an administrator, an instructional supervisor, or a designated curriculum planner, the job at hand involves identifying desired academic outcomes. Gay (1980, p. 120) explains:

> Curriculum theorists and practitioners agree that, in one form or another, curriculum development includes: identification of educational goals and objectives.

Curriculum developers need to differentiate between several terms used to express desired outcomes. Among these educational outcomes, or expectations, are aims, goals, and objectives (see Figure 6.1).

## AIMS

Of the different types of educational expectations, *aims* are the most general. Educational aims are lifetime aspirations. They provide long-term directions for students. Most aims are written for groups, as opposed to individuals. A good example of educational aims is the Seven Cardinal Principles of Secondary Education, given in Chapter 3.

Like a cross-country road map, aims help us guide our lives in general and positive directions. They can never be fully attained.

## GOALS

Like aims, educational *goals* are group expectations, and they may take weeks, months, or even years to attain. Goals differ from aims in that they are attainable, yet many go unattained. A high school may have as one of its goals that the mean achievement scores for all classes that are tested next year will equal or exceed their counterparts' scores on this year's tests. Because goals are group-oriented, the successful attainment of goals does not require each and every student to succeed.

**Figure 6.1** The relationships between aims, goals, and objectives

## OBJECTIVES

To avoid confusion, we will use the term *objectives* to refer to what is expected of students daily. We could also use the term *performance objectives*, for each objective refers to the ability of students to perform selected tasks in one or more specific ways.

Returning to the road map analogy, objectives are like statewide maps in that they chart the course for each day. Many educators have insisted that all worthwhile expectations that schools have of students be stated in objectives. The author disagrees and insists that some of the most valuable services provided by schools, some of the most important effects of schools and teachers, can never be stated in terms of objectives. For example, by definition, objectives must be measurable; yet how can the growth of a student's self-concept or appreciation for learning be measured?

Objectives clarify the expectations teachers have of student performance. As Wulf and Schane (1984, p. 117) have said, when objectives are used, "there are no unexpected or surprise results since both parties have agreed upon the end product." When students know the expected outcomes, they usually become more involved in their assignments (Unger, 1994). Because performance objectives are the most specific of all expressions of educational expectations, they must be written in great precision and detail. The following sections introduce techniques for writing performance objectives.

## CRITERIA FOR WRITING PERFORMANCE OBJECTIVES

The exact steps teachers use when writing objectives may vary according to the preferences of their administrators and according to the content being studied. Yet most authorities appear to agree that all statements of performance objectives must meet at least three criteria:

1. Objectives must be stated in terms of expected student behavior (not teacher behavior).
2. Objectives must specify the conditions under which the students are expected to perform.
3. Objectives must specify the minimum acceptable level of performance.

Look again at these criteria. Stating objectives in terms of expected student behavior is important because all lessons are developed for students. For each student, the success of each lesson depends on appropriate student involvement.

Reform efforts are bringing pressure from many directions. Emphasis is usually on test scores, with teachers pressured to raise the scores of their students. Some educators feel that our nation has gone overboard with accountability and testing. LaBonty and Everts-Danielson (1992, p. 186) have said:

"We are, in fact, a nation engulfed in testing." Educators must remember that schools exist for students, not for educators or even parents, but for *students*. Cole and Schlechty (1992, p. 11) express this concern:

> Students, and the work students are expected to do, should be the focus of all school activity. Schools should, therefore, be organized around the work of students, not around the work of teachers, administrators, or the particular interests of school boards, political factions, or interest groups.

To be more precise, the school exists to guide the development of students mentally, physically, socially, emotionally, and even morally. When teachers state all objectives in terms of desired student performance, and when they use language that describes observable and measurable actions, they and their students more clearly understand what the expectations are and the degree to which these expectations are being met. Table 6.1 lists the types of verbs that

**Table 6.1  Performance Objective Terms**

| Yes (Specific and measurable) | No (vague and not measurable) |
| --- | --- |
| Build | Appreciate |
| Classify | Consider |
| Contrast | Desire |
| Demonstrate | Feel |
| Distinguish | Find interesting |
| Evaluate | Have insight into |
| Identify | Know |
| Interpret | Learn |
| Label | Like to |
| List | Love to |
| Match | Really like to |
| Measure | Recognize |
| Name | Remember |
| Remove | See that |
| Select | Think |
| State | Understand |
| Write | Want to |

describe specific, observable, and measurable actions and those that are too general and vague to do this.

Because students can grasp only a limited number of major ideas in a class period of 45 or 50 minutes, the daily lesson plan should contain only four or five major ideas. Suppose an English teacher wants to teach composition writing. The teacher could select four or five of the most important ideas about capturing and holding a reader's attention. These ideas will become the content for the first day's lesson in a unit titled Composition Writing. Suppose that the teacher determines that five ideas are essential to capturing the reader's attention and that, once the reader's attention is captured, four ideas are essential to holding it. If so, the teacher could plan one lesson on how to capture the reader's attention and a subsequent lesson on how to hold the reader's attention.

Objectives should be written in terms of desired student behavior. The emphasis should not be "Today I'll teach" but (as a result of the lesson) "Each student will be able to . . . " Second, teachers should state the conditions under which the students are expected to perform: "When given a list containing vertebrates and invertebrates . . . " Third, teachers should state the expected level of performance ("with 80 percent accuracy" or "without error") and should avoid using vague verbs describing actions that cannot be observed or measured, such as *appreciate, learn, know,* and *understand.* Instead of such general verbs, specific, action-oriented verbs such as *identify, list, explain, name, describe,* and *compare* should be used.

## WRITING OBJECTIVES

Some educational aims and goals deal with thinking (for example, command of the fundamental processes), others involve attitudes (for example, development of moral character), and still others focus on physical skills (for example, art, music, and sports). Many educators say that performance objectives for each of these categories, called *domains* (cognitive, affective, and psychomotor) should be written for each class. Although this may not always be practical and sensible, perhaps you will agree that teachers should be able to do this and should also be able to write objectives at varying levels of difficulty in each domain.

### The Cognitive Domain

The first really systematic approach to helping teachers write objectives at specified levels came in 1956, when Benjamin S. Bloom and a group of students at the University of Chicago developed a taxonomy of educational objectives in the cognitive domain that included six levels:

Level 1: Knowledge
Level 2: Comprehension

Level 3: Application
Level 4: Analysis
Level 5: Synthesis
Level 6: Evaluation

Involving students in tasks that cause them to operate at these different levels requires the ability to write objectives for each level.

## Level 1: Knowledge

Mastery of facts and concepts is a prerequisite for performing higher mental operations. For example, many mathematics problems require students to multiply. Learning the multiplication tables can probably be done best by simple rote memorization. Objectives that focus on memorization are the easiest to write. Unfortunately, many lessons fail to go beyond this most elementary level. Some assignments or tasks at the knowledge level are essential, but they should not dominate the curriculum.

An example of an objective written at the knowledge level would be: "When given a list of 10 elements and a list of atomic weights, the student will be able to correctly match 8 of the 10 elements with their correct atomic weights." Or: "When given a list containing 10 vertebrates and 10 invertebrates, the student will correctly identify 8 of the 10 vertebrates and 8 of the 10 invertebrates."

Both objectives begin with a statement of the conditions under which students are expected to perform the task ("When given . . . "), and both objectives are written in terms of desired student performance ("the student will . . . "). In addition, both objectives contain active verbs that describe actions that can be observed and measured (*match, identify*) and both objectives end with a statement of the minimum acceptable level of performance ("8 of the 10").

## Level 2: Comprehension

Objectives at the comprehension level require that students do more than memorize; they require students to translate, interpret, or predict a continuation of trends.

For example, an English teacher who wants students to know the differences between phrases and clauses may set the following objective: "When given a paragraph containing two clauses and three phrases, the student will correctly underscore the phrases using a single line and underscore the clauses using double lines." Can you identify the minimum acceptable level of performance for this objective? Actually, because there is no mention of an acceptable level, it must be assumed that the students are expected to perform with 100 percent accuracy.

Since the comprehension level requires students to translate, interpret, and predict, charts, maps, graphs, and tables are useful when writing objectives at the comprehension level.

## Level 3: Application

Objectives written at the application level require students to use principles or generalizations to solve a concrete problem. For example, a mathematics teacher might write the following objective for geometry students: "Given the lengths of both legs of a right triangle, the student will use the Pythagorean theorem to find the length of the hypotenuse." Or an English teacher might write the following objective: "Given the beats and measures in iambic pentameter, the student will write a five-verse poem in iambic pentameter without missing more than one beat per verse."

Chapter 4 stressed the important role of generalizations in learning. It is at the application level that students learn to generalize. Thus it is important that objectives written at this level help students to apply a principle to more than one situation.

## Level 4: Analysis

Like the application-level objectives, analysis-level objectives require students to work with principles, concepts, and broad generalizations—but the students must do this themselves. Students are required to break down the concepts and principles in order to better understand them, and to do this, they must understand not only the content but also the structural form of the content.

For example, a government teacher might write the following objective for a class that is studying how a bill becomes a law: "Given a particular law, students will trace its development from the time it was first introduced as a bill, listing every major step without missing any." A teacher of auto mechanics might write the following objective for a group of students who have been studying the electrical system in an automobile: "Starting with the positive battery terminal, the student will trace the flow of current through the automobile until the current returns to the negative battery terminal, stating what happens in the coil, alternator, distributor, and condenser without getting more than one of these steps out of sequence." A biology teacher might ask students to trace the human circulatory system in a similar manner.

## Level 5: Synthesis

In a way, the synthesis-level objective is the opposite of the analysis-level objective because it requires the student to take several parts and put them together. But the synthesis-level objective is more demanding because it requires students to form a new whole. Unlike the analysis-level objectives, synthesis-level objectives require students to change their way of thinking and to use creativity.

The student's attitude is especially important at the synthesis level. Synthesis requires experimentation—investigating the new. Furthermore, the student must understand that the teacher does not have in mind a definite solution or predetermined conclusion for the student to reach.

For example, a history teacher who wants students to understand the problems faced by the early settlers might preface the unit with an assignment involving the following objective: "Suppose you are a member of a team of explorers who are going to another inhabited planet to start a new colony. List at least ten rules you would propose to guide the new nationals, making sure that at least five of the rules would serve to protect the interests of all the native inhabitants."

Because of their open-ended and creative nature, synthesis-level objectives are difficult to write. Generally, practice is a prerequisite to competence in writing objectives at this level.

At the beginning of Chapter Four, a teacher education student expressed concern over what he perceived as shallow teachers using shallow lessons that produce shallow learning. The need for the ability to write higher-level objectives is great. For without them, classroom thinking will remain dominated by rote memorizing. Stefanich (1990, p. 49) says:

> Higher level thinking cannot be demanded. We must learn it through nurturing a series of successfully more advance learning tasks until the student reaches the desired level of performance.

## Level 6: Evaluation

The highest level in Bloom's cognitive domain is the evaluation level. Here the student is required to make judgments, but judgments based on definite criteria, not just opinions. Evaluation-level objectives contain various combinations of elements from the first five levels.

A speech teacher might use the following objective with students who are studying diplomatic and persuasive techniques: "After viewing a video recording of the President's two most recent public addresses, each student will rate the speeches in terms of tact and persuasion, pinpointing in each address at least three areas of strength and three areas of weakness."

The ability to write objectives at each cognitive level is crucial, because this is the only way to be sure that students will learn to develop intellectual skills at each level. Because this is the most important work a teacher does to affect learning, teachers must be able to state objectives clearly.

But not all educators agree that such distinct steps parallel the actual development of youths. One skeptic is Donald Orlich (1991, p. 160), who says:

> For over a quarter of a century, I have assumed and taught my students that the four upper levels of the taxonomy had to be taught in a sequence. But the

more that I observed young students in hands-on classes . . . the less support I found for the linear assumption. . . . I can no longer assume a linear connection to the four upper levels of the cognitive taxonomy. Nor can I support the idea of hierarchical arrangement of the entire model!

Orlich (1991, p. 236) uses the following quote from John Goodlad's 1984 study, *A Place Called School*, to point out that other educators also have concerns over the levels of objectives that are represented in high school curricula:

Only rarely did we find evidence to suggest instruction likely to go much beyond mere possession of information to a level of understanding its implications and either applying it or exploring its possible applications. Nor did we see activities likely to arouse students' curiosity or to involve them in seeking a solution to some problem not already laid bare by teachers or textbook. . . . And it appears that this preoccupation with the lower intellectual processes pervades social studies and science as well. An analysis of topics studied and materials used gives not an impression of students studying human adaptations and exploration, but of facts to be learned.

Others criticize the use of goals and objectives because of a concept called *goal displacement*. Faidley and Musser (1991, p. 24) explain this criticism:

It is a commonly known and widely studied phenomenon in organizations that when people are given a specific objective, they will often reach that objective at the expense of the overall purpose that objective was established to attain.

Paradoxically, if students are to reach the upper levels of the taxonomy, it will be the result of purposeful planning by the teacher, yet teachers often hold expectations that are beyond students' levels of development.

## The Affective Domain

As mentioned in Chapter 3, teachers have no choice but to affect students' values, and there is no doubt that teachers have the responsibility to teach values such as honesty and citizenship.

An important role of the school and the teacher in the realm of values is to help students become aware of their own values, to question their values, and to discover the origin of their values, whether they are based on fact and logical or based on myth and illogical.

David R. Krathwohl was a leader in the development of a system to categorize values. Through his work, a hierarchy of objectives in the affective domain was established (Krathwohl et al, 1964):

Level 1: Receiving

Level 2: Responding

Level 3: Valuing

Level 4: Organization

Level 5: Characterization

## Level 1: Receiving

*Receiving* refers to students' awareness of new information or experiences. Students receive information in varying ways and degrees. In a single class, some students absorb information like sponges, some may not receive the information at all, and others may attend, or receive, at a low level of awareness. Still others may be very selective, attending only to the things that are most meaningful to them. Of course, students can be encouraged and taught to develop attention skills.

## Level 2: Responding

At the *responding* level, a student reacts to whatever has attracted his or her attention. This requires physical, active behavior. Some responses may be overt or purposeful, as opposed to simple or automatic. A student who becomes involved at the responding level might, at the teacher's instruction or even voluntarily, go to a library and research a topic. Or a student involved at this level may obey the rules set forth in the class.

## Level 3: Valuing

A *value* is demonstrated when someone prizes a behavior enough to be willing to continue with the behavior even in the face of opposition. A value has not necessarily been demonstrated when a person reacts without having had time to think. In other words, if people really value a behavior, they are likely to continue it even though they know the unpleasant results it may bring, and they will do so repeatedly (Simon, Howe, & Kirschenbaum, 1972).

For example, a mathematics teacher whose students are learning to use simulation games might write the following valuing objective: "When given free time next week at the end of each period to read, play simulation games, talk to friends, or sleep, each student will choose to play simulation games at least two out of the five days." Note that the objective asks students to choose individually of their own free will and to repeat that choice. Also notice that there are alternatives from which to choose.

## Level 4: Organization

The *organization* level of behavior requires individuals to bring together different values to build a value system. Whenever there is conflict between two or more of their values, they must resolve the conflict. For example, from the elementary grades through high school students frequently encounter the conflicting expectations of their friends and parents. As students mature, their behavior should be influenced less by the expectations of the people (either friends or parents) they are with at the moment; they should be able to combine the values of those people with their own beliefs and knowledge about themselves. In so doing, they will develop their own value systems.

For example, a teacher might assign students to defend both sides of a controversial issue. Doing this will enable the students to compare the two points of view and possibly even to learn to compromise.

A teacher of a class in U.S. government might introduce a hypothetical bill and have students form two teams, one composed of those who favor the bill, the other team composed of those who oppose it. The objective might read: "After having had the opportunity to support the bill, and the opportunity to try to defeat it, the students will combine all the information and write a statement that expresses their feelings for and against the bill. Given the opportunity, the students will choose to modify the bill to make it reflect their own value systems."

## Level 5: Characterization by a Value or a Value Complex

At the *characterization* level, students have already developed their own value systems. Their behavior is consistent and predictable. At this level, students also demonstrate a degree of individuality and self-reliance.

An example of an objective written at the characterization level is: "Each student will bring one newspaper article or news report to class and explain at least two ways in which the article caused the student to change his or her mind from a previously held position on a controversial issue." Does this objective prove that the student has really changed his or her mind? What if the student just says that the change has occurred? At the moment, the student may hold a particular belief, but what about a week from now or a year from now? This objective can be rewritten so that this doubt will be reduced or removed. For example, without further instruction from the teacher, the student will continue reading controversial articles and these articles will continue shaping the student's behavior.

## The Psychomotor Domain

The *psychomotor domain* involves development of physical skills that require coordination of mind and body. It has always been especially relevant to physical education, art, drama, music, vocational courses, and the like. The current emphasis on interdisciplinary, integrated curricula and performance evaluation makes the psychomotor domain particularly relevant.

Although this domain was the last for which a taxonomy was developed, at least two scales have been established. The following taxonomy is based on a scale developed by E. J. Simpson (1972):

Level 1: Perception

Level 2: Set

Level 3: Guided response

Level 4: Mechanism

Level 5: Complex overt response

Level 6: Adaptation

Level 7: Origination

## Level 1: Perception

Purposeful motor activity begins in the brain, where stimuli received act as guides to motor activity. A Person must first become aware of a stimulus, pick up on cues for action, and then act upon these cues. For example, a writer may discover that she is separating her subjects and verbs, thus diluting the impact of her sentences. Or a batter may notice that he is flinching and taking short steps away from the plate when swinging, causing him to miss the ball. Or a piano student may realize that he is failing to reduce the interval between double notes.

A sample objective at the perception level would be: "Following a demonstration, a geometry student who has been confusing $x$ and $y$ axes in plotting graphs will notice that the $x$ axis always runs horizontally and the $y$ axis always runs vertically."

## Level 2: Set

In the psychomotor domain, *set* refers to an individual's readiness to act, mentally, physically, and emotionally. For example, divers pause before diving to get a psychological, emotional, and physical set. Emotionally, they must feel confident about their ability to make a safe and accurate dive. Psychologically, although they may have performed the same dive hundreds of times, they must think through the sequence of steps before each dive. Physically, they must ready their muscles in order to respond quickly and accurately. On a less dramatic scale, students preparing to take notes or do a writing assignment may flex their fingers or rub their eyes—in short, they are getting set to perform at their best.

An example of a psychomotor objective at this level for piano students is: "Upon the signal 'Ready,' each student will assume proper posture and place all fingers in correct keyboard position." Is a minimum level of performance specified in this objective?

## Level 3: Guided Response

Once students have perceived the need to act and are set to act, they may find that whenever the act involves complex skills, they need to be guided through their first few responses. For example, students in a photography club may need oral guidance as they process their first negatives.

An example of an objective designed to help the development of these skills would be: "When given step-by-step directions in the darkroom, each student will open the film cylinder, remove the film, and, without touching the surface of the film, wind it on a spool so that the surface of each round does not touch previous rounds."

## Level 4: Mechanism

This level involves performing an act somewhat automatically without having to pause to think through each separate step. For example, the photography teacher might want students eventually to be able to perform the entire sequence of development operations while simultaneously counting the number of seconds required to wait between each step. Or a chemistry teacher might write the following objective at the mechanism level: "Given a series of compounds to analyze, the student will operate the electron microscope without having to pause even once to think about the sequence involved in mounting the slide, focusing the projector, and changing the lens size."

## Level 5: Complex Overt Response

The *complex overt response* is an extension of the mechanism level, but it involves more complicated tasks. For example, a driver education teacher may write an objective at this level such as: "When given an unexpected and abrupt command to stop, the student will immediately respond by applying the correct amount of pressure to the brakes, giving the correct signal, and gradually pulling off the road."

## Level 6: Adaptation

At this level students are required to adjust their performance in response to different situations. For example, when encountering an icy surface, a driver would adjust her brake pressure. Or a cook would adjust the timing when using an electric stove instead of a gas stove. A boxer would alter his style to adjust for a left-handed opponent.

An example of a psychomotor objective at the adaptation level is: "When planning a budget vacation, the student (without being reminded of the gas shortage and cost increases) will avoid unnecessary automobile travel and adopt gas-saving strategies."

## Level 7: Origination

At the *origination* level, the highest level of the psychomotor domain, the student creates acts creatively. For example, the cook adds his own touch of genius, and the pianist alters her style or the music itself.

An art teacher might write the following objective: "Given a mixture of powders and compounds of varying textures, students will use them to accentuate the feeling they are trying to communicate in an oil painting."

## SUMMARY

Throughout the United States, education reform efforts are increasing the level of accountability of teachers, administrators, and other curriculum developers, making them responsible for the academic success of their students. By learning to write aims, goals, and objectives, educators can increase the level to which they serve the reform efforts in their state.

Aims, goals, and objectives also serve the education reform goals of curriculum alignment, cooperative learning, and restructuring. Many education reform movements focus on empowering teachers to become more involved in the total school activities. Expertise in writing aims, goals, and objectives is one way for teachers to do this.

Objectives are essential to carry the more theoretical aims and goals to their practical attainment. Teachers should be able to write objectives in the three domains (cognitive, affective, and psychomotor). Objectives should always be expressed in terms of individual student performance, and they should always specify the conditions under which the student must perform and the minimal acceptable level of performance. Only verbs describing actions that are observable and measurable should be used in writing objectives.

Not everyone supports the use of objectives. Some critics believe that some of the most important functions of schools cannot be expressed in terms of objectives. Other critics say that setting objectives lowers students' levels of aspirations. Still other critics question the traditionally held belief that the levels of the taxonomies must be taught in sequence.

## QUESTIONS

1. What implications does the increased emphasis on academic accountability have for teachers' competence in writing aims and goals?

2. If educational aims can never be reached, why, then, are they needed?

3. How can tests be used to raise students' levels of thinking?

4. How can teachers involve students in planning?

5. Do you believe that educators have gone too far in using objectives? If so, what are some effective teacher responses to the demands that objectives be used?

6. Why should teachers include affective and psychomotor objectives in their curricula?

7. How do education reform programs intensify the curriculum developer's need for competence in writing performance objectives?

## SUGGESTED FURTHER ACTIVITIES

1. Select an educational film, videotape, or book and write one aim, two goals, and five objectives for a lesson that uses the medium you chose.

2. Think about the world in which we live. What one thing would you most like to see changed? Write one objective in each of the domains that will help bring about this change.

3. Check your personal philosophy statement, if you wrote one while studying Chapter 3. Otherwise, write a statement of your beliefs about the main purpose of schools. From this statement write one goal. Next, write at least two affective objectives to help your students reach this goal.

4. Make a list of verbs to use when writing objectives; they should describe observable and measurable actions.

5. An example of a psychomotor objective was given at the end of the discussion of Level 2: Set. Can you rewrite this objective in a more meaningful way? List two ways in which you could establish minimum levels of performance. Does either of your objectives explain what is meant by *correct posture* or *correct keyboard position*? Do both of your suggested changes help make the act measurable?

6. Suppose that you are teaching the circulatory system to a biology class. Write an objective that will enable students to understand the sequence in which the blood travels throughout the body. (Hint: Designate one of the heart's chambers as a beginning point.) Be sure that your objective meets the three criteria for writing performance objectives: Is it written in terms of expected student performance? If so, underscore the part of the objective that identifies both the performer and the performance. Does the verb you used express action? Can the action described be observed or measured? Is your statement of conditions clear? Circle it. Does it accurately describe the conditions under which you expect the student to perform? Did you begin the objective with a statement like "Given . . . " or "When given . . . "? This is an easy way to be sure that you have included a statement of conditions in each objective. Is your statement general, for example, "When giving a test . . . " or "Following a lesson . . . "? Can you make it more specific? Can you think of a way to alter the task, making it easier to perform, simply by changing the conditions?

  Finally, examine your objective to see whether it includes a statement of minimum acceptable level of performance. Draw a box around this statement. Does it tell the student exactly how accurately the task must be performed before the results will be acceptable? Is it expressed as a percentage or fraction, such as "with 80 percent accuracy" or "four out of five times"? Can you think of other ways to express your concept of the minimum acceptable level of performance without using percentages or fractions? By now you would probably like to start over and rewrite your original objective, improving each part.

Now examine your evaluation-level objective. Does it require that decisions be based on supportive data or on internal or external standards?

7. Because of the lack of emphasis on concepts and the lack of opportunities to develop concepts, principles, and other content generalizations, our students are often deficient in their ability to grasp the structure of the disciplines. Suppose that you are an art teacher. In your class, you have presented such concepts as cubism (using cubes to form objects) and pointillism (using points to form shapes). Can you write an objective at the synthesis level? (Hint: You might begin by identifying a particular effect you would like your students to achieve through the use of cubism and pointillism, for example, a specific feeling or mood.)

One example of such an objective might be: "After reviewing the use of cubism in Picasso's paintings and the use of pointillism in Seurat's paintings, the student will combine these two techniques with a new technique to create at least three of the following feelings: happiness, surprise, sadness, anger, love."

At the synthesis level, be sure to provide enough structure to make the assignment meaningful and yet allow students enough freedom to put themselves into the work.

# BIBLIOGRAPHY

Bloom, B. S. (1956). *Taxonomy of educational objectives. The classification of educational goals. Handbook I: Cognitive domain.* New York: McKay.

Bushman, J. H. (1991). Reshaping the secondary curriculum. *The Clearing House, 65*(2), 83–85.

Cole, R. W., & Schlechty, D. C. (1992). Teachers as trailblazers in restructuring. *The Education Digest, 58*(6), 8–12.

Dagenais, R. J. (1994). Professional development of teachers and administrators: Yesterday, today, and tomorrow: The views of Robert H. Anderson. *Kappa Delta Pi Record, 30*(2), 50–54.

English, F. (1992). *Curriculum alignment.* An Eastern Kentucky University/Phi Delta Kappa Conference. Richmond, KY.

Essex, N. L. (1992). Educational malpractice: The price of professionalism. *The Clearing House, 65*(4), 229–232.

Faidley, Ray, & Musser, Steven (1991). National educational standards: The complex challenge for educational leaders. *NASSP Bulletin, 75*(537), 23–27.

Gay, G. (1980). Conceptual models of the curriculum planning process. In A. W. Foshay (Ed.), *Curriculum improvement*. (p. 120) Alexandria, VA: Association for Supervision and Curriculum Development.

Good, T., Reys, B. J., Grouws, D. A., and Mulryan, C. M. (1990–91). "Using work groups in mathematics instruction." *Educational Leadership, 47*(4), 52–55.

Goodlad, J. I. (1984). *A place called school*. New York: McGraw-Hill.

Haberman, M. (1992). The role of the classroom teacher as curriculum leader. *NASSP Bulletin, 76*(547), 11–19.

Henson, K. T. (1976). Behavioral objectives: Over light. *Contemporary Education, 47*, 250.

Kearns, D. T. (1994). Foreword to Siegel, P., & Byrne, S. *Using quality to design school systems*. San Francisco: Jossey-Bass.

Krathwohl, D. R., Bloom, B. S., & Masia, B. B. (1964). *Taxonomy of educational objectives: The classification of educational goals. Handbook II: The affective domain*. New York: McKay.

LaBonty, Jan, & Everts-Danielson, Kathy (1992). Alternative assessment feedback techniques in methods courses. *The Clearing House, 65*(3), 186–190.

Orlich, D. (1991). A new analogue for the cognitive taxonomy. *The Clearing House, 64*(3), 159–161.

Ornstein, A. C. (1992). Essay tests: Use in development and grading. *The Clearing House, 65*(3), 175–178.

Siegel, P., & Byrne, S. (1994). *Using quality to design school systems*. San Francisco: Jossey-Bass.

Simon, S., Howe, L. W., & Kirschenbaum, H. (1972). *Values clarification*. New York: Hart.

Simpson, E. J. (1972). The classification of educational objectives in the psychomotor domain. *The psychomotor domain*. (Vol. 3). Washington, DC: Gryphon House.

Stefanich, G. P. (1990). Cycles of cognition. *Middle School Journal, 22*(2), 47–52.

Towers, J. M. (1994). The perils of outcome-based teacher education." *Phi Delta Kappan, 75*(8), 624–627.

Unger, C. (1994). What teaching for understanding looks like. *Educational Leadership, 51*(5), 8–10.

Wulf, K. M., & Schane, B. (1984). *Curriculum design*. Glenview, IL: Scott, Foresman.

Zlatos, B. (1994). Outcomes-based outrage runs both ways. *Education Digest, 59*(5), 26–29.

# Chapter 7

# SELECTING CONTENT AND ACTIVITIES

## OBJECTIVES

This chapter should prepare you to:

1. Develop a multipurpose activity to achieve two objectives that you consider important.
2. Draw a model to explain your conceptualization of constructivism.
3. Defend, from the point of view of a curricularist, education reform's goal to empower teachers.
4. Give two reasons for including problems when selecting curriculum content and activities.
5. Defend the inclusion of multicultural content in the curriculum.
6. React to the statement "In selecting content, more is less."
7. Develop a table of specifications to achieve a goal which you consider important for one of your courses.

## BUILDING BRIDGES TO REFORM: THE MODEL LABORATORY SCHOOL[1]

Wednesday is a special day at Model Laboratory School in Richmond, Kentucky. Walk the halls, and you will see a bustle of educational activity. Something exciting is going on. A group of students sit on the floor in a classroom working on a weather map that shows lows, highs, and fronts. But upon closer inspection you realize that all the words on the map are in Spanish and that this is a Spanish class for young children. In the cafeteria, students are participating in a simulation that challenges them to consider the relationship between power and authority in a democratic society. In one of the school's three computer labs,

---

[1]Appreciation is given to Dr. Bruce Bonar, the director of Model Laboratory School, for providing the information for this case.

students are learning the intricacies of the WordPerfect word processing program. In the chemistry classroom, teachers, playing the roles of pharmacists, clerks, and sales representatives in a simulation, are questioned by students using forensic chemistry to sort out the facts in a "murder case." The two school administrators, the librarian, the gifted program coordinator, and the two counselors are teaching today. A local college dean and a writer from the College's English department are team-teaching a Writing for Publication class to high school sophomores, juniors, and seniors.

What's happening at Model Laboratory School is one attempt to reform a school program at the grassroots level. The impetus for the Wednesday activities was provided by the passage of the Kentucky Education Reform Act (KERA) of 1990. By now the story of KERA has been heard nationwide. The Kentucky State Supreme Court declared the state's entire public school system unconstitutional, based upon a case claiming that educational funding in Kentucky was insufficient and the funds were being distributed unfairly among Kentucky's school districts. The result was the passage of legislation that created a new way to fund and run schools, different ways to measure student progress, and different techniques for teaching kids.

The Model Lab teachers, already advocates of experimentation, enthusiastically embraced the Kentucky school reform movement. As members of an institution whose aims are to test and disseminate innovative projects, the faculty at Model immediately jumped onto the reform bandwagon. The laboratory school formed a site-based council during the first year of KERA. It began the first nongraded primary program in the area. As part of a grant, a writing resource teacher worked with the faculty to facilitate the writing process in all subjects, the goal being to train all faculty to teach writing.

The faculty received enormous amounts of training both within and outside the school building. The primary teachers attended a total of 80 workshops in preparation for teaching nongraded classes. All faculty were trained in performance-based instruction and academic theme building. Other teachers and administrators attended meetings on portfolio construction in math and language arts, assessment, and technology. All teachers and administrators attended a five-day curriculum alignment workshop.

Having received all this extensive training, the teachers searched for ways to put it into practice. During the early days of reform, there were no KERA models and the reforms were in a developmental stage, with new required practices surfacing daily, it seemed. Implementing Kentucky education reform during its development was characterized by one educator as "building an airplane while you're flying it."

For a time, the changes that took place were tentative and limited in scope. Despite the demands of KERA and the extensive training of the faculty, the structure of the high school and middle school remained unchanged. Teachers began to develop event and portfolio tasks that demonstrate student competency in learning, either individually or within a group. Some teachers joined with colleagues to teach integrated units and tasks. Yet the reform attempts remained sporadic, with some teachers readily aligning their classes with the KERA curriculum elements and others remaining tied to more traditional educational practices.

Finally, through the efforts of the teachers and the on-site decision-making council, a new curriculum, called the *alternative schedule*, was proposed and then adopted. The developers had taken their cue from the emphasis on alternative curricula in the state reform legislation. The Wednesday program was the result. It has caused everyone at the school to focus on reform. It has given teachers an almost threat-free environment in which to try new curricula, experiment with KERA reform, and to cover topics often neglected in traditional curricula.

The all-day Wednesday program consists of classes that meet for one hour or for two consecutive hours. The courses are designed to fulfill at least one of four reform criteria:

1. Meet the needs of students who work at different learning rates (KERA states that *all* children can and will learn).
2. Integrate learning experiences with the real world.
3. Demonstrate performance-based learning and evaluation.
4. Increase social awareness and cooperative behavior.

Teachers submit proposals that are reviewed by faculty and evaluated on the basis of the efficacy of the offering and its match to the criteria. In some classes, parents assist teachers; in others, parents teach and faculty serve as supervisors. Courses are designed in two-hour blocks for high school students. One-hour classes are given to middle school students, except for students taking high school offerings.

Working with administrators, teachers use student choices and faculty recommendations to set up schedules. Students needing remediation and those who benefit from accelerated curricula are assigned to the same offerings, particularly labs in math, social studies, and language arts. Students receive most, but not all, the classes they request. In the middle school, students have fewer choices, and some of the younger children are required to take certain classes in math.

Evaluations were carried out after the first year of the Wednesday classes. More than 90 percent of the students enthusiastically endorsed the project. Only 3 of the school's 25 faculty members opposed the alternative schedule. Many parents commented positively about the minicourses, stating that children seemed more enthusiastic for school on Wednesday. School attendance records indicated that, on the average, 98 percent of the students came to school on Wednesdays as compared to the overall 95 percent daily rate. Teachers reported that students seemed to be more productive on Fridays while the alternative schedule was in place, perhaps because of the variety they experienced in their weekly schedule.

The alternative schedule is an attempt by one school to cope with the demands of local school change. Whether this program remains intact and becomes institutionalized or whether the ideas in the alternative schedule become incorporated into a larger and more comprehensive restructuring of the school remains to be seen. For the moment, the teachers and students at Model Laboratory School are looking forward to Wednesdays. Figure 7.1 shows the course offerings in this program.

## THE IMPORTANCE OF CONTENT AND ACTIVITIES SELECTION

Almost 150 years ago, at the beginning of the American Civil War, British educator Herbert Spencer (1861) posed the simple and yet profound and enduring question "What knowledge is of most worth?" Before Spencer's question can be answered, other questions must be asked: "Of most worth for what? Of most worth for whom?" We can begin to find the answers to these questions by examining the purposes of our schools. Although these questions are, by their very nature, philosophical, they have highly practical implications. Selecting content and activities is a responsibility shared by all teachers. Since different individuals and groups do not agree on what the purpose of school is, the job of selecting content and activities is not simple. Before reviewing the purposes of schools, let's look at some current practices that contribute to the complexity of content and activities selection.

Curriculum development, if it is effective at all, is an ongoing activity, every day throughout the year. Even so, most schools lag in their efforts to provide relevant and current content and activities. Anderson and Pavan (1993, p. 207) explain:

> Even though the review and revision of curriculum is a perennial and essential task in every school district, it is probable that 99 percent of American school districts are significantly behind schedule in so far as updating is concerned.

The demand for ongoing updating requires teachers and other curricularists to stay on top of the job. At a time when political leaders in many states are pressing for education reform, the importance of selecting the most appropriate content for K–12 classrooms cannot be overstressed. As expressed by Anderson and Pavan (1993, p. 190):

> The K–12 curriculum is in almost desperate need of streamlining and reform. The question "What should be taught?" and the even more relevant question, "What must be learned?" deserve top priority on every campus.

## PROBLEMS IN CONTENT AND ACTIVITIES SELECTION

A major problem that has persisted through the years, and which has accelerated in recent years, is the amount of information from which curriculum developers must choose. The "knowledge explosion" highlights the lack of a rational system for selecting content and activities.

## Block A

APPLIED PROBLEM-SOLVING:
The students will have the opportunity to use many types of media and machine or processes to solve problems by designing and building a prototype. GEVEDON

DATABASES AND SPREADSHEETS:
This course will explore uses of databases and spreadsheets. Students will create, edit, and update data and investigate given sets of data for research and finance problems. FIND OUT WHY DATABASES AND SPREADSHEETS SPARKED THE PC REVOLUTION! CYRUS

HISTORICAL RESEARCH:
Students will explore a topic of history, using secondary and primary resources. Students will produce a product depicting some aspect of the topic. WHAT DO YOU KNOW ABOUT LIFE ON THE FRONTIER IN MADISON COUNTY 200 YEARS AGO? DR. BONAR

*THE INKWELL:*
This is a practical, hands-on course in the production of a student magazine. Students will write, select, edit, and use desktop publishing technology, including the scanning of images and artwork. RHODUS/CARTER

LAB SKILLS:
Required of all freshman science students and all new sophomores. Students will learn and practice skills required for success in labs in earth science, biology, chemistry, and physics. ALEXANDER & SHUTTLEWORTH

## Block B

AMERICAN STUDIES LAB:
Offers opportunity for study in topics of interest in American culture, whether historical, literary, or pop. A variety of interests and purposes will be tolerated and encouraged. Students requiring additional time and/or guided practice in reading, notetaking, or communicating may be assigned to laboratory on a contract basis, with improved performance keyed to grades in regular classes. ROBERTS

ATHLETIC TRAINING:
Students will be familiarized with trainer's techniques for prevention of sports injuries and will have the opportunity to learn basic equipment, safety tips, and taping procedures. Students will study topics related to elite athletes and athletic performance. GALLOWAY

CHORUS:
Students will learn and perform choral music with a concert October 15th at 7:30 in Edwards Auditorium. Everyone join! Everyone attend! HENRICKSON

CREATIVE FOODS:
This course includes the study of planning, preparing, serving, and eating regional and foreign foods, for occasions such as holidays, receptions, and company meals. A $20 fee will be required to cover the cost of foods. WHERE ELSE CAN YOU GET 8 OR 9 MEALS FOR $20? ADKINS

## Block C

ACADEMIC TEAM:
Think you're smart? Wish you were? Or just want to sit around and watch a bunch of people who are? Take Academic Team and you will have time to study areas of strength or weakness, to develop the all-important coordination of your right hand (beep, beep!), and to interact with some of Model's most interesting people. ROBERTS

ART APPRECIATION & STUDIO WORK: FEE: $6.
Students will explore a different type of art each week. Learn about famous artists and different cultures and then create an art project that uses similar ideas, materials, and techniques. ISAACS

DIPLOMACY:
**Diplomacy** is a role-playing board game of skill and cunning in which chance plays no part. Game recreates events in pre-WWI Europe. Tests ability to plan a campaign and outwit one's fellow in negotiation. Students of Machiavelli's Prince should enjoy this game! Only 18 high school students can participate in teams of three. STEPHENS

FROM EXECUTIONS TO EXPLORATIONS: MEDIEVAL AND RENAISSANCE WORLD
Is it better to be beheaded with a sword or an axe? Did Robin Hood fear the Black Death? Did knights wear clothing under their armor? Can you turn other metals into gold? Were damsels really in distress? What would have happened if Columbus had stopped

**Figure 7.1** Courses Offered in the Wednesday Alternative Curriculum at Model Laboratory School.

## Block A

**MATHEMATICS LABORATORY:**
Students will be allowed extra computer time and assistance in exploring mathematics and computer topics of interest. Students experiencing difficulty in math classes may be placed into the lab with contract tying improved performance back to the classroom grade. ALLEN

**MOCK TRIAL, AN INTRODUCTION:**
Students will receive an in-depth introduction to the mock trial and will participate as attorneys or witnesses in several "class" mock trials. Interested students will be encouraged to try out for Model's immensely successful Mock Trial Team. **Not open to students who took this class last year.** DR. EDWARDS

*THE OBSERVER:*
Monthly newspaper—works with everyone/every aspect of the school! Must be able to sell ads, write articles, do layouts, take and print pictures, and meet deadlines. COMBS

**RED, YELLOW, BLACK AND WHITE: EXPLORING CULTURAL DIVERSITY**
This class will explore the cultural diversity of the United States and the world through a variety of experiences. Students will read both fiction and nonfiction, view films/movies, participate in role-playing games, meet guest speakers from diverse cultures, and

## Block B

**"HERSTORY": WOMEN IN HISTORY**
It is said that "The hand that rocks the cradle rules the world!" Join Herstory and examine the impact the hands of women have had throughout history. SIMS

**INSTRUMENTAL MUSIC:**
If you never started on a band instrument but would like to, or you started and dropped but would like to try again, or scheduling kept you out of Band, or you are in Band and would like to learn a different instrument, this course is for you! Course teaches basics of instrument and music reading, enabling students to develop skills leading to performance with the Band. **REQUIRED: You must have your own band instrument to use!** STEPHENS

**MATHEMATICS LABORATORY:**
Students will be allowed extra computer time and assistance in exploring mathematics and computer topics of interest. Students experiencing difficulty in math classes may be placed into the lab with contracts keying improved performance back to the classroom grade. CYRUS

**SEIKO YOUTH CHALLENGE:**
Would you like to solve a real environmental problem in our community? In this class we will form teams who will then identify, investigate, and prepare a solution to be entered into the

## Block C

and asked for directions? The answers to these and other exciting questions will be explored by students through films, readings, guest speakers, music, discussions, projects, role-playing, and games. Activities will culminate with a school-wide Renaissance fair. SHUTTLEWORTH & SIMS

**INTRODUCTION TO WORD PERFECT:**
This word processing course will meet in the high school computer lab and will teach beginning or advanced students how to create letters and other personal-use documents using Word Perfect. DR. EDWARDS

**LIGHTS, CAMERA, ACTION: BEGINNING VIDEO PRODUCTION**
The students will be actively involved in the proper usage of the camcorder, and will plan and produce a video! MCILVAIN

**PUBLIC SERVICE COOPERATIVE:**
Students will be placed in a public work setting, attend seminars, and participate in field trips, to increase social awareness and allow career exploration through interaction with the public. Students should increase their understanding of the importance of community service and of the diversity of the community. ADKINS

**TEST PREPARATION: THE PSAT**
Students will have pre-and post-

**Figure 7.1**   Courses Offered in the Wednesday Alternative Curriculum at Model Laboratory School.
(continued)

## Block A

visit the displays of the Cultural Festival at EKU. JACOBS

**SOCIAL STUDIES—CAFETERIA STYLE!**
Students will be free to select from a variety of experiences in the rich world of social studies. CAMPAIGN '92 students will study and debate the issues Americans **should** be talking about and have the opportunity to get involved in the election. **1792–1992**—students interested in Kentucky's **only** Bicentennial will be able to study issues of local or statewide interest. Students will be encouraged to produce **scholarship-winning** products for the Kentucky Junior Academy of History. ROBERTS & SIMS

**WEIGHT TRAINING:**
An introduction to and application of weight training principles. Avoid HEART ATTACKS! GET YOUR IRON THE SAFE WAY—PUMP IT! AMBROSE

**AMATEUR RADIO:**
Operate Model's Amateur Radio Station. Current equipment puts us on 80, 40, 20, 15, and 10 meters, capable of 180 watts CW or SSB, and 150 watts AM phone. We plan to expand to 160 meters and into VHF range as equipment and antennas become available. Must have valid amateur radio license on file with Mr. Stephens and be checked out on equipment. STEPHENS.

**All Blocks   All Day**

## Block B

Seiko Youth Challenge Competition. WOLFE

**SPEECH LEAGUE:**
This class will offer students the opportunity to explore their public speaking and dramatic talents by participating in the Kentucky High School Speech League. Students may choose from a variety of categories, such as Oratory, Debate, Extemporaneous Speaking, Radio Broadcasting, Duo Interpretation, Dramatic and Humorous Interpretation, Storytelling, Poetry, Prose, etc. This offering will require students to participate in two Speech League competitions at a small entry fee. JACOBS

**WEIGHT TRAINING**
An introduction to and application of weight training principles. GIVE YOUR BODY A WEIGHT BREAK! TAKE YOUR IRON THE HEALTHY WAY—PUMP IT! AMBROSE

**WRITER'S WORKSHOP:**
Students will increase their writing skills in a broad range of areas, from writing mechanically correct, killer themes to creative writing. RHODUS

## Block C

assessments with the PSAT. Use of test scores, strategies for testing, and content area review will be the major focus of the course. RECOMMENDED FOR ALL JUNIORS AND THOSE SOPHOMORES PLANNING TO TAKE THE PSAT THIS YEAR. MCCREARY

**WINDOWS ON ARCHAEOLOGY:**
This nine weeks students will examine the basic tools and techniques of field archaeology, including the study of rock formations, artifacts, fossils, carbon dating, statistical methods of "dig" site identification, layout of a "dig" site. Students will participate in a "dig" at an artificially "salted" site. They will have field trips to the Universities of Kentucky and Cincinnati where they will see museums and archaeology departments. This project, partially funded by a grant from GTE, will offer students exciting, in-depth exploration of archaeology and will develop skills and attitudes crucial to success in science in today's world. ALEXANDER & ALLEN

*THE EXEMPLAR:*
This course is for the yearbook staff which will have the practical experience of designing and producing another outstanding, award winning, annual for the school. Students will write copy, work on layouts, use computer equipment, and meet deadlines—all valuable experiences today. COMBS

**Figure 7.1** Courses Offered in the Wednesday Alternative Curriculum at Model Laboratory School. (continued)

The historical reliance (or overreliance) on the textbook is another problem. As mentioned in Chapter 2, the number one curriculum determiner throughout the history of our schools has been the textbook. Applebee, Langer, and Mullis (1987, p. 2) reviewed the results of several studies on the extent to which textbooks shape the curriculum:

> Numerous studies report that textbooks structure from 75 to 90 percent of classroom instruction.

This reliance on the textbook would be more acceptable if textbook writers and publishers used a logical system to select content, but they do not. In fact, the content in textbooks is usually a hodgepodge of topics. Referring to the constant adding of content to textbooks, Tyson and Woodward (1989, p. 15) have said:

> It is not surprising then, that American textbooks have become compendiums of topics, none of which are treated in depth.

Another problem with letting the textbook determine the curriculum is the failure of textbooks to cover pertinent concepts, that is, concepts whose understanding is a prerequisite to understanding the discipline being studied. In particular, most textbooks do not cover the major concepts that are essential to understanding their respective disciplines.

Further, when textbooks determine the curriculum, higher levels of thinking and understanding are not promoted. Davis and Hoskins (see Orlich, 1980) found that over 85 percent of textbook content is written at the recall level. Trachtenberg (1974) analyzed more than 61,000 questions in workbooks, texts, and teachers' manuals accompanying nine world history textbooks and reported that 95 percent of the questions were lower-order.

Another variable that affects, indeed often *dictates*, content selection is personal preference. Scheville et al. (1981) reported that an elementary teacher who enjoyed teaching science taught, not just 2 or 3 times as much science as a colleague who said that she did not enjoy teaching science but 28 times as much!

The search for the "best" content and activities for the curricula of any era must be an ongoing activity. Consequently, the search for the best system for selecting content and activities must never stop. It is clear that such determiners as textbooks and personal preference do not contribute to the search for an answer to Spencer's question "What knowledge is of most worth?"

In any era, a search for the best content should include, at a minimum, (1) consideration of the known information, that is, the body of knowledge, or the knowledge pool, which the curriculum developer has available, (2) society's needs, including current trends and perceived future needs, (3) the needs and interests of learners, and (4) human development, that is, the social worth of education. See Figure 7.2.

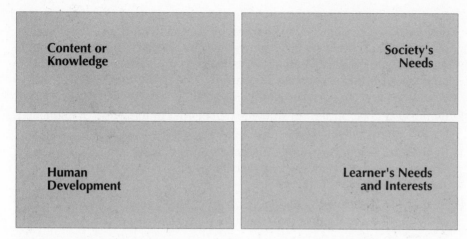

**Figure 7.2** Foundations for selecting content.

## NATIONAL GOALS

Since curriculum development is a continuing process, and since the purposes of schools change, the selection of content should begin by considering existing aims and goals. For example, the Seven Cardinal Principles of Secondary Education, which have been listed earlier on two occasions, may be revisited:

1. Health
2. Command of the fundamental processes
3. Worthy home membership
4. Vocational efficiency
5. Worthy use of leisure time
6. Citizenship
7. Ethical character

The importance of these goals for today's schools has already been discussed in Chapter Three. Another source for a system to guide in the selection of content and activities is the more recent Goals for 2000. From Chapter 3 you will recall this list as follows (National Education Goals Panel, 1991):

A. By the year 2000, all children in America will start school ready to learn (i.e., in good health, having been read to and otherwise prepared by parents, etc.).

B. By the year 2000, the high school graduation rate will increase to at least 90% (from the current rate of 74%).

C. By the year 2000, American students will leave grades 4, 8, and 12 having demonstrated competency in challenging subject matter, including English, mathematics, science, history, and geography. In addition, every school in America will insure that all students learn to use their minds, in order to prepare them for responsible citizenship, further learning, and productive employment in a modern economy.

D. By the year 2000, American students will be first in the world in mathematics and science achievement.

E. By the year 2000, every adult American will be literate and will possess the skills necessary to compete in a global economy and to exercise the rights and responsibilities of citizenship.

F. By the year 2000, every school in America will be free of drugs and violence and will offer a disciplined environment conducive to learning.

An examination of the Seven Cardinal Principles and the Goals for 2000 shows that both hold the schools responsible for serving both the society and the students.

We have identified four important factors in the search for the best content: knowledge or information, the needs of society, student needs, and human development. Now let's examine each of these factors.

## THE NATURE OF KNOWLEDGE

Many criticisms are heard today about the schools' failure to teach students how to master the subjects they study. Standardized tests which have been *nationally* normed show that an alarming number of students fail to develop a clear understanding of the content which they encounter in their classrooms.

Because the subject-centered design has dominated the curricula in American schools throughout their existence, concern for content mastery has always been present. Initially, there was little question of what content was most important. The Puritans created the schools to teach the laws of the colony (that is, God's laws), which were determined by the Scriptures. This curriculum quickly gave way to the practical curriculum of the Franklin Academy. The English secondary schools' curricula seemed to take over and serve the schools for many decades.

Content plays a dominant role in subject-centered curricula. First, *information*, often in the form of seemingly unrelated facts, is selected for inclusion in the curriculum. Once selected, this information becomes curriculum content. *Content* is defined as the information selected to be part of a curriculum. The aim is for this content to become knowledge. *Knowledge* is defined as the content that students have connected to their previous experiences. The relationship between information, content, and knowledge is shown in Figure 7.3. Although the differences between these three terms may appear

**Figure 7.3** The relationship between information, content and knowledge.

slight, their effects on students make the difference between memorizing and understanding.

Constructivists stress the importance of students being able to relate newly acquired information to previously acquired understandings. "According to constructivist views, when presented with new information individuals use their existing knowledge and prior knowledge to help make sense of the new material" (King & Rosenshine, 1993, p. 127). Markle, Johnston, Geer, and Meichtry (1990, p. 53) explain:

> Constructivists describe learning in terms of building connections between prior knowledge and new ideas and claim that effective teaching helps students construct an organized set of concepts that relates old and new ideas.

Teachers generally recognize the importance of students learning the main concepts in each lesson; yet Perkins and Blythe (1994, p. 4) report that students often do not clearly understand the major concepts:

> Teachers were all too aware that their students often did not understand key concepts nearly as well as they might. Research affirms this perception. A number of studies have documented students' misconceptions about key ideas in mathematics and the sciences, their parochial views of history, their tendency to reduce complex literary works to stereotypes, and so on.

This concern was further expressed by Gardner and Boix-Mansilla (1994, p. 14), who said:

While students may succeed in "parroting back" phrases from lectures and texts, they often falter when asked to apply their understanding to new situations.

## THE NEEDS OF SOCIETY AND STUDENTS

From the time of the English classical school until *Sputnik* (1957), curriculum content received little attention. In fact, throughout our nation's history, unfortunately, the schools have been taken for granted, except in times of national emergencies. After *Sputnik*, the next national "emergency" came in the early 1980s, when it became obvious that the nation's dominant position in world productivity was being seriously threatened. For the first time, it was recognized that other nations could mass-produce higher-quality automobiles and equally good electronics at prices that were competitive in the national and international markets. To the writers of many education reform reports, this constituted a national emergency, and the schools were held accountable for putting the nation in jeopardy. Consequently, the education reform movement exemplified society's perceptions of its needs.

John Dewey believed that each generation brings on a new culture. If this is so, then with each new generation, a new curriculum must be developed to serve the unique needs of the new culture.

To understand the needs of learners, curriculum developers can begin by examining their most basic beliefs about the youths they know. Although this list is far from exclusive, the following questions might be asked. By nature, are young people:

- Social?
- Curious?
- Self-centered?
- Active?
- Passive?
- Competitive?
- Cooperative?

These traits can be studied merely by observing the behavior of a group of young people. If left to choose, will most young people work with others or will they work alone? Do most have more questions than answers?

Although most young people are social, are they not also self-centered? Do they not perceive the world as revolving around them and their wants? As they mature, many young people are taught by their parents or peers to be more considerate of others. Are not young people both cooperative and competitive? These paradoxes (social and yet self-centered, cooperative and yet competitive) allow curriculum developers to choose. For example, suppose that a teacher believes that young people are basically social. Then suppose that this teacher notices that the behavior of a group of children contradicts this assumption. The curriculum must be adjusted to correct this behavior.

Among learners' needs are their interests. Rousseau's book *Emile* stressed the need to give students complete freedom. This meant that they could study what they pleased. A. S. Neil (1960) described his school, Summerhill, as giving students the freedom to study what they wished and the freedom to attend only the classes that interested them. The Progressive Education Movement gave students choice of content. Contemporary curriculum leaders stress the need to involve students in the selection of content.

## Human Development

John Dewey believed that the schools had a responsibility for improving humankind. Newton (1989, p. 91) said:

> According to Dewey, "The aim of education is not merely to make citizens of workers, but to make human beings who will continuously add to the meaning of their experience and to their ability to direct subsequent experience." He

wanted each generation to go beyond its predecessors in the quality of behavior it sought to nurture in children.

Thus, some content should (must) be selected on the basis of its potential for helping improve the quality of thinking and the quality of behavior of humankind. The definition of philosophy as the "pursuit of wisdom" (see Chapter 3), coupled with the definition of wisdom as the "knowledge of things beautiful, first, divine, pure, and eternal," seems to guarantee a place in the curriculum for the study of philosophy, values, and the arts.

## The Comprehensive High School

One of the most far-reaching efforts to ensure that schools develop the full potential of their students occurred in the late 1950s, when James Conant, who had been a chemistry professor and later was president of Harvard University, began openly expressing his dissatisfaction with the American high school. He put his concern in print in his book *The American High School Today* (1959), in which he defended the concept of large, comprehensive schools with core curricula. He especially wanted the schools to offer vocational and precollege programs along with a strong general studies program. The comprehensive high school, which was first recommended in 1918 by the NEA Commission on the Reorganization of Secondary Education, publishers of the Seven Cardinal Principles of Secondary Education, had come under major attack.

Through his contributions as a chemist, writer, researcher, and president of Harvard, Conant had earned the respect of the public at large and especially the scientific community. He was commissioned by the Carnegie Corporation to write *The American High School Today*, a report designed to strengthen the education of all students. The report was highly prescriptive, requiring of all students four years of English, three or four years of social studies, one year of math, and one year of science. A heavier curriculum was prescribed for gifted students. The report recommended both heterogeneous groupings (homerooms) and ability groupings. It also set a minimum number of hours of homework. To achieve currency and to respond to the nation's needs, he recommended requiring all seniors to take a course on American problems. Conant's critics questioned that a single course could achieve so much, especially since a large portion of students dropped out before reaching the senior year. However, Conant's recommendations were widely adopted, reaffirming the credibility of the comprehensive school and the Carnegie unit.

## Personalizing the Classroom

This book embraces and endorses the development of classrooms in which everyone cares about the feelings of others. Because of their home and neighborhood environments, many students may experience culture shock in such a classroom. Initially, some students may resist such personalized environments, in the same way some students are ashamed of earning good grades.

Yet, most people want others to respect and care for them. Wolfgramm (1993, pp. 102–103) explains:

> There is a critical need for educational environments that encourage kindness and concern. In our efforts to improve schools we must not lose sight of the most important part of the process—the students themselves. Students must know that they are valued as individuals. Their needs are important. They are not pawns in an international game of economic survival. The question, "For whom are our schools?" must be central to the debate on school reform. Educational environments that stress student interest, personal choice, first hand experience, thoughtfulness, and humanness need to be encouraged. At no time in world history has the international community been more sensitive to the need for the democratic values of individual worth and personal freedom than today.

Unfortunately, many young people grow up on the streets or in homes where the first and only rule is survival. In such environments, youths appear to have no choice but to be tough, if, indeed, they are to survive. But, given a choice, many—perhaps all—of these youngsters would prefer a safer climate such as that offered by the schools. Harkins (1992, p. 62) says this quite effectively:

> Despite widespread portrayals of schools as deserts, the local school is for many youngsters an oasis. At least it has that possibility. A safe, consistent, and caring school setting is for many students a complete contrast from life at home or in the neighborhood.

Referring to their vision of what schools can be, Ponder and Holmes (1992, p. 409) described the ideal relationship between teachers and students:

> Children will feel close to their teachers and will "experience teachers enjoying them and enjoying being with them." Teachers will be involved with kids both educationally and personally and "they will value their relationships with the kids. . . . In this ideal school, being a content expert is not enough"—"teachers need to be good at relating."

Such curricula will require a combination of the educational domains. "Teachers must be knowledgeable about people and not just subjects, and they must have counseling and social work skills. Humor, openness, and energy are the instructional tools these teachers will use to build relationships with everyone" (Ponder & Holmes, 1992, p. 409).

This personal approach includes respecting students' perspectives. As Fielding and Pearson (1994, pp. 66) have said, "Recently, the process of allowing students to build, express, and defend their own interpretations has become a revalued goal of text discussions."

Nowhere in the accountability-based, content-focused education reform reports is anyone likely to find suggestions for developing this type of curriculum; yet for proactive teachers the opportunity is there.

## At-Risk Students

One condition of modern society with which future curricula must deal, in order to remove a major learning barrier, is the growing number of at-risk students. Defined in many ways, *at-risk students* are more likely than average students to drop out of school. Wanat (1992) says that the school is a refuge for these children because it provides them with needed stability. These youths know that the schools and teachers can be counted on. If students obey the policies, they can expect to get along fine. If they put forth the required effort, the chances are good that they will succeed in the school environment. This is far from the case in other aspects of their lives. Also, unlike the families of a large percentage of today's youths, the school is not going to fall apart; it is not subject to divorce. In discussing what this comforting quality of consistency means to children of divorces, Wanat (1992, p. 59) says:

> Schools provide structure and stability and maintain a foundation that's not going to come apart like the family came apart.

Unlike the competitive, norm-referenced systems used in many traditional schools, a system using clear, criterion-based objectives which specify definite results of specific behaviors instills a sense of security in students. A curriculum that supports reasonably high expectations of all students communicates that the school has confidence in students' capabilities.

## SELECTING ACTIVITIES

For the sake of simplicity, the early part of this chapter was limited to a discussion of the importance of content and the need for curriculum developers to use a logical strategy to select the best content for their schools. In reality, of course, to separate content from the activities students need in order to master this content is to take a superficial approach. If educators accept John Locke's concept of *tabula rasa* (that everyone is born with a blank mind and the only way to put anything on it is through experience), or if educators accept John Dewey's philosophy of "learning by doing," then the fact that content and activities are inseparable is evident.

The process of selection of content, then, is meaningless unless it includes the selection of activities through which that content can become meaningful. Yet, educators focus on content while ignoring activities. For example, although the textbook remains the dominant curriculum determiner, and although many studies have analyzed textbook content, unfortunately, few studies analyze the uses that teachers make of textbooks (Garcia, 1993). Educators need to conduct more investigations on both planned teacher activities and student activities. Such investigations should include determining which instructional methods are best suited to specific disciplines. As Gardner and Boix-Mansilla (1994, p. 18) have explained:

> Different disciplines call on different analytic styles, approaches to problem solving, and findings, temperaments, and intelligences . . . effective teachers should help youngsters to appreciate that what counts as cause and effect, data and explanation use of language and argument, varies across the disciplines."

## The Knowledge Base

In a chapter written for an Association for Supervision and Curriculum Development (ASCD) yearbook, Hopkins (1990, pp. 64–65) concluded with the following message:

> We now know a great deal about the conditions that make for high school achievement and what a school is like that is dedicated to the learning of both students and teachers. We need to use this knowledge creatively, and humanly to create the vision we now know is possible.

Hopkins suggests that we employ our accumulated knowledge to uncover the conditions that lead to increased learning. It becomes more important to do this as our teaching knowledge base increases. Within the past few years, researchers have collected more information about effective teaching than had been accumulated over the previous two centuries. This fact alone demands that, when selecting teacher activities and learner activities, teachers make full use of the existing knowledge base, keep abreast of the findings reported in professional journals, and whenever possible contribute to the knowledge base. However, caution should be used to avoid the temptation to overgeneralize data and draw unfounded conclusions. Joyce (1990, p. 26) explains:

> It is easy to underplay the research base and fail to locate some of the solid material that has been accumulated. On the other hand, it is equally easy to make too much of some provocative but thin findings and imbue them with qualities of substance that are not yet warranted.

The message in Joyce's words seems to be that teachers should be encouraged to use the knowledge base when selecting teacher activities and learner activities, but to proceed with caution. An equally strong suggestion can be found in these words for teacher education programs. To be capable of achieving the desired balance, that is, to select and use valid research without imbuing the findings with unwarranted substance, requires knowledge of and skills in using research. Teacher education programs, undergraduate and especially graduate, should include research across the curriculum. Without a research component, the potential for in-service faculty development programs to help teachers build the necessary research skills—indeed, the potential of a single research course to achieve this goal—is extremely limited.

## Problem Solving

Since the Woods Hole Conference in 1959 (discussed in Chapter 3), problem solving has been emphasized in curricula in both elementary and secondary schools. Its heavy emphasis during the early 1960s was predicated on its effectiveness in helping students understand the content they studied. Richards (1993, p. 29) stresses the acuteness of this need in the 1990s:

It only makes sense in a world that encourages problem solving, more corporate decisions being reached through employer-employee think tanks, and doctors including their patients in their diagnosis process, that students should be encouraged to be more actively involved in their own educational pursuits; in order to make them more capable, proficient, and responsible for the employment work.

When students solve problems in a cooperative manner, additional benefits accrue: They can achieve several goals simultaneously. Cooperation leads to increased and deeper understanding (O'Donnell & Dansereau, 1993). After studying the cognitive effects of guided cooperative questioning, King and Rosenshine (1993, p. 143) reported:

> Results of this study show that children at fifth-grade level can be trained to use the highly elaborated question seems to generate thought-provoking questions about material presented in classroom lessons.

Since many problem-solving situations are open-ended, students learn from dealing with them that knowledge seeking does not stop with a single answer. Often one answer may lead to additional questions. Novak (1993, p. 53) agrees with this perception:

> And students need to know that understanding is never complete. It is an iterative process where the learner moves gradually toward greater understanding.

Some teachers have mistakenly thought that effective use of activities requires choosing one activity to help students meet one objective; they have assumed that there should be a separate activity for each objective in their curriculum. But this is not so: Carefully designed, a multipurpose activity can serve several objectives. Dormody (1991, p. 4) talks about this advantage of multipurpose activities when he addresses some of the benefits of group problem solving:

> Group problem solving has something for everybody, and can motivate different students in many different ways. While solving group problems, students can learn about teamwork, leadership, the subject matter area of the problem and problem solving itself.

Problem solving is so entrenched in today's curricula that Zurbrick (1991, p. 3) apologizes for having to remind readers of its importance:

> Given the eminence of problem solving as an accepted teaching methodology and the fact that the ability to solve problems is a nearly universally acknowledged outcome for all educational programs, it seems sacrificial to question problem solving in an education journal.

Multipurpose activities are especially needed to meet some education reform requirements. Anderson and Pavan (1993, pp. 208–209) made this clear through a couple of activities which they offer for nongraded classes:

> One specific and immediate activity, in schools where a nongraded program is being launched, could be the development of two (or more) interdisciplinary "units" that can be launched during the first few months. A possible theme for

one of these could be "Exploring Our Own Back Yard." This might be taken literally in at least three ways: making descriptive reports on the school building and its contents (human as well as physical), collecting similar data about the school site (including area dimensions, varieties of plants and trees, unique topological features, birds, insects and animals sighted, etc.), and looking at the total geographic area, or a designated portion thereof, served by the school.

A variation of the latter could be for each child (perhaps with parental assistance) to take a "census" of the neighborhood area within which his/her own residence is located, and then for each class (or preferably team) to organize the resulting data. As some examples, it might be discovered that this multi-aged team of 106 children identified 631 family pets, including 37 dogs (broken down by breed, or color, or age, or whatever), 48 cats, 17 gerbils (and more on the way), 18 white mice, 11 snakes(!), 165 goldfish, etc. That same group may have located 431 trees, of which 183 were maples, 69 were oaks, etc. Ditto for flowers; for colors of houses; for skateboards, bicycles, backboards, musical instruments, jungle gyms, television sets, boats, or whatever else could be tallied and described. The sheer variety of interesting items within their collective environments is likely to surprise, and hopefully delight, the children.

It might be noted that the "census" activities could also include taking note of anomalies or problems in the neighborhood. For example, notes on the quantities and types of trash found on urban streets might be put to good use in social action efforts.

It is easy to see how such an exercise could involve learning at many different developmental levels in mathematics, language, social studies, science, art, music, physical education, and other content areas. Culminating activities could involve songs, plays, murals, TV documentaries, "census" reports, and all sorts of other products. The explorers, though of differing ages, would have come to know and respect each other in a working situation, and it is to be hoped that some of the most fascinating discoveries will have been made, and shared with enthusiasm, by the youngest children in the class or team.

An immediate activity when moving to multi-aged grouping will be to assign themes to certain years so children do not experience repeated themes. A two-year sequence is needed if the multi-aging spans two years; three-year sequence for three years, etc.

In summary, problem solving is a strategy which offers tomorrow's citizens opportunities to prepare for the type of lifestyle that will require the ability to think critically and solve a vast array of problems. Alvarez (1993, p. 13) says:

> If we expect critical thinking to take place, we need to provide students with problem solving lessons in meaningful learning contexts.

Alvarez (1993, p. 14) also suggests that a viable way for students to develop critical thinking skills is through the case study method. "Self-selected cases spurred curiosity and invited students to initiate critical and imaginative thinking." Cases provide an open invitation to generalize (Biddle & Anderson,

1986), and they allow students to be creative and imaginative (Kowalski, Henson, & Weaver (1994).

## Internationalization

Chapter 1 discussed the high level of panic expressed in the education reform reports of the 1980s and 1990s. Setting the pattern, the title of one report, *A Nation at Risk*, suggested a crisis, speaking of "a rising tide of mediocrity." That concern over the ability of the United States to compete internationally suggests how important it is for American students to be knowledgeable about the world at large. King (1991, p. 18) stresses this need:

> The infusion of international knowledge, skills, and attitudes should take place at all levels and within all courses in the curriculum. International concepts should be integrated directly into subject matter.

If a school's curriculum is to serve society by providing leadership, it must incorporate technological developments and international trends and must include content and activities to prepare the current generation of youth for their contemporary and future roles in the community and in the world.

To survive, all societies depend on the cooperation of the rest of the world. As this dependency increases, another responsibility of the curriculum is to recognize, and help others to recognize, the importance of global awareness. Decker (1992, pp. 5–6) says, "A sound source of impact is recognition of the vital role of education in helping members of all societies understand and discharge their global responsibilities." There is evidence that an increased global awareness can help prepare students to make better decisions on world issues. Dennee (1993, p. 368) explains:

> Incorporating a global perspective into your curriculum is both practical and beneficial. By recognizing our increased worldwide independence and by developing empathy with humankind, we develop the ability to make intelligent decisions regarding our world.

## EDUCATION REFORM'S IMPACT ON THE SELECTION OF CONTENT AND ACTIVITIES

Throughout the country, education reform is altering the selection of curriculum content and activities. The curriculum has always attracted reformers. Cuban (1993, p. 183) addresses this irresistible quality of the curriculum: "Hence, changing the official curriculum is the bright brass luring reformers. Such issues fire passions, grab headlines, and lead off the evening news." The *official curriculum* is the planned curriculum. *That* the curriculum will be altered significantly is fact; *how* it will be altered depends on teachers. The point here is that teachers need not and, indeed must not, wait to see how tomorrow's content and activities will look; rather, responsible teachers must be proactive and must shape the new curricula by choosing the content and activities needed to prepare students for the twenty-first century. Recognizing the need for ongoing improvement does not imply that all change or all reform is good. Teachers should not blindly accept all reform as improvement; rather, they should continually evaluate the worth of new as well as old practices.

## A Need for Increased Flexibility

A proactive role will require teachers to think and even feel in different ways. In the past, the curricula demanded compliance from students. But such curricula no longer work. Brimfield (1992, p. 386) explains:

> For many children the curriculum is neither the content, nor the one of compliance which I experienced as a student. It is a curriculum of endurance and apathy. They simply do not care about what is happening in their classes either because its value has not been emphasized at home or because their own needs for survival must take precedence.

The time is ripe for contemporary teachers to ask what they want of tomorrow's schools. Although this Tylerian (ends-means) approach is sometimes criticized, it is an excellent beginning. The reform reports call for more science and mathematics and for students to develop the ability to apply their knowledge in their adult lives. The reports call for American students to be able to achieve the highest scores on national achievement tests and to outperform their counterparts internationally. Although these goals may have merit, teachers must look beyond them, for, by themselves, the goals do not address the need to prepare students for the future. For example, the new century will require high levels of flexibility—in thinking, in accepting the differences between people, in accepting the ideas of others, and in relating to errors (i.e., accepting mistakes as a part of the learning process). As role models, teachers must excel in their flexibility, and curricula must be designed to nurture flexible behavior.

In their article "Purpose, Products, and Visions: The Creation of New Schools," Ponder and Holmes (1992, p. 414) describe their concept of the ideal curriculum for tomorrow's schools:

> Risk taking will be supported and rewarded; mistakes will be expected as a natural by-product of experimentation. . . . Like an experienced traveler, teachers will know many different routes to each learning destination. Teachers will look to each student's unique needs to determine which route is best. They will consider different cognitive styles and modality preferences. They will design activities that appeal to both left and right brain learners. They will also vary the pace at which they drive students toward the learning objectives.

Flexibility must go even further: Teachers who use authoritarian methods must learn to relinquish some of their authority; they must learn how to feel comfortable in letting students set some of their own objectives, knowing that objectives will be different for different students and knowing that mistakes will be made.

Robert Anderson (see Dagenias, 1994, p. 53) offers his vision of the school climate of the future; his thinking parallels that of Ponder and Holmes:

> The school environment must become and remain dynamic. There must be a feeling of adventure in the air. Learners, adults as well as children, must behave like explorers in the risk-taking sense. . . . The culture of the school must be such that there is a maximum(s) of opportunity for working together, sharing, trading secrets, and celebrating.

The expansion of flexibility must be a personal goal of experienced and new teachers alike, and a curriculum goal for students. Chapter 10 discusses Abraham Maslow's view that a human being's cognitive and emotional selves are inseparable. Interestingly, Maslow became increasingly aware of this relationship in his later years. In fact, he wrote the quote given in Chapter 10 just weeks before his death. Piaget's thinking paralleled that of Maslow, and not long before his own death, Piaget also wrote about the inseparable connection between the cognitive self and the emotional self.

## Teacher Empowerment

Current education reform efforts emphasize the need to empower teachers. Teachers who traditionally have remained in self-contained classrooms must assume a larger role in the entire operation of the school if, indeed, education reform efforts are to succeed.

Teacher empowerment is more than a fad of current education reform, and its purpose goes beyond the securing of higher pay and better working conditions for teachers. As much as higher pay and improved working conditions may be needed, some educators believe that teacher empowerment is indispensable to meaningful reform. Ayers (1992, p. 260) has this perception:

> In a sense, all education is about power—its goal is for people to become more skilled, more able, more dynamic, more vital. Teaching is about strengthening, invigorating, and empowering others.

Teacher empowerment requires teachers to develop greater expertise in curriculum development. Klein (1992, p. 196) emphasizes the role of knowledge in this empowering act:

> If teacher empowerment extends to curriculum decision making, as some leaders propose, the need for teachers to become more knowledgeable about and sophisticated in the field of curriculum—including theories and alternative ways of conducting classroom practice—becomes critical. For this to occur, all practitioners—teachers, supervisors, and administrators—will need to have the study of curriculum as a fundamental part of their preparation.

Notice in these discussions that it is virtually impossible to distinguish between curriculum content and curriculum activities. Teacher empowerment requires the ability to select both content and activities to promote the empowerment of students.

## THE NEED FOR SECURITY

Teacher empowerment also requires a safe climate. As Greenlaw (1993, p. 120) says, "Some teachers do not have the confidence in themselves or the courage to act to make empowerment work." The best confidence builder is acceptance, and self-acceptance is achieved best through success. Too often, educational reformers and reform policies unintentionally and unknowingly send the message that teachers' prior efforts have been futile. For example, consider what happens when, without their involvement in and input into decisions to alter the curriculum, teachers are told to replace existing practices with new ones. A common interpretation of this directive is that someone—usually an outsider who knows little about the characteristics and needs of students and the community—has decided that the current practices are all wrong, which means that teachers have failed. The harm that this conclusion brings to schools can easily be avoided by involving teachers in decisions and by letting teachers know that reform can occur by building on the existing curriculum; indeed, destroying or replacing an existing curriculum is seldom, if ever, necessary or desirable.

For example, during a workshop designed to help teachers develop an integrated curriculum, one teacher was overheard saying, "When we collapsed four subjects to form a central integrated theme, and designed 120-minute periods, some of the teachers insisted on having 30 minutes to devote exclusively to their discipline." Although success with integrated programs requires teachers to give up the idea of having time exclusively for their discipline, reprimanding a teacher who balked at this would gain nothing. A far better approach would be to compliment such teachers on their level of dedication to their discipline and explain that they will not have to give up their level of commitment to their subject but will be required to forgo spending *exclusive* time on their discipline.

Teachers are not alone in their need for confidence building. Students also need self-confidence for the future, when new types of demands will be made of all citizens. One of these demands will be to deal with uncertainty. Eisner (1992, p. 723) says it clearly: "Education is about learning how to deal with uncertainty and ambiguity."

Uncertainty is a zone of high discomfort. As mentioned in Chapter 2, in the past, schools have been bastions of tradition protecting teachers from the unknown. Like other adults, many teachers fear the uncertainty because, when they went to school, they were punished for making errors. Of course, the all-too-logical conclusion is that the best way to avoid errors is to avoid experimenting with new approaches. This condition can be rectified for both the teachers and their students by curricula that make mistakes acceptable. The best way to drive out fear of the unknown is to make the unknown familiar; in the classroom this means taking risks, making mistakes, and using mistakes, instead of hiding from them.

Another way to help teachers overcome their fear of reform is to assure them that they have the time needed to implement reform. Unfortunately, the tone of urgency expressed in some of the reform reports has intensified teachers' anxieties; yet curricularists know that significant educational change comes slowly. A timetable can be used to assure teachers that they are making progress at a rate that is both reasonable and acceptable.

Still another way to build self-confidence is through helping others increase their self-esteem. Canfield (1990, p. 49) offers nine suggestions for teachers to use to help their students develop self-esteem. The teacher:

1. Accepts total responsibility for the learner's self-concept.
2. Focuses on the positive.
3. Monitors his or her comments.
4. Uses student support groups in the classroom.
5. Identifies strengths and resources.
6. Clarifies the learner's vision.
7. Sets goals and objectives.
8. Takes appropriate action.
9. Responds appropriately to feedback.

The curriculum should offer an effective route whereby students can succeed, and self-esteem should come from self-improvement rather than from self-concept development programs that rely on telling students that they are important.

## CHECKLIST FOR REVISING CURRICULA

The Association for Supervision and Curriculum Development (1992, p. 137) offers the following questions which can be used as a checklist when revising curricula. Does your curriculum:

1. Provide a balanced core of common learning?
2. Focus on results with multiple assessments?
3. Integrate subject areas?
4. Involve students in learning?
5. Recognize and respect student diversity?
6. Avoid tracking plans?
7. Develop student thinking skills?

In one or more ways, most of these questions relate directly to the selection of content and activities. By planning activities to help their students increase their self-esteem, teachers can enhance their own self-concepts, and by covering all the reform practices endorsed by their district, teachers can feel more comfortable about education reform. A description of a system teachers can use to ensure that they are achieving local education reform expectations follows.

## TABLES OF SPECIFICATIONS

Because curriculum development is a complex process, and because it is rapidly becoming more complex, (through the pressure of education reform), including the most important content in the curriculum has become a formidable challenge. A system is needed to ensure that the most important content and activities are being covered so that the expectations of the curriculum are met. One such system is a *table of specifications*.

Tables of specification vary, but their principle is constant. Each table uses a matrix. The columns and lines are labeled. For example, Table 7.1 is a sample table of specifications designed to ensure that the local education reform practices are being covered in a teacher education curriculum.

In this example, the teacher education courses are listed horizontally across the top of the chart, and the reform elements are listed vertically at the left.

The table of specifications can be used in two ways. First, the left side of the matrix can be used as a point of origin. For example, this approach would be used if you wanted to know how thoroughly a particular reform element is being covered. Or you might wish to know how comprehensive a particular course is in covering education reform. You can determine this by using the top as your point of origin; locate the course in question and move down the column in the table to see how many reform elements are addressed in the course. This matrix goes further: A 1 to 3 numbering system is assigned to show the depth to which a reform element is covered. Coverage at level 1 is an introduction; level 3 is mastery; level 2 is between introduction and mastery.

On a smaller scale, a table of specifications can be designed for each course. Across the top you can list the objectives you want students to master. The first column can list the content generalizations (concepts) needed to achieve these objectives. Once the top row and the first column are filled in, you can use the chart to check each objective to determine whether the content needed to achieve the objective is covered. Table 7.2 is a sample table of specifications for a high school class in world history.

Similar tables of specifications can be developed to ensure coverage in the affective and psychomotor domains. An advantage of tables of specifications is

**Table 7.1   Table of Specificaitons for Educational Reform**

| KERA topics | Courses in the Program Area | | | | | | | | | | | |
|---|---|---|---|---|---|---|---|---|---|---|---|---|
| | ELE 361 | ELE 362 | ELE 445 | ELE 446 | ELE 490 | ELE 491 | ELE 492 | ELE 493 | ELE 499 | ELE 530 | ELE 541 | ELE 551 |
| 1. Curriculum goals | 2 | 2 | 1 | 2 | 1 | 3 | 3 | 2 | 3 | 2 | 1 | 2 |
| 2. Performance-based student assessment | 1 | 2 | 0 | 2 | 2 | 3 | 1 | 2 | 2 | 1 | 2 | 1 |
| 3. Nongraded primary | 2 | 1 | 0 | 2 | 3 | 3 | 1 | 2 | 2 | 2 | 1 | 1 |
| 4. Site-based decision making | 1 | 0 | 1 | 1 | 1 | 2 | 1 | 1 | 1 | 0 | 1 | 0 |
| 5. Instructional uses of technology | 1 | 0 | 1 | 1 | 1 | 3 | 2 | 1 | 2 | 0 | 1 | 1 |
| 6. Research-based instructional practices | 3 | 1 | 1 | 2 | 3 | 1 | 3 | 2 | 2 | 2 | 1 | 3 |
| 7. Extended school programs | 0 | 0 | 0 | 2 | 1 | 0 | 0 | 0 | 1 | 1 | 1 | 0 |
| 8. Motivating students of diverse cultures | 3 | 1 | 1 | 1 | 1 | 1 | 2 | 2 | 3 | 3 | 2 | 3 |
| 9. School finance | 0 | 0 | 0 | 0 | 0 | 0 | 1 | 0 | 1 | 0 | 0 | 0 |

Rating scale: 1—Awareness of topic; 2—topic is reinforced; 3—mastery of topic is achieved.

that they can be used to ensure coverage of objectives at varying levels of the three domains of the educational taxonomies. Table 7.3 provides this type of table of specifications for an art class.

Still another use of the table of specifications is to ensure that a curriculum contains activities covering each major concept or objective. List the objectives or concepts on one axis, and the activities on the other. When the table is used for this purpose, one activity should correspond to each objective or concept; however, the same activity may be assigned to more than one objective or concept.

For example, Table 7.4 shows a table of specifications for a grade 4–6 unit on weather. Major concepts are expressed briefly so that they will fit in the table. Whenever possible, concept statements should be kept to simple sentences.

The number of ways teachers can use tables of specifications is limited only by their imaginations. Certainly, discovering creative applications of this instrument to solve contemporary problems epitomizes the exhilarating

**Table 7.2   Table of Specifications to Ensure Content Coverage for All Objectives**

| Content generalizations | Obj. 16 | Obj. 17 | Obj. 18 | Obj. 19 | Obj. 20 | Obj. 21 | Obj. 22 | Obj. 23 | Obj. 24 | Obj. 25 | Obj. 26 | Obj. 27 |
|---|---|---|---|---|---|---|---|---|---|---|---|---|
| 1. Concept of power and authority and law and order | | | | | | | | | | | | |
| 2. Generalizations on social orders of feudal classes | | | | | | | | | | | | |
| 3. Little representation of lower classes | | | | | | | | | | | | |
| 4. Foundations of democracy laid in medieval period, quality of life and secularism increased | ✔ | | ✔ | ✔ | | | | | | | ✔ | ✔ |
| 5. Value of art created by many great artists during this period | ✔ | ✔ | ✔ | ✔ | | | ✔ | | ✔ | ✔ | ✔ | ✔ |
| 6. Even though centuries pass, life remains the same | ✔ | ✔ | | | ✔ | ✔ | | ✔ | ✔ | ✔ | ✔ | ✔ |
| 7. Past contributions relate to total picture of history | | ✔ | ✔ | ✔ | ✔ | ✔ | ✔ | | ✔ | | ✔ | ✔ |

nature of curriculum improvement and the challenges that face today's teachers. As teachers' roles in curriculum development grow, so will the need to be skilled in discovering new ways to use this and other versatile instruments.

## SUMMARY

A major role of the curriculum is to help students make meaning out of newly acquired information. Achieving this goal requires the ability on the part of teachers to make careful selections of content and activities. Yet, in the past,

**Table 7.3  Table of specifications to ensure coverage of all levels of the three domains**

The levels of each domain are arranged in a hierarchy from left to right at the top. Each level assumes inclusion of lower levels. The highest targeted level is checked.

| | Cognitive | | | | | | Affective | | | | | Psychomotor | | | | | | |
|---|---|---|---|---|---|---|---|---|---|---|---|---|---|---|---|---|---|---|
| | Knowledge | Comprehension | Application | Analysis | Synthesis | Evaluation | Receiving | Responding | Valuing | Organization | Characterization | Reception | Set | Guided Response | Mechanism | Comp. Overt Resp. | Adaption | Origination |
| 1. Name materials | ✔ | | | | | | | | | | | | | ✔ | | | | |
| 2. Select materials | | ✔ | | | | | | ✔ | | | | | | ✔ | | | | |
| 3. Identify terms | ✔ | | | | | | | ✔ | | | | | | ✔ | | | | |
| 4. Spell terms | | | ✔ | | | | | ✔ | | | | | | | ✔ | | | |
| 5. Name design element | ✔ | | | | | | | ✔ | | | | | | ✔ | | | | |
| 6. Name design principle | ✔ | | | | | | | ✔ | | | | | | ✔ | | | | |
| 7. Iden. design elem. | | | | ✔ | | | | ✔ | | | | | | ✔ | | | | |
| 8. Iden. comp. prin. | | | | ✔ | | | | ✔ | | | | | | ✔ | | | | |
| 9. Iden. comp. areas | | | | ✔ | | | | ✔ | | | | | | ✔ | | | | |
| 10. Iden. comp. in pix | | | | ✔ | | | | ✔ | | | | | | ✔ | | | | |
| 11. Mix colors: hue | | | ✔ | | | | | | ✔ | | | | | | | ✔ | | |
| 12. Create: tint, shade | | | | | ✔ | | | | | ✔ | | | | | | | | ✔ |
| 13. Create: mood | | | | | ✔ | | | | | ✔ | | | | | | | | ✔ |
| 14. Create: design elem. | | | | | ✔ | | | | | ✔ | | | | | | | | ✔ |
| 15. Compare pictures | | | | ✔ | | | | | ✔ | | | | | | | | | |
| 16. Compare sculpture, pictures | | | | ✔ | | | | | ✔ | | | | | ✔ | | | | |
| 17. Use technique | | | ✔ | | | | | ✔ | | | | | | | | ✔ | | |
| 18. "Wait turn" | | | | ✔ | | | | ✔ | | | | | | ✔ | | | | |
| 19. Choose for group | | | | ✔ | | | | | | ✔ | | | | | | ✔ | | |
| 20. Properly use mat'l & equipment | | | | ✔ | ✔ | | | ✔ | | | | | | | | ✔ | | |
| 21. Construct 3-D objects | | | | ✔ | | | | | | ✔ | | | | | | | ✔ | |
| 22. Store materials | | | | ✔ | | | | ✔ | | | | | | | | ✔ | | |
| 23. Store equipment | | | | | | | | ✔ | | | | | | | | ✔ | | |
| 24. Share with instr. | | | | | | | | ✔ | | | | | | ✔ | | | | |
| 25. Share with group | | | | | | | | ✔ | | | | | | ✔ | | | | |
| 26. Share with the class | | | | | | | | ✔ | | | | | | ✔ | | | | |
| 27. Display, classroom | | | | | | ✔ | | | | ✔ | | | | | | | | |
| 28. Display, other | | | | | | ✔ | | | | ✔ | | | | | | | | |
| 29. Prepare display | | | ✔ | | | | | | ✔ | | | | | | | ✔ | | |
| 30. Select group | | | | ✔ | | | | | | ✔ | | | | ✔ | | | | |
| 31. Show followership | | | | ✔ | | | | | | ✔ | | | | ✔ | | | | |
| 32. Show leadership | | | | | | ✔ | | | | ✔ | | | | ✔ | | | | |
| 33. Accept others' work | | | | | | ✔ | | | | | ✔ | ✔ | | | | | | |
| 34. Evaluate products | | | | | | ✔ | | | ✔ | | | | | | | ✔ | | |
| 35. Evaluate process | | | | | | ✔ | | | ✔ | | | | | | | ✔ | | |
| 36. Work alone, cooper. | ✔ | | | | | | | ✔ | | | | | | ✔ | | | | |
| 37. Cooper. in group | ✔ | | | | | | | ✔ | | | | | | ✔ | | | | |
| 38. Adapt techniques | | | | | | ✔ | | | ✔ | | | | | | | | ✔ | |

**Table 7.4   Table of specifications for a unit on weather**

Goals

| Objectives | 1. Processes | 2. Knowledge | 3. Curiosity | 4. Independence | 5. Group participation | 6. Communication | 7. Economics | 8. Culture | 9. Reduce fear |
|---|---|---|---|---|---|---|---|---|---|
| 1. Apply symbols | ✔ | ✔ | | | | | | | |
| 2. Identify terms | | ✔ | | | | | | | |
| 3. Write paragraph | | ✔ | | ✔ | | | | | ✔ |
| 4. Record weather | ✔ | ✔ | | ✔ | | | | | |
| 5. List effects | | | | | | | ✔ | | |
| 6. Identify clouds | ✔ | ✔ | | ✔ | | ✔ | | | |
| 7. Design mural | | | | | ✔ | | | | |
| 8. Research climate | | | | ✔ | | | ✔ | ✔ | |
| 9. Complete activity | ✔ | ✔ | ✔ | ✔ | | | | | |
| 10. Apply symbols | ✔ | ✔ | | | | | | | ✔ |
| 11. Complete evaluation | ✔ | | | ✔ | | | | | |
| 12. Resupply center | | | | ✔ | ✔ | | | | |
| 13. Perform in grade | | | | | ✔ | | | | |
| 14. Label measurements | ✔ | ✔ | | | | | | | |
| 15. Interview | | | | ✔ | | ✔ | | ✔ | |
| 16. Record forecasts | | | ✔ | | | ✔ | | | |
| 17. List machines | ✔ | | | | | | | | |
| 18. Construct instructions | ✔ | | | ✔ | ✔ | ✔ | | | |
| 19. Write questions | | | ✔ | | | | | | |
| 20. List rules | | | | | | | | | ✔ |
| 21. List services | | | | | | | ✔ | | ✔ |
| 22. List variables | | | | | | | ✔ | | |
| 23. Make graph | ✔ | ✔ | | | | | | | |
| 24. Make puppets | | | | ✔ | ✔ | | | | |
| 25. Write letter | ✔ | | | ✔ | ✔ | | | | ✔ |
| 26. Write story | | | ✔ | ✔ | | ✔ | | | ✔ |
| 27. Create game | | | | ✔ | ✔ | | | | |
| 28. Write review | ✔ | ✔ | | | | | | | ✔ |
| 29. Develop problem | ✔ | | | | ✔ | | | | |
| 30. Construct satellite | | ✔ | | | ✔ | ✔ | | | |

most teachers have not selected content and activities logically. The textbook, a very poor source for determining content, remains the dominant curriculum determiner, followed closely by another equally poor curriculum determiner, personal choice.

Constructivists believe that the only way to make sense of newly acquired information is by integrating it into previously acquired understandings. This requires using concepts and themes and selecting appropriate student activities designed to enable students to use new information.

The curriculum should serve the student and the society. Content selection should use human development (the improvement of society through improving individuals) in the selection of content. Multipurpose activities serve a multiple number of objectives. Problem solving is an excellent form of multipurpose activity, since the future will require individuals to solve more problems.

Current world events, current education reform goals, and the future welfare of students should govern the selection of content and activities.

## QUESTIONS

1. How should one's knowledge of constructivism affect the selection of content and activities?

2. What is the difference between *content* and *knowledge*, and what can the curriculum developer do to alter this relationship?

3. Which of the four major factors—society's needs, knowledge, students' needs, or human development—do you think is most important to curriculum development? Why?

4. What should receive more emphasis in curriculum development: the present or the future? Why?

5. Which factors in Table 7.2 can you use most to guide your curriculum work? How?

## SUGGESTED FURTHER ACTIVITIES

1. Research the topic *human development*. Begin by finding three definitions of this term and then write your own definition. Next, make a list of actions you can take to help achieve this goal as you plan curricula.

2. Choose one lesson that you enjoy teaching. List and describe one activity that you might include in that lesson to address human development.

3. Write a one- or two-page statement concerning your beliefs about the nature of youth. Include your perceptions of young peoples' nature to be (*a*) curious or apathetic, (*b*) active or passive, (*c*) cooperative or competitive, (*d*) self-centered or social, and (*e*) honest or dishonest.

4. With regard to John Dewey's admonition to redesign our curricula to fit the rebirth of a new culture with each generation, make a list of important factors in the lives of contemporary youths that are unique to this generation.

5. Develop a system that you can use to gather information about student preferences.

6. Examine a state study guide or your state's reform program. Then select two or three goals and develop a multipurpose activity to serve them.

## BIBLIOGRAPHY

Alvarez, M. C. (1993). Imaginative uses of self-selected cases. *Reading research and instruction, 32*(2), 1–18.

Anderson, R. H. & Pavan, B. N. (1993). *Nongradeness: Helping it to happen.* Lancaster, PA: Technomic.

Applebee, A. N., Langer, J. A., & Mullis, I. V. S. (1987). *The nation's report card: Literature and U.S. history.* Princeton, NJ: Educational Testing Service.

Association for Supervision and Curriculum Development. *1992 ASCD curriculum handbook.* Alexandria, VA.

Ayers, William (1992). The shifting ground of curriculum thought and everyday practice. *Theory into practice, 31*(3), 259–263.

Berliner, D. C. (1984). The half-full glass: A review of research on teaching. In P. A. Hosford (Ed.), *Using what we know about teaching.* Alexandria, VA: Association for Supervision and Curriculum Development.

Biddle, B., & Anderson, D. (1986). *Theory, methods, knowledge, and research on teaching.* In M. Wittrock (Ed.), *Handbook of research on teaching* (3rd Ed.) (pp. 230–252). New York: Macmillan.

Brimfield, R. M. B. (1992). Curriculum! What's curriculum? *Educational Forum, 56*(4), 381–389.

Canfield, J. (1990). Improving students' self-esteem. *Educational Leadership, 48*(1), 48–50.

Conant, J. B. (1959) *The American High School Today.* New York: McGraw-Hill.

Cuban, L. (1993). The lure of curricular reform and its pitiful history. *Phi Delta Kappan, 75*(2), 182–185.

Dagenais, R. J. (1994). Professional development of teachers and administrators: Yesterday, today, and tomorrow/The views of Robert H. Anderson. *Kappa Delta Pi Record, 30*(2), 50–54.

Decker, L. E. (1992). Building learning communities: Realities of educational restructuring. In L. E. Decker and V. A. Romney (Eds.), *Educational restructuring and the community education process.* Alexandria, VA: National Community Education Association.

Dennee, J. (1993). Developing a global perspective through cooperative learning. *Contemporary Education, 66*(6), 367–369.

Dormody, T. J. (1991). Getting the most out of group problem solving. *The Agricultural Education Magazine, 64*(3), 4, 10.

Eisner, E. (1992). The federal reform of schools: Looking for the silver bullet. *Phi Delta Kappan, 73*(9), 722–726.

Erb, T. O. (1991) Preparing middle grades teachers to understand the curriculum. *Middle School Journal, 23*, 24–28.

Fielding, L. G. & Pearson, P. D. (1994). Reading comprehension: What works. *Educational Leadership, 51*(5), 62–68.

Fogarty, R. (1992). Ten ways to integrate curriculum. *Education Digest, 57*, 537.

Garcia, J. (1993). The changing image of ethnic groups in textbooks. *Phi Delta Kappan, 75*(1), 29–35.

Gardner, H. & Boix-Mansilla (1994). Teaching for understanding—within and across disciplines. *Educational Leadership, 51*(5), 14–18.

Greenlaw, M. (1993). Do teachers really want to be empowered? *Contemporary Education, 64*(2), 119–122.

Harkins, W. (1992, Fall). A practical approach to organizing curriculum. *NASSP Bulletin, 76*, 54–62.

Hopkins, D. (1990). Integrating staff development and staff improvement: A study of teacher personality and school climate. In B. Joyce (Ed.), *Changing school culture through staff development* (ASCD Yearbook, pp. 41–67). Arlington, VA: Association for Supervision and Curriculum Development.

Joyce, B. (1990). The self-education teacher: Empowering teachers through research. In B. Joyce (Ed.), *Changing school culture through staff development*. (ASCD Yearbook, pp. 26–40). Arlington, VA: Association for Supervision and Curriculum Development.

King, A., & Rosenshine, B. (1993). Effects of guided cooperative questioning on children's knowledge construction. *The Journal of Experimental Education, 61*(2), 127–148.

King, D. R. (1991). Changing the curriculum: Will it never end? *Agricultural Education Magazine, 63*: 18–19.

Klein, M. F. (1992). A perspective on the gap between curriculum theory and practice. *Theory into Practice, 31*(3), 191–197.

Kowal, Jerry (1991). Science, technology, and human values: A curricular approach. *Theory into Practice, 30*(4), 267–272.

Kowalski, T., Henson, K. T., & Weaver, R. A. (1994). *Case studies of beginning teachers*. New York: Longman.

Markle, G., Johnston, J. H., Geer, C., & Meichtry, Y. (1990). Teaching for understanding. *Middle School Journal, 22*(2), 53–57.

National Education Goals Panel (1991). *Goals Report*. Washington, DC: U. S. Government Printing Office.

Neil, A. S. (1960). *Summerhill*. New York: Hart.

Newton, B. T. (1989). Democratic aims of education-revisited. *Education, 110*(1), 87–93.

Novak, J. D. (1993). How do we learn our lessons? (helping students learn how to learn). *The Science Teacher, 60*(3), 50–55.

O'Donnell, T., & Danserau, D. F. (1993). Learning from lectures: Effects of cooperative review. *The Journal of Experimental Education, 61*(2), 116–125.

Orlich, D. (1980). *Teaching strategies: A guide to better instruction.* Lexington, MA: D. C. Heath.

Perkins, D., & Blythe, T. (1994). Putting understanding up front. *Educational Leadership, 51*(5), 4–7.

Ponder, G. A., & Holmes, K. M. (1992). Purpose, products, and visions: The creation of new schools. *The Educational Forum, 56*(4), 405–418.

Richards, P. M. (1993). A step beyond cooperative learning. *Middle School Journal, 24*(3), 28–29.

Scheville, J., et al. (1981). Teachers as policy brokers in the content of elementary school mathematics. In L. S. Schulman and E. G. Sykes (Eds.). *Handbook of teaching and policy.* New York: Longman.

Schomoker, M. (1990). Sentimentalizing self-esteem. *The Education Digest, 60*(7), 55–56.

Spencer, Herbert (1861). *Education: Intellectual, moral and physical.* New York: D. Appleton.

Taba, Hilda (1962). *Curriculum development: Theory and practice.* New York: Harcourt Brace Jovanovich.

Trachtenberg, D. (1974). Student tasks in text material: What cognitive skills do they tap? *Peabody Journal of Education, 52,* 54–57.

Tyson, Harriet, & Woodward, Arthur (1989). Why students aren't learning very much from textbooks. *Educational Leadership,* 14–17.

Wanat, C. L. (1992). Meeting the needs of single-parent children: School and parent views differ. *NASSP Bulletin, 76*(543), 55–60.

Wiske, M. S. (1994). How teaching for understanding changes the rules in the classroom. *Educational Leadership, 51*(5), 19–21.

Wolfgramm, H. F. (1993). For whom are our schools? *Contemporary Education, 64*(2), 99–103.

Woods, R. K. (1994). A close-up look at how children learn science. *Educational Leadership, 51*(5), 33–35.

Zurbrick, P. R. (1991). Problem solving? *Agricultural Education Magazine, 63*(12), 3, 11.

Chapter 8

# HELPING PEOPLE CHANGE

## OBJECTIVES

This chapter should prepare you to:

- Explain how the curriculum role of the educational leader has changed in recent years.
- Tell why teachers need to conduct research and describe the extent to which they should carry out research.
- Describe some of the benefits of teacher involvement in research.
- Explain the effect that education reform has had on teacher involvement in schoolwide matters.
- Describe how education consortia can contribute to school reform.
- Justify teacher empowerment as a prerequisite to (a) improving a school's curriculum and (b) implementing education reform.
- Discuss the use of power in education reform.

## EDUCATIONAL EXCELLENCE LABORATORY CONSORTIUM

In a state where education reform was raging, no money had been appropriated to higher education institutions to enable them to help the public schools, yet some of the state universities and colleges had a long-standing record of providing faculty development and other services to the schools. These educators had a deep commitment to helping the schools reform. Furthermore, the leaders at these colleges and universities anticipated that their institutions would be held accountable for the schools' success or failure in implementing the new laws.

Like a number of other state universities, Regional University has a fully staffed Office of Field Services and Professional Development. For 12 years Regional University has hosted monthly meetings for about 40 public school superintendents. In addition, Regional's in-service director has met regularly with the superintendents and instructional supervisors in the 22 counties in its service region and has provided numerous staff development workshops. Other universities in the state have similar arrangements and a history of providing strong support to the schools in their respective regions.

When the winds of school reform began blowing across the state, Regional's president and education dean spent time in the capital with the general assembly at open debates on education. As radical change became imminent, Regional was self-designated as a leader in mapping the state's school reform, and its College of Education was named as the organizer and leader for the university. As soon as the education reform bill was drafted, Regional began holding trainer-of-trainer workshops on the major reform issues contained in the bill, such as nongraded primary curricula, valued outcomes, alternative curricula, integrated curricula, portfolios, alternative assessment, performance evaluation, multicultural education, curriculum alignment, site-based decision making, educational technology, and research-based teaching. It was expected that, as new reform elements were introduced, new workshops would be developed.

With the news that the state was appropriating additional funds to the public schools for education reform (increased dollars based on average daily attendance) but that no additional money would be provided to the universities, Regional University made the following proposal to the school districts in its service region.

## EDUCATIONAL EXCELLENCE LABORATORY
## A PROPOSED STAFF DEVELOPMENT CONSORTIUM
## PROPOSAL ABSTRACT[1]

The State General Assembly, as a part of its education reform package, has identified staff development as a serious need in improving the state's public schools and has recommended that regional centers and consortia be established to address this need. In response to this recommendation, it is proposed that a staff development consortium, the Educational Excellence Laboratory, be established at Regional University. The Educational Excellence Laboratory would utilize the existing facilities and expertise of the university to provide effective staff development programs targeted to the identified needs of the participating school districts.

### Statement of Need

1. Many state school districts lack the fiscal resources to provide staff development activities that have the necessary breadth and depth to effect change.

2. The districts lack a sufficient number of supervisory personnel necessary to plan and manage long-range staff development programs.

3. Many districts are in remote and isolated areas, far removed from access to exemplary programs. More programs, addressing areawide concerns, need to be located in the various areas.

---

[1]Special thanks to Dr. William R. Thames for his developmental and leadership roles in the Educational Excellence Laboratory consortium.

4. Assistance in the design, analysis, and application of school-based research, addressing local problems, is critical.

## Regional's Role

Regional University has a definite role to play in this effort to enhance staff development activities in the public schools. An office to assist the schools in staff development already exists in the College of Education. The faculty members of the College of Education have close, trusting relationships with the teachers and administrators in the schools. Regional's leadership role in teacher education, both preservice and in-service, is recognized and accepted.

## Goals

The Regional University Educational Excellence Laboratory will revitalize school districts in the consortium through programs designed to provide continuous in-depth professional development opportunities. Extensive assessment will determine local needs related to the recommended education reforms. Utilizing the nursery through 12th grade laboratory school at Regional, along with on-site assistance, Regional will help local districts improve their staff development programs through:

1. *Staff development:* Continual training will be offered to effect positive school changes.
2. *Curriculum and instruction research:* This will focus on assessing local needs and on designing and conducting research related to effective instructional techniques and curricula.
3. *Technology services:* The future of education reform is related to the efforts of schools to use computers as instructional and administrative tools.
4. *Diagnostic, assessment, and assistance services:* Students placed at risk or with handicapping conditions are in need of diagnoses and assessments for individualized educational plans.
5. *Learning resource center:* Teachers need accessible locations where they can review materials, create instructional materials, and share ideas.
6. *Needs assessment and evaluation:* Continued progress in education requires assessing needs and evaluating expected outcomes in order to tailor the professional development program to the school level.
7. *Professional renewal opportunities:* Practicing teachers and administrators need opportunities for professional renewal which will motivate them and bring about their commitment to education reform.

## Organizational Structure

The proposed Educational Excellence Laboratory consortium would provide professional development services at several sites on the Regional campus and in the field. The consortium would be operated through the existing Office of

Field Services and Professional Development located in the College of Education. This office has the responsibility for assisting the school districts in the planning, implementation, and delivery of quality staff development activities. The director of this office would serve as the director of the consortium under the guidance of a steering committee composed of representatives from participating school districts.

The Educational Excellence Laboratory consortium would have five sites, each with a distinct function in professional development. The sites and their functions would be as follows:

1. *Assessment and evaluation site:* Located in the College of Education's Office of Research and Planning, this site will conduct needs assessments, long-range planning, and program evaluation.

2. *Training sites:* Located at Regional's off-campus center and at the on-campus Sam Ervin Center, these sites will provide easy access for training that reflects the best practices and is responsive to participants' needs.

3. *Demonstration site:* The laboratory school, located on Regional's campus, will serve as the demonstration site for innovative approaches to instruction and curriculum.

4. *Resource sites:* The off-campus facility and the Horns Library will provide instructional materials libraries for use by participating districts. Other sites to be utilized would be the Tri-Lakes Environmental Center, the Planetarium, the Department of Special Education (with its communication disorders laboratories), the College of Allied Health and Nursing, and the Department of Health Education.

5. *Research and development site:* Located within the laboratory school, this site will provide assistance in identifying the best of the developing instructional practices and assistance in conducting research with and disseminating results to participating school districts.

The establishment of the Regional University Educational Excellence Laboratory, as outlined above, would result in more effective professional development and improvement of instruction for school districts participating in the consortium.

## EDUCATIONAL EXCELLENCE LABORATORY PROPOSED INITIAL FUNDING

Funding for the initial activities of the consortium would be provided jointly by Regional University and the participating school districts. Regional University will seek outside funding for its initial share, and participating districts will match that amount dollar for dollar. The exact amount required from each participating district will depend upon the amount of outside funding secured by Regional and the number of school districts participating in the consortium.

Funding for the continuing operation of the consortium would come from the monies provided to the districts through the reform package in the following manner:

| Year 1 | $1 per child |
| Year 2 | $5 per child |
| Years 3–5 | $25 per child |

Twenty-one school districts joined the new consortium, each agreeing to pay a fee based on the number of students in its region. After two years, the consortium expanded its services to include purchasing goods (food, instructional supplies, and cleaning materials). During the following year, purchases of goods exceeded $2 million, saving the districts thousands of dollars.

During the second half of the consortium's third year (June through December) 598 reform workshops were provided to 15,990 teachers. Most of the workshops were delivered on site in the local districts.

## INTRODUCTION

Improving schools involves changing the curriculum and changing the behavior of those who implement the curriculum. It is a long-standing axiom that good leaders are good agents for change.

Historically, the appropriate leadership role in the schools has been that of ridding schools of their problems. Responsibility for providing this leadership belonged to the principal and the principal's assistant. Basically, the charge of these administrators was to fix or have fixed whatever went wrong, from leaky roofs to student behavior, sometimes even teacher behavior.

## A NEW CONCEPT OF LEADERSHIP

These perceptions have changed. First, the charge is no longer to maintain the status quo. The academic expectations of all schools have been raised, making the curriculum the center of attention. Second, the administrator is very much in the center of efforts to improve curriculum and instruction. Third, the curriculum is being improved on a continuous, nonstop basis; curriculum improvement does not wait until "problems" are identified.

Many changes in today's schools are impacting beyond the traditional classroom-level curriculum. In fact, the most common change today is to restructure the organization. *Restructuring* means comprehensive curriculum change to attain the school's mission. Education reform is a major catalyst for much of this change. Fullan and Stiegelbauer (1990) say that, without question, education reform and the process of change are intertwined. In fact, change is a prerequisite for meeting any of the elements of education reform. Because of this dependency on change, Kowalski and Reitzug (1993, p. 305) stress the need for educators to pursue further study to learn more about the way organizations change. They say:

> Without question, the goal of reform and the process of change are intertwined. For this reason, a clear perspective of the former cannot be achieved without an understanding of how the latter does or does not occur. Your understandings of organizations at the early stages of professional study are critically important.

## Resistance to Change

Changing organizations is difficult because organizations have a built-in resistance to change. Because of their fundamental nature, schools are especially resistant to change. Fullan and Stiegelbauer (1990, p. 12) describe this property of schools:

> On the one hand schools are expected to engage in continuous renewal, and change expectations are constantly swirling around, on the other hand, the way teachers are trained, the way schools are organized, the way the hierarchy operates, and the way political decision makers treat educators result in a system that is more likely to retain the status quo.

Tyack (1990) has pointed out that most of the changes which have occurred in the schools over the past 30 years have not resulted from local initiation; most important changes in our schools have been unplanned and have been stimulated by external forces such as federal laws. Kowalski and Reitzug (1993) devised a chart to show some of the forces that lead to change (see Figure 8.1) and how most schools change.

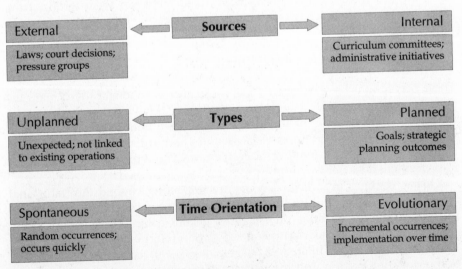

Figure 8.1  Conditions leading to education change.

The left side of Figure 8.1 lists the ways most schools have changed; the right side lists types of behaviors that are foreign to most twentieth-century schools.

## Some Barriers to Change

Changing the behavior of organizations requires changing the behavior of the individuals in the organizations. It is an accepted and well-documented fact that teachers have historically avoided involvement in the organization in which they work.

### Barrier 1: Failure to Use Research

Chapter 1 identified one of the barriers that keep teachers from getting involved with organizational change: Most teachers do not use research (Egbert, 1984; King, 1991). An examination of the reasons why teachers choose to ignore research might give some clue as to how the problem could be corrected. King (1991, p. 43) says that the reasons teachers give for not using research are:

1. Lack of confidence in their ability to understand the studies reported in research publications.
2. Confusion over contradictory research results.
3. Inability to apply research findings immediately in the classroom.

An examination of these reasons suggests that teachers may have little choice; many teachers don't use research because they can't. Bellon et al (1992, p. 3) agree: "Many experienced teachers are not conversant with the recent research on teaching."

### Barrier 2: Teachers Are Classroom-Bound

The inability to use research may also explain why teachers shun curriculum planning at levels beyond their own classroom. Young (see Haberman, 1992, p. 15) concludes that most teachers are ambivalent toward curriculum development beyond the classroom level and that, when they do develop curricula, they stay at the classroom or instructional level:

> The data presented clearly indicates that teachers' primary interest was in translating curriculum into instruction.

The idea that teachers tend to shun curriculum involvement at levels beyond their own classrooms is reinforced by Young (1985, p. 14), who discovered that the degree to which teachers feel alienated from the decision-making hierarchy relates directly to their sense of involvement in curriculum decisions at a level beyond the classroom. Perhaps Eisner (1990, p. 525) says it best with simple words. Referring to teachers, he says, "We do what we know how to do."

## Barrier 3: Perceptions of Teachers

Teachers' proclivities to avoid research and schoolwide involvement have caused other educators, and perhaps even teachers themselves, to view teachers as incapable of contributing meaningfully to schoolwide change. To a degree, this thinking is a self-fulfilling prophecy.

The evidence that teachers prefer not to get involved with curriculum development outside their classrooms and that they purposely avoid dealing with research is convincing; yet one should not conclude that teachers cannot or should not be prepared for using research and working with the total curriculum. Haberman (1992, p. 17) discusses how teachers are perceived and alludes to how this view must change:

> Another barrier to change in schools has been the perception that teachers are part of the existing problems and that any successful attempt to improve the schools must first be teacher-proof. . . . Classroom teachers must be viewed as part of the solution, never as the problem."

Teachers' reluctance to change perhaps can be attributed, at least in part, to the failure of schools to involve teachers in change. Barth (1990, p. 513) discusses this reluctance and some possible consequences when teachers do get involved:

> The lives of teachers and principals more closely mirror the cultivation of mushrooms: "You're kept in the dark most of the time, periodically you're covered with manure, and when you stick your head out it gets chopped off."

Apparently, major education reform is required in order to involve teachers and administrators in change.

## A NEED FOR INVOLVEMENT

Staying in the classroom and attending only to instruction and other "classroom matters" seemed appropriate until states and school districts began gathering research data on effective schools. These data have indicated that changing ineffective schools into effective schools requires teacher involvement with the total school, especially with curriculum matters. Haberman (1992, p. 14) explains:

> Recently, more attention has been given to the concept of the teacher as a professional with specialized knowledge and a pragmatic approach to curriculum planning that is derived from classroom experience. At the classroom level, the teacher would carry out action research to provide knowledge about the needs of students and their relationship to the curriculum.

There are several reasons why contemporary educators insist that teachers should be involved in changing the curriculum at levels beyond their own classroom. Cuban (1993, p. 182) says that improving schools requires more than just changing the curriculum; it also requires changing people; which is neither simple or easy:

> It is humbling to realize how little each generation learns from the experience of its equally earnest forebears about just how crude a tool curriculum change is for transforming student knowledge and behavior.

Kirk (1988) reports that teachers who are directly involved in curriculum development tend to shift their teaching style from prescriptive to interactive, causing them to increase their interactions with students and more effectively evaluate the needs of their students. Haberman (1992, p. 15) confirms this:

> As teachers feel more involved in the development of curriculum, it is clear that their personal commitment will be a primary factor in motivating the student to be more interested in the material being presented. Further, improvements in teacher-student relationships will not only enhance teaching, but will be evidenced in student achievement as well. Thus, curriculum development becomes curriculum renewal as the chain of communication from student to teacher to curriculum committee becomes a continuous cycle of analysis and problem solving.

When teachers are encouraged to become involved and to contribute to curriculum improvement at levels beyond the classroom, they influence the degree to which their peers accept change. It is not surprising that teachers are willing to follow the lead of their peers rather than mandates imposed by outsiders. Ambrosie and Hanley (1991, p. 78) discovered that when change directives come from the central office, teachers react positively 38 percent of the time; when the impetus for change comes from other teachers, they react positively 86 percent of the time.

Educators (Kirk, 1988; Haberman, 1992; Ravitch, 1992; Fullan, 1993) agree that in the future teachers should and must be involved more in the curriculum than they have been in the past. In an article titled "Why Teachers Must Become Change Agents," Fullan (1993, p. 17) says:

> In the future the teacher must be equally at home, in the classroom, and in working with others to bring about continuous improvements.

## The Use of Incentives to Involve Teachers

Persuading teachers to expand their levels of involvement in curriculum matters will require special incentives, and although more money may contribute to this persuasion, money is not always the strongest motivator. Wright (1985) found that of the several incentives that are used to motivate teacher involvement, the most frequently identified incentives are intrinsic rewards, such as increased self-confidence, a sense of achievement or challenge, or the opportunity to develop new skills. Young (1985, p. 14) agrees that the power of intrinsic motivators is important, reporting that the number one motivator for teachers to become involved in curriculum development is their desire for personal involvement in decision making.

It should not be surprising that intrinsic motivators are influential on teachers' involvement in curriculum development within or outside their school; Maslow's hierarchy of needs clearly explains the force of such motivation. Yet one should not conclude that extrinsic motivators are unimportant. Psychologist Frederick Herzberg (Herzberg, Mausner, & Snyderman, 1959) uses Figure 8.2 to show the relationships between factors which prevent workers from being dissatisfied and factors which motivate individuals to do their best.

Through a series of teacher interviews, Young (1985) learned that lack of compensation for extra time spent working on committees and the absence of released time deterred teachers from considering involvement in curriculum development.

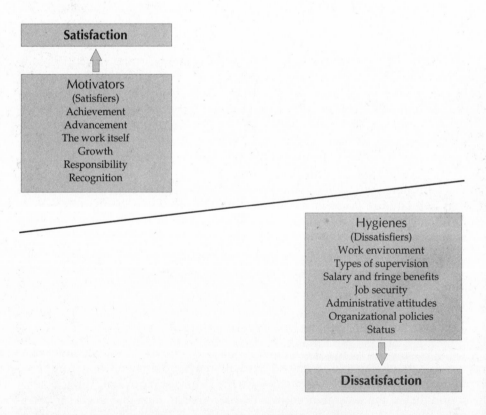

**Figure 8.2** Model of Herzberg et al, Two-Factor Motivation Theory.

## Providing Staff Development to Involve Teachers

Klein (1992, p. 96) says that one type of support-staff development is very important and explains why:

> Teachers will become more involved in curriculum decision making, which will require significantly more curriculum development skills and knowledge than they typically now have.

A major factor that inhibits many teachers from expanding their involvement arena is their uncertainty about what activities are appropriate for teachers. Obviously, as the teacher's role rapidly changes, the array of appropriate teacher activities increases. Some teachers are uncertain about what behavior is appropriate. A review of the literature (Joyce, 1990; Little, 1989; Rosenholtz, 1989) suggests that most teacher behavior is individualist, dealing with day-to-day operations because the culture of schools supports it. Yet Joyce (1990, p. 33) warns, "Without a balance between operations and the study of teaching and curriculum, the school is liable to drift toward obsolescence and fail to adapt to the needs of the surrounding society."

## Involving Teachers in Planning

The literature also provides suggestions as to how teachers can best be enticed to get involved. Early involvement, that is, during the planning stage, is especially important. Ravitch (1992) says that teachers should be involved in setting high standards and in rethinking the school's curriculum. This suggestion seems timely, because the U.S. Department of Education has begun to issue grants to several agencies to support the development of national educational standards. Haberman (1992) suggests that all who work on curricula have a responsibility for communicating the new curriculum to their peers and to the community at large. With all of these needs for techer involvement in school-wide planning, historically teachers have not been given adequate time to plan. Darling-Hammond (1993) concludes that American teachers are denied adequate time to plan because they are stereotyped as being relatively unimportant.

## Involving Teachers with Research

From its inception until the mid-twentieth century, the American school was the hub of all sorts of community activities. Cake walks and fish fries were common means of raising money for the schools; money which was given to the teacher to buy supplies which the teacher used to develop all aspects of the curriculum. In rural areas, the school building was the meetinghouse for the vocational associations (Farm Bureau, Future Farmers of America, Future

Homemakers of America, and 4-H Clubs), and in town the schoolhouse was used by civic groups. In both rural and urban settings, schools have served as polls. A special meeting at school brought in not only mom and dad but the entire extended family including grandparents, uncles, aunts, and cousins.

During this time, teachers were in charge of the entire curriculum. But increased urbanization, school growth and consolidation, and forced busing destroyed the concept of the school as the hub of the community. Federal and state curriculum mandates reshaped the curricula. By the early 1960s, prefabricated curricula were being manufactured at research and development centers and sent to the schools. The results of these changes have been (1) a diminishing of the *level* of the teacher's responsibility for curriculum development, and (2) a reduction in the *range* of teacher involvement in curriculum development, from schoolwide control to projects that are limited to their own classrooms.

Removing teachers from the center of schoolwide curriculum development has isolated them from research activities and kept them from seeing the need to verify their practices. It has also left teachers feeling left out of schoolwide decisions. Carson (1990, p. 167) expresses the problem this way:

> Rather than being active participants in school change, teachers have found themselves on the receiving end of criticism, new regulations, having to implement new programs, answering to external evaluations, and being responsible for more layers of bureaucratic management.

On the positive side, there have been some recent increases in the level of teacher involvement with research. And it has an historical precedent; a recent review of the literature revealed that, as early as 1908, efforts were made to involve classroom teachers in research (Lowery, 1908). The purpose of early teacher-conducted research was to develop curricula (McKernan, 1988), and this purpose has remained constant throughout the century. In recent years the term *action research* has been applied to teacher-conducted research. McCutcheon and Jung (1990, p. 144) define action research as "inquiry teachers undertake to understand and improve their own practice." When conducting action research, teachers may work alone or collaborate with others (Shalaway, 1990).

In spite of an enduring involvement by some teachers in research not all, or even many, teachers conduct research. On the contrary: Most teachers have purposefully avoided research, and for a number of reasons. For example, teachers often perceive research topics as too theoretical and too superficial (Chattin-McNichols & Loeffler, 1989). At least in part, this perception may result from the different natures of the teacher's world and the researcher's world. Cuban (1992) contrasts the two worlds, saying that the teacher's world is characterized by action and concrete facts, whereas researchers deal with abstractions and theory. Teachers want concrete answers to questions such as "What should I do?" Researchers are comfortable exploring possibilities.

But when teachers do become involved with research, significant gains are realized. For example, in general their teaching improves. Kirk (1988) says that, as teachers become involved with research, their style shifts from prescriptive to interactive. Stevens, Slaton, and Bunny (1992) say that, through involvement with research, teachers experience a renewed desire to stay current (see Sardo-Brown, 1992). As Boyer (1990, p. 57) expresses it, "As teachers become researchers they become learners." Nixon (1981, p. 9) says that "Action research serves primarily to sharpen perceptions, stimulate discussion, and energize questioning."

After becoming involved in conducting research, teachers are more critical, questioning their own beliefs and the assertions of others (Neilsen, 1990). Lytle and Cochran-Smith (1990, p. 101) say:

> As teachers begin to participate in the generation of knowledge about teaching, learning, and schooling, they become more critical of both university-based research and standard school practices. They challenge taken-for-granted assumptions about theory and practice.

Improved teacher attitude is another benefit that arises from teacher involvement with research. Bennett (1993, p. 69) says:

> I noted that teachers went into the research component of the program feeling anxious and hostile, but emerged feeling positive about the experience and their newly found identities as teacher-researchers.

Involvement of teachers in action research is viewed in contemporary literature as contributing to *teacher empowerment*. According to Carson (1990, p. 167), "Action research has been seen as a way of giving teaching back to teachers. As Tripp (1990, p. 165) says, "Action research enables teachers both to formulate and act upon their own concerns, thereby personally and professionally developing themselves within and through their practice."

Action research brings both perceptual and phenomenological benefits to teachers. First, involvement in research makes them more aware. One way to think about perceptual benefits is to consider what happens to teachers' perceptions when they are not involved in ongoing research: Sanger (1990, p. 175) says, " . . . as teachers, we gather to ourselves that which confirms our deepest underlying prejudices and attitudes."

Involvement in action research can move teachers beyond their perceptions, into their understandings and feelings about themselves and how they relate to their work. It can help teachers understand that, although they often believe that they have all the answers they need to do their daily work, they never really do. Each of us interprets the world about us in unique ways. Involvement in research can help teachers view their professional role more open-mindedly. As Carson (1990, p. 172) explains, "This requires an openness to our own experience and the experience of others, putting aside dogmatic arguments and preconceived opinions."

Increased understanding about ourselves in relation to the world around us opens the way to clearer, more honest relationships with others. Most current action research projects are collaborative efforts. McElroy (1990, pp. 209, 213) says that, "Being authentic (or real), for example, in our relationship with another is at the heart of collaborative action research, and is at the heart of a matter of ethics." He reports that his collaboration action research efforts have caused him to replace his concern for self with a greater connection, a freeing to experience more authentically. "This ego-less is not weakening; rather, it provides a feeling of strength, of standing firmly on a formless, shifting ground."

As faculties throughout the country are being "forced" to implement educational reform, it is evident to the outside observer that egos are threatened. Much, if not most, resistance comes from the threat teachers feel from the forced changes. When told that we must change, we infer that we have been doing something wrong; the message is that our performance is unacceptable. Few forces can fire the level of resistance that follows when individuals are told, either overtly or covertly, that they are unworthy. If, indeed, involvement in collaborative action research can free teachers from some of their need to protect their egos, the way to progress for school reform may be cleared.

Like theory, research and development are not linear, problem-answer processes. Since the goal is often to change the infrastructure of the school's curriculum, and since lasting change is a slow process, action research requires patience and commitment. Jack Sanger, an action research trainer (1990, p. 175), says, "The deepest and least changeable levels seem to accrete slowly through experience. Rather like a coral reef, 'significant' bits are drawn down from the surface of daily events and settle and fuse with deeper layers. They add to and complement what is already there."

There is also evidence that involvement with research prepares teachers for future change by making them more flexible and accepting to change. Bennett (1993, p. 69) addresses this idea:

> As teachers gained experience and success with research, their attitude toward research greatly improved. Teacher-researchers viewed themselves as being more open to change.

## Helping Teachers Become Researchers

Teacher research occurs in many different ways. One variable among the organizational structures of research activities is the teacher's role, which can range from that of passive assistant to that of an independent researcher or a full partner in research.

Not all teachers want to conduct research. Therefore, success in promoting teacher research depends on the selection of appropriate teachers, that is, teachers who have qualities conducive to conducting research. An obviously necessary quality is curiosity; teacher researchers must have questions for which they want answers—questions about their own teaching.

Another quality that facilitates the conducting of research is the habit of constant reading. Teacher researchers must read professional journals in their fields. As Shalaway (1990, p. 37) says, "Teacher researchers agree that all teachers can benefit by keeping up with the professional literature." This practice is essential because regular reading of the professional literature keeps teachers current and reflects an attitude of intellectual flexibility (Hattrup & Bickel, 1993).

An analysis of the benefits teachers derive from being involved with research found that most benefits are realized only when teachers are involved at the highest level. This type of involvement occurs only when teachers identify a problem that is important to them. As Chattin-McNichols and Loeffler (1989, p. 21) explain, identifying an important problem is easy:

> Classroom teachers are faced, on a daily basis, with questions that puzzle and concern them in their interactions with children. Many of these questions provide appropriate material for microresearch projects for teachers to carry out in their classrooms.

Once a problem is selected for study, the investigator must define the problem. Part of this identification might include establishing a baseline, which the Reading/Language in Secondary Schools Subcommittee of the International Reading Association (1989) says is essential. A baseline or benchmark provides a starting place for measuring improvement. A baseline can be established by using a pretest or simply by gathering data.

Once the baseline is established, the investigating teacher(s) should implement the change strategies and then follow up by testing to determine the amount of progress. Chattin-McNichols and Loeffler (1989) stress the importance of full teacher involvement in every stage of the research. Cardelle-Elawar (1993) developed the model for initiating teacher research shown in Figure 8.3.

## The IDEA Model

Cardelle-Elawar (1993) developed the model shown in Figure 8.3 to show a linear set of steps that leads to problem solving. Since good changes often involve solving problems, this model is ideal for helping teachers change. Although it was designed to help teachers become classroom researchers, its implications for helping teachers change are much broader.

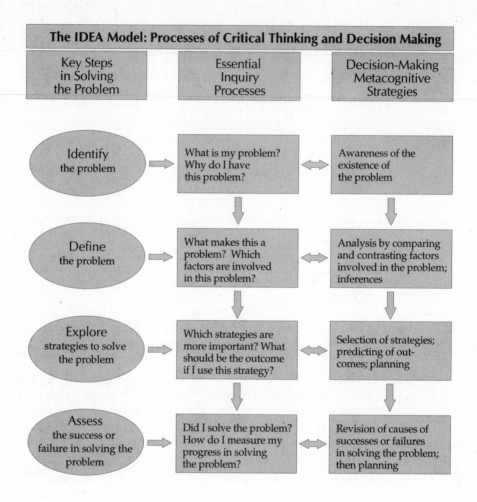

**Figure 8.3**  A strategy for helping teachers become researchers in the classroom.

## STAFF DEVELOPMENT

Staff development first became popular as a way to improve schools in the early 1940s as a result of the Eight-Year Study (Schubert, 1986), which was described in Chapter 2. For almost two decades the National Council of States on In-Service Education (NCSIE) has provided a forum for staff developers to share their research and experiences. Current education reform programs have raised the level of support provided for teachers to unprecedented heights. A description of the history and goals of the NCSIE follows.

## The NCSIE[2]

The National Council of States on In-Service Education (NCSIE), founded in 1975, is dedicated to a collective and shared approach to improving education and empowering all educators through effective, proactive leadership and continuing professional development. The organization enables state education agency personnel to work in coequal partnerships with personnel from schools, colleges and universities, professional organizations, and the private sector on topics such as educational reform, school empowerment, site-based and collaborative management, leadership development for educators, systemic planning, total quality management, recruitment and retention of minorities, at-risk teachers and students, alternative delivery systems, accountability, outcomes-based education, and equitable opportunities for all students. NCSIE is a cohort of dedicated and enthusiastic people with a unique vision of how to deal with the problems of education and professional development that we are facing today. It is a collection of educators who possess a solid understanding of what constitutes good education and how to provide it. NCSIE members are committed to working jointly with the "family of educators" locally, statewide, and nationally. They are concerned with empowering the individual and enriching the lives of all Americans.

The goals of NCSIE are:

- To provide positive, proactive leadership at the national, state, and local levels, within and among the states.
- To provide leadership at the national level in the identification, development, and dissemination of exemplary staff, leadership, and faculty development programs.
- To improve education through effective leadership and professional development.
- To assist educational agencies in accomplishing their goals, particularly as they relate to planning, implementing, and evaluating staff development programs.
- To assist in the development of national, state, and local educational priorities and to provide optimal solutions to the problems and concerns of members of the NCSIE organizations, including a comprehensive view on preservice, induction, and professional development.
- To empower people and thereby reform and renew education.

---

[2]For further information, contact NCSIE, 402 Huntington Hall, Syracuse University, Syracuse, NY 13244-2340.

- To work with states and, through them, professional organizations, schools, universities, and so on, to develop frameworks and systems for relevant and authentic educational reform.

- To encourage systemic and coherent policy development and implementation.

- To develop broad-based frameworks for decision making at the national, state, and local levels.

- To create strategies for coordinating systemic, state-initiated reform with local school-based reform.

- To develop flexible governance structures that allow for sufficient local autonomy to ensure that local needs can be met.

- To serve as a vehicle to bring together all members of the profession in a "partnership for the improvement of education."

For almost 20 years, the NCSIE has been involved in a succession of national and statewide programs and activities. Among its many accomplishments, the NCSIE has played an active role in:

- Facilitating statewide and multistate planning and national coordination of professional development programs.

- Awarding subcontracts to provide consultant and technical assistance to states and to facilitate the development and implementation of statewide leadership and staff development programs in conjunction with the Council of Chief State School Officers and other organizations.

- Coplanning, implementing, and monitoring state and local meetings as part of state minicontracts.

- Designing, developing, conducting, and evaluating hundreds of national, regional, statewide, and local meetings, including 17 large annual national conferences.

- Developing numerous manuscripts and position papers as well as publishing the Professional Development Monograph Series.

- Disseminating information, articles, and publications nationally via the National Dissemination Center.

- Publishing a national newsletter.

The NCSIE is an organization of and for educators who want to be on the cutting edge of education—educators who want a stake in the future of education and the opportunity to be part of a network to improve education as the United States heads into the twenty-first century (Collins, 1993).

## Consortia

Like the NCSIE, other professional organizations—especially state education association chapters—are dedicated to helping teachers become empowered and prepared to assume greater curriculum leadership roles. Many workshops are required to prepare in-service teachers and administrators for the reform challenges in their state, but even the best workshops are no better than the degree to which the objectives, content, and skills they cover match the needs of the teachers and administrators who attend the workshops. One organizational structure used to achieve the match of content and needs is the consortium.

An *educational consortium* is a formal coalition of two or more school districts designed to aid them in achieving common goals. Educational consortia work much like traditional agricultural and vocational education cooperatives. Member school districts pool their resources to purchase services which no district could afford by itself.

## Staff Development Problems

Staff development makes specific demands of its leaders. When those demands are not met, problems arise. Reporting on a study by the Southern Education Consortium, Purvis and Boren (1991, p.21) identified three major problems related to staff development: "(1) "Incentives for attendance are lacking, (2) programs are not related to teachers' needs and interests, and (3) staff development programs are not well organized and thought out carefully enough."

## Responsibilities of Staff Development Leaders

Myrick and Jones (1991, pp. 3–6) suggest the following roles and responsibilities of staff development leaders:

- Leaders must be aware of new practices in curriculum and instruction.
- Leaders must help develop a vision for their school.
- Leaders must communicate the school's or department's mission and goals.
- Leaders must be team members.
- Leaders must secure financing.
- Leaders must conduct assessments.
- Leaders must value growing.
- Leaders must earn trust.

- Leaders must remain open-minded.
- Leaders must recognize contributions by others.

Interestingly, some of these responsibilities seem to apply to any educational leader, not just to the staff development leader. Clearly, the education reform reports have changed the role of education leaders quite dramatically, making it broader and increasing their management responsibilities. Education reform has pressed for participation in management as a means of empowering teachers because, as indicated earlier, there is evidence that successful involvement of teachers in managing the schools is essential to maximum educational improvement.

Poplin (1992) discusses this shift in the role of educational leaders, making several points that deserve repeating. First, the role of educational leaders has, indeed, changed, becoming much broader. The teacher must be prepared to manage a broad spectrum of the school's business, including financial and curriculum decisions, heretofore outside the teacher's purview. Second, today's leaders must provide a climate that lets teachers expand their horizons. Third, the contemporary leader must help teachers develop skills they can use to evaluate their own performance. Fourth, today's leaders must protect teachers' time (this translates into providing released time from regular assignments). In short, Poplin describes today's leader as a highly skilled manager, able to provide latitude, freedom, support, and encouragement for teachers to grow and become less dependent on their leadership.

All curriculum leaders, including department and grade-level chairs, need these types of skills. For many leaders, the greatest challenge may be to bring about the changes in attitude that will be required to provide leadership or managership while working alongside other teachers.

## A NEED TO GO BEYOND CURRENT HORIZONS

This chapter has stressed the need to examine the teacher's work environment and to provide fiscal and physical support to curriculum leaders and to their colleagues as they work together to improve the curriculum. As discussed, this kind of support is essential for effective leadership, but success requires more. Curriculum leaders must be motivated to achieve beyond their previous levels. Remember John Dewey's human development goal: That each culture would be elevated above its previous culture through the development of individuals. In other words, as essential as the tools needed to do the job are, success requires more: teachers must be motivated to want to exceed the accomplishments of the previous generation.

# SCHOOL CULTURE AND CLIMATE

Anyone who has worked with schools knows that each school has its own culture, its own ethos. Schools are like homes: Some make you feel welcome; others don't. Some schools send a message that they are exciting places to be. Some schools are threatening; others offer security. Some are as dead as a petrified forest; others are like a freeway during rush hour—people have places to go and they are eager to get there. As McNeil (1990, p. 196) says, "The idea of a school having an ethos, being distinct from other schools, and subjecting all aspects of school life to this quality is powerful."

Kowalski and Reitzug (1993, p. 311) describe the relationship between a school's climate and the variables that interact to form its climate: culture, milieu, ecology, social system, and organization. They emphasize the important role that school culture plays in changing schools:

> There are three common perspectives of how change occurs in organizations. The first is a technical view erected on an assumption that increased knowledge and technical assistance produce change. This approach assumes rationality and focuses on the nature of the innovation (e.g., a new program). The second perspective accounts for power and influence that may be used by groups and individuals to support or ward off change. The focus is political behavior, and attention is given to both the innovation and the context of the organization. The third perspective looks at the shared values, beliefs, and norms of the organization. It is identified as the cultural perspective and emphasizes the importance of organizational context (Rossman, Corbett, & Firestone, 1988). After more than ten years of attempted reform, educators and the general public are recognizing the limitations of the first two approaches. Hence, more recent reform efforts have focused largely on the third category. More precisely, second wave change efforts are inquiring about the ways in which culture produces barriers that prevent change.
>
> Imagine a situation in which a third-grade teacher is considering whether to administer corporal punishment to a disruptive student. What factors affect the decision? First, the teacher's behavior is influenced by personal values, experiences, and beliefs regarding the moral and practical dimensions of hitting a child. Additionally, the teacher hopefully considers whether corporal punishment is acceptable professionally and legally. The third, and often most influential, component is the teacher's perception of what the school expects from him or her. In other words, the teacher considers the school's norms. Do other teachers use corporal punishment? Does the principal advocate it? In some combination, the teacher weighs personal considerations (e.g., personal beliefs, motivations), legal and professional dimensions, and school-specific norms. Thus, even though the teacher may reject the use of corporal punishment, both personally and professionally, the act still may be carried out because of social pressures maintained by the school.

Sagor (1992) testifies to the importance of school culture and to the contribution that good leaders make to their school's culture. Sagor says that these principals use three building blocks of transformational leadership: (1) a clear and unified focus, (2) a cultural perspective, and (3) a constant push for improvement.

Good leaders may have highly different styles, but they also have some qualities in common. According to Sagor, good leaders never quit asking questions about practices that affect learning, and they give their teachers latitude and meaningful personal support.

## FORCES THAT PROMOTE AND IMPEDE CHANGE

At any school, forces work to make improvements, and other forces work to impede change. Basom and Crandall (1991, pp. 74–75) have identified seven common barriers to change:

- A discontinuity of leadership deters change (many schools have frequent personnel changes in key leadership positions).
- Many educators view change as unmanageable (administrators and teachers do not believe that they can bring about purposeful change).
- Educators have not been properly prepared to deal with the complexity of restructuring schools (administrators and teachers know little about organizational behavior, conflict management, and other related topics).
- In following a "top-down" approach to making decisions, educators have not relied on research and craft knowledge to inform their decisions (decision makers have not been required to justify their decisions).
- Educators are conditioned and socialized by the format of schooling they experienced and understand (they believe that school structure is not the problem).
- There are conflicting visions of what schools should become (teachers and administrators cannot agree on what changes are needed or what goals should be established).
- Time and resources have been insufficient (time and money are not available to conduct necessary staff development).

As you read this list, you may have noticed that some items are conceptual, relating to traditional ideas about the schools and how improvement should occur (e.g., top-down approach) and some are real barriers (e.g., lack of funds, hopeless attitude). Other barriers result from the newness of restructuring and can be reduced as the knowledge base on restructuring grows. Hopefully, in the 1990s educators now realize the importance of collecting data and writing cases that reflect the problems they face, and that they recognize the victories they will win when they overcome these problems as they accept new challenges such as restructuring. For example, leaders often need help in convincing their peers that their school really does have a problem, and they need the skills to lead their teachers to develop a clear mission and goals.

## LEADERSHIP

Good leaders have the capacity to go beyond their own goals and help teachers exceed the leader's imagination. Tewel (1991, p. 13) explains what the leader should do:

- Offer a menu of ideas.
- Encourage teachers to plan new initiatives on their own.
- Reward teacher independence and creativity.
- Decentralize decision making.

All designated curriculum directors, principals, vice principals, department and grade-level chairs, and individuals designated or elected to effect changes in the curricula at some point must deal with diversity among their team (the teachers). The emerging natural leaders who stand like the U.S. Marines, ready to go into action at any moment, are an asset to any organization, but their value is defined by the support they receive from their leaders. The naysayers, who have perhaps the clearest vision of their role in life—to share their cynicism, doubts, and complaints with anyone who will listen—have the power to sabotage almost any operation, if they are neglected by the school's leaders. The contributions of the members of the critical mass, who absorb conflicting messages from the other groups as they wait to do what they must, will be determined by the leadership they receive. Left alone, the majority will do little or nothing; correctly motivated, they often surprise even themselves with their contributions.

No leader knows exactly how much time and energy to assign to these different groups; yet experienced leaders know that because the naysayers are the loudest they often get the most attention. The "squeaky wheel" often forces leaders to focus their attention, and to use most of their time and resources, to try to redirect, appease, or subdue this group. This is usually a mistake, because this group can seldom be redirected or subdued.

Although the naysayers seem to be aggressive, and aggressiveness suggests self-confidence, they may be suffering from low self-esteem. Research (Schomoker, 1992, p. 94) has suggested that the best way to help individuals improve their self-esteem is to direct them to goal-oriented activity that is linked to some social or positive purpose. Although this approach sounds logical and simple, building self-esteem is not easy. Research done by the California Task Force (Dettloff, 1993) shows a low success rate for self-esteem programs.

## Using Power

Leaders have several types of power at their disposal. By being aware of the sources of power, leaders can often increase their power and improve the ways they use it. Steers, Ungson, and Mowday (1985) have identified five types of leadership power: (1) reward power, (2) punishment power, (3) legitimate power, (4) expert power, and (5) referent power. In addition, the ability to build consensus confers power.

*Reward power* and *punishment power* are often combined and collectively called *coercive power*. Of the first two types, reward power is the more appropriate power to wield when dealing with professionals; merit pay is an example of the use of reward power. However, many current state school reform programs are using both reward power and punishment power to increase academic achievement. Baselines for performance are established for each school. If the achievement scores fall significantly below the baseline, the school may be put on warning or probation and given a designated time to raise its achievement scores to an acceptable level. If the school fails, a variety of punishments, including removal of the local governing body, may be implemented. It is not out of the question for the local administrators to be fired.

Current education reform programs are also using reward power. Again, baselines are set. In addition, levels above the baseline are established. A school can earn a dollar amount for each level achieved above the baseline. In some instances, this money can even be used as bonus pay for teachers.

*Legitimate power* is power sanctioned by the organization. For example, the chair of the high school science department has power simply because of holding this position.

Educational leaders rely heavily on *expert power*, derived from having special knowledge and skills, and *referent power*, which comes from the ability to get others to identify with their leader and imitate their leader. As teachers themselves become empowered and educational leaders become better managers, referent power grows increasingly indispensable for educational leaders.

Expert power, too, is indispensable for educational leaders. But the type of expertise required of educational leaders has changed. More than ever before, this expertise comes not so much from acquired cognitive knowledge but from growth in the affective domain. Future educational leaders will have to be experts in coping with the unknown. Much security is relinquished as fellow teachers are placed in leadership roles. A power shift occurs when site-based decision-making teams (often called *school councils*) take on problems and make decisions that a single individual (for example, the principal or superintendent) lacks the expertise to handle.

Another type of expertise that is quickly becoming indispensable for the educational leader is consensus development. No longer can the leader make unilateral choices; rather, a leader must lead the team to consensus. Interestingly, as a local decision-making team perfects this skill, the team also gains power. Steers, Ungson, and Mowday (1985, p. 436) acknowledge this type of power:

> In general, the more cohesion and homogeneity a group or collection of groups has on a particular issue, the greater its influence.

Of the various types of power, some are derived from the organization, and some are inherent in the leader. True leaders always depend on expert, referent, and consensus-building power. Steers, Ungson, and Mowday (1985, p. 307) have said that "Leadership exists when subordinates *voluntarily* comply because of something the leader has done."

## The Future of Educational Leadership

Predicting the future is always risky, but leaders have the responsibility to do just that. The risk can be reduced by gathering as much information as possible and using that information in predicting. Notice that the task is to predict the future of educational leadership, *not* to predict what type of leadership the future will bring. There is a subtle but powerful difference between the two concepts. The latter assumes that educational leaders will exist in some form; the former makes no such assumption.

There is reason to consider the possibility that educational leadership is becoming moribund, and education reform is the likeliest culprit. Holzman (1992, p. 36) asks, "Are we sure that leadership itself and the cult of personal leadership are not in large measure the problem with public education in the United States today?" There has been a radical shift in the role of the leader, away from leadership as we have known it.

Sergiovanni (1992, pp. 41, 42, 45) says that teachers become more committed and self-managing when schools become the committees, freeing principals from the burden of trying to control people. He blames leadership for standing in the way of an exploration of alternative ways to run the schools. He also points out that leadership is something that someone does to others, whereas the greatest improvement in our schools and teachers is likely to come from within the teachers. Although he never says it, Sergiovanni "leads" his readers to suspect, if not conclude, that leadership also hampers professionalism:

> Both professionalism and leadership are frequently prescribed as cures for school problems, but in many ways the two concepts are antithetical. The more professionalism is emphasized, the less leadership is needed. The more leadership is emphasized, the less likely it is the professionalism will develop.

Sergiovanni concludes by saying, "In time, direct leadership will become less and less important, self-management will take hold, and substitutes for leadership will become more deeply embedded in the school."

## SUMMARY

The role of educational leaders is changing dramatically and rapidly. In the past, these leaders served as curriculum troubleshooters who located and fixed problems. Now, curriculum development is a continuing process that does not require problems to get attention. Education reform has brought curriculum development to the center of attention.

Traditionally, most teachers have handicapped themselves by avoiding involvement with research and with the school outside their classroom. However, to bring student performance to the levels called for in the reform reports will require teachers to become involved with the total curriculum.

Successful teacher involvement in restructuring will require that they develop skills in research, in curriculum development, and in working cooperatively with other teachers, administrators, and parents. The leader must help by providing staff development and by managing teams of teachers as they work on the curriculum. Such successful management will require skills in using power, especially expert power and referent power. As teachers become empowered, educational leaders will no longer be able to depend on traditional types of power (legitimate and coercive) but will be required to become more proficient in developing and using referent power.

Contemporary and future leaders must determine the needs of individuals and faculties and arrange for staff development that addresses these needs. One method that has proved to be effective is the consortium.

In the future, educational leaders, as they have been viewed in the past, may no longer be in demand. If the term *leader* continues to be used in this context, the "leaders" will have to be adept in management skills and will have to trust their colleagues to set goals and make all types of important decisions.

## QUESTIONS

1. How are educational research and education reform related?
2. Why do teachers avoid research?
3. Why does education reform require teachers to expand their horizons?
4. What are some intrinsic motivators that can be used to help teachers become involved in improving their schools?
5. How can educational leaders ensure that staff development workshops will match the teachers' needs?
6. What are some responsibilities of staff development leaders?
7. How have the education reform reports altered the role of educational leaders?

8. Why is teacher empowerment a major goal of education reform?

9. How does Herzberg's two-factor theory relate to educational leadership?

10. What types of power do educational leaders need most? Why?

11. Why must educational leaders change their perception of their need for security?

## SUGGESTED FURTHER ACTIVITIES

1. Curriculum change has become a continuous process. Develop a calendar which you can use to help fellow teachers make curriculum improvements throughout the year. Designate times for (1) developing a needs assessment, (2) conducting a needs assessment, (3) setting goals, (4) planning workshops, (5) advertising workshops, and (6) giving the workshops.

2. The success of an educational consortium depends on a match between the staff development offered and the needs and desires of its members. Design a system that will communicate the relevance of programs offered throughout the year and will show the relationship between the goals of the workshops and the needs of the consortium members.

3. As leaders prepare for their new roles as managers, their success requires good human relations skills. Choose a current education reform practice from the list in paragraph 1, page 2, and prepare a presentation to use during an open house to convince parents of the importance of this reform element.

## QUESTIONS ON THE EDUCATIONAL EXCELLENCE LABORATORY CONSORTIUM

1. What responsibility do you believe the directors of such consortia have for determining the most critical needs of their clients?

2. How do you think consortia directors can learn what services a district needs most?

3. Most of the workshops the consortium provided were given on site in the school districts. How important is this? Why?

4. The membership cost for each school district is based on the number of its students. Why is this important?

5. How can a consortium afford services that a district cannot afford? After all, the consortium gets no funding beyond that given to the schools.

## BIBLIOGRAPHY

Ambrosie, Frank, & Hanley, P. W. (1991, October). "The role of the curriculum specialist in site-based management." *NASSP Bulletin, 75*(537), 73–81.

Barth, R. S. (1990). A personal vision of a good school. *Phi Delta Kappan, 71*(7), 512–516.

Basom, R. E., & Crandall, D. P. (1991). Implementing a redesign strategy: Lessons from educational change *Educational Horizons, 69*(2), 73–77.

Bellon, J. J., Bellon, E. E., & Blank, M. A. (1992). *Teaching from a research knowledge base.* New York: Macmillan.

Bennett, C. K. (1993). Teacher-researchers: All dressed up and no place to go. *Educational Leadership, 51*(2), 69–70.

Boyer, E. (1982). A conversation with Ernest Boyer. *Change, 41*(1), 18–21.

Boyer, E. (1990). *Scholarship reconsidered.* New York: Carnegie Foundation for the Advancement of Teaching.

Bracey, G. W. (1991). Teachers as researchers. *Phi Delta Kappan, 72*(5), 404–405.

Brown, D. S. (1990). Middle level teachers' perceptions of action research. *Middle School Journal,* pp. 30–32.

Bushman, J. H. (1991, November–December). Reshaping the secondary curriculum. *The Clearing House, 65*(2), 83–85.

Cardelle-Elawar, M. (1993). The teacher as researcher in the classroom. *Action in Teacher Education, 15*(1), 49–57.

Carson, Terry (1990). What kind of knowing is critical action research? *Theory Into Practice, 29*(3), 167–173.

Chattin-McNichols, J., & Loeffler, M. H. (1989). Teachers as researchers: The first cycle of the teachers' research network. *Young Children, 44*(5), 20–27.

Collins, James (1993). Unpublished statement of policy.

Cooper, L. R. (1991). Teachers as researchers. *Kappa Delta Pi Record, 27*(4), 115–117.

Conley, D. T. (1991, September). Eight steps to improved teacher remediation. *NASSP Bulletin, 75*(536), 26–39.

Cornett, J. W. (1990). Utilizing action research in graduate curriculum courses. *Theory into Practice, 29*(3), 185–193.

Csikszentmihalyi, M. (1990). *Flow: The psychology of optional experience.* New York: Harcourt Brace Jovanovich.

Cuban, L. (1992). Managing dilemmas while building professional communities. *Educational Researcher, 21*(1), 4–11.

Cuban, L. (1993). The lure of curricular reform and its pitiful history. *Phi Delta Kappan, 75*(2), 182–185.

Darling-Hammond, L. (1993). Reframing the school reform agenda. *Phi Delta Kappan, 74*(10), 753–761.

Dettloff, E. (1993). "Go slow on self-esteem." *Phi Delta Kappan, 74*(6), 504.

Egbert, R. L. (1984). The role of research in teacher education. In R. L. Egbert & M. M. Kluender (Eds.), *Using research to improve teacher education.* Lincoln, NE.: American Association of Colleges for Teacher Education.

Eisner, E. W. (1990). Who decides what schools teach? *Phi Delta Kappan, 71*(7), 523–526.

Enns-Connolly, E. (1990). "Second language curriculum development as dialectic process." *The Canadian Modern Language Review*, 46, 500–513.

Fullan, M. G. (1993). "Why teachers must become change agents." *Educational Leadership, 50*(6), 12–17.

Fullan, M. G. & Stiegelbauer, S. (1990). *The new meaning of educational change* (2nd ed.). New York: Columbia University Teachers College Press.

Garrison, J. W. (1988). Democracy, scientific knowledge, and teacher empowerment. *Teachers College Record, 89*(4), 487–504.

Haberman, Martin (1992, November). The role of the classroom teacher as a curriculum leader. *NASSP Bulletin, 76*(547), 11–19.

Hattrup, V., & Bickel, W. E. (1993). Teacher-researcher collaboration: Resolving the tensions. *Educational Leadership, 50*(6), 38–40.

Henson, K. T. (1996). Teachers as researchers. In J. Sikula, T. J. Buttery, & E. Guyton (Eds.), *Handbook of Research on teacher education* (2nd ed.). Arlington, VA: Association of Teacher Educators.

Henson, K. T. & Saterfiel, T. H. (1968, June). These schools join forces to share the research load and their findings. *The American School Board Journal, 173*(6), 40–42.

Herzberg, F., Mausner, B., & Snyderman, B. (1959). *The motivation to work.* New York: Wiley.

Holzman, Michael (1992, February). Do we really need "leadership"? *Educational Leadership, 49*(5), 36–40.

Houser, N. O. (1990). Teacher-researcher: The synthesis of roles for teacher empowerment. *Action in Teacher Education*, 12(2), 55–60.

Joyce, B. (1990). "The self-educating teacher: Empowering teachers through research." In B. Joyce (Ed.), *Changing school culture through staff development* (ASCD Yearbook). Arlington, VA: Association for Supervision and Curriculum Development.

Kant, Immanuel (1793). *On the old saw: That may be right in theory but it won't work in practice* (E. B. Ashton, Trans., 1974). Philadelphia: University of Pennsylvania Press.

Kearney, K., & Tashlik, P. (1985). Collaboration and conflict: Teacher and researchers learning. *Language Arts, 62*(7), 765–769.

King, Margaret (1991, September). Cooperative planning workshops: Helping teachers improve. *NASSP Bulletin, 75*(536), 42–46.

Kirk, D. (1988). Ideology and school-centered innovation: A case study and a critique. *Journal of Curriculum Studies, 20*, 449–464.

Klein, M. F. (1992, Summer). A perspective on the gap between curricula theory and practice. *Theory Into Practice, 31*, 191–197.

Kowalski, T. J., & Reitzug, V. C. (1993). *Contemporary school administration*. New York: Longman.

Little, J. (1989). The persistance of privacy: Autonomy and initiations in teachers' professional relations. Paper presented at the annual meeting of the American Educational Research Association in San Francisco.

Lowery, L. (1908). *The relation of superintendents and principals to the training and professional improvement of their teachers*. Seventh yearbook for the National Society for the Study of Education. Pt. I. Chicago: University of Chicago Press.

Lytle, S. L., & Cochran-Smith, M. (1990). Learning from teacher research: A working topology. *Teachers College Record, 92*(1), 83–103.

McCutcheon, C., and Jung, B. (1990). Alternative perspectives on action research. In A. Oberg and G. McCutcheon (Eds.), *Theory into Practice, 29*(3), 144–151.

McElroy, Lon (1990). Becoming real: An ethic at the heart of action research. *Theory into Practice, 29*(3), 209–213.

McKernan, J. (1988). Teacher as researcher: Paradigm or praxis. *Contemporary Education, 59*(3), 154–158.

McNeil, J. D. (1990). *Curriculum: A comprehensive introduction* (4th ed.). New York: HarperCollins.

Myrick, Paula, & Jones, Ron (1991, September). "How instructional leaders view staff development." *NASSP Bulletin, 75*(536), 1–6.

Neilsen, L. (1990, November). Research comes home. *Reading Teacher, 44*(1), 248–250.

Newsome, G. L. (1964). In what sense is theory a guide to practice in education? *Educational Theory, 14*, 36.

Nixon, (1981). *A teacher's guide to action research*. London: Grants McIntyre.

Poplin, M. S. (1992, February). The leader's new role: Looking to the growth of teachers. *Educational Leadership, 49*(5), 10–11.

Purvis, J. R., & Boren, L. C. (1991, September). Planning, implementing a staff development program. *NASSP Bulletin, 75*(536), 16–24.

Ravitch, Diane (1992, December). National standards and curriculum reform: A view from the Department of Education, *NASSP Bulletin, 76*(548), 24–29.

Reading/Language in Secondary Schools Subcommittee of the International Reading Association (1989). Classroom research: The teacher as researcher. *Journal of Reading, 33*(3), 216–218.

Reis, S. M., and Renzolli, J. S. (1992, October). Using curriculum compacting to challenge the above average. *Educational Leadership, 50*(2), 51–57.

Rosenholtz, S. J. (1989). *Teachers' workplace: The organization of schools*. White Plains, NY: Longman.

Rossman, G. B., Corbett, H. D., and Firestone, W. A. (1988). *Effectiveness in Schools: A cultural perspective*. Albany: State University of New York.

Russell, B. (1958). *Religion and science*. Oxford: Oxford University Press.

Sagor, R. D. (1992, February). Three principals who make a difference. *Educational Leadership, 49*(5), 13–18.

Sanger, Jack (1990). Awakening a scream of consciousness: The critical group in action research. *Theory Into Practice, 29*(3), 174–178.

Sardo-Brown, D. (1992). Elementary teachers' perceptions of action research. *Action in Teacher Education, 14*(2), 55–59.

Schomoker, Mike (1992, November). What really promotes self-esteem? *Educational Leadership, 50*(3), 94.

Schubert, W. H. (1986). *Curriculum: Perspective, paradigm, & possibility*. New York: Macmillan.

Sergiovanni, T. J. (1992, February). Why we should seek substitutes for leadership. *Educational Leadership, 49*(5), 41–45.

Shalaway, L. (1990). Tap into teacher research. *Instructor, 100*(1), 34–38.

Stefanich, G. P. (1990). Cycles of cognition. *Middle School Journal, 22*(2), 47–52.

Steers, R. M., Ungson, G. R., & Mowday, R. T. (1985). *Managing effective organizations*. Boston: Kent.

Stevens, K. B., Slaton, D. B., & Bunny, S. (1992). A collaborative research effort between public school and university faculty members. *Teacher Education and Special Education, 15*(1), 1–8.

Taba, Hilda (1962). *Curriculum development: Theory and practice*. Orlando, FL: Harcourt Brace Jovanovich.

Tewel, K. J. (1991, October). Promoting change in secondary schools. *NASSP Bulletin, 75*(537), 10–17.

Tripp, D. H. (1990). Socially critical action research. *Theory Into Practice, 29*(3), 158–166.

Tyack, D. (1990). Restructuring in historical perspective: Tinkering toward utopia. *Teachers College Record, 92*(2), 170–191.

Wright, R. (1985). Motivating teacher involvement in professional growth activities. *The Canadian Administrator, 5*, 1–6.

Young, J. H. (1985). The curriculum decision-making preferences of school personnel. *The Alberta Journal of Educational Research, 25*, 20–29.

# Chapter 9

# EVALUATING INSTRUCTION AND THE CURRICULUM

## OBJECTIVES

This chapter should prepare you to:

- Discuss the impact of education reform on curriculum evaluation.
- Explain the role of curriculum alignment in education reform.
- Give an example of progress reporting and either challenge or defend its use in the schools.
- Differentiate between the use of norm-referenced evaluation and criterion-referenced evaluation in elementary and secondary schools.
- Write a brief mission statement for a school and use this statement to write three aims for the school.
- Give two ways that curriculum balance should be evaluated.
- Give an example of the proper relationships among curriculum articulation, continuity, and scope.

## REGIONAL ACCREDITATION SITE VISIT

By Sunday afternoon, cars from across the state and a few from out of state begin converging at a local motel. The next three days will be grueling for these university professors, public school administrators, and teachers, for as a regional accrediting team, these 12 educators will arrive each morning by 7:30 a.m. at Hillsboro Middle School, where they will visit classes, study records, and interview administrators, teachers, counselors, and students. Even the custodians and lunchroom workers will not escape their scrutiny. Each day, about 4 p.m., the team members will reassemble in their workroom at the school, drive back to their hotel, have an hour for dinner, and begin discussing what they saw and making plans for the next day. If all goes well, they will get to bed about midnight. If not, they will work until 2 or 3 o'clock in the morning. They all know what lies ahead. They also know that, if they are lucky, there will be some good humor along the way. But the real reward from working these long hours with-out pay will come from the knowledge that, by conducting a thorough evalua-tion of the entire school, they will be helping this school improve itself.

The next two days prove to be both successful and enjoyable. The team members who are teachers spend several hours in classrooms watching teachers in their respective disciplines teach. Ironically, teachers rarely have an opportu-nity to see how other teachers organize their curricula and manage their lessons. This is one of the professional benefits of participating on such a team. The counselor and the two administrators on the team also spend time with their counterparts at Hillsboro Middle School.

But the classroom and office visits are only part of the overall observations of this school. As these team members walk down the halls, and even during lunch, they constantly observe the teachers and students.

Several team members notice that the school's faculty has practically no minority members. The minority student representation at Hillsboro is also extremely low, and this, too, concerns some of the team members.

Because of the hectic schedule, Wednesday comes faster than the team thought possible and the visit is complete, except for the detailed written report that the chair must prepare and mail to the principal. As they anticipated, the work was hard, but they did have some chuckles. Mr. Sims, a member of the team, is a veteran superintendent who is proud of his school district and likes to talk about his schools. But during their initial meeting, the team chair had set a rule that any members who talked about their own professional experiences would have to put a quarter in the kitty. At the end of the visit, the money would be used to buy refreshments for the group to enjoy while celebrating the com-pletion of the evaluation.

Each time Mr. Sims started to talk about his schools, he was interrupted and reminded to put a quarter in the pot. In one meeting, after he had deposited three quarters, he became so frustrated that he raised his hand to silence every-one, reached into his wallet, took out a $10 bill, and, dropping it into the kitty, said, "Now all of you are going to shut up until I finish my story." And they did! After that, Mr. Sims received a lot of respect.

Accreditation visits can have some surprises. On this visit, the surprise came early. Sunday evening was special because the administrators and the school board had an opportunity to express their appreciation to the team members for giving their time and energy to the important goal of helping the school improve. The dinner was nice—very nice. But it was the entertainment that surprised the team members most. They had not expected to be entertained by an orchestra, but the fact that the school's students made up the orchestra was astonishing. None of the evaluators had ever known of a middle school that had an orches-tra, and the youngsters performed like professional musicians.

Accreditation visits usually reveal some weaknesses, too, and this one was no exception. Apart from the lack of minority representation, the greatest disap-pointment was in the science department. More accurately, it *would have been* in the science department, had there been one. Actually, the entire three grades offered only one course in science, and that course wasn't required of all students. This meant that some graduates of the school entered high school having had no science in their program. A closer look revealed that the school's outstanding music curriculum was complemented by a superb art curriculum. In other words, the school had an outstanding fine arts curriculum at the expense of having no science program.

One of the team members, a professor of curriculum and instruction, was assigned the task of coordinating the part of the report that focused on the school's instructional program. She referred to her notes as she described to the team her impressions of the English curriculum:

> The English curriculum has a purposeful sequence. Within the year, each topic leads to the next, and each year builds on the preceding year.
>
> Within and between years, the content is continuous and free of disruptions. I would say that the English curriculum has excellent sequence and continuity.
>
> I do question the scope of this curriculum. It seems a little skewed, a little narrow in that there is more literature than composition. I wonder whether this arrangement is used to raise the achievement test scores.
>
> As you know, each year this school ranks near the top on the state achievement test scores.
>
> As for the social studies curriculum, it seems to be in good shape. It has both good scope and good sequence. Nothing major is missing. The math curriculum is about the same. I saw one thing that bothered me: an absence of integration. For example, I didn't find any trace of math in the social studies department, and vice versa. I wonder why the math department doesn't have assignments that address social problems. I didn't see much in the way of writing assignments being required outside the English Department. Thus, I would say that the curriculum lacks integration. I believe that many of these shortcomings could be overcome if the school's curriculum had a more contemporary focus. More topics such as urban living and cultural pluralism are needed.
>
> I also examined the testing program. The curriculum content and the tests are aligned with the state's valued outcomes. In other words, the taught curriculum is tied to the tested curriculum. I'm sure that this contributes to the success the students have on the state's achievement tests.

When all reports are completed, the team chair will have the responsibility of writing the summary report. This task will require checking the individual reports to determine whether any elements are missing from the major curriculum. He will then consolidate the oral reports with his own observations on the major components of the curriculum.

# INTRODUCTION

Historically, teachers have been responsible for using measurement and evaluation in their classes to assess the outcomes of their instruction. Ironically, most teacher preparation programs have not required a course designed to prepare them for this important task. Even more ironic, when a course in evaluation is required, the emphasis is on standardized tests. But teachers spend much more of their planning time and classroom teaching time preparing, administering, and scoring tests they create themselves than they spend on standardized tests. This statement is not intended to downplay the need teachers have for understanding standardized tests but, rather, to point out a serious failure in most teacher education curricula to prepare teachers to develop, administer, and score teacher-made tests.

A second major curriculum shortcoming in many teacher education programs is the failure to offer instruction on testing, measurement, and evaluation. At both the college and the K–12 level, the overwhelming emphasis has been placed on summative evaluation while ignoring formative evaluation.

A third concern, which makes evaluation more significant than ever as a topic for teachers and all curriculum workers to study, is the emphasis that education reform is placing on evaluation and the manner in which it is using evaluation to determine progress in education reform.

All these concerns focus on instruction and learning. As mentioned in Chapter 8, perhaps through no fault of their own, historically teachers have limited their involvement in the schools to their own classrooms, and their attention to that part of the education process with which they are most comfortable—instruction. Administrators have accepted this limitation of teacher involvement and, in fact, have often promoted it (Habermann, 1992).

Yet, as pointed out in Chapter 1, maximum success with education reform will require teachers to become intensely involved with the total school program, including its evaluation.

Given the history of teachers' isolation from the school outside their own classroom, it is not surprising that they have not been involved in curriculum evaluation. Yet there is a special need for teachers to be involved with the whole school curriculum. Oliva (1992, p. 480) addresses this need:

> The field of evaluation often calls for the services of specialists in evaluation and research. Some large school systems are able to employ personnel to direct, conduct, and supervise curriculum evaluation for their school systems. These people bring to the task a degree of expertise not shared by most teachers and curriculum planners. Some school systems, which do not hire their own evaluation personnel, invite in outside consultants to help with particular curriculum problems and research. However, most valuative studies must be and are conducted by the local curriculum planners and the teachers. The shortage of trained personnel and the costs of employing specialists are prohibitive for many school systems. Even in large systems that employ curriculum evaluators, many curriculum evaluation tasks are performed by teachers and curriculum planners.

Only when teachers are involved in designing the curriculum are they capable of implementing it, and only when they are involved with developing the curriculum are they committed to work to make it succeed. Reconstructionists are calling for teachers to become intensely involved in redesigning the entire school structure. But successful contribution to the restructuring of school programs will require skills which most teachers are currently lacking. Central to these necessary skills is the ability to evaluate the school's curriculum. The following definition of curriculum evaluation should help clarify the need for all teachers to develop skills in curriculum evaluation (Hill, 1986, p.5):

> The purpose of the curriculum of the school is to arrange for the situations, materials, and processes by which learners can engage in activities which will promote new meaning, enhanced skills, and growth. The function of instruction in school is to facilitate directly and indirectly the learner's engagement with curriculum.
>
> Curriculum evaluation gathers evidence and promotes understanding of how to bring about the optimum arrangement of the curriculum, the most skillful facilitation of instruction, and the potentials of learners in order to increase, extend, and deepen the learner's ways of knowing, valuing, acting, and growing. It is not a procedure focused only on the identification of curriculum materials and textbooks or the assessment of learner achievements according to program objectives. Rather, it is the meaning making technology which is applied to the curriculum, instruction, and learning potentials of a school. These three—curriculum, instruction, and learning—are inseparably linked in synergy as a whole system. They are the core technology, the productive functions, which are the work of the school. This comprehensive definition of curriculum evaluation is basic to conceptions of curriculum development.

The first part of this chapter examines the roles of testing, measurement, and evaluation in instruction, reviewing the past and current roles of these processes in instruction. The second part examines the role that evaluation must play in curriculum. Finally, several models for evaluating the curriculum will be examined.

# EVALUATING INSTRUCTION

## A Look at the Past

The literature sends a convincing message about the ways teachers have misused and underused evaluation (Frymier, 1979; Fielding & Shaughnessy, 1990; Parsons & Jones, 1990; Wiggins, 1989; & Winton, 1991). All who have come through the American educational system know how frequently tests are used as instruments to enforce good behavior and punish misbehavior. Winton (1991, p. 40) addresses this concern:

> Teachers sometimes use grading to motivate, punish, or control. In this they frequently have parents as allies. It is assumed that students with poor grades will naturally work harder to achieve better grades. Good marks become the objective of learning. Grades become the currency which students, teachers, and parents may use for different purposes.

Others have noticed further misuses of evaluation. One concern is the record teachers have of ignoring the knowledge base on evaluation. Parsons and Jones (1990, p. 17) have said clearly that we fail to use all that we know about evaluation, "Unfortunately, the litany of our knowledge about classroom evaluation does not match our usual practices as teachers." Teachers' failure to use the existing knowledge base on evaluation and testing is pervasive, and thus the potential that tests offer to improve instruction is being wasted. Fielding and Shaughnessy (1990, p. 90) say, "The gap between the potential of testing as a teaching-learning tool and the reality of current practice is wide."

The failure of teachers to use current knowledge on evaluation and testing parallels their failure to use research in general (Egbert, 1984; Brown, 1990), and this failure can be attributed to the same reasons teachers give for ignoring the research (Marshall, 1991). Another factor which contributes to teachers' failure to use available data is their misconceptions about the proper use of evaluation and testing. For example, many teachers are criticized for "teaching to the test." But, as Wiggins (1989, p. 41) has said, "To talk with disdain of 'teaching to the test' is to misunderstand how we learn."

Just how pervasive is the practice of adjusting curricula and instruction to help students score higher on the exams? A survey of 1200 teachers from across the country found that fewer than 20 percent report having made no changes in their teaching as a result of standardized tests. Thirty percent said that they give more emphasis to basic skills, and one-fourth said that the exams prompt them to emphasize paper and pencil computation. About a fourth (24 percent) reported that they spend more time studying the topics that are covered on the test (Chambers, 1993, p. 80).

## A Need for Formative Evaluation

Initiated by Carroll (1963) and promoted by Bloom, Hastings, and Madaus (1971) and Block, Efthim, and Burns (1989), *formative evaluation* is now receiving a resurgence of attention stimulated by the current education reform efforts. Unlike its counterpart, *summative evaluation,* which is used to determine grades and to differentiate between passing students and failing students, formative evaluation has one ultimate purpose—to promote learning. It achieves this goal through improving study habits, instruction, and the curriculum.

Dagley and Orso (1991, p. 73) comment on the purpose of formative evaluation: "Formative evaluation is an ongoing process, designed to improve the teacher's performance." Formative evaluation enables teachers to monitor their instruction and keep it on course (Oliva, 1992). "If any student cannot learn excellently from the original instruction, the student can learn excellently from one or more correctives" (Block & Henson, 1986, p. 24). Put simply, students often need a chance to test their knowledge without penalty so that they will know how to adjust their study techniques. According to Markle, Johnston, Geer, and Meichtry (1990), tests can become strong clarifiers of teacher expectations, thereby guiding students toward expected outcomes.

Although most teachers agree that going over test answers in class can help some students learn more about the material, they are aware that this approach is not likely to result in total mastery of the material.

Students do not usually see the potential that tests have for promoting learning. At least this is what their behavior after they complete a test suggests. "After a test is finished, it is time to shut down the schema. Teachers are sometimes frustrated because students do not exhibit any interest in reviewing their tests" (Stefanich, 1990, p. 50). A much more systematic use of evaluation is needed, one that will separate evaluation from grading, a system that is aimed only at promoting learning.

One example of formative evaluation is the *take-home test*. This type of test gives students access to information sources and provides students with more time to internalize that information. According to Parsons and Jones (1990, p. 17): "Take-home tests can provide an answer for teachers who wish to evaluate student progress with longer and more complex problem situations."

## Progressive Reporting

Letter grades are being replaced with *progress reports*, which can be far more revealing than traditional grades. Winton (1991, p. 40) explains:

> The use of progress reporting is a viable alternative since it imparts information—information about what is being taught, alternative activities the student has completed, and how he or she is coping with the course. No individual letter grade can do this. Direct conferences supplement narrative reports and a portfolio of student work is much more revealing and reliable.

Another advantage of progress reporting is its ongoing nature. Unlike traditional exams, which give only one-time results, ongoing testing produces a much more comprehensive view of student progress, which often varies continuously. As Perrone (1994, p. 13) says, "On-going assessment is critical."

## Summative Evaluation

Dagley and Orso (1991, p. 73) present one use of *summative evaluation:* "The purpose of summative evaluation is to decide if the teacher meets minimal accountability standards." Summative evaluation is also used to measure student performance to determine such major decisions as grades, passing, and failing.

Since teachers have used tests almost exclusively for the purpose of determining student grades, it might be assumed that, with all that practice, teachers are systematic in the way they convert raw scores into letter grades. But this is not so: Each teacher seems to have an individual system, and many teachers use a different system from one grading period to the next. Why? Because most teachers never find a system with which they are satisfied. There is no single system that is right for evaluating all classes. An awareness of the strengths and weaknesses of various grading systems empowers teachers to choose wisely.

## Norm-Referenced versus Criterion-Referenced Evaluation

Evaluation systems that force a student to compete with other students are called *norm-referenced*, and those that do not require interstudent competition but instead are based on a set of standards of mastery are called *criterion-referenced*. Traditionally, by using norm-referenced evaluation, our schools have required students to compete with their classmates. Many teachers believe that competition among students is necessary for motivating, but classroom competition is often damaging, especially when the competition is excessive and when students of unequal abilities are forced to compete. Winton (1991, p. 40) expresses concern over the excessive use of competition: "Over and over again in homes and in schools we set up situations which guarantee that children will feel defeated and inept." Winton challenges this practice: "Evaluation should be for the purpose of promoting further learning. It should be a positive, supportive experience."

## Standardized Tests

Education reform has increased the use of *standardized tests*. Standardized tests have several features in common. First, they are based on norms derived from the average scores of thousands of students who have taken the test. Usually these scores come from students throughout the nation, so each student's performance is compared with that of thousands of other students.

Standardized tests are usually used to measure or grade a school's curriculum. Seeking to make teachers more accountable, state officials have forced schools to give standardized tests to students to measure both student success and teacher success. On the one hand, standardized tests provide a means of comparing local performance with state and national means; on the other, standardized tests may unintentionally shape a school's curriculum. Most educators think that several other factors should also be major influences in shaping the curriculum.

Misuse of standardized test scores has always been a problem. Education reformers' emphasis on increased accountability, as measured by standardized tests, will intensify this misuse unless teachers and other curriculum directors work to prevent this from happening.

Box 9.1 discusses the magnitude of error in standardized test scores.

## The Normal Curve

Students are also placed in competition with others when grading is done with the *normal curve* (also called the *normal probability curve* or the *probability curve*). The curve could well be called the *natural curve* or *chance curve*, because it reflects natural or chance distribution. This distribution is shown in Figure 9.1.

---

## Box 9.1    A Very Standard Error

### Let's Ponder

*The following passage illustrates the magnitude of the standard of error in geology and demonstrates why standardized test scores often have an equally alarming high standard error.[1] Read the passage, then think about this as you respond to the questions below.*

A Very Standard Error

*My friend was a geologist. We were in his backyard, awed by the majesty of the Rocky Mountains. The monstrous flat sloping rocks that are the hallmark of Boulder, Colorado, were the subject of our conversation.*

"Do you know how old those rocks are?" my friend inquired.

"I have no idea at all," I replied.

"They are about four hundred million years old," he said, "give or take a hundred million years."

1. Do you think the general public is aware of the large standard of error common to many standardized test scores? What evidence can you offer to support your answer?

2. What do educators do that suggests that they do not consider the fallability of standardized test scores?

3. Realizing that standardized tests frequently have large standards of error, how do you think this should affect a teacher's use of standardized test scores? Why?

[1]*The passage is from J. Frymier (1979). On the way to the Forum: It's a very standard error. Educational Forum, 36, 388–391.*

---

The normal curve is divided into equal segments. The vertical line through the center (the mean) represents the average of a whole population. Each vertical line to the right of the mean represents one average (or standard) unit of deviation above the mean. Each vertical line to the left of the mean represents one standard unit of deviation below the mean. As the figure shows, about 34 percent of the population is within one standard deviation unit above the mean, and about 34 percent of the population is within the standard deviation below the mean. Only about 14 percent of the population is in the second deviation range above the mean, and about 14 percent is in the second deviation range below the mean. A very small portion of the population (approximately 2.3 percent) deviates enough from the mean to fall within the third unit of deviation above the mean; an equal portion deviates three standard units below the mean.

Teachers who use the normal curve to assign grades in a school classroom make several bold assumptions. First, like other evaluation schemes based on competition among students, the normal curve rests on the assumption that

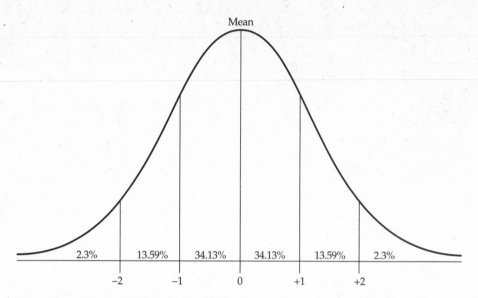

**Figure 9.1** Normal distribution curve.

the level of a particular student's performance compared with that of the average of a group of students (usually the student's classmates) is important. Second, use of the normal curve assumes that all students have an equal opportunity to succeed—as though all have equal study opportunities, equal encouragement and help from home, and equal potential; this is extremely unlikely. Third, the use of the normal curve assumes that the number of students used as a norm is large enough to reflect the characteristics of all students at the particular grade level. Unless the class size exceeds 100 students, this is a bold assumption, indeed. The use of the normal curve assumes that 68 percent of the students will earn C's, 13.5 percent will earn B's and 13.5 percent will earn D's, and 2.5 percent will earn A's and 2.5 percent will fail. Its use is appropriate only to the degree to which these percentages actually reflect the subjects' distribution.

## Stanine Scores

*Stanine* (from *standard nine*) *scores* are derived by using the normal distribution curve to group test scores into nine categories. This modification of the normal curve eliminates the A's, B's, C's, D's, and F's. An advantage of stanine scores is that they remove the stigma associated with letter grades. Another advantage stanine scores have over the normal curve is the use of nine categories instead of the normal curve's five categories, giving the teacher more groups in which to place projects that must be subjectively evaluated. Stanines may become more useful as educational reform programs press for the use of more self-evaluation instruments (such as portfolios) and for other qualitative evaluation instruments.

## Schoolwide Standards

Even more popular than the normal curve is the practice of schools setting their own standards. Most teachers are undoubtedly familiar with the system shown in Box 9.2.

This type of evaluation makes an important and often false assumption: That the level of difficulty of a test fits the abilities of the students exactly. Student teachers usually realize this error as they begin marking their first set of papers, discovering that most of their students failed the test. Although the exact percentage used to define the boundaries of each grade may vary from school to school, the system remains a common method of evaluation.

## The Case Against Competitive Evaluation

Researchers and educators have recently discovered much evidence that shows that grading in the high school should be strictly an individual concern—involving the teacher and the student. "Criterion-referenced tests (which do not force competition among students) contribute more to student. . . progress than (do) norm-referenced tests" (Fantini, 1986, p. 132). Once it was thought that competition for grades was necessary because it motivated students to do their best. This may be true for students who have the most ability, but forcing the less capable students to compete with their more academically capable classmates can discourage the less capable students, causing them to concentrate on their inadequacies. Competition can also be bad for the more capable students in that it can cause them to have a superior attitude toward their less capable classmates. Teachers can reduce these problems by refraining from making test scores and grades public.

Many contemporary educators believe that grades should reflect a student's effort—that no students should receive an A without really trying and no students who are exerting themselves to their full potential should receive an F. These teachers hold that the purpose of grading is not to acknowledge high ability levels and not to punish those who do not have high ability;

---

### Box 9.2   Traditional Grading Scale

90 percent and above = A

80–89 percent = B

70–79 percent = C

60–69 percent = D

Below 60 percent = Failure

rather, each grade should reflect the degree of progress a student makes relative to that student's ability. Consider the following report (Brogdon, 1993, pp. 76–77):

> An accrediting team member reports being approached by a student named Darlene. "Is it fair for them to keep my diploma?" she asked, fighting back the tears. She talked about kids who fought and sassed the teachers, who cut class and took dope, who acted up and interfered with instruction, lazy kids who refused to do homework. After each example, she would say, "I didn't do that; I did what they told me to do." Three times during our conversation she sobbed, "I know I'm in special education and we're slow. But I tried hard and did my work. I didn't cause trouble."
>
> Darlene's counselor supported her. "She tried so hard and worked so hard; she came early and stayed late on test days." Near the end of the conversation, the counselor talked about Darlene's strengths. "She knew how to get along with people. Her clothes were always clean and ironed, and that's impressive, especially for a student as poor as Darlene. (She lived in a run-down mobile home with her mother who was on welfare and several brothers and sisters). The kindergarten teachers who supervised her in the program loved her. She would have a diploma and a job if it weren't for that stupid test."
>
> Although she started to school at age 7 and repeated the first grade, Darlene made good grades in every subject, except social studies, throughout elementary and middle school. Her high school grades were low average.
>
> The counselor reminded her colleagues of a similar student who now holds a responsible position with a major firm. "Like Darlene, Suzanne, too, could barely read, but she worked hard and she got along. She got the opportunity to work there because she got a diploma. Suzanne probably couldn't read above the 4th grade level, but she has kept a job because of other traits; being responsible, courteous, dependable, and hardworking."

To realize how far we have come with testing, contrast the level of confidence in tests held by those who permitted her failure on a single test to deny her a high school diploma with the crude teacher certification evaluations that were conducted a century earlier (Huggest & Stinnett, 1958, p. 416):

> Grandfather was on the school board in the little rural community in which he lived. He and another board member had in mind a young man named Matthew as a teacher of their school. Matthew had little "book larnin." He attended church regularly and his character seemed to be quiet satisfactory. So far as was known he did not use intoxicating beverages. . . . But he had only attended and finished the local one-room school. The certification law at that time stated that all candidates must be examined in respect to character, ability to teach, and soundness of knowledge of the subject taught. . . . Matthew was examined by Grandfather—who commanded him to open his mouth. . . . Grandfather peered inside the tobacco stained cavity and then ran his fingers over the blackened teeth. Grandfather said to the other member of the board. . . "Write Matthew out a certificate to teach. . . . I find him sound in every way."

## Competition and At-Risk Students

The need for continuous curriculum evaluation has already been emphasized. Because local communities and the American society change continually, teachers and curricularists must align the curricula with both the environment and the school's mission. For example, the curricula and practices at many schools do not make a connection between the classroom and students' lives in their homes and communities. Failure to tie school experiences to nonschool experiences causes dissonance, which is counterproductive to achieving schools' instructional and social goals. Cognitive achievement is made more difficult for students who encounter incongruence between their school life and home life (Delgado-Gaitan, 1991).

Competition also impedes the attainment of current multicultural goals. Banks (1993, p. 26) expresses this concern:

> Cultural conflict occurs in the classroom because much of the personal/cultural knowledge that students from diverse cultural groups bring to the classroom is inconsistent with school knowledge and with the teacher's personal cultural knowledge. For example, research indicates that many African American and Mexican American students are more likely to experience academic success in cooperative rather than in competitive learning environments.

To succeed, students of many different backgrounds must figure out the school's culture. Without a curriculum that provides assistance, many minority students will not be able to cross the bridge to academic success. Continuous curriculum evaluation is needed to ensure that this assistance is, indeed, being provided.

## Portfolios

A *portfolio* is a collection of tangible products that provides evidence of a student's skills. Many educators believe that there are benefits in involving students in their own ongoing evaluation. The success of portfolios is contingent upon establishing the purpose of the portfolios when they are assigned. As Barton and Collins (1993, p. 202) explain:

> The first characteristic of our portfolio development is explicitness of purpose. Teachers by themselves and teachers and learners together must explicitly define purposes of the portfolio so that learners know what is expected of them before they begin developing their evidence file.

According to Pratt (1980, p. 258), "Many schools allow students to write their own self-appraisal. . . . This encourages students to reflect on their own learning." Portfolios also have the power to motivate students. Portfolio development shifts the ownership of learning to students (Wiggins, 1992; Barton & Collins, 1993). Portfolios should include projects involving writing across the curriculum. As Perrone (1994, p. 13) says, "If students are not regularly writing across a variety of topics and in a variety of styles for diverse purposes, then promoting self-evaluation has limited value."

The use of portfolios fosters the idea that students' judgment should be sought and used in determining their grades. A couple of relevant questions commonly asked regarding portfolios are: "How do you believe the quality of your present work compares with your previous work?" " Do you believe this sample of your work represents the best you can do?" Of course, this approach requires that the teacher know each student, not merely as a recognizable face but as a developing human being.

Portfolios function much as a commercial artist's portfolio shows the artist's skills in several related areas. The portfolio shown in Box 9.3 is typical in that it requires a variety of products such as writing, artwork, and oral presentations. Such variety is a strength of most portfolios. Since a portfolio is part of a student's curriculum, this quality makes this portfolio a good example of curriculum alignment.

An example of a portfolio is shown in Box 9.4. This is an oral history project for ninth graders designed by Albin Moser at Hope High School, Providence, Rhode Island. The project has two outstanding strengths: It requires the student to reflect and to be creative.

As stated earlier, most portfolios require a variety of products from the students; this is considered a strength. But not all portfolios are multidisciplinary. Some focus only on an activity required to develop a particular skill. For example, Abruscato (1993) describes a portfolio that is used in Vermont schools in grades 4 and 8 and is designed to enhance the development of writing skills (see Box 9.5).

## A Need for Complementary Grading Systems

A strength of many education reform programs is the fact that they require a combination of types of measurements of student performance. Epstein and MacIver (1990, p. 39) recommend blending performance evaluation and progress grades: "A school that officially rewards improvement by using progress grades along with performance grades can expect at least 1.7 percent fewer of its male students to eventually drop out."

## A Need for Multicriteria Grading

Ironically, although some reform programs are strengthened by the use of nontraditional evaluations, a major weakness in other education reform programs is their exclusive use of standardized test scores to hold teachers and administrators accountable for student performance. No test has the ability to accurately measure student progress in all desired learner outcomes.

---

## Box 9.3    A Sample Portfolio

## The Rite of Passage Experience (R.O.P.E) at Walden III, Racine, Wisconsin[1]

*All seniors must complete a portfolio, a study project on U. S. history, and 15 oral and written presentations before a R.O.P.E. committee composed of staff, students, and an outside adult. Nine of the presentations are based on the materials in the portfolio and the project; the remaining six are developed for presentation before the committee. All seniors must enroll in a yearlong course designed to help them meet these requirements.*

The eight-part *portfolio*, developed in the first semester, is intended to be "a reflection and analysis of the senior's own life and times." The requirements include:

- a written autobiography
- a reflection on work (including a resume)
- an essay on ethics
- a written summary of coursework in science
- an artistic product or a written report on art (including an essay on artistic standards used in judging artwork)

The *project* is a research paper on a topic of the student's choosing in American history. The student is orally questioned on the paper in the presentations before the committee during the second semester.

The *presentations* include oral tests on the previous work, as well as six additional presentations on the essential subject areas and "personal proficiency" (life skills, setting, and realizing personal goals, etc.). The presentations before the committee usually last an hour, with most students averaging about 6 separate appearances to complete all 15.

A diploma is awarded to those students passing 12 of the 15 presentations and meeting district requirements in math, government, reading, and English.

*Note:* This summary is paraphrased from both the R.O.P.E. Student Handbook and an earlier draft of Archbald and Newmann's (1988) *Beyond Standardized Testing*.

[1]*From G. Wiggins (1989, April). Teaching to the authentic test.* Educational Leadership, *46(7) pp. 4–47.*

---

Although the terms *grading* and *testing* are often used synonymously, this is a mistake. Most teachers believe that a student's grade should reflect more than test scores. Fantini (1986, p. 112) has said, "No test reveals all there is to know about the learner, and no test should be used as an exclusive measure for any student's capacity." Because no single test can measure all a student knows about any topic, and some things other than the acquisition of knowledge are important in school, a variety of measurements is needed. For example, teachers are responsible for seeing that each student develops certain

---

## Box 9.4   An Oral History Project for Ninth-Graders[1]

*To the student:*

You must complete an oral history based on interviews and written sources and then present your findings orally in class. The choice of subject matter is up to you. Some examples of possible topics include: your family, running a small business, substance abuse, a labor union, teenage parents, and recent immigrants.

Create three workable hypotheses based on your preliminary investigations and four questions you will ask to test out each hypothesis.

Criteria for Evaluation of Oral History Project

*To the teacher:*

Did student investigate three hypotheses?

Did student describe at least one change over time?

Did student demonstrate that he or she had done background research?

Were the four people selected for the interviews appropriate sources?

Did student prepare at least four questions in advance, related to each hypothesis?

Were those questions leading or biased?

Were follow-up questions asked where possible, based on answers?

Did student note important differences between "fact" and "opinion" in answers?

Did student use evidence to prove the ultimate best hypothesis?

Did student exhibit organization in writing and presentation to class?

*Note:* This example is courtesy of Albin Moser, Hope High School, Providence, Rhode Island. To obtain a thorough account of a performance-based history course, including the lessons used and pitfalls encountered, write to Dave Kobrin, Brown University, Education Department, Providence, RI 02912.

[1]*From G. Wiggins (1989, April). Teaching to the authentic test. Educational Leadership, p. 44.*

---

behavioral patterns and attitudes, such as honesty, promptness with assignments, the ability to work with others, and respect for others. Therefore, each of these traits should be reflected in a student's grade. Evaluation of these qualities is essentially subjective, and to avoid being prejudiced, teachers should decide at the beginning of the year just how much weight these parts of the total evaluation have and take care not to depart from the guidelines.

Grades should represent all the major activities a student engages in while in the classroom. Daily work and term projects may, and perhaps should, carry as much weight toward the final grade for the term as the tests. The use of several tests (weekly or biweekly), daily assignments, term projects, and daily discussions provides more satisfactory material on which to base the

---

## Box 9.5 The Writing Portfolio

*The writing portfolio used in Vermont schools at grades 4 and 8 includes two types of products: (1) a collection of six pieces of writing done by the student during the academic year; and (2) a "uniform writing assessment," a formal writing assignment that is given by all teachers to all students in the grade level.*

Examining a student's writing portfolio reveals the following:

1. a table of contents
2. a "best piece"
3. a letter
4. a poem, short story, play, or personal narrative
5. a personal response to a cultural, media, or sports exhibit or event or to a book, current issue, math problem, or scientific phenomenon
6. one prose piece from any curriculum area other than English or language arts (for fourth-graders) and three prose pieces from any curriculum area other than English or language arts (for eighth-graders)
7. the piece produced in response to the uniform writing assessment, as well as related outlines, drafts, etc.

---

final grade. Winton (1991, p. 40) gives a good summary of the use of multicriteria grading: "Good middle school philosophy limits competition and substitutes direct conferences and written evaluations for formal grading systems."

## Assignments for Extra Credit

To challenge the most capable students, some teachers include a bonus question on every major test. This is fine if those who do not choose to answer this question and those who answer it incorrectly are not penalized. Some teachers offer extra credit to students who attend special sessions and complete extra assignments in areas in which they are having difficulties. This practice can also be helpful in motivating students.

When a student asks for an assignment for extra credit at the end of the grading period, however, the student may be less interested in learning than in raising a grade. The student may really be asking, "Will you extend an assignment which failed to motivate me the first time I was confronted with it so that my grade can be elevated?" Sometimes such requests prompt teachers to assign additional problems which the student already knows how to work, or they may prompt the teacher to assign the task of copying hundreds of words from an encyclopedia, library book, or magazine without requiring the student to understand or use the content. This practice is most undesirable, for it encourages some students to procrastinate until the last minute and then subject themselves to X amount of punishment rather than attaining X amount of understanding. Students may also associate the undesirable assignment with the subject and learn to dislike the subject that produced the meaningless assignment.

Decisions on whether to honor students' requests to do extra work for credit should be based on the probability that the students will learn from the task. More aware teachers may ask the students what type of assignment they propose to do and what they expect to learn from it. If they can convince their teacher that they can and will learn as a result of the task, the assignment may be warranted.

## Grading Systems

Since most teachers have considerable latitude in choosing whatever criteria they use to assess grades, all grading, including criterion-referenced systems, is essentially subjective. One question should preface all grade assignments: What grade will be the best for this student? The answer will be determined, at least in part, by each individual student's ability and by the level to which the student applies this ability. To assign a grade that is higher than deserved is certainly not good for the student, nor is assigning a grade lower than the student has earned.

Obviously, each teacher's philosophy on grading shapes the teacher's choice of grading systems, but having a philosophy of grading is not enough. The teacher's choice of grading systems shapes their instructional program, yet often teachers must base this choice on the information they have at hand, and making decisions without all the needed information is difficult and is seldom appreciated. Pratt (1980, p. 259) explains, "Grading is a sensitive area, one in which the teacher can feel uncomfortably exposed and can be subject to powerful pressures to make decisions that are in conflict with the educator's professional judgment."

Too often teachers rely on test scores alone to determine student grades. As Parsons and Jones (1990, p. 20) explain, there is strength in using a variety of criteria to assign grades: "In fact, the more diverse and imaginative the evaluation activities used by the teacher, the more all-encompassing and valid the evaluation is likely to be."

Ideally, teachers have a variety of activities upon which to base each grade; for example, there may be class projects, presentations, classwork, homework, and tests. Box 9.6 lists the type of activities that can be used to determine the grade at the end of a six-week grading period (weekly tests, final exam, term paper, oral presentation, 30 homework assignments, and so on).

In order to arrive at the grade for the six-week period, the teacher can assign equal or varying values to each item on this list. Consideration should be given to the amount of time the student has spent on each activity. As shown in Box 9.6, ordering the elements according to the time invested may simplify the process.

## Box 9.6  Grade Relative to Time

| Activity | Time Required |
| --- | --- |
| Homework 30 × 40 minutes | 20 hours |
| Classwork 20 × 30 minutes | 10 hours |
| Group project | 6 hours |
| Six weekly tests at 50 minutes | 5 hours |
| One term paper | 4 hours |
| Oral presentation of project (including preparation) | 3 hours |
| One final exam | 1 hour |

The activities in Box 9.6 required 49 hours of student time. To simplify the process, an additional hour of credit can be added to class participation. With a total of 50 hours, each hour spent in an activity could account for 2 percent of the grade. Thus the percentage assigned to each activity could be as shown in Box 9.7.

But suppose the teacher of this class does not like the fact that the final exam counts for 2 percent versus 10 percent for classroom participation. This is no problem—the distribution can be changed (6 percent assigned to the final exam and 6 percent to participation, or 7 percent and 5 percent, and so on).

The distribution will not be identical from one teacher to another. This does not matter, so long as each grade is based on the chosen system. Criteria other than the time spent on each activity may also be considered when determining the value of each activity, for example, the degree of emphasis given to each topic in class and the degree to which the student has cooperated with other students.

Traditionally, most schools have required students to earn a designated percentage of the possible points to receive an A, a B, a C, or a D. Contemporary educators question this rather rigid approach: Will such systems meet the needs of future citizens? Smith (1991, p. 21) comments: "Traditional evaluation, on the other hand, is not likely to provide the clarity and focus students need."

## Performance-Based Assessment

According to Guskey (1994, p. 51), "Few innovations in evaluation have caught on as quickly as performance-based assessment." Yet there is no unanimity of agreement on its definition (Kennedy, 1992). Performance-based assessment requires students to create an answer or a product (Fever &

**Box 9.7**

| Activity | Percentage of Grade |
| --- | --- |
| Homework | 40 |
| Classwork | 20 |
| Group project | 12 |
| Weekly tests | 10 |
| Term paper | 8 |
| Oral presentation | 6 |
| Final exam | 2 |
| Classroom participation | 20 |

Fulton, 1993). It is not a new idea. Winograd and Jones (1992, p. 37) say that "Historically, good teachers have used performance assessment to monitor the progress of their students." Education reformers of the 1990s place much confidence in performance-based assessment as a means of motivating teachers and students to increase the level of academic attainment. As Aschbacher (1992, p. 51) explains, "The current enthusiasm for performance assessment reflects a hope that it can drive school reform and improvements in student performance, particularly complex thinking skills."

Performance-based assessment exists in many forms. It can require verbal performance (e.g., music voice majors or an oral dissertation defense), writing (e.g., an essay exam), or manipulative skills (e.g., a science laboratory assignment). Fever and Fulton (1993, p. 478) say that "It [performance evaluation] is best understood as a continuum of formats that range from the simplest student-constructed response to comprehensive demonstrations or collections of large bodies of work over time."

Another form of performance-based assessment is exhibitions between students or between groups of students. For example, a simulation baseball game can be used in any subject at any grade level.

Performance-based assessment can be defended by the fact that it requires students to go beyond the simple recall of knowledge and causes them to use the newly acquired knowledge. At a higher level, performance-based assessment, as Goldberg (1992) said of the arts, can provide opportunities and motivation for students to transform meaning.

Guskey (1994, p. 51) said that the value of performance assessment goes further:

Some educators have carried this vision a step further, suggesting that authentic, performance-based assessments could actually drive instructional improvements. This approach is called measurement-driven-instruction or MDI.

Offering such meaningful advantages as it does, one might think that performance-based assessment would be universally accepted, but it is not. Because performance evaluation sparks competition, it also sparks controversy. Worthen and Leopold (1992, p. 1) discuss its controversial nature:

> Despite the surge of interest in alternative assessment (alternative ways of assessing student performance), criticism of this movement by those who favor more traditional means of assessment creates a strong undertow.

## Outcomes-Based Education

No reform practice has caused more controversy than *outcomes-based education (OBE)*. Although to most educators, it means simply that educational planning should begin by determining the desired outcomes and should end by having students perform the activities needed to achieve those outcomes, not all people see it so simply. Brandt (1994) says that the OBE controversy itself is confusing because the term means different things to different people. As Spady (1994) has said, the disagreement is not so much over whether to target outcomes as it is over *what* outcomes we should have.

Adding clarity, and therefore meaning, to our teaching, although very important, is just one advantage of using OBE. Marzano (1994, p. 44) says:

> One common argument for their increased use is that many provide information about students' abilities to analyze and apply information—their ability to think.

With the recent emphasis on promoting higher-order thinking, this goal itself is enough to garner the support of many for OBE.

## Authentic Tests

Tests designed to cause students to develop the skills measured by standardized tests are called *authentic tests*. Authentic tests get their name from the fact that they test for valuable understanding and that the test activities themselves are valuable (Guskey, 1994). The Special Study Panel on Educational Indicators for the National Center for Education Statistics (1991) says that *authentic*, *alternative*, and *performance* are all terms applied to the emerging assessment techniques. Whatever names they go by, their common denominator is that they call on students to apply their thinking and reasoning skills to generate often elaborate responses to the problems put before them. Successful authentic testing requires teachers to (1) begin planning by examining the types of skills they wish their students to have, (2) design their tests to meet these aims, and (3) teach accordingly.

## EVALUATING THE CURRICULUM

As education reform and its required restructuring advance, the need for teachers to become involved in evaluating the school's curriculum will continue to increase. This book has not reported on teachers' failures to use research and the knowledge base on testing and evaluation in an attempt to engage in teacher bashing, for this would do nothing but impede or prevent the success of the education reform efforts. Teacher education colleges must share any blame that might be directed at teachers, for undergraduate teacher education programs have failed to prepare teachers to conduct research and to provide an adequate knowledge base on evaluation and testing. The point of mentioning these shortcomings again is to stress the critical need for teachers to develop curriculum evaluation skills.

### Curriculum Alignment

In addition to meeting the demands that education reform reports have made with regard to ongoing increased evaluation of the entire school program, evaluating the curriculum provides needed direction, security, and feedback for teachers. Consider, for example, the concept of *curriculum alignment*. A faculty that is unaware of this concept is unlikely to align the taught curriculum with the tested curriculum and even more unlikely to try to align the implied curriculum with the other taught and tested curricula. If caught teaching test items, these teachers are inclined to invent explanations or excuses to justify this practice.

Yet, when teachers understand the relationships between these curricula, they are apt to feel good about their efforts and to derive a sense of security from knowing that they are doing what they should be doing.

### A Need to Involve Teachers

Chapter 8 stressed the need to involve teachers in curriculum matters of all types. Involving teachers in evaluating the curriculum requires early and continuous involvement. To understand the relationships among such curriculum components as philosophy, aims, goals, objectives, content, teacher activities, student activities, and evaluation, teachers must be involved in writing the school's mission statement and in writing their department or grade-level goals, so that they can see how the components are interrelated and understand the basis on which all curriculum decisions are made, that is, the school's philosophy.

Needless to say, historically most teachers have not been involved continuously with shaping the school's written philosophy. Nor have teachers been involved continuously in relating their grade-level objectives to the objectives of the subjects at the grade levels that immediately precede and follow their own grade level.

## A Need for Integration

Teachers' inability to expand their understanding of the curriculum either vertically (to grades above or below their own) or horizontally (to other subjects) without working with teachers at these levels is obvious. Although this process will be discussed further in Chapter 11, it must be understood that effective curriculum evaluation begins in the classroom and spreads throughout the school. Curriculum evaluation cannot occur in isolated classrooms. Each individual teacher's curriculum must be assessed *always* in relation to the school's overall mission.

## The CIPP Model

One of the most popular curriculum evaluation models developed in recent years is the *CIPP model* (see Figure 9.2). A Phi Delta Kappa committee chaired by Daniel Stufflebeam developed this comprehensive model (CIPP is an acronym for *context, input, process,* and *product*). Context evaluation involves defining the environment of the curriculum. This part of the model is similar to the concept Beauchamp (discussed in Chapter 4) called the *arena* in his curriculum theory model. It includes a needs assessment. The input part of the CIPP model involves determining appropriate and available resources to use to attain the objectives. Process evaluation is an ongoing monitoring of the evaluation to detect flaws. This information is used to revise the model. The evaluation stage refers to assessing the product to determine whether to continue the use of the model.

## Evaluating Curriculum Components

Another way to evaluate a curriculum is to examine each of its components, beginning with the institution's mission statement (see Figure 9.3).

Perhaps the most underappreciated and certainly the most underused curriculum component is the philosophy statement, which either *is* or reflects the institution's mission. The mission statement is the rudder that steers the ongoing curriculum. Usually dusted off and tinkered with only just preceding an accreditation visit, the school's written philosophy is quickly put back on the shelf and thought of only as a document.

Yet the philosophy should give rise to the curriculum's aims (remember the Seven Cardinal Principles) and goals (remember the Goals for 2000). In

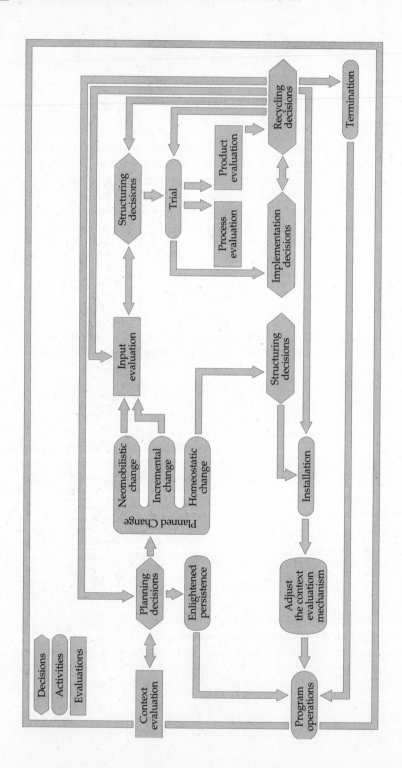

**Figure 9.2** The CIPP model.

Eastern Kentucky University shall serve as a residential, regional university offering a broad range of traditional programs to the people of central, eastern, and southeastern Kentucky. Recognizing the needs of its region, the University should provide programs at the associate and baccalaureate degree levels, especially programs of a technological nature.

Subject to demonstrated need, selected master's degree programs should be offered, as well as the specialist programs in education. The elimination of duplicative or nonproductive programs is desirable, while development of new programs compatible with this mission is appropriate.

The University should continue to meet the needs in teacher education in its primary service region and should provide applied research, service, and continuing education programs directly related to the needs of its primary service region.

Because of the University's proximity to other higher education and post-secondary institutions, it should foster close working relationships and develop articulation agreements with those institutions. The University should develop cooperative applied research and teaching programs using resources such as Maywoods and Lilley Cornett Woods and Pilot Knob Sanctuary.

**Figure 9.3**   University Mission Statement

most states, reform efforts are strong enough to require an evaluation and revision, if necessary, of a school's philosophy. Interestingly, the philosophy affects all components, *and* all components have an impact on the philosophy.

Curriculum evaluation is multidirectional. Because of the complexity of the curricula any attempt to adjust one part is likely to require adjusting other parts accordingly. Curriculum evaluation, then, is not a simple, one-way, linear process. Second, since the needs of students and the community change daily, curriculum evaluation must be continuous.

The exact amount of impact of each part of the curriculum on other parts varies; it can be minimal, or monumental. For example, consider the effect that one part of society, for example the economy, has had on today's curricula. The success of education reform practices in each state hinges on that state's economy. The economy also has a significant effect on the implementation of technology in the schools. Or consider the impact that a federal law such as Public Law 94-142 (now Public Law 101-476; *Education for All Handicapped Children*) has had on the curriculum in every school in the country. Innovative teaching practices and their accompanying philosophies (such as mastery learning or the nongraded primary program) can reshape an entire curriculum.

## Evaluating Curriculum Sequence

The curriculum *sequence*, the order in which objectives, content, and activities are presented, can significantly determine the level of difficulty or ease with which students can comprehend the content. The attainment of some objectives would be impossible without first attaining some prerequisite objectives. Parallel sequence among schools prevents disruptions for students who move from one district to another. The children of migrant farm workers exemplify the need for consistency in sequence.

When curriculum sequence is disrupted, continuity cannot be maintained. Lack of sequence can also cause unintentional redundancy and omission.

## Evaluating Curriculum Continuity

*Continuity* is the absence of disruptions in the curriculum. Failure to maintain continuity contributes to learning difficulty. To illustrate the need for continuity, consider the difficulty in remembering the following letters: NISEYLAN-NAPV. These letters lack continuity because they lack sequence. There are two reasons why a curriculum might lack continuity: either it lacks sequence or it has gaps. The letters in our example lack sequence. Ordered correctly, they are much easier to remember: PENNSYLVANIA. Curricularists—including teachers—are responsible for ensuring that the school's written curriculum and taught curriculum offers content that progresses from one day to the next and one year to the next with disruptions.

## Evaluating Curriculum Scope

Curriculum evaluations should also examine the curriculum's scope. The *scope* of a curriculum refers to its breadth; it is a horizontal dimension or a snapshot of the curriculum. For example, one might wish to examine the number of subjects a middle school curriculum offers at the eighth-grade level. Or when helping a high school student plan his or her curriculum for the senior year, the counselor might examine the number of subjects the student would have on Tuesday. Curriculum evaluations should consider, in addition to the number of subjects in a curriculum, the variety or breadth of content that each offers.

## Evaluating Articulation

Curriculum developers want to be sure that each part of the curriculum fits the other parts. This "smoothness" quality is called *articulation*. When evaluating the curriculum for its articulation, the curriculum developer examines both the vertical dimension (through the grades) and the horizontal dimension (across the grades).

## Evaluating Balance

One of the most important characteristics of any curriculum is *balance*. The balance of a curriculum should be examined from several perspectives. Since most schools have some graduates who enter the world of work, care should be taken to offer a balance between college preparation courses and vocational or business courses. College entrance examinations measure both quantitive and qualitative abilities, so care should be taken to offer a balance between quantitive subjects such as mathematics and the hard sciences and qualitative subjects such as English, social studies, and the fine arts. Since good health requires exercise, each curriculum should offer some types of physical education.

Even within the disciplines, care should be taken to offer a balance of subjects. For example, the hard science curriculum is often expected to offer some physics, chemistry, biology, and earth science. A junior high earth science curriculum might be evaluated to ensure that it contains some geology, oceanography, meteorology, astronomy, and physical geography. Although some educational reform programs stress the need to integrate the curriculum, increased integration of the disciplines does not negate the importance of balance among the subjects offered.

Curriculum balance is equally important to each student's individual curriculum. The value placed on a "well-rounded" education reflects a history of concern for curriculum balance.

Chapter 7 described a teacher who taught 28 times as much science as a colleague who did not feel comfortable with science. The educational reform reports have consistently recommended more science and mathematics for public school curricula. Perhaps the imbalance of these subjects from one classroom to another will be rectified by their recommendations. However, most reform reports have consistently ignored the fine arts. Contemporary teachers and other curriculum directors have a shared responsibility for protecting these subjects and thus contributing to the maintainance of balance in the curriculum.

## Evaluating Curriculum Coherence

A common flaw in curricula is the failure to connect or relate the components to each other. As stated earlier, aims must flow from the philosophy or mission statements, and goals must flow from aims. Such relationships among the curriculum components is called *coherence*.

An example of the common lack of coherence occurred in a college which offered a course in music appreciation. Some students elected the course because they wanted to increase their understanding and appreciation of classical music; others elected it because of its reputation for awarding an easy A. The word spread about the course's reputation for being easy, and adjustments in the course were made. Rigid, objective, pencil-paper exams were administered. Dissatisfied and discouraged with their first scores, some students dropped the course. Of those who remained, few students earned an A. Ironically, most students exited the course having developed a disdain for classical music. Curriculum evaluations should ensure that *all* parts of the curriculum complement the other parts. Students benefit from the increase in perceived relevance that occurs when the relationships between the mission and content are clear.

Content mastery is facilitated when today's content matches today's objectives, tomorrow's content, and today's content across the disciplines. These benefits result from evaluating curriculum for coherence.

## EVALUATING SCHOOL REFORM

School reform (or education reform) inevitably involves changing the curriculum, for by changing the curriculum, reformers can shape the nature of schools and, indeed, of entire communities. Cuban (1993, p. 183) explains the impact that curriculum change can have on society, at large, "To change the curriculum is to fiddle with important values in American culture."

### School Transformation

Education reform can start at the top or at the bottom or anywhere that someone has the energy and commitment to work to make it happen. But, as Schlechty (1990, p. 8) has said, "change can be most effectively implemented when those whose energy, commitment, and goodwill are needed to support the change believe in, understand, and support the change." True education reform requires effecting substantial changes in the schools, and evaluation is needed to determine when this is needed and when this has happened. Evaluation is essential to avoid the dead-end trap of rhetoric that characterizes so much of today's "reform." It is also needed because transformation itself is often part of the rhetoric and, when applied to schools, its meaning is unclear.

School transformation is more than changing the curriculum. Goodman (1992) says that school transformation is partly ethereal, referring to its temporary nature and also to its emotional or attitudinal quality. Like *curriculum* itself, school transformation should be defined at each school. The following list contains questions that can be used to determine whether your school needs to be transformed.

What kinds of questions do we want our students to ask?

What kinds of attitudes do we want our students to have?

What are the desired values that our faculty agrees should be promoted at our school?

What is the teacher's role in promoting attitudes?

How can we help our students develop the sense of efficacy required for success?

How does our faculty define true success?

What is the future of our culture, and how can our curricula be adjusted to prepare students for the future?

What barriers does our school present to minority students, and what adjustments are needed to help them cope with these barriers?

What types of desirable and undesirable attitudes, beliefs, and behaviors does our evaluation system reward?

What kinds of real passions should our school promote, and how can we adjust the curriculum to promote them?

What kinds of values does our school's hidden curriculum promote?

What additional or currently unused resources does our community have that can be tapped to achieve our school's major goals?

## Retreats

Measuring school transformation requires getting beyond surface answers. Retreats are a valuable transformation evaluation tool because they offer an opportunity to assess difficult-to-measure feelings and impressions. Retreats give teachers time to think about important questions such as the purpose of school. Goodman (1992) reported that, at the beginning of a two-day retreat, one fifth-grade teacher responded to the question What is the purpose of the fifth-grade curriculum? by saying that it was to prepare students for grade six. At the end of the retreat, the same teacher said that the purpose of the fifth-grade curriculum was to prepare students to live in a democracy.

## *Restructuring*

Another term closely related to transformation is *restructuring*. Schlechty (1990, p. xvi) defines restructuring as "altering systems of rules, roles, and relationships so that schools can serve existing purposes more effectively or serve new purposes altogether."

## SUMMARY

In the past, teacher education programs have neglected to prepare teachers to construct, administer, and score tests. Most programs that require a measurement or evaluation course offer a course that deals almost exclusively with standardized tests, ignoring teacher-made tests.

Education reform has stressed accountability as measured by student performance on standardized exams. Education reform is also stimulating the restructuring of the school's curriculum. Maximum success with this process requires teacher involvement in evaluating the total curriculum. Effective evaluation is continuous and comprehensive, covering all parts of the curriculum.

Teachers have often been accused of teaching to the test. Today, teachers are being taught to align the taught curriculum with the tested curriculum.

Historically, most tests used in elementary and secondary schools were summative tests administered at the end of the teaching unit. Today, teachers are learning that a far more powerful tool to promote learning is formative tests, which are administered prior to and throughout the unit and which can promote learning by improving instruction, study skills, and the curriculum.

Instead of using objective test scores exclusively as grade determiners, as has been a common practice, schools are being encouraged to use a combination of test scores and portfolios or other subjective criteria.

Curriculum evaluators should examine such qualities as articulation, balance, continuity, scope, and sequence; these qualities must be tied to the school's philosophy or mission statement. The mission statement should produce the curriculum's aims, and the aims should produce the goals, which in turn produce the objectives. Unfortunately, the philosophy or mission statement has often been overlooked.

Several curriculum evaluation models, which can be useful in planning curriculum evaluation, are available.

## QUESTIONS

1. Why must teachers become more knowledgeable about curriculum evaluation?

2. What relationship should exist between the curriculum and the school's testing program?

3. Why have teachers ignored formative evaluation, and why is it important?

4. Why is criterion-referenced evaluation more appropriate for use in elementary and secondary schools than norm-referenced evaluation?

5. What impact is education reform having on testing, and how should teachers respond?

6. What advantages do progressive reporting systems have over traditional testing?

7. Why do curriculum developers need evaluation models?

8. Which of the following curriculum elements relate to the vertical curriculum and which elements relate to the horizontal curriculum: scope, sequence, articulation, continuity, balance, and coherence?

9. What general advice would you give beginning college students to help them plan their curricula?

10. Why is continuous curriculum evaluation necessary?

11. Is it ever acceptable to sacrifice one discipline to achieve excellence in another? Why or why not?

12. If a school invested all its resources and time in academics at the expense of a physical education program, would that practice be more acceptable than Hillsboro Middle School's curriculum?

13. Usually when economic recessions occur, the first program to be eliminated is fine arts. Is this practice acceptable? Why or why not?

14. What do you suppose could have motivated the faculty members at Hillsboro to shape their curriculum as they did?

15. The current education reform programs are pressing for more math and science. What precautionary measures should school personnel take to ensure curriculum balance?

## SUGGESTED FURTHER ACTIVITIES

1. Draw a diagram to show your own concept of the CIPP evaluation model and, for each part, write a descriptive paragraph.

2. Draw a chart and contrast formative and summative instruction according to when they occur and according to their purpose.

3. Make your own portfolio. Include at least five of the following six items: (*a*) formative test, (*b*) summative test, (*c*) objectives (*d*) essay test, (*e*) your philosophy of evaluation (how you believe it should and should not be used), and (*f*) a sample simulation you will use to teach a future lesson.

4. Identify the two curriculum elements that you believe are the most important and write a paper telling why you believe they are important.

5. Identify the major strengths in your curriculum model and identify relationships among its parts.

## BIBLIOGRAPHY

Abruscato, J. (1993, February). Early results and tentative implications from the Vermont portfolio project. *Phi Delta Kappan, 74*(6), 474–477.

Archbald, D., & Newmann, F. (1988). *Beyond standardized testing: Authentic academic achievement in the secondary school.* Reston, VA: National Association of Secondary School Principals.

Aschbacher, P. R. (1992). Issues in performance assessment staff development. In J. R. Craig (Ed.). *New directions for education reform.* Bowling Green, KY: Western Kentucky University.

Banks, J. A. (1993). Multicultural education: Development, dimensions, and challenges. *Phi Delta Kappan, 75*(1), 22–28.

Barton, J., & Collins, A. (1993). Portfolios in teacher education. *The Journal of Teacher Education, 44*(3), 200–210.

Block, J. H., Efthim, H. E., & Burns, R. B. (1989). *Building effective mastery learning schools.* New York: Longman.

Block, J. H. & Henson, K. T. (1986). Mastery learning and middle school instruction. *American Middle School Education, 9*, 21–29.

Bloom, B. S., Hastings, J., & Madaus, G. F. (1971). *Handbook of formative and summative evaluation of student learning.* New York: McGraw-Hill.

Bracey, G. W. (1993). Restructuring: Achievement and engagement outcomes. *Phi Delta Kappan, 75*(2), 186–187.

Brandt, R. S. (1994). Overview: Is outcome based education dead? *Educational Leadership, 51*(6), 5.

Brogdon, R. E. (1993). Darlene's story: When standards can hurt. *Educational Leadership, 50*(5), 76–77.

Brown, D. S. (1990). Middle level teachers' perceptions of action research. *Middle School Journal, 22*(1), 30–32.

Carroll, J. B. (1963). A model of school learning. *Teachers College Record, 64*, 723–733.

Chambers, D. L. (1993). Standardized testing impedes reform. *Educational Leadership, 50*(5), 80.

Craig, J. R. (1992). Performance assessment: A new direction in education reform. In J. R. Craig (Ed.). *New directions in education reform.* Bowling Green, KY: Western Kentucky University.

Cuban, L. (1993). The lure of curricular reform and its pitiful history. *Phi Delta Kappan, 75*(2), 182–185.

Dagley, D. L. & Orso, J. K. (1991, September). Integrating formative and summative modes of evaluation. *NASSP Bulletin, 75*, 72–82.

Delgado-Gaitan, C. (1991, November). Involving parents in the schools: A process of empowerment. *American Journal of Education, 100*(1), 20–46.

Egbert, R. L. (1984). The role of research in teacher education. In R. L. Egbert & M. M. Kluender (Eds.). *Using research to improve teacher education.* Lincoln, NE: American Association of Colleges for Teacher Education.

Epstein, J. L. & MacIver, D. J. (1990, November). National practices and trends in the middle grades. *Middle School Journal, 22*(2), 36–40.

Fantini, M. D. (1986). *Regaining excellence in education.* Columbus, OH: Merrill.

Fever, M. J. & Fulton, K. (1993). The many faces of performance assessment. *Phi Delta Kappan, 74*(6), 478.

Fielding, G. & Shaughnessy, J. (1990, November). Improving student assessment: Overcoming the obstacles. *NASSP Bulletin,* 90–98.

Frymier, J. (1979, February). Keynote speech at Southwest Educational Research Association, Houston, TX.

Goldberg, M. R. (1992). Expressing and assessing understanding through the arts. *Phi Delta Kappan, 73*(8), 619–623.

Goodlad, J. I. (1984). *A place called school.* New York: McGraw-Hill.

Goodman, J. (1992). Towards a discourse of imagery: Critical curriculum theorizing. *The Educational Forum, 56*(3), 269–289.

Guskey, T. R. (1994). What you assess may not be what you get. *Educational Leadership, 51*(6), 51–54.

Habermann, M. (1992, November). The role of the classroom teacher as a curriculum leader. *NASSP Bulletin, 76*(547), 11–19.

Hill, J. C. (1986). *Curriculum evaluation for school improvement.* Springfield, IL: Charles C. Thomas.

Huggest, A. J. and Stinnett, T. M. (1958). *Professional problems of teachers.* New York: Macmillan.

Kanpol, B. (1993). Critical curriculum theorizing as subjective imagery: Reply to Goodman. *The Educational Forum, 57*(3), 325–330.

Kennedy, R. (1992). What is performance assessment? In J. R. Craig (Ed.). *New directions for education reform.* Bowling Green, KY: Western Kentucky University.

Markle, Glenn, Johnston, J. H., Geer, C., and Meichtry, Y. (1990, November). Teaching for understanding. *Middle School Journal, 22*(2), 53–57.

Marshall, C. (1991, March–April). Teachers' learning styles: How they affect student learning. *The Clearing House, 64*(4), 225–227.

Marzano, R. J. (1994). Lessons from the field about outcome-based performance assessments. *Educational Leadership, 5*(6), 44–50

Oliva, P. F. (1992). *Developing the curriculum.* New York: HarperCollins.

Parsons, J. & Jones, C. (1990, September–October). Not another test. *The Clearing House, 64*(1), 17–20.

Perrone, V. (1994). How to engage students in learning. *Educational Leadership, 51*(5), 11–13.

Pratt, D. (1980). *Curriculum design and development.* New York: Harcourt.

Schlechty, P. C. (1990). *Schools for the 21st century: Leadership imperatives for educational reform.* San Francisco: Jossey-Bass.

Smith, M. (1991, January). Evaluation as instruction: Using analytic scales to increase composing ability. *Middle School Journal, 22*(2), 21–25.

Spady, W. G. (1994). Choosing outcomes of significance. *Educational Leadership, 51*(6), 18–22.

Special Study Panel on Education Indicators for the National Center for

Educational Statistics (1991). *Education counts*. Washington, DC.: U.S. Department of Education.

Stefanich, G. P. (1990). Cycles of cognition. *Middle School Journal*, 22(2), 47–52.

U.S. Department of Education (1994). *A Nation at Risk*.

Wiggins, G. (1989, April). Teaching to the authentic test. *Educational Leadership*, 46(7), 41–47.

Wiggins, G. (1992). Creating tests worth taking. *Educational Leadership*, 49(8), 26–35.

Winograd, P., & Jones, D. L. (1992). The use of portfolios in performance assessment. In J.R. Craig (Ed.). *New directions in education reform*. Bowling Green, KY: Western Kentucky University.

Winton, J. J. (1991, January). You can win without competing. *Middle School Journal*, 22(3), 40.

Worthen, B. R. & Leopold, G. D. (1992). Impediments to implementing alternative assessment: Some emerging issues. In J. R. Craig (Ed.). *New directions in education reform*. Bowling Green, KY: Western Kentucky University.

# Chapter 10

# PLANNING AND CONVERTING THE CURRICULUM INTO INSTRUCTION

## OBJECTIVES

This chapter should prepare you to:

- Explain the relationship between curriculum and instruction.
- Develop a plan for ensuring that the major concepts in each lesson will be understood by all students.
- Choose a lesson plan and adjust it to prepare students to discover new concepts and relate these concepts to existing knowledge.
- Develop a multipurpose activity to achieve some of the daily objectives.
- Develop a set of guidelines for assigning students to groups and for using group assignments to meet individual student needs.
- Develop a contract to be used with students whose needs differ significantly from those of their classmates.
- Make a list of the qualities and advantages of mastery learning and a similar list for matching teaching and learning styles. Using some of these qualities, design a lesson to meet the needs of a class of at-risk students.

## A SCHOOL DISTRICT MATCHES LEARNING STYLES AND TEACHING STYLES

Welcome to Wichita, Kansas, and to the Wichita School District. Traditionally, many teachers throughout the country have been expected to stay in their rooms, apply the approaches that are "tried and proven," and keep things under control. With little or no encouragement to try new approaches, many teachers who have chosen to experiment with new educational theories have had to do so in the isolation of their classrooms with little or no support. But teachers who accept the responsibility not only for what they teach but also for what is learned are eager to use any technique that they believe might help them in diagnoses, prescription, and treatment of their students.

Fortunately, today most districts are encouraging teachers to experiment with innovations through exposing the teachers to the most current educational approaches. Such is the case here in Wichita. The following passages offer a glimpse of several settings which reflect some of the diverse approaches individual teachers, departments, schools, and school districts can use to update their curricula.

## LEARNING STYLES THEORY

One Wichita junior high school teacher attended a district in-service meeting where he learned about learning styles theory and its application. Deciding to experiment with the theory, he invited a consultant from the teacher center to visit one of his classes and explain the concept to the students. The teacher and the consultant spent a considerable amount of time making sure that the students understood the implications of learning styles theory and the teacher's interest in using it.

The teacher administered a learning style preference questionnaire, and the students scored the survey, developed their profiles, and shared the results with the class. The students were then encouraged to contribute ideas for classroom organization that would take advantage of the variety of preferred learning modalities within the class. They helped set up areas where students could listen to tapes or join in discussion groups. They also arranged areas where students could read or work on written assignments.

Student enthusiasm soon spread, and parents became interested. The teacher decided to carry the program further and arranged a parent meeting where he explained the learning styles concept and how he was implementing it. He then administered the survey to the parents and helped them interpret the results regarding their own preferences. To explain the use of styles management and thus earn potential support, the teacher began using the parents' learning styles when he conducted parent-teacher conferences.

The results of this experiment were very positive. The students and the teacher increasingly shared in the planning of learning procedures and outcomes. Students' willingness to accept learning differences in others also increased. In addition, the parent-teacher conferences became more effective and mutually appreciated. The success in this classroom led the teacher to introduce the learning style concept in his other classes. Other teachers in the school began experimenting with the concept in their classrooms.

There's a lesson here: When teachers want to introduce a new program or an innovation, others must be sold on the idea, because innovations often require additional facilities, materials, space, and program flexibility. The success of innovations depends on the cooperation of administrators, teachers, and others who understand the importance of the change. A simple approach is first to inform others about the process and then to involve them with the innovation. The success of the junior high school teacher in applying learning styles theory to his class was due, in part, to his awareness of the importance of support from others.

## IGE

Another Wichita school, Cloud Elementary School, adopted the Individually Guided Education (IGE) program as its basic instructional process. The IGE approach to schooling provides a framework for individualized instruction and continuous progress. Instead of being organized into the usual self-contained classes in which all students of one age are grouped together, students and teachers are organized into "learning communities." Each learning community is composed of students of several age-groups and teachers of varying talents and backgrounds.

This elementary school program had several goals, one of which was to determine students' learning styles. After experimenting with several assessment techniques, the teachers decided that the locally developed learning styles inventory gave them usable and practical information that they could easily manage. They arranged for the local district's computer department to put student data from the locally developed learning styles inventory into a computer. The computer-based analysis was designed to identify students who fell below a previously defined score.

Learning style data were shared with the students in the advisement programs and with the parents during conferences. A profile for each student was developed, and the results were used to determine the best way for individual students to reach their learning objectives. In addition to developing learning objectives to complement each student's learning preference, the teachers identified students whose styles preference analysis revealed a possible inability to use a wide range of learning styles successfully. These students were then given help in expanding their styles. Thus, one major learning goal was to increase "style flex" among students.

Results of the experiment were encouraging; student achievement and parental satisfaction were increased. Teachers were pleased with the effort because they had acquired an additional tool for individualizing instruction. They also believed that student attitudes toward the classroom were improved.

The conclusion here is that, even when a student has a preferred learning style that works well, introducing the student to other styles is essential. Students who have only one preferred learning style are in trouble when they are assigned to a teacher whose teaching style varies drastically from their learning style. By introducing students to a variety of styles, teachers can give students an opportunity to expand their style flex.

## EXPERIENCED-BASED LEARNING

In response to the career education movement, many high schools throughout the United States have established special programs to provide selected students with an opportunity to participate in experience-based learning in the community. This concept provides a less formal learning environment and meets the needs of certain students more effectively.

The Experience-Based Career Education Program at Wichita High School East is one such program. It was organized as a school within a school. Soon after the program was instituted, its director became aware that the learning styles concept was being increasingly used. After appropriate planning, the program staff decided to include a learning preference assessment—the student learning styles instrument—as one of the diagnostic procedures used to determine whether a student would be admitted to the program.

When a student applied for admission to the program, the student learning styles inventory was administered as one of the standard battery of tests. The results were used to determine the preferred basic learning modalities of the applicants. Faculty served as both teachers and counselors in the program. These teacher-counselors established job and job skill categories based on nine characteristics identified in the learning styles inventory. Style preferences were strongly considered in job placement procedures and were openly shared with prospective employers as an aid to developing programs for the students. (Some employers later requested permission to administer the learning styles inventory to other employees. They saw it as potentially useful in developing training programs for full-time employees and in hiring procedures.)

The positive outcomes of the program, and the student successes, indicated that the assessment of learning modalities helped the program meet the needs of students through a closer match of work experience and learning style preferences. There was also evidence that students' confidence in the success of the program was increased, that students' self-concepts were enhanced, and that students performed better in other phases of their learning experiences as well.

## AN ALTERNATIVE SCHOOL

Another approach to dealing with students' differences is through creating a school designated for this purpose. Munger Junior High School (now Alcott Alternative Learning Center) was established in 1978 as an alternative for Wichita youth who had experienced frustration in previous learning environments. Some students were drug abusers, some were school dropouts, and others were family dropouts. All had been discipline problems in school. The staff members were selected because of their special interest in "reluctant learners" and their proven ability to work with them. Each teacher functioned as both teacher and counselor.

The principal and staff decided to administer the locally developed student learning styles survey to determine the learning preferences of the students and to use the information to develop individual learning programs. Many students reported that this was the first time they felt that their own needs were being considered. They were very interested in the concept and its outcomes and began to question the teachers regarding their (the teachers') learning styles. As a result, the program was carried one step further to identify the learning styles of the entire staff. Survey results were posted publicly, and students and staff became aware of the various learning styles each represented.

One unexpected benefit of the program was the increased communication that occurred as a result of greater awareness of cognitive styles. For example, students who were auditory learners made counseling appointments with staff members who had complementary preferences. When teachers had the opportunity to use their own cognitive preferences, they found it easier to work effectively with students. Administering the learning styles inventory became a standard procedure for admitting both students and staff members to this alternative junior high school.

One benefit from a situation in which teachers teach students whose learning styles are similar to their own (the teachers') is the probability that a teacher will be able to recognize student problems and limitations more readily. Teachers automatically select methods that they, as learners, find effective.

## ANOTHER KANSAS DISTRICT

Learning style theory embraces the concept that both students and instructors are accountable for learning. The Remington district, a small rural district near Wichita, decided to experiment with learning style theory by applying it on a districtwide basis. The district administered the student learning styles survey to every student.

The initial purpose of the districtwide project was to confirm the effectiveness of existing classroom management techniques and teaching strategies. To implement the plan, a consultant was scheduled for a series of sessions designed to acquaint the entire professional staff with the concept of learning styles, techniques for administering the survey, analysis of the results, and possible teacher-student applications for the classroom.

The survey was then administered to every student in the district. Teachers analyzed their students' scores and used the scores to confirm the various learning groups they had already established in their classes. To expand the use of the survey results, teachers then met as grade-level committees to develop curriculum goals and instructional processes using the styles data for each student. Where team teaching existed, the results were also used to assign students to teams that emphasized certain styles.

Districtwide use of the learning styles data was the goal. To date, satisfaction with the process has been high. School officials report increased student learning, improved self-concepts, and better communication within the district. The district also anticipates that continued improvement in student learning will be evident as students move through a school system in which their learning styles are taken into consideration each year of their education.

Districtwide implementation of an innovation often increases the chances of success by showing that the district supports the change. Teachers and other curriculum directors who can persuade the district office to try a new approach are academically empowered. Certain steps can be taken to establish credibility for the proposed change.

First, the teacher needs evidence that the approach is effective. The literature can be used to show the success that other teachers or districts have had with the innovation. Also, the teacher might ask permission to try the innovation at the classroom or department level, collecting test data to show how effective the new approach is compared with the approach currently in use.

These examples show some of the ways school districts can, and indeed are, using learning styles theory to improve the educational experiences of all students.

## INTRODUCTION

This book began by examining a variety of definitions of *curriculum*. Although the perceptions of curriculum are many and diverse, the ultimate purpose of the curriculum is universally accepted: All curricula exist to provide the basis for effective instruction, that is, instruction that maximizes learning. To the degree that any curriculum succeeds in improving instruction and learning, that curriculum is successful; conversely, any curriculum that fails to improve learning cannot claim success.

This interpretation of the role of the curriculum, predicated on the assumption that all children can learn, makes the curriculum accountable for the academic success of all students. An effective curriculum requires effective planning.

This chapter begins by examining long-term curriculum strategies: daily lesson planning follows. The chapter ends with a discussion of ways to adjust the curriculum to meet individual student needs.

## LONG-RANGE PLANNING

### Concept Development

Sometimes students need help in focusing on the major concepts in a lesson. Just prior to or at the beginning of a lesson, teachers may ask questions, present a simple outline, or give students a few key words to help them focus on the major concepts. Such strategies, called *advance organizers*, can be an effective means of gaining student attention and directing it to the lesson. Snapp and Glover (1990, p. 270) found that middle school students who read and paraphrased an advance organizer prior to study correctly answered more lower-order and higher-order study questions than did students who did not encounter the organizer. "The educational implications of the current study seem straightforward. If a reasonable academic goal is to improve the quality of answers that students construct for study questions, we recommend that one method of so aiding students is through the use of advance organizers."

Harrison (1990, pp. 503–504) offers the following 10 steps for teachers to use to help students identify and become familiar with each lesson's (or unit's) major concepts:

1. Present a nominal definition of a concept and give examples.
2. Emphasize the common attributes and ask students to name further attributes.
3. Ask students to generate examples.
4. Have students give totally opposite examples.
5. Have students name metaphors to compare and contrast to the original idea.
6. Have students review contexts in which the concept takes place.
7. Describe the overt application of the concept.
8. Identify factors in the environment that facilitate or hinder the application of the concept.
9. Formulate an operational definition involving the last steps of this process.
10. Discuss consequences in terms of viable solutions to a given problem.

Harrison (1990, p. 203) reminds teachers that just understanding concepts is not enough: "Instruction must focus on the use of the concepts and the context in which they occur in order to ascertain their practical connotations." Perkins (1994, p. 23) says that teachers must induct students into each discipline they study:

> Concepts and principles in a discipline are not understood in isolation. Grasping what a concept or principle means depends in considerable part on recognizing how it functions within the discipline. This requires a sense of how the discipline works as a system of thought.

One method teachers can use to help students apply concepts is the case study (Kowalski, Weaver, & Henson, 1994), which enables students to separate relevant information from irrelevant information. In doing so, they can gain a clearer grasp of the concepts.

Van Gulick (1990) believes that the decline in performance on standardized tests is the result of the way our students store information. To be able to use newly learned information, students must see how the new information relates to a larger whole as they learn it.

The implications for teachers and other curriculum developers are great. "The teachers' role will no longer be to dispense 'truth' but rather to help and guide the student in the conceptual organization of certain areas of expertise" (Von Glasersfeld, 1988). Such guidance is best achieved through the use of group assignments which require students to describe the process they use to explore the new content as it relates to what they already know (Markle, et al, 1990, p. 54).

## The Unit Plan

Chapter 6 focused on setting appropriate aims, goals, and objectives, and Chapter 7 focused on selecting appropriate content and activities needed to reach the aims, goals, and objectives. Reaching aims, goals, and objectives also requires a long-term plan, or unit plan. For example, a teacher of junior high earth science would probably want each student to acquire some understanding of astronomy, ecology, geology, meteorology, oceanography, paleontology, mineralogy, and physical geography. For each of these areas, the teacher should plan a unit of study that will last from a few days to a few weeks and contain the topics that the teacher believes are essential to a general understanding of earth science.

### *Planning the Unit*

The unit planning should be a joint effort by the teacher and students; their roles are different. Teachers' extensive study of their subjects gives them insights into what students need to know about the subject of the unit—insights students seldom have. Therefore, the teacher is accountable for identifying some of the important ideas or concepts that will be developed in the unit and explaining the importance of this material to the students. Students may want to have some ideas or sections of the unit deleted solely on the basis of a dislike for certain material, but teachers are responsible for including concepts that they believe are essential to attaining the unit objectives.

An important function of the teacher's role in planning a unit is to give students the opportunity to suggest topics that they think should be studied, even though the teacher might question the importance of these topics. Involving students in planning has another important advantage: It helps avoid the prescribed, step–by–step, sequential approach that often limits learning. According to Hart (1983, p. 77), "Because the ordinary classroom does not provide this richness in learning and, in most instances, limits what the brain can do, students become addicted or habituated to this limited, sequential approach." Involving students can also increase their emotional commitment to the material, which is important because it enhances their learning of the material. According to Levy (1983, p. 70), "If students are engaged [in learning activities, as opposed to remaining passive], both sides of the brain will participate in the educational process regardless of subject matter."

The third part of the teacher's role in planning a unit is to help students select activities necessary for learning the content. Doyle (1979, p. 47) expresses the importance of activities: "The immediate task of teaching in classrooms is that of gaining and maintaining the cooperation of students in activities that fill the available time." This does not mean that the teacher selects some of the activities and the students independently select other activities. When presenting the option of selecting class activities, teachers should have on hand a list of activities from which the class can choose and should permit students to add activities that are feasible, safe, and consistent with school policy. Student interest in a particular activity may of itself make the activity worthwhile by raising the level of motivation in the class.

Another group of individuals who are far too important to ignore when planning the curriculum is parents. Because of their vested interest in the schools and because of their ability to influence students positively, parents have always been included in good curriculum planning. The recent popularity of school-based decision making has intensified the need to include parents in all parts of schools, especially academics. O'Neal, Earley, and Snider (1991, p. 123) stress this need:

> Research has constantly indicated that parent and family involvement is critical to the academic success of many children.

Reporting on a research and development study for the National Center for Education Statistics, Finn (1993, p. 72) said, "Overall, parents' direct involvement with their youngsters regarding school work is positively associated with academic performance." Interestingly, if parental involvement is to increase achievement, this involvement must occur during planning.

## Parts of the Unit Plan

The learning unit, or unit plan, is much more than an outline of subject material to be explored. Although there are many variations, most unit plans contain most of the following parts: a title; a statement of philosophy; a statement of purposes (aims, goals, and objectives); content to be covered; teacher and student activities designed to enhance the attainment of the objectives; and a method of evaluating the degree of understanding developed during the unit. See Figure 10.1. The unit plan may also include a list of resource people (consultants) and resource materials (bibliography).

A statement of philosophy is a declaration of a teacher's beliefs about such issues as the purposes of the school, the nature of youth, how youngsters learn, and the purposes of life in general. Because teachers spend too little time reflecting on their beliefs about these all-important issues, the philosophy statement is the most neglected part of learning units.

**Figure 10.1** Anatomy of a learning unit.

Yet the first question teachers hear at the beginning of a new unit is often "Why do we have to study this stuff?" Only by thinking through these broad issues can teachers be prepared to answer this question intelligently.

The statement of purposes is a list of the general expectations the teacher has of the unit. For example, the general expectations of a tenth-grade unit in government may include an understanding of how a bill is introduced, increased tolerance of the opinions of others, or an appreciation of democracy as a type of government. Unlike the performance objectives used in daily planning, which are stated in specific, observable, and measurable terms, the purposes for a unit should be general.

The selection of content for any unit should be based on three broad considerations: (1) the significance of the content in attaining the purposes of the particular unit (in other words, it must be content that is necessary to master in order to reach the general objectives), (2) the importance of the content to society, and (3) the needs and interests of the learners.

Activities should be chosen on the same basis, with experiences selected that will enable students to learn the content. Teachers need not feel obligated to select one activity for each objective, for some of the best activities serve multiple purposes and lead to the attainment of several objectives. For example, one activity for a senior English class might be to write a composition contrasting Shelley's poetry with that of Byron. Such an activity would undoubtedly provide opportunities for both gaining writing skills and sharpening concepts of one author's style by contrasting it with another author's style. Some teachers believe that they do not have enough time to achieve multiple objectives in their classes, but they should realize that several objectives can be met simultaneously. Further, planning activities with multiple objectives does not necessarily promote inefficiency, as some teachers may fear.

Each learning unit should contain two or three types of student performance (affective, cognitive, and psychomotor) and include different types of measurement, such as written tests, oral tests, debates, term projects, homework assignments, classwork, and perhaps performance in class or group discussions. This type of evaluation, which examines the quality of a product, is called *product evaluation*.

Another type of evaluation that should be applied to each learning unit is called, *process evaluation*. This is a description of the effectiveness of the teaching or the unit. Process evaluation analyzes the various parts of the unit in isolation to determine whether the unit needs improvement. It also involves looking at all parts together to see how they relate to one another. Teachers should ask themselves such questions as Is my philosophy sound? Does it convince these students that the unit is important? Are the purposes important? Am I being realistic in expecting students to achieve them in this length of time? Is the content in this unit what is needed to achieve the unit's stated purposes? Are these activities helpful in attaining these objectives? Is the evaluation fair to everyone? Does it discriminate between those who have met the objectives and those who have not?

Learning units should include certain practical information, including the title, subject, grade level, and a list of resources—consultants, equipment, facilities, and supplies—needed to teach the unit, especially audiovisual aids. Learning units should also include a list of references that support the unit and can be used to pursue the topic further. Each unit should contain performance objectives that (1) are stated in terms of student behavior, (2) describe the conditions, and (3) specify the minimum acceptable level of performance.

## Sample Unit Plans

Two sample unit plans are shown here. The title of each unit describes the unit; the statement of purpose or objectives describes a desired change in the students; and the evaluation is related to the objectives stated at the beginning of the unit.

The unit plan in Box 10.1 was chosen for its brevity and simplicity. This does not make it a superior plan, but such brief plans are often used. Perhaps the unit plan is too skimpy. What would you say about the format? Is the outline adequate? Figure 10.2 shows the parts commonly found in a unit. Notice that some of the parts in Figure 10.2 are not included in the sample unit given in Box 10.1.

The meteorology unit has neither a statement of philosophy nor a statement of rationale to show the significance of the unit. Many educators feel that a statement of philosophy is needed to help teachers clarify their basic beliefs about life, school, and adolescents and how adolescents learn. Goals and objectives should coincide and should reflect the teacher's basic beliefs. Other educators prefer to have a statement of rationale instead of a statement of phi-

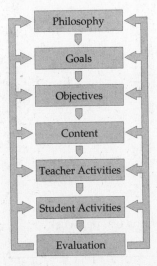

**Figure 10.2** A learning-teaching unit.

## Box 10.1  Unit Plan – Metorology

Meteorology Unit Plan: What Meteorology Means to You

I. Purpose
   A. Knowledge: To understand—
      1. The different types of weather
      2. The principles of weather formation
      3. The role of the weatherperson
      4. The names and principles of commonly used weather instruments
      5. Weather vocabulary
   B. Attitudes: To appreciate—
      1. The damage weather can do
      2. The advantage of good weather
      3. How weather affects our daily behavior
      4. The rate of accuracy of weather predictions
      5. The precision use of weather instruments
      6. The fallacies of superstitions about the weather
   C. Skills: To develop the ability to—
      1. Read and interpret weather instruments
      2. Read and interpret weather maps
      3. Predict future weather

II. Daily Lessons
   A. Definition of weather
   B. Precipitation
      1. The different types of precipitation
      2. How each type of precipitation is formed
   C. Reading the weather map
   D. Reading weather instruments
   E. Predicting weather
   F. Effects of geographic location on weather
   G. Effects of the earth's rotation on weather
   H. Effects of the earth's tilting on weather
   I. How to change weather that can hurt you

III. Materials
   A. Weather reports from newspapers
   B. Weather maps
   C. Equipment for making fog: air pump, water, jar
   D. Barometer, thermometer, anemometer, wind vane
   E. Graph paper for each student

IV. Evaluation
   Tests for each section of the unit: approximately one test per week's study of the topic.

losophy. By writing a statement of rationale, teachers justify the unit to themselves; then they can use the rationale to convince students that the unit is worth their time and energy.

The meteorology unit has no sections titled "Teacher Activities" or "Student Activities." This is unfortunate, because at the time of planning the unit the teacher should make decisions about activities, such as taking the class to a weather station and showing films on meteorology. The weather station may need advance notice, and for field trips students will have to identify in advance what information they will attempt to obtain during the visit. Films must be scheduled and ordered in advance so that they will be available when they are needed, and time will be required to preview them. You can probably identify other weaknesses in this unit plan.

Box 10.2 shows a chemistry unit plan designed for use in an eleventh-grade class. This more comprehensive plan has fewer weaknesses because it has most of the parts that educators consider essential to any unit. Examine its strengths and weaknesses. Pay particular attention to the plan's overall structure and organization, and you will probably be able to improve it.

## DAILY LESSON PLANNING

As essential as they are by themselves aims and goals are no more than elusive generalities. Making them attainable requires designing daily lesson plans that include the general expectations (goals) but that can also be translated into more specific terms. Each daily lesson plan should be developed to achieve a particular part of the unit; in fact, most units contain a series of daily lesson plans.

### The Daily Lesson Plan

Because the teaching unit is usually content-oriented and may not specify the experiences needed for learning each day's lesson, daily strategies are required to help students move nearer to the unit goals. For most teachers, this organized approach is the *daily lesson plan*. A teacher who attempts to teach without a lesson plan is like a pilot taking off for an unknown destination without a map. Like the map, the lesson plan gives directions to the lesson objectives. If the lesson begins to stray, the lesson plan brings it back on course. Staying on course is difficult without a lesson plan. However, despite the emphasis teacher education places on the ends-means approach, there is much evidence that experienced teachers do not begin the planning process by determining lesson objectives. Studies show that most teachers begin by determining the content to be covered and then design or select learning activities for students (Zahorik, 1975; Walter, 1979; Shavelson & Stern, 1981). One study, which examined planning in middle-level school laboratories, found that teachers spend most of their planning time focusing on content, a moderate

## Box 10.2  Chemistry Unit

*Chemistry Unit Plan: The Organization of Chemistry*

I. Statement of Purpose. The chapters covered in this unit are designed to introduce the beginning chemistry student to the basic background and structural knowledge needed for further studies in chemistry. Topics include Atomic Structure and the Periodic Table.

II. Performance Objectives

A. Chapter I: Atomic Theory. The eleventh-grade general chemistry student will be able to—

*Lesson 1*

1. Define an atom correctly in a closed book test.
2. Give the size of an atom in the unit posttest.
3. Identify the parts of an atom by name and describe them, given an unlabeled diagram of the atom. Four or five parts must be correctly labeled and described.
4. Match the mass of the parts of the atom to the correct path, given a list of masses.

*Lesson 2*

1. Define the atomic number of an atom.
2. Define the mass number of an atom in a closed book test.
3. Utilize the concept of isotopes by correctly grouping given atoms into isotopic groups.
4. Apply the concept of energy level shells by designating the number of electrons in each shell, given an atomic number.

*Lesson 3*

1. Correctly define atomic mass in a closed book test.
2. Define Avogadro's number in a closed book test.
3. Apply the concept of a mole by the amount of a substance in a mole of a given substance.
4. Define the atomic weight of an atom in a closed book test.
5. Apply the concept of atomic number, Avogadro's number, mole, and gram atomic weight in solving simple stoichiometric problems. Given the problem and required information, the student must solve for the asked-for information, correctly answering 80 percent of the problems to receive credit. (Partial credit given for correct setups).

B. Chapter 2: Periodic Table. The eleventh-grade general chemistry student will be able to—

*Lesson 1*

1. List at least three of the four basic elements.

## Box 10.2 (Continued)

**Lets Talk**

Each performance objective should contain four parts. Check the above objectives against these criteria. It is as simple as A, B, C, D.

Audience:     The student should be the subject of each objective.

Behavior:     The student's behavior should be the verb of each objective.

Conditions:   The objective should describe the conditions under which the student is expected to perform

Degree:       The degree or level of performance required of the students should be specified.

   2. Identify the common elements by symbol. This will be shown by correctly giving the elements or symbol asked for in 15 of 18 questions in two in-class quizzes.

*Lesson 2*

   1. Obtain atomic numbers of elements from the periodic table with an accuracy level of 80 percent.

   2. Obtain the mass number of elements from the periodic table with an accuracy level of 80 percent.

   3. Obtain a given element's electron configuration from the periodic table.

*Lesson 3*

   1. Define periodic law.

   2. Define "group of elements."

   3. Define "period of elements."

   4. Distinguish the characteristics of families of elements by matching the correct family with the given characteristic with a minimum accuracy level of 80 percent.

   5. With 80 percent or above accuracy, match the correct family with the given element.

III. Attitudinal Objective. The eleventh-grade general chemistry student will be able to participate in class discussions. This objective will be met when 80 percent of the class answers general questions, directed to the class as a whole, during the course of the discussion.

## Box 10.2 (Continued)

**Lets Talk**

Below are lists of concepts and content generalizations under topics to be studied. A check to see whether students know these terms can help the teacher begin at the appropriate level. The second list—generalizations—is even more important. These are the major understandings that should come from the unit. Notice that they are essential for achieving the preceding objectives.

IV. Concept and Generalizations

    A. Topic 1: Atomic Structure

| *Concepts* | *Generalizations* |
|---|---|
| Atomic theory | Atomic theory has been developed to |
| Atom |     support observations |
| Proton | Each subparticle composing the atom |
| Neutron |     (electron, neutron, proton) has certain |
| Electron |     characteristics and is unique in energy |
| Nucleus |     levels or shells |
| Element | Each atom has its electrons arranged. |
| Mole | |
| Avogadro's number | |
| Angstrom A | |

    B. Topic 2: Arrangement of Electrons in Atoms

| *Concepts* | *Generalizations* |
|---|---|
| Orbitals | Quantum numbers describe the |
| Orbital notation |     orientation of an electron in an |
| Electron configuration notation |     atom in terms of (a) distance from |
| Electron dot notation |     the nucleus; (b) shape; (c) position |
| |     in space with respect to the three |
| |     axes (x, y, z); and (d) direction of spin. |

    C. Topic 3: Periodic Table

| *Concepts* | *Generalizations* |
|---|---|
| Periodic table | The periodic table organizes |
| Series (period) | the elements; properties can |
| Group (family) | be predicted from the |
| Noble gas family | elements' positions. |
| Sodium family | Elements with similar arrangements |
| Calcium family | of outer shell electrons have |
| Nitrogen family | similar properties. |
| Oxygen family | |

amount of time selecting strategies, and the smallest amount of time establishing objectives (Peterson, Marx, & Clark, 1978). Furthermore, even when teachers modify their teaching approaches, they seldom consider the lesson objectives (Clark & Peterson, 1986).

## Lesson Plan Factors Affecting Achievement

Recent data provide a framework for developing daily lesson plans. Romberg and Carpenter (1986) reviewed studies of mathematics classes and discovered three significant variables associated with student achievement. First, instead of teaching the concepts needed to understand their subject, teachers of the same subject and grade level may cover very different topics within their subject. This unfortunately reduces the time spent studying the important concepts, and "classes in which less time is allocated to mathematics instruction (or instruction in any subject) are likely to have relatively poorer achievement in the subject" (Romberg, 1983, p. 60). Yet as we saw in Chapter 7, the most frequent determiner of content—the textbook—usually does a poor job of covering concepts that are essential to understanding a discipline.

Another factor affecting achievement is the amount of engaged time teachers spend on a topic or concept compared to the time that is allocated for the subject. For example, during a 50-minute period, one class may spend 20 minutes on the day's lesson (engaged time), whereas another class may spend 40 minutes on the lesson and therefore be likely to achieve more. Thus it is obvious that each lesson should be planned so that it engages students with the important concepts and skills for the subject.

The time students spend identifying and developing concepts, as opposed to the time they spend just studying the concepts, also affects achievement. Des Dixon (1994, p. 362) criticizes our schools for failing to involve students in meaningful curriculum development:

> We have Mickey Moused the lives of children by denying them control, the very thing we should be teaching them so they can find meaning in life and learn to survive in the real world of childhood.

In the developmental portion of a lesson, students should spend time discussing such issues as why the concept is true, how skills or concepts are interrelated, and how to use broader relationships to estimate answers to problems. In other words, developmental time should put the important concepts and skills in a broader context in order to extend the students' understandings of those ideas.

Class size has been studied for over 50 years to determine its effect on achievement. Carson and Badarack (1989, p. 9) reviewed the research studies and reported that "studies of the achievement effects of substantial reductions in class size indicate that smaller classes do have more positive effects than large ones, but the effects are small to moderate." Class size may negatively affect the teacher, however, but research is not conclusive on this subject.

Although the research shows that the positive effects of smaller classes are minimal, Carson and Badarack (1989) argue that, over time, the cumulative effect may be significant. Johnston (1990) reports that one advantage of smaller classes is improved teacher morale. Fowler (1992) stresses the need for additional research to determine the effect of class size on the level of student participation since participation directly correlates with achievement.

Traditionally, clear concepts in each discipline, and effective models and strategies for teaching them, have not been available because they have not been identified. As Armento (1986, pp. 948–949) states, "Methodological advances have outpaced conceptual advances in the last 10 years." Although Armento is referring to the field of social studies, the same is true of all disciplines. But there is hope, because more studies that identify important concepts in disciplines are being conducted today, and there is an increase in metacognitive studies, which will help determine more effective ways to teach students to analyze their individual conceptual development processes. For the present, prospective teachers should seek out the concepts and skills needed to achieve the objectives of each lesson, and plan to use them as focal points for studying. These concepts and principles should become the content portion of each lesson plan.

## What Makes a Lesson Plan Good?

Lesson plans come in many sizes and varieties. The length or style of a plan does not make one plan better than another. A good lesson plan can be a comprehensive outline that is worded formally, neatly typed on bond paper, and enclosed in a plastic binder, or it can be a brief outline written in pencil on 3- by 5-inch cards. The styles of good lesson plans vary as much as their length. A good lesson plan contains material that challenges and engages students throughout the class period with activities that involve every student, and a format that is easy to follow and does not require the teacher to stop the lesson to read it.

The lesson plan should be thought of as a tool, and like any tool, it will be only as effective as the person using it; yet the worker who has good machinery has an advantage over the worker who has faulty equipment. The important point is that teachers should develop and correctly use a lesson plan that works for them.

## Setting Objectives

As in planning an entire unit, planning a daily lesson always begins by thinking as follows: In what ways do I want this lesson to change my students? Or: What will they be able to do as a consequence of the lesson? When stated at the outset, these proposed behavioral changes can give direction to daily activities. Writing performance objectives was the focus of Chapter 6.

## Organizing Materials

Chapter 5 provided assistance in organizing material. Having decided what material to include in the lesson, the teacher must next decide on the sequence in which the material will be presented. Sometimes the nature of the subject dictates the order of presentation, so the teacher should check the major ideas to be covered to determine whether there is a natural sequence.

For example, a physical education teacher who wants to provide experiences that are essential for learning to drive a golf ball will think, "What few ideas are important to understanding this process?" The answer is: "Addressing the ball, the backswing, the downswing, and the follow-through." The answer to the question of what sequence to follow is obvious because a natural process is involved. Another example would be the home economics teacher planning a lesson on how to bake a chiffon cake. Again, the process dictates the sequence of the content. A history teacher, too, would prepare many lessons in which the sequence of the content would follow the chronological order of the historical events.

If the four or five objectives of a day's lesson have no natural order, the teacher can try to determine whether a particular sequence would make the lesson more easily understood. For instance, a chemistry teacher would probably not teach the formula of a compound until the students had learned to recognize the symbols of the elements contained in the compound.

## Selecting Experiences

Generally, more emphasis should be placed on experiences than on content, because today's educators recognize that the experiences students have are major avenues for learning. For this reason, a lesson plan must describe what experiences the teacher expects to use to teach the content. Further, because students learn more when they participate in lessons (Finn, 1993), each lesson plan should provide meaningful experiences.

At this point, the teacher should review the partly completed lesson plan. A statement of how the lesson should change the students—that is, the objectives of the lesson—has been made. Some major ideas to be developed have been selected and organized. The next step is to plan involvement by assigning a task that will require the students to use each of the major ideas in the lesson. Questions can be used to focus students' attention on the lessons. Snapp and Glover (1990) found that questions can be used as advance organizers to improve student achievement.

The English teacher who is planning a lesson on How to Capture the Reader's Attention would assign tasks that make the students use what they have just learned. Presented with several compositions, the students could be asked to identify the principles of capturing the reader's attention each time they occur. Later in the class period, each student could write the lead paragraph of a composition, employing the techniques of capturing the reader's attention introduced earlier in the lesson.

The physical education teacher who wants to teach the correct procedure for driving a golf ball may demonstrate each step and ask students to identify mistakes that the teacher deliberately makes in each phase. Eventually, the students could go through the process themselves, while other students critique. A vocational shop teacher would follow a similar process, as would math, science, history, English, music, and art teachers.

Each of these experiences is an assigned task which requires students to do things they could not do correctly unless they understood the content taught in the earlier part of the lesson.

## Implementing the Lesson Plan

The results of any lesson are likely to be no better than the daily lesson plan, yet the lesson plan does not guarantee learning success. Even the best plans may need modification as the students interact with the materials and activities (Green and Smith, 1982). In summarizing several studies on planning, Shavelson (1984) suggests that prolific planning may be counterproductive if the teacher becomes single-minded and does not adapt the lesson to the students' needs. As teachers develop planning skills, they should consider ways to alter their plans in case the plans are not effective with a particular group at a particular time.

## Time Management

Ciscell (1990, p. 217) explains the importance of time management skills for teachers:

> Teachers' inefficient use of their professional time recently has become the focus of much attention within the educational community. What started out as simple efforts to measure the amount of on-task behavior have resulted in somewhat alarming reports concerning the ways elementary and secondary teachers manage the school day. In the last decade, educational time has taken on a vocabulary all its own: Researchers now talk in terms of allotted time, engaged time, and academic learning time. Almost inevitably, teachers' use of classroom time has been blamed for declining achievement in America's schools.

Ciscell (1990, p. 218) goes on to suggest that teachers can improve how they use their time by delegating tasks to others and by letting others know that they are time-conscious. He suggests the following steps to achieve this goal:

- Keep an appointment calendar.
- Always be on time for meetings and appointments.
- Start and end meetings on time and follow an agenda.

- Limit time spent in idle chitchat in the teacher lounge.
- Keep your classroom door closed to avoid spontaneous walk-ins by colleagues.
- Organize and manage your classroom efficiently.
- Forget trying to work in the teachers' workroom—find a place to hide.

An important management skill is to learn to say no. When asked to fill in for a friend on a committee or assignment, refuse or negotiate: "I'm sorry, but I'm tied up at that time." "I'll be happy to if you will take my place selling football tickets Friday night." With practice, these strategies will become natural and easy, and your colleagues will find a target elsewhere. "Benefits accrue not only for teachers themselves but also for students as they take on the responsibility and challenge of a well-planned assignment" (Ciscell, 1990, p. 218).

Effective teachers distinguish between important information and other information (Corno, 1981) and simplify major concepts for their students; less effective teachers attempt to deal with great quantities of issues (Morine & Vallance, 1975). Because beginning teachers often lack the ability to simplify and make sense of classroom events (Calderhead, 1981), the time spent identifying the major principles and concepts in a discipline will be a wise investment.

## Summarizing the Daily Lesson

The lesson plan should end with a review of the main ideas covered in the lesson, but the summary should not be an attempt to review every detail covered in the lesson, nor should it merely list the main parts of the lesson. Harrison (1990, p. 503) makes an excellent suggestion for summarizing or reviewing a lesson: "Have students name analogies and metaphors, and compare and contrast these with the original idea." The review should show the relationships among the major ideas, tying together the parts of the lesson.

For example, the physical education teacher planning a lesson on how to drive a golf ball would include in the review each of the major ideas—the address, the backswing, the downswing, and the follow-through—and go over the major issues related to each. The review would begin with the first idea—how to address the golf ball—and include the major points involved in the proper address as they were mentioned in the lesson. Likewise, the English lesson on How to Capture the Reader's Attention would include each point and its development.

## Learning Cycle Theory

An instructional theory called the *learning cycle theory* (Lawson, Abraham, & Renner, 1989) uses a learning cycle approach to instruction to help students move through the levels of understanding. The program has three parts:

exploration, concept introduction, and application. The hands-on introduction enables students to develop descriptive and qualitative understandings. The concept introduction stages let them talk about their experiences, with the teacher or in cooperative learning groups where the teacher guides the discussion. During the application phase, students are given assignments that let them apply the concepts in different ways.

Markle et al (1990) caution the teacher to guard against making assumptions about what students know. They advise teachers to provide a procedural structure that tells students in advance what they are going to do, what the key points are, and what they should know when the lesson is completed.

## Sample Daily Lesson Plans

Two sample daily lesson plans are shown here. (See Boxes 10.3 and 10.4.) They differ in style, but each contains a few major ideas and is arranged in a sequence that facilitates learning. Note that each major idea is followed by an assigned task that requires students to use the idea. Note also that each sample lesson ends with a review that ties together the major ideas in the lesson.

# INDIVIDUALIZING INSTRUCTION

## The Need to Individualize

Without adequate planning, teachers can be overwhelmed by the challenge of designing instruction for students who have a broad range of abilities and levels of motivation. The need for individualized instruction, that is, instruction that meets the needs of all students, is clarified in Marshall's statement (1991, p. 225) "If students do not learn the way we teach them, then we must teach them the way they learn." Individualized instruction is based on the premise that students are different and each student has unique learning needs that each teacher must make special efforts to meet. Failure to plan for the variety of student needs results in some students becoming bored because they are inadequately challenged and others becoming discouraged by expectations that are beyond their abilities.

While educators recognize the need to individualize instruction, few agree on how to meet the great range of learning needs. The following are some common approaches that schools and teachers use to individualize instruction. The discussions are far from all-inclusive, though. Every day new approaches are being applied. Some of the more successful innovations may never get beyond the walls of the classroom. Others may be studied and tested, and the results disseminated through the professional literature. This is the case with the approaches described in the following passages.

---

**Box 10.3**

**Daily Lesson Plan—Business**

I. Title of Lesson: How to Read and Analyze a Newspaper's Financial Page Effectively.

II. Reason for Lesson: To show how a stock exchange allows people to put their capital to work whenever and however they choose.

III. Points to be reviewed

    A. Just what common stock is

    B. What common stock means to an issuing corporation

    C. What common stock ownership means to the investor

    D. Advantages and disadvantages of common stock

IV. Content and Activities

| *Content* | *Activity* |
|---|---|
| A breakdown of the different headings contained in the stock quotes. | Each student will be asked in advance of my explanation as to their meanings. |
| The prices will be analyzed as to what they actually mean. | Different prices will be put on the board with students giving the answer in dollars and cents. |
| Actual examples from a newspaper will be analyzed as to their meanings in relation to other stock quotes. | Each student will recite the quotes from a newspaper handout and will tell what they mean. |

*Summarizing the above concepts:*

V. Evaluation: A simple quiz on the material just covered and the review work will be given. A simulated paper quote will be provided so that I can test whether they understand all the aspects of the heading and the prices contained in the quote.

VI. Assignment: They will be given a project of keeping the daily price quotes of a particular stock, which will be turned in at the end of the week and evaluated. Each student will be assigned a different stock.

---

## In-Class Ability Grouping

A common approach to reducing the task of teaching 30 or so students of varying abilities and needs is to form subgroups of students who have abilities and interests in common. Simple arithmetic would suggest that dividing a class of 30 students into five groups of six students per group would reduce the range to which the instruction must be adapted to one-fifth the original range.

---

**Box 10.4**

**Daily Lesson Plan—Speech**

---

1. Title: "How to Use *Time* When Reading with Expression." Establish set by reading a poem ("Richard Cory") aloud as monotonously and ineffectively as possible, no pauses, no variation in speed.

2. The essential concepts of time: pause, rate, duration. Introduce these concepts (pause, rate, and duration) in that order because we go from time where no words are involved to time that involves several words, down to time that involves just one word.

3. (a) Pause—the pregnant space of time when no sound is uttered, the dramatic pause after a heavy statement—give an example; the anticipating pause—slight hesitation before key word, often used both in dramatic and comedy punch line—give an example.

   (b) Duration—the amount of time spent on just one word. Used for emphasis and imagery. Show how one can stretch out a single word and how it highlights the meaning of a passage.

4. Assignment: Go around the room and have each one say "Give me liberty, or give me death" using the three concepts of time for more expression.

5. Summary: Read the same poem ("Richard Cory") as in beginning, only read it well and with expression. Then ask class if they've heard it before. Tell and then show how important the proper use of those three concepts is for effective communication. In the second reading, demonstrate how those three concepts worked.

---

Unfortunately, the results of ability grouping are not usually dramatically successful; yet ability grouping does tend to improve student learning (Nye et al., 1994). An analysis of more than 40 studies of ability grouping found that grouping makes a small contribution to the improvement of learning and a larger contribution toward improvement of student motivation (Julik, 1981).

## Individualizing Instruction

How effectively ability grouping improves learning depends on how the teacher adjusts the instruction to each group. In general, less capable students need concrete material and examples of ways to apply newly learned concepts to real-world experiences, and more capable students need greater challenges, but challenges of different types. For example, rather than assigning a high-ability group of math students a much larger number of the same type of problems given to less capable groups, the teacher might assign more creative challenges requiring divergent thinking to the more capable students.

Advanced groups might even be assigned to develop problems instead of finding solutions, or to find a variety of solutions to a problem.

The teacher using ability grouping should expect to spend more time with the less capable students, especially after the more capable groups get on task. Slower students may require more careful monitoring and guidance. Good, Reys, Grouws, and Mulryan (1990–1991) say that when groups are established, higher-ability students tend either to dominate the group or not participate in the group. Furthermore, low-ability students perform less well when placed with other low-ability students (Calfee & Brown, 1979). This is probably partly because teachers usually spend less time with the less capable groups. Oakes (1990) reported that schools serving mainly non-English-speaking students offer less breadth and depth of content coverage. A review of the literature found that the amount of time teachers devote to direct instruction is closely related to student achievement (Centra & Potter, 1980). Yet, taking time to ask higher-order questions and encouraging students to ask each other questions are imperative. Students must be given time and encouragement to reflect on their thinking. Sigel (see Ellsworth & Sindt, 1994) discovered that children's ability to move from the concrete to the symbolic level requires distancing themselves from the present. Higher-order questions can be used to make this necessary cognitive linking occur. Self-assessment which requires students to use writings, charts, graphs, and drawings to document their progress can be used to help young children make this necessary time transition (Phillips, Phillips, Melton, & Moore, 1994).

## Unintentional Differential Treatment

Ability grouping requires different treatment for different groups at different levels, but differential treatment must be avoided. For example, while it is realistic to expect high-ability students to cover more material faster than less capable groups, teachers often make unrealistically different demands of the groups. Shavelson (1984) found that high-ability groups were paced as much as 15 times faster than groups of lesser ability, increasing dramatically the difference in amounts of material covered by the two groups.

Teachers tend to treat students for whom they hold low expectations in several different ways. For example, Brophy (1983, p. 274) reports that teachers treat these students in the following unique ways. The teacher will:

1. Wait less time for lows to answer questions.

2. Give lows the answer or call on someone else.

3. Provide inappropriate reinforcement.

4. Criticize lows more than highs for failure.

5. Praise lows less than highs for success.

6. Fail to give lows feedback on their public responses.

7. Interact with lows less and pay less attention to them overall.

8. Call on lows less often in class.

9. Ask for lower performance levels from lows.

10. Smile less, have less eye contact, have fewer attentive postures towards lows.

## Differences in Evaluation

The teacher may find it desirable to devise nontraditional ways of evaluating advanced students and students with limited ability. For example, objective tests may not measure the kinds of growth anticipated for these groups. Such methodology as oral discussions or one-on-one questioning may be needed to discover the depth of insights developed by advanced students and to detect progress made by students with limited ability. Term projects may be preferable to exams. For example, the teacher of a student who accepts responsibility for writing a computer program to breed plants may find that the resulting product—that is, the computer program—is itself the best measure of success for this assignment.

## Precautions

Whenever students are grouped by ability, the teacher must take certain precautions. There is a certain prestige in being affiliated with the upper group(s), whereas a certain disgrace befalls students who are assigned to the lower group(s). Attempts to disguise the ranking or ordering of groups usually fail. Indeed, students often know the level to which they will be assigned even before their teachers know it.

Teachers should not make comments that compare ability groups, and they should not allow students to make judgmental or derogatory comments about any group. Sometimes teachers contribute to the caste problem without even realizing their error, as is evident from the following narrative.

> Mrs. Bentley's Typing I class was made up of about 30 girls and 10 boys, none of whom had previously taken typing. She had a unique system for reporting individual grades. Along one wall she posted a white sheet of paper on which there was a landscape. A fence was in the foreground, and a blue sky was above the fence. Near the top there were beautiful, fluffy cumulus clouds. About 40 bluebirds perched on the fence. Each bluebird had a label on which the name of a student appeared.
>
> The namesake of the bird called James lived in one of the city's worst ghettos. As each student developed the ability to type 25 words a minute, his or her namesake bird would leave the fence and begin to ascend. Right away, several birds made their departures. These birds represented students who owned a typewriter and had some familiarity with typing at the beginning of the class. James was frustrated because he was still learning the keys when others were typing more than 25 words per minute—and more.

Each day James tried a little harder but made more mistakes (each mistake carried a five-word penalty). By the end of the year, some of the bluebirds were flying into the clouds. James's bluebird was still sitting on the fence.

The high premium placed on peer approval in middle, junior, and high schools can exacerbate the emotional damage caused by ability grouping. Also, higher-ability groups tend to become snobbish and condescending toward members of lower-ability groups.

## Interclass Ability Grouping

In some schools, ability grouping is done independently of teachers—standardized intelligence tests determine the placement of students in groups. Under these circumstances, teachers are still responsible for protecting the lower-ability groups from ridicule.

Interclass grouping and intraclass grouping produce different types of competition. When students are grouped within one class, they compete with classmates, but when the grouping is interclass, the competition is between two or more classes.

For several centuries, schools in England have had houses. A *house* is a group of students whose abilities are heterogeneous, that is, each house contains students who have a wide range of abilities. The houses frequently compete in oral debates, in sports, and so on. This encourages cooperation, not competition, among the members of a house.

Other schools choose homogeneous ability grouping. For example, five groups of students may be formed, producing five "tracks," each representing a different level of general ability. Here is an example:

Suppose you enter a seventh-grade classroom and see groups of students located throughout the room. On closer observation, you notice that group A is collecting weather data, using a weather vane, thermometer, and hygrometer; group B is constructing a map of the United States with a weather symbols key at the bottom, and group C is shading the map to show rainfall, altitude, and temperature. Groups D and E are competing vigorously, developing new ways of forecasting the weather one year into the future. On the wall are color-coded charts that show at a glance the group to which each student belongs.

You notice that Bobby Burns belongs to group A in English, group B in social studies and science, group C in mathematics, and group D in spelling. A small square is added above Bobby's name as he completes a unit in a particular subject. It doesn't seem to bother Bobby that he belongs to groups of different academic levels; his rate of performance in each group appears to be more important to him.

This example is typical of a classroom in one of the nation's largest and most progressive school systems; all 185 schools use the approach just described. Several similar approaches to cooperative learning have been developed. With one system, called teams-games-tournaments (TGT), hetero-geneous groups compete for academic awards. It enables low-ability and high-ability students to contribute the same number of points to the team. TGT has been used in more than 2000 schools. Group games make it possible for each group member to have some of the information needed to solve a problem, ensuring that everyone is responsible for group success.

## Grade Contracts

Grade contracting is a method that recognizes that students are more highly motivated by some topics than by others. It permits an individual to place more emphasis on certain topics.

At the beginning of each unit of study, students are issued contracts. According to the student's ability and interest in the topic, the student agrees to perform a certain amount of work in order to earn a certain grade. Box 10.5 is a sample grade contract. Contracts can also be used to provide students with opportunities to earn free time and other rewards.

## Using Instructional Models

Another way to organize lessons is to use the formats provided by instruction-al models. An advantage to using models is that they have been examined, tested, and proved to be theoretically and practically sound. Lewellen (1990, p.

---

**Box 10.5**

**Student Contract for Art History**

| Grade | Requirements |
|-------|-------------|
| A | Meet the requirements for the grade of B and visit a local art gallery. Sketch an example of a gothic painting. Visit a carpenter gothic house and sketch the house. Show at least three similarities in the two products. |
| B | Meet the requirements for the grade of C and name and draw an example of each of the major classes of columns used in buildings. |
| C | Meet the requirements for the grade of D and submit a notebook record of the major developments in art since 1900, naming at least six major painting styles and two authors of each style. |
| D | Attend class regularly and participate in all classroom activities. |

I _____ agree to work for the grade of _____ as described
  (Student's name)                                      (specify grade)
in this contract.

63) says that a model should be "systematic, descriptive, explanatory, and widely applicable." Examples of instructional models are direct instruction, scientific inquiry, concept attainment, and the Socratic questioning model. Reyes (1990, p. 214) endorses the use of such models to plan lessons:

> Models provide a convenient organizer for teaching the precepts of effective teaching or for teaching the steps of lesson planning. For the teacher in the classroom at any level, models of instruction can structure his or her decision making. For example, the teacher's choice of classroom questions, homework assignments, introductions to lessons, and so on are typically influenced by the instructional model being used as an organizer.

## Information Processing Model

A popular contemporary way to examine and describe learning is by viewing it mechanically, as you might describe the process computers use to store and retrieve information. Using the five senses to gather information (see Figure 10.3), human beings immediately decide which information to store. A perceptual screen is used to filter out unwanted information (see Figure 10.4).

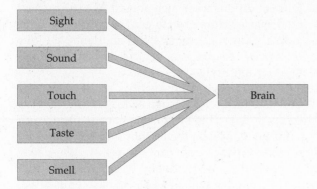

**Figure 10.3** The five senses act as receptors.

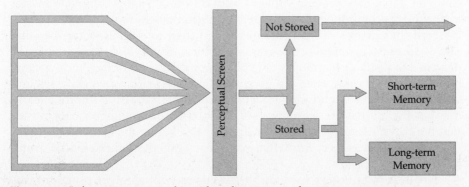

**Figure 10.4** Information is stored in either short-term or long-term memory.

Information selected for keeping is stored in one of two places. Information which is going to be used immediately or in the near future is stored in the short-term memory; the other information is stored in the long-term memory. Van Gulick (1990) believes that students cannot possess information unless it is stored in a manner that allows them to make use of it. He stresses the need for interconnections.

As you introduce new information to students, you can use advance organizers to point students toward the most important information, thus affecting the information that is retained. Then, by helping students relate new information to previously acquired information, you can help them derive meaning from the new information which might otherwise be meaningless to them.

## Mastery Learning

In 1963 J. B. Carroll, a professor at Harvard University, wrote an article titled "A Model of School Learning," in which he challenged the then-accepted belief that students' IQs are a major factor in determining academic success. Carroll hypothesized that, if four conditions were met, at least 90 to 95 percent of all high school students could master class objectives. The four conditions were: (1) give each student enought time, (2) motivate all students, (3) give opportunity to remediate, and (4) present subject matter in a manner compatible with the individual student's learning style.

Using Carroll's model, Benjamin S. Bloom and his students at the University of Chicago developed an educational system called *learning for mastery (LFM)* (see Block & Henson, 1986). This system is teacher-paced and group-based. In other words, the teacher leads the lessons and the class as a group follows. Most mastery learning programs, however are student-paced (that is, the students set the pace) and are individually based. Each student pursues learning individually—at that student's preferred pace (Guskey & Gates, 1986).

All mastery learning programs have several important characteristics in common. First, they provide students with different lengths of time to master each topic. Second, they give students opportunities to remediate or restudy material that proves difficult for them, and then to retest without penalty. Third, all mastery learning programs use formative evaluation—evaluation designed to promote learning, not to be computed as part of the grade system. Short daily or weekly tests are given to diagnose learning weaknesses and teaching weaknesses, and then teachers and learners adjust to improve learning. Finally, all mastery learning uses criterion-based evaluation. This means that the criteria essential for success are revealed before the study unit begins. (For further discussion of formative evaluation and criterion-referenced evaluation, see Chapter 9.)

Finally, with mastery learning programs, as with all other programs, the success depends on how it is used. Cunningham (1991, p. 84) explains:

There are two essential elements of the mastery learning process. The first is an extremely close congruence between the material being taught, the teaching strategies employed, and the content measured. The second essential element is the provision of formative assessment, opportunities for students followed by feedback, corrective and enrichment activities.

To determine the effectiveness of mastery learning compared with traditional programs, Burns (1979) examined results from 157 mastery learning studies and discovered that 107 studies found that mastery learning students significantly outscored their traditionally taught counterparts; 47 of the studies showed no significant differences. Only 3 of the 157 studies reported that traditionally taught students outscored mastery learning students. One study of mastery learning, spanning 15 years in 3000 schools, concluded that mastery learning was consistently more effective than traditional curriculums (Hyman & Cohen, 1979). Guskey and Gates (1986) reviewed 25 studies of group-based and teacher-paced mastery learning in elementary and secondary schools. In all cases, the students in the mastery learning groups outlearned their counterpart control groups.

But mastery learning is not without its critics. In a review of studies on mastery learning, Arlin (1984) reported some of the more popular criticisms. Some critics say that the claim that mastery learning equalizes students' learning abilities is an overstatement. Some critics describe mastery learning as a "psychological trap": It does not have a proper conceptual base. Some critics even call mastery learning a "Robin Hood phenomenon" that takes from advanced students and gives to the poor students. Arlin himself argues that studies that find all students equally capable should be interpreted more cautiously. Slavin (1989, p. 79) says that "if school districts expect that by introducing group-based mastery learning. . . . They can measurably increase their students' achievement, there is little evidence to support them."

Readers of professional journals must remember that any innovation may meet either astounding success or total failure, depending on the conditions of the moment. The old adage "Never believe anything you hear, and believe only half of what you see" is good advice as you interpret research findings. Proceed with caution. Curricularists must also carefully examine the studies being reported. Not only are they not without flaws but there are so many flaws that Bracey (1993, p. 85) was prompted to write, "Far too many flawed studies are getting through the seams of peer review and into print. Mislabeled and misleading graphs and figures abound."

## Matching Teaching Styles and Learning Styles

Dunn, Brennan, DeBello, and Hodges (1984) began an article by quoting the following words from a National Association of Secondary School Principals' publication (see Keefe, 1979, p. 132): "Learning style diagnosis . . . gives the most powerful leverage yet available to educators to analyze, motivate, and assist students in school. . . . It is the foundation of a truly modern approach to education." Dunn and coworkers followed this quotation with one taken from *Redbook* magazine: "You can determine a lot about your own child's learning style, share the information with teachers, challenge any facile diagnosis . . . or any remedial work that isn't working. . . . You can be instrumental in making educators realize that children of different needs need to be taught differently" (Ball, 1982). Like the first quotation, the *Redbook* quotation urges readers to become familiar with techniques for measuring learning styles. For more than a decade, educators have conducted research to discover more about various learning styles.

Figure 10.5 shows five categories of characteristics, or stimuli, that affect learning: environmental, emotional, sociological, physical, and psychological. Although the effects of the environment on learning may be obvious, the other elements may affect learning without the teacher's being aware of it.

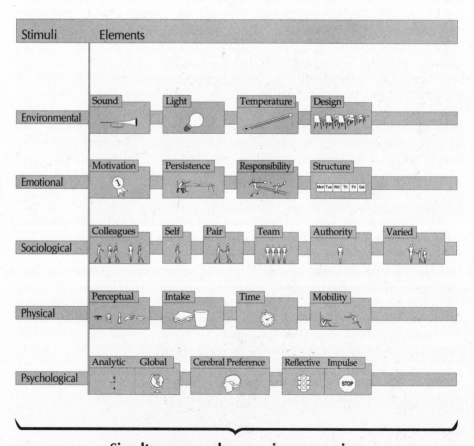

**Simultaneous and successive processing**

**Figure 10.5** Diagnosing learning styles.

Several research studies have reported successful applications of the matching styles movement. Sixth-graders who had been matched with their learning style preferences had significantly higher reading scores than their counterparts who had not been matched with learning style preferences. Their attitudes were also better (Pizzo, 1981). High school students who were matched with teachers of similar styles had more positive attitudes (Copenhaver, 1979), and in a high school English class, students who were matched with their time-of-day preferences had less truancy (Shea, 1983). Dunn and colleagues (1984) perceive learning style preferences as strengths teachers can use to design more effective learning experiences. Geisert and Dunn (1991, p. 223) say that "difficult material needs to be introduced through each student's strongest perceptual modality (preferred learning style) and then reinforced through supplementary modalities."

Studies show that such matching consistently increases academic achievement, improves attitudes toward school, and reduces discipline problems. This last finding is consistent with the often heard statement that a well-planned lesson is the greatest deterrent to discipline problems.

## How to Match Styles

There are several ways to attain a match between teaching style and learning style. First, teachers can be matched with students who have similar personalities, but there are mixed results with this method. For example, Thelan (1960) found that such personality matches produced more "manageable" classes and increased student satisfaction with classroom activities. Yet Jones (1971) matched introverted teachers with introverted students and extroverted teachers with extroverted students and found that the matchings failed to foster productive relationships. McDonald (1972) found that compatibility between teachers and students did not affect classroom interaction patterns.

A second approach to matching is to have the teacher select teaching methods that correspond to student learning styles. The teacher who discovers that a particular class of students responds favorably to simulations and not to lectures would use more simulations than lectures with that class. Another way to match methods with learning styles is to administer a learning style inventory to an entire class. The teacher can then group students according to their style preferences.

Should teachers always try to accommodate students by using instructional methods that the students prefer? Probably not. In fact, to provide students with opportunities to develop new styles teachers should purposely expose students to a variety of styles. Of course, this means that each teacher must master a variety of teaching styles. Changing styles may be difficult for many teachers, however, because it requires a change of attitudes. Marshall (1991, p. 226) explains:

> Consequently, for teachers to change their teaching styles, to understand and
> risk planning instruction on the basis of learning style patterns of students—
> and, therefore, to teach successfully a wider range of learners—they must

come to recognize, respect, and support the learning differences of students. If students do not learn the way we teach them, then we must teach them the way they learn.

## The Matching Learning and Teaching Styles Movement

Not everyone believes in the powers of matching teaching styles with learning styles. For example, consider the following hypothetical statement:

> The movement to match learning styles with teaching styles is a fluke that several educators dreamed up to get attention. Little quality research has been conducted in this area, and some of the limited studies on matching styles found little or no difference in learning. Some studies suggest that teachers should expose students to several styles, but teachers naturally tend to alter their approaches according to students' responses. So matching teaching and learning styles is nothing new—it's the same old wine in a new bottle. To quote Shakespeare, it's "much ado about nothing."

1. How consistent must research findings be to be considered conclusive? In other words, must all studies produce the same answer before the answer can be considered factual?

2. Choose one of your favorite teachers. Does this teacher use different teaching styles? List three or four of this teacher's styles.

3. Do you have a single preferred style? To reach an intelligent answer to this question, draw a vertical line down the middle of a sheet of paper. On the left side, list variables that enhance learning for you. On the right side, list variables that impede learning for you.

4. Challenge or defend this statement: All teachers should purposely increase their repertoire of teaching styles.

5. Do you think teachers should spend more or less time developing new styles? Why?

## Using Microcomputers to Individualize

Microcomputers offer teachers unprecedented opportunities to individualize instruction. As Magney (1990, pp. 55–56) so aptly notes, "Computer games can be a window [through] which students can enter many academic realities. . . . Prior to the microcomputer, computers were used primarily to give rules and other information to players but now the computer often makes decisions for the players. Unlike most of the older games, and simulations, which focus on group work, those computerized activities can be easily designed for individual use."

## Programs for At-Risk Students

Much attention is being given to increase the success of at-risk students. These are the millions of students whose likelihood of dropping out of school is great. These students often come from poor families or have no family at all.

The characteristics that identify at-risk students are well documented. They include low achievement, retention in grade, behavior problems, poor attendance, low socioeconomic status, and attendance at schools with large numbers of poor students (Morris, 1991). Many of these factors cause stress among students; they ultimately affect classroom performance.

According to Levin (1987), approximately one-third of secondary school students are at risk of dropping out of school. Other reports estimate that the percentage of secondary students who are at risk is even higher, perhaps approaching 50 percent (Aksamit, 1990).

Several societal conditions have contributed to the large number of at-risk students. For example, one-half of American families in all social groups will at some time become involved in dangerous behavior, the United States leads the entire industrialized world in the rate of adolescent pregnancy, 1 million children run away from home every year, adolescents are the only age-group in the United States for which the statistics for suicide, obesity, sexually transmitted diseases, drug and alcohol abuse, and violent death keep increasing (Banks, Kopassi, & Wilson, 1991).

Even the schools conduct activities that seem to work against the best interests of students. For example, the Phi Delta Kappa study of at-risk students found that failure to promote students is clearly harmful because it increases the likelihood that students will drop out and diminishes the probability that they will raise their achievement levels (Frymier & Gansneder, 1989). Many at-risk students are vulnerable to failure of any kind because they do not have the confidence lent by academic success; therefore, their blossoming depends upon a supportive, warm, confidence-building environment (Blumenthal, Holmes, & Pound, 1991).

At-risk students have developed counterproductive behaviors. Wellington and Perlin (1991, p. 88) say, "We need innovations for 'unteaching' counterproductive behavior." The use of alternative learning styles can help at-risk students. One program director (Friedman, 1991, p. 89) says, "We respect the fact that individuals learn differently and we empower our students to accept responsibility for maximizing their learning potential."

Other appropriate qualities for at-risk curricula include high involvement, high reinforcement, and personalization. But each program must be designed or adapted to meet the particular needs of the students. Elkind (1991) cautions that making programs more rigorous is an oversimplistic approach that is both mindless and destructive.

Today, educators realize that, if the needs of at-risk students are to be met, the schools must begin addressing them early in their school experiences, preferably even in preschool. Karweit (1987) found that full-day kindergarten programs, as opposed to half-day programs, improved the performance of at-risk students. Day-long programs provide the time needed to bring about attitude changes. These children need to develop self-confidence. But students do not outgrow this type of problem, and teachers at all grade levels have a big role to play in educating at-risk students.

Successful programs for at-risk students have several common characteristics. Most have close relationships between schools, other community agencies, and the homes. Successful classrooms for at-risk students also have several common characteristics, including:

Using classroom rules

Setting clear expectations

Using directed teaching

Monitoring student behavior

Because at-risk students often need more than educational support, one program provides students a minimum of 30 minutes each day for discussion of whatever the students want to talk about (Blumenthal, Holmes, & Pound, 1991).

In response to the isolation that at-risk students experience in our society, most programs require them to work cooperatively with their classmates. For example, in a program called Writing Roulette, one participant identifies a problem in writing, another suggests ways for solving the problem, and a third concludes by solving the problem. This cooperative approach encourages students who may be reluctant to express their ideas in writing (Lile, Lile, & Jefferies, 1991). Because at-risk students are often alienated from the mainstream in our society, successful at-risk programs tend to be personal, stressing one-on-one attention (Coleman, 1991).

In a research and development at-risk study for the National Center for Education Statistics, Finn (1993, p. 77) concluded that "More attention should be given by educators and researchers to encouraging the potential of 'marginal' students." These students do not display the behaviors of at-risk students, for example, absenteeism, failure to do homework assignments, and failure on tests.

## Other Ways to Involve Students

In addition to varying lesson plans, a variety of learning avenues, such as textbooks, discussions, field trips, oral reports, term projects, and homework, is necessary. We now turn to the use of these approaches and the teacher's role in each.

### Textbooks

As discussed in Chapter 7, throughout the history of education in the United States, one type of textbook or another has dominated the curriculum. At first, the textbook determined the content to be studied. There were virtually no experiences other than rote memorization and recitation, which often resulted in a boring, irrelevant curriculum. To a large extent, this is still true: Many teachers still consider the textbook to be the major (and usually only) source of content. Although the role of the textbook as the sole determiner of content is changing, the textbook can still be important in today's planning.

For example, textbooks can be used along with other materials. Instead of the textbook leading the teacher and students in the selection of content and experiences, the teacher can take a proactive posture and lead the designing of the curriculum. For example, instead of following the textbook organization from Chapter 1 to Chapter 2, the teacher can determine the sequence of topics. The teacher may decide that some chapters are not worth including in the curriculum. Teachers are becoming increasingly competent in curriculum development, and more and more teachers insist on having the freedom to shape the curricula in their classes as they see fit. For example, reform programs may provide teachers with curriculum frameworks (guidelines for selecting curriculum content and activities) and require teachers to design the curriculum.

But not all school systems provide teachers with the freedom to develop their own curricula. Concern that students may not "cover" all the content needed for the following year or for college is always present, and this concern is legitimate. School administrators know that they are responsible for seeing that the total school curriculum does not have major content gaps. Many larger secondary schools hire a curriculum director, a curriculum supervisor, or an assistant principal who is directly responsible for this. Teachers should work with the curriculum leader and/or other teachers to avoid curriculum redundancy and gaps.

Other teachers make even less use of the textbook; some almost totally avoid it. They substitute current problems, learning activity packages, or learning units they have developed themselves. Of course, these teachers are in school systems that permit an unusually high degree of teacher freedom.

Whatever freedom your system permits you in using the textbook, be sure that you do not spend most of the class period reading the text or requiring students to read it. It is much better to assign a chapter as homework the evening before a lesson and to use class time to discuss what was read.

## Discussions

Today's students want to be involved. They feel that their own opinions and judgments are worthwhile, and they want to share them. For this reason, the discussion method has increased in popularity. A good discussion involves all participants. Everyone has an opportunity to relate the topic to his or her own experiences. This sharing of various perspectives can enrich the knowledge and understanding of individual participants. But discussions that are merely rambling gossip sessions and that do no more than share ignorance should be avoided.

Plan discussion carefully. Grouping students according to their interest in a topic and letting students choose discussion topics can encourage total participation. Avoiding groups made up of both passive and expressive students can serve both the expressive and the reserved students. Putting the reserved students together forces one or more of them to assume leadership, and placing expressive students in the same group forces some of them to learn to yield the floor to others. Assigning roles, such as "discussion moderator" and "recorder," and then varying these roles, will prompt all group members to participate even further.

Selecting topics that have answers, even though there may be multiple answers depending upon individual perspective, and letting students know that a definite outcome of their discussions is expected can give students a sense of purpose and responsibility.

A student moderator's difficulty in keeping group discussion progressing and on target can prompt teacher intervention, but too much interference will cause a group to become dependent on the teacher's leadership. Take care, also, to ensure that the group moderator does not dominate the discussion. The discussion must proceed on the basis that all serious comments are worth hearing, regardless of how inaccurate or insignificant others may consider them.

A free-flowing discussion provides a valuable opportunity to develop social skills, which is in itself an important goal for middle-level and secondary students. It also helps students identify with their peers. All adolescents need to belong, and all need positive recognition and approval from peers. Group discussions should help fill these needs.

The participants need to know that each person has a definite role in every discussion. First, each participant is obligated to read the assignment so that the discussion will begin from a common base. Second, each person is responsible for contributing information to the discussion. Opinions and contributions of knowledge should be prized only when the participants can present evidence or knowledge to support them. Third, each participant is responsible for listening to others and, when possible, for referring to specific comments of others. This assures all participants that their comments are being considered.

The teacher is responsible for seeing that the environment remains informal, pleasant, and nonthreatening. The teacher's role is that of facilitator, helping students to locate appropriate resources and to plan their discussion. Following the discussion, teachers can help students evaluate discussion techniques and redesign their strategies for future discussions.

## Field Trips

Like many fine inventions of the past, the field trip has become almost moribund, even though it has many unique advantages. The reasons for its loss of popularity are many. First, there has been a growing trend of lawsuits against schools, and the courts have begun to find more schools liable as charged. Because administrators and teachers can also be found liable, many are reluctant to encourage field trips, perceiving them as unnecessary risks.

This is unfortunate, because field trips have unique potential. There is no better way for a social studies class to study the habits of an ethnic group than to visit a local community. And a group of students interested in aerodynamics could find nothing more meaningful than a visit to a wind tunnel. An agriculture class may benefit tremendously from a visit to an agricultural agency, an experimental station, or a local farm.

Before arranging a field trip, the teacher should check school policy, because many schools now forbid field trips of any type. But even in schools that forbid field trips, teachers can "bring the field to the school." For example, a middle school or junior high earth science teacher might arrange for a few truckloads of several types of soil and rocks to be deposited on school grounds so that students can make an "on-site geology field trip."

Teachers in schools that permit field trips can let their students suggest the need for one, assuming that they are mature and self-disciplined enough to be trusted. Some groups of students simply present too great a risk, and a teacher would be foolish to pursue a trip with such students. If the idea comes from the students, they may be willing to work harder and organize better.

Every field trip should be necessary and purposeful, and each student should have definite responsibilities for gathering, processing, and reporting specific data. Students may also share the responsibility for organizing the trip, clearing it with the principal's office, arranging the visit, filling out the necessary insurance forms, and securing the necessary permissions and financing.

Afterward, a follow-up lesson in which students report their data and discuss implications will accentuate the trip's accomplishments. As with all other instructional approaches, evaluation of one field trip will improve the quality of future trips. Evaluations are more effective when done immediately after the trip while the teacher and students still remember specifics.

## Oral Reports

For several decades, oral reports have been popular in elementary, middle, and secondary schools, but the success of this technique depends on its use. When you are considering using oral reports, first decide on the purpose of each report. Too often, teachers give assignments without really thinking through the purpose. Oral reports can have several purposes that may be considered important goals.

For example, if an oral report is assigned to an advanced student who is delving into one aspect of a topic, the report can provide the student with an opportunity to share information and can simultaneously enable the rest of the class to benefit from the information. Or assigning a report to a group of students of diverse backgrounds can give them an opportunity to learn to work together cooperatively. Other reports might give shy and insecure students experience in public speaking.

Each of these purposes is legitimate and worthwhile so long as the teacher communicates the main purpose(s) of the reports to the students. However, assigning a report to punish misbehavior or to substitute for effective planning is not wise. Students will quickly connect the report with these purposes and probably will not expect any significant learning to result. This is the case when reports are used at the end of a grading period to give students an opportunity to improve their grades.

Whatever the reason for assigning oral reports, teachers must communicate to the reporter(s) the primary purposes of the assignment. Other members of the class should be told what is expected of them during the report. Should they take notes? Ask questions? Take issue with the speaker? Should they ask for clarification when they do not understand? Should they interrupt the speaker with comments or wait until the end of the presentation? Will they be held accountable on the next test for information presented orally by their peers? By answering these questions before the report is delivered, teachers can draw each student into the oral presentations of their peers and thereby maximize interest and involvement.

To avoid students' taking reports too lightly, credit might be given for oral reports—and perhaps to the rest of the students for their responses. To avoid threatening students, a positive reward system can let them earn credit for participation in the discussion without penalizing those whose contributions are minimal.

The timing of oral reports can be critical, and care should be taken to avoid scheduling too many reports in succession. The student who is giving the twelfth consecutive report in class is at a definite disadvantage. The repetition and the boredom students experience when too many reports are given can be avoided by spreading out the reporting so that no more than two are given during any week.

Students need ample time to prepare reports. Depending on the level of sophistication of the subject, a minimum of one weeks' to several weeks' lead time will be needed. Because many secondary school students and some middle school students hold part-time jobs, and extracurricular activities consume much of their out-of-class time, time should be allotted for preparing oral presentations. This is needed especially when students are planning group presentations.

Teachers should never make assignments without giving students an opportunity to present the results. This is especially detrimental when oral presentations are involved. Scheduling the reporting dates at the time the assignments are made, helps prevent this from happening. Then students will not be disappointed, and they will see oral presentations as worthwhile.

## Projects

Whatever the subject, assigning projects is a valuable option for a teacher. There many types of projects: long-term projects, which may last for a grading period or even a semester; short-term projects; and individual projects. Not all projects must end with an oral presentation; some may conclude with written reports or with presentations of products that have resulted from the assignment. Regardless of the product, students should be given an opportunity to show their creations. For example, a science teacher might want to arrange a local science fair to display students' insect collections, or a music teacher might want to set up a student recital.

Teachers who offer projects as options (not required of all students) may use a liberal grading system. One great advantage of projects is that they permit students who for one reason or another do not benefit from didactic forms of instruction to become totally involved. Many teachers take advantage of the opportunity to grade these activities in a way that rewards student effort. Many students who appear to be failures on tests can produce excellent projects. Perhaps it is because they want to do the projects, or perhaps they feel more competent doing something with their hands, or it may be a combination of the two. Therefore, many teachers view projects as an opportunity to provide successful experiences for everyone by assigning A's and B's to all projects.

## Homework

According to Solomon (1989, p. 63), "The purpose of homework is to prepare the student for his/her next lesson and/or reinforce concepts and skills learned in the previous lesson."

Solomon says that homework can play a positive role in student achievement. "A search of the literature proves that homework, assigned by a mentor for practice, participation, preparation, personal development, reinforcement, or as an extension of class study, will increase individual achievement."

During the 1960s and 1970s, homework for the public school student lost much of its prestige, but by the end of the 1970s it had regained some of its reputation. In fact, half of secondary school students themselves said that the homework was not challenging enough (Elam, 1979).

Cooper (1990, p. 88) researched the effect of homework on achievement across grade levels and reported:

> Homework has a positive effect on achievement, but the effect varies dramatically with grade level. For high school students, homework has substantial positive effects. Junior high school students also benefit from homework, but only about half as much. For elementary school students, the effect of homework on achievement is negligible.
>
> The optimum amount of homework also varies with grade level. For elementary students, no amount of homework—large or small—affects achievement. For junior high school students, achievement continues to improve with more homework until assignments last between one and two hours a night. For high school students, the more homework, the better achievement—within reason, of course.
>
> I found no clear pattern indicating that homework is more effective in some subjects than in others. I did conclude, however, that homework probably

works best when the material is not too complex or completely unfamiliar. Studies comparing alternative feedback strategies revealed no clearly superior approach.

But not all homework results in improved learning. For example, in a review of 24 studies on the effects of homework given in elementary and secondary schools, Friesen (1979) found that 12 reported positive effects on achievement and 11 found no difference or negative effects; the remaining study showed that the homework group did better on investigator-designed tests but worse on standardized tests.

One reason why students who have homework may score less well than would be expected is that teachers often do not have a definite purpose for homework assignments. This can lead to busywork. Here are some of the major uses teachers can make of homework assignments (Lee & Pruitt, 1978, p. 31):

1. Practice—designed to reinforce skills and information covered in class

2. Preparation—given to prepare students to profit from subsequent lessons

3. Extension—provided to determine whether a particular student can extend the concept or skill learned in class to a new situation

4. Creative—designed to require students to integrate many skills and concepts in producing some project

This list shows that homework can be used for different purposes and that it can also be used to develop higher-order skills. The purpose of homework should determine the teacher's instructional behavior. Teachers should always base a decision to use homework on a purpose for which it is suited and should introduce it accordingly. Far too often, homework is used only for practice. Because many states now require all teachers to give homework (many districts specify the number of hours a night), it is imperative that teachers become familiar with the variety of uses for which homework is suited. The four uses listed above are a good place to begin. The following suggestions will help with the design and implementation of a system for assigning homework.

## Homework Guidelines

### Clarify the Assignment

Homework assignments must be clear. Assignments that involve problem solving can be clarified and simplified by giving students an opportunity to work at least one problem of each type in class before asking them to do problems at home. Simply using verbal instructions and explanations may not be enough. Perhaps you can remember a time when, as a student, you thought you understood how the teacher wanted you to complete an assignment, but when you got home, you found that you didn't know how to begin. Had you been given an opportunity to work just one problem in class, you could have raised questions at that time.

## Individualize Homework Assignments

Students who cannot understand how to do their classwork even with the help of the teacher will benefit little from a homework assignment of more of the same type of problems. The teacher assigning homework must consider the abilities and needs of each student. Certain homework assignments for slower students will help them catch up with the rest of the class, and other types of assignments for the more advanced students can help them explore areas of special interest to them in depth. Such an individualistic approach to homework assignments can relieve the ever-present dilemma of teachers— how to challenge the brightest students without losing the slower students.

## Make Homework Creative

Teachers today realize that the old practice of assigning students to "read the next chapter and work the problems at the end of the chapter" is not challenging or stimulating. Homework assignments are more interesting when they contain variety. Students can be asked to respond to something that is on the evening news, in the newspaper, or on an educational television program. Multisensory activities can replace written assignments. Creativity cannot be forced, but a climate that stimulates and nourishes creativity can be established by letting all students investigate problems that have no fixed answer.

## Be Reasonable

Contemporary teachers should avoid making too many demands on students' time at home because many students come from homes that have no books or no place that is well-lighted or quiet enough for studying. Disruptions from brothers and sisters make homework difficult for many students. Then, too, many secondary school students and some middle school students use after-school hours for part-time jobs on which their families depend for some essentials. For such students, homework assignments that require a few hours each evening are impossible to complete. Secondary school teachers must also remember that students have several other courses and may be receiving homework assignments in all of them.

Evaluations of homework should take into account the conditions under which students must perform and should be lenient enough so that students who are faced with adverse environments will not become discouraged.

## Follow-Up

Nothing can be more disheartening than spending time and energy on an assignment only to have the teacher forget about it or push it aside for more critical matters. By scheduling a follow-up at the time of the assignment, teachers can prevent these annoying situations. Follow-ups also let students know that they are expected to complete each assignment. According to Phelps (1991, p. 242), regular follow-ups result in improved results: "When students are held responsible for assigned work, they are more likely to do the work than when their efforts go unnoticed."

### Steps in Assigning Homework

The following steps can be used as a guideline for making homework assignments (Berry, 1977, p. 52).

1. As an alternative, plan for assignments to be completed at some time during the school day in a supervised area.

2. Be sure the purpose of every homework assignment is clear in your mind and that you have made it clear to the students.

3. Try to match assignments with students, making sure each student is treated fairly and equally.

4. Be sure every student knows exactly what is required.

5. Check the assignment when it is due.

6. Don't expect homework to teach a student who is not learning properly in the classroom.

7. Remember that assignments that use a multisensory approach are most effective in teaching.

Although these seven steps were designed for elementary school teachers, they are appropriate guidelines for secondary and middle school teachers.

We have now discussed the uses of textbooks, discussions, field trips, oral reports, term projects, and homework. When a teacher makes any of these assignments, perhaps the most important question to ask is: What will this homework assignment permit students to do that they cannot do in class? And how can I design the assignment to benefit the student and perhaps the rest of the class?

### Parent Involvement

Parents' responsibility for helping their children succeed with homework has been recognized for many years; yet their exact role has not been clear. Solomon (1989, p. 63) offers the following suggestions for teachers to help guide parents who wish to help their children achieve in their homework assignments:

Teachers should encourage parents to: (1) set a definite time for study each day with a beginning and ending time and no interruptions; (2) provide the proper environment; (3) provide the materials needed; (4) require the student to organize school materials including books, notes, assignments, and papers,;(5) require a daily list of homework assignments; and (6) provide support and guidance if the child becomes discouraged or frustrated.

The site-based decision-making movement that is sweeping the country offers much hope for garnering the support of family members. Most teams will include parents. These teams will make decisions on curriculum, financing, and all other major school matters.

## SUMMARY

This chapter encourages the matching of styles in the classroom. There are, indeed, a number of advantages to matching teaching and learning styles, but this method is not a solution for all educational problems, and teachers should be aware of the limitations and criticisms of this movement. Good and Stipek (1983) identified the four following concerns:

1. There is no single dimension of learners that clearly dictates an instructional prescription. A style the student may find motivating might not be consistent with the student's ability or prior knowledge. Sometimes, a mismatch might be preferable.

2. Matching styles does not account for the relationship between the student and teacher, the nature of the learning task, and other important variables that affect learning.

3. Such important variables as task clarity, feedback, and opportunities for practice are often ignored, yet these affect learning.

4. Uniform classroom instructional treatments are often superior to differentiated treatment because they are compatible with the teacher's skills.

These criticisms seem fair, and there are others. The general approach of grouping, itself, may present overwhelming problems. Studies show that many teachers, especially inexperienced teachers, find it too much of a challenge to monitor different groups in classrooms (Doyle, 1980; Good & Brophy, 1987). Studies show that a degree of discomfort can be an asset in learning, rather than a problem to be circumvented (Harvey, Hunt, & Schroder, 1963; Piaget, 1952). Thus the major purpose of style grouping—to accommodate students—may be based on a faulty premise. Even the term *learning styles* is not clearly defined in the literature. Hyman and Rosoff (1984) say that a clear definition in terms of student performance would be helpful. They further point out that learning style is not static, because learning itself is a highly complex activity. Indeed, learning is such a broad activity that it cannot be confined to the cognitive domain.

The study of the effects of matching learning and teaching styles is still in its infancy. The findings hold promise, but the claims of the studies should be viewed critically.

As many as one-third of all students face obstacles—at home, in the community, and at school—which make them at risk of failing and dropping out. Schools and teachers are using many approaches to make school more meaningful for these and other students by attempting to individualize learning. A variety of instructional models are being used. Mastery learning has proved to be both successful and controversial. Some of its major strengths for learners include unlimited time on each topic, opportunities to remediate without penalty, and the absence of grades. Ironically, each of these strengths can cause major administrative headaches. Flexible time for individual students may not fit the school calendar, and many parents may insist on receiving traditional A–F grade reports based on competition. Another approach to individualizing learning which has been highly successful with many classes is grade contracts.

Such successful approaches to teaching at-risk students have some common elements. They spell out the expectations the teacher has of students, and the teacher carefully monitors student behavior. Maximum success usually requires involving parents, and site-based decision-making teams are doing just that.

## QUESTIONS

1. What is the difference between long-range planning and unit planning?
2. What are some ways that a constructivist perception should affect (a) long-term planning? (b) daily planning?
3. How can assignments of students to groups be made to ensure that all students will participate?
4. What are some advantages of mastery learning, and what is one planning step teachers can use to ensure that a lesson realizes each advantage?
5. How can teachers plan so that students' self-images will be enhanced?
6. How would you relate the terms *individualized instruction, grouping, mastery learning*, and *academic contracts* to each other?
7. Is the current reform practice of providing a curriculum framework to introduce students to activities adequate, or must teachers also lead students to identify major concepts within each discipline? Explain your answer.

## SUGGESTED FURTHER ACTIVITIES

1. Develop three separate ways of using advance organizers to introduce one lesson.
2. Develop a set of guidelines for teachers to use to involve students in planning.
3. Describe the strengths and limitations of two sample daily lesson plans given in this chapter in meeting the needs of at-risk students. Tell how each plan can be adjusted to reach the needs of these students.
4. Make a chart showing some obstacles to implementing mastery learning in K–12 schools. Describe a planning adjustment teachers and other curriculum developers can make to overcome each obstacle listed.
5. Draw a model to show your perception of the relationship between curriculum and instruction.

6. Develop a contract to be used in a class of students with diverse needs.

7. Choose a lesson plan and convert it into a mastery learning plan.

## BIBLIOGRAPHY

Aksamit, D. (1990). Mildly handicapped and at-risk students: The greying of the line. *Academic Therapy, 25*(3), 227–289.

Applebee, A. N., Langer, J. A., & Mullis, I. V. S. (1987). *The nation's report card: Literature and U.S. history.* Princeton, NJ: Educational Testing Service.

Arlin, M. (1984). Time, equality, and mastery of learning. *Review of Educational Research, 54*; 71–72.

Armento, B. J. (1986). Research on teaching social studies. In M. C. Wittrock (Ed.), *Handbook of research on teaching* (3rd ed.) New York: Macmillan.

Ball, A. L. (1982, November). The secrets of learning style: Your child's and your own. *Redbook, 160,* 73–76.

Banks, R., Kopassi, R., & Wilson, A. M. (1991). Inter-agency networking and linking schools and agencies: A community based approach to at-risk students. In R. C. Morris (Ed.), *Youth At-risk Students* (pp. 106–107). Scranton, PA: Technomic.

Beauchamp, George A. (1975). *Curriculum Theory* (3rd ed.). Wilmette, IL: Kagg.

Berliner, D. C. (1984). The half-full glass: A review of research on teaching. In P. A. Hosford (Ed.), *Using what we know about teaching.* Alexandria, VA: Association for Supervision, and Curriculum Development.

Berry, K. (1977). Homework: Is it for elementary kids? *Instructor, 86,* 52.

Block, J. R., & Henson, K. T. (1986). Mastery learning and middle school instruction. *American Middle School Education, 9*(2), 21–29.

Blumenthal, C., Holmes, G. V., & Pound, L. (1991). Academic success for students' at-risk. In R. C. Morris (Ed.), *Youth at-Risk.* Scranton, PA: Technomic.

Bracey, G. W. (1993). Tips for researchers. *Phi Delta Kappan, 75*(1), 84–86.

Brophy, J. (1983). Classroom organization and management.*Elementary School Journal, 83,* 265–285.

Burns, R. B. (1979). Mastery learning: Does it work? *Educational Leadership, 37,* 110–113.

Calderhead, J. (1981). *Research into teachers' and student teachers' cognitions: Exploring the nature of classroom practice.* Paper presented at the annual meeting of the American Educational Research Association, Montreal, Canada.

Calfee, R., & Brown, R. (1979). *Grouping students for instruction.* 78th Yearbook of the National Society for the Study of Education. Pt. 2, 144–148. Chicago: University of Chicago Press.

Carnahan, R. S. (1980). *The effects of teacher planning on classroom processes.* Unpublished doctoral dissertation. University of Wisconsin at Madison.

Carroll, J. B. (1963). A model of school learning. *Teachers College Record, 64,* 723–733.

Carson, M. D., & Badarack, G. (1989). *How changing class size affects classrooms and students.* Riverside, CA: University of California at Riverside, California Educational Research Cooperative.

Centra, J., & Potter, D. (1980). School and teacher effects: An interrelational model. *Review of Educational Research, 50,* 273–291.

Ciscell, R. E. (1990). A matter of minutes: Making better use of teacher time. *The Clearing House, 63*(5), 217–218.

Clark, C. M. & Peterson, P. L. (1986). Teachers' thought process. In C. M. Whittrock (Ed.), *Handbook of research on teaching* (3rd Ed.). New York: Macmillan.

Coleman, J. G. (1991). Risky business: The library's role in dropout prevention. In R. C. Morris (Ed.), *Youth at-risk* (pp. 61–62). Scranton, PA: Technomic.

Cooper, H. (1990). Synthesis of research on homework. *Educational Leadership, 47*(3), 85–91.

Copenhaver, R. (1979). *The consistency of student learning as students move from English to mathematics.* Doctoral dissertation. Bloomington, IN: Indiana University.

Corno, L. (1981). Cognitive organizing classrooms. *Curriculum Inquiry, 11,* 359–377.

Cunningham, R. D. Jr. (1991). Modeling mastery teaching through classroom supervision. *NASSP Bulletin, 75*(536), 83–87.

Des Dixon, R. G. (1994). Future schools and how to get there from here. *Phi Delta Kappan, 75*(5), 360–365.

Doll, R. C. (1978). *Curriculum improvement: Decision making and process* (4th ed.). Boston: Allyn & Bacon.

Doyle, W. (1979). Making managerial decisions in classrooms. In D. L. Duke (Ed.), *Classroom management.* 78th Yearbook of the National Association for the Study of Education, Pt. 2. Chicago: University of Chicago Press.

Doyle, W. (1980). *Classroom management.* West Lafayette, IN: Kappa Delta Pi.

Doyle, W. (1983). Academic work. *Review of educational research.* Washington, DC: American Educational Research Association, *53*(2), 176–177.

Drucker, Peter F. (1954). *The Practice of Management.* New York: Harper & Bros.

Dunn, K. (1981). Madison Prep: Alternative to teenage disaster. *Educational Leadership, 39*(5), 386–387.

Dunn, R., Brennan, P., DeBello, T., & Hodges, H. (1984, Winter). Learning style: State of the science. In K. T. Henson (Ed.), *Theory Into Practice, 23,* 10–19.

Elam, S. M. (1979, June). Gallup finds teenagers generally like their schools. Report made in November, 1978. *Phi Delta Kappan, 60,* 700.

Elkind, R. (1991). Success in American education. In R. C. Morris (Ed.), *Youth at Risk.* Lancaster, PA: Technomic.

Ellsworth, P. C. & Sindt, V. G. (1994). Helping "Aha" to happen: The contributions of Irving Sigel. *Educational Leadership, 51*(5), 40–44.

Finn, J. D. (1993). *School engagement and students at-risk.* Washington, DC: National Center for Education Statistics, U.S. Department of Education.

Finn, J. D. & Pannozzo, G. M. (1992). *Classroom behaviors that detract from learning.* Unpublished manuscript.

Flantzer, H. (1993). What we say and what we do. *Phi Delta Kappan, 75*(1), 75–76.

Fowler, W. J., Jr., (1992, April). What do we know about school size? What should we know? Paper presented at the annual meeting of the American Educational Research Association, San Francisco.

Friedman, R. S. (1991). Murray high school: A nontraditional approach to meeting the needs of an at-risk population. In R. C. Morris (Ed.), *Youth At Risk.* Lancaster, PA: Technomic.

Friesen, C. D. (1979, January). The results of homework versus no homework research studies. Educational Resources Information Center (ERIC) 167–508.

Frymier, J., & Gansneder, B. (1989, October). The Phi Delta Kappa study of students at risk. *Phi Delta Kappan, 71,* 142–146.

Geisert, G., & Dunn, R. (1991). Effective use of computers: Assignments based on individual learning style. *The Clearing House, 64*(4), 219–223.

Good, T. L., & Brophy, J. (1987). *Looking in classrooms* (4th ed.). New York: Harper & Row.

Good, T. L., Reys, B. J., Grouws, D. A., & Mulryan, C. M. (1990-1991). Using work-groups in mathematics instruction. *Educational Leadership, 47*(4), 56–62.

Good, T. L., & Stipek, D. J. (1983). Individual differences in the classroom: A psychological perspective. In G. D. Fenstermacher (Ed.), *Individual differences and common curriculum.* Eighty-Second Yearbook of the National Society for the Study of Education, Pt. 1, Chicago: University of Chicago Press.

Green, J., & Smith, D. (1982). *Teaching and learning: A linguistic perspective.* A paper presented to the Conference on Research and Teaching, Airlie House, VA.

Guskey, T. R., & Gates, S. L. (1986). Synthesis of research on the effects of mastery learning in elementary and secondary classrooms. *Educational Leadership, 43*(8), 73–80.

Harrison, C. J. (1990). Concepts, operational definitions, and case studies in instruction. *Education, 110*(4), 502–505.

Hart, L. A. (1983). *How the brain works.* New York: Basic Books.

Harvey, O. J., Hunt, D. E., & Schroder, H. M. (1963). *Conceptual systems and personality organization.* New York: Wiley.

Hubbuch, S. M. (1989, April-May). The trouble with textbooks. *The High School Journal, 72*(4), 203–209.

Hyman, J. S., & Cohen, A. (1979). Learning for mastery: Ten conclusions after fifteen years and 3,000 schools. *Educational Leadership, 37,* 104–109.

Hyman, R. T., & Rosoff, B. (1984, Winter). Matching learning and theory styles: The jug and what's in it. In K. T. Henson (Ed.), Matching learning and teaching styles. *Theory Into Practice, 23,* 35–43.

Johnston, J. M. (1990, April). *What are teachers' perceptions of teaching in different classroom contexts?* Paper presented at the annual convention of the American Educational Research Association, Boston, MA.

Jones, V. (1971). *The influence of teacher-student introversion achievement, and similarity on teacher-student dyadic classroom interactions.* Doctoral dissertation, University of Texas at Austin.

Joyce, B. (1979). Toward a theory of information processing in teaching. *Educational Research Quarterly, 3,* 66–77.

Julik, J. A. (1981, April). *The effect of ability grouping on secondary school students.* Paper presented at the American Educational Research Association, Los Angeles.

Karweit, N. (1987). *Effective kindergarten programs and practices for students at-risk.* Report No. 21. Baltimore: The Johns Hopkins University Center for Research on Elementary and Middle Schools.

Keefe, J. W. (1979). *School applications of the learning style concept: Student learning styles* (pp. 123–132). Reston, VA: National Association of Secondary School Principals.

Kowalski, T. J., Henson, K. T., & Weaver, R. A. (1994). *Case studies on beginning teachers.* New York: Longman.

Kowalski, T. J., Weaver, R. A., & Henson, K. T. (1990). *Case studies on teaching.* White Plains, NY: Longman.

Lawson, A. E., Abraham, M. R., & Renner, J. W. (1989). *A theory of instruction: Using the learning cycle to teach science concepts and thinking skills* (NARST Monograph No. 1). Cincinnati, OH: University of Cincinnati, National Association for Research in Science Teaching.

Lee, J., & Pruitt, K. W. (1978). Homework assignments: Classroom games or teaching tools? *Clearing House, 53,* 31.

Levin, H. M. (1987). *New schools for the disadvantaged.* Unpublished manuscript. Stanford, CT: Mid-Continent Regional Laboratory.

Levy, J. (1983). Research synthesis on right and left hemispheres: We think with both sides of the brain. *Educational Leadership, 40* (4), 66–71.

Lewellen, J. R., (1990, Oct.–Nov.) "Systematic and effective teaching." *The High School Journal. 63* (1), 57–63.

Lile, B., Lile, G., & Jefferies, B. (1991). Project rebound: Effective intervention for rural elementary at-risk students. In R. C. Morris (Ed.), *Youth at-risk* (pp. 40-41). Scranton, PA: Technomic.

Little, D. (1985). *An investigation of cooperative small-group instruction and the use of advance organizers on the self-concept and social studies achievement of third-grade students.* Doctoral dissertation, University of Alabama.

Magney, J. (1990). Game-based teaching. *The Education Digest, 60*(5), 54–57.

Markle, G., Johnson, J. H., Geer, C., & Meichtry, Y. (1990, November). Teaching for understanding. *Middle School Journal, 22*(2), 53–57.

Marshall, C. (1991, March-April). Teachers' learning styles: How they affect student learning. *The Clearing House, 64*(4), 225–227.

McDonald, C. (1972). *The influence of pupil liking the teacher, pupil perception of being liked, and pupil socioeconomic status on classroom behavior.* Doctoral dissertation. University of Texas at Austin.

Morine, G., & Vallance, E. (1975). *Special study B: A study of teacher and pupil perceptions of classroom instruction* (Technical Report No. 75-11-6). San Francisco: Far West Laboratory.

Morris, R. C. (1991). (Ed.). *Youth at-Risk.* Lancaster, PA: Technomic.

Nye, B. D., Achilles, C. M., Boyd-Zaharias, J., Fulton, B. D., Wallenhorst, M. A. (1994). "Small is far better." *Research in the schools, 1* (1), 9–20.

Oakes, J. (1990). *Multiplying inequalities. The effects of race, social class and tracking on opportunities to learn mathematics and science.* Santa Monica, CA: The Rand Corporation.

Oliva, Peter F. (1992). *Developing the curriculum* (2nd ed.), New York: Harper Collins.

O'Neal, Michael, Earley, Barbara, & Snider, Marge (1991). Addressing the needs of at-risk students: A local school program that works. In Robert C. Morris (Ed.), *Youth at risk* (pp. 122–125). Lancaster, PA: Technomic.

Orlich, D. C. (1980). *Teaching strategies: A guide to better instruction.* Lexington, MA: D. C. Health.

Perkins, D. (1994). Do students understand understanding? *Education Digest, 59*(5), 21–25.

Peterson, P. L., Marx, R. W., & Clark, C. M. (1978). Teacher planning, teacher behavior, and student achievement. *American Educational Research Journal, 15,* 555–565.

Phelps, P. H. (1991). Helping teachers excel as classroom managers. *The Clearing House, 14*(3), 241–242.

Phillips, D. R., Phillips, D. G., Melton, G., & Moore, P. (1994). Beans, blocks, and buttons: Developing thinking. *Educational Leadership, 51*(5), 50–53.

Piaget, J. (1952). *The origins of intelligence in children.* New York: International University Press.

Pizzo, J. (1981). *An investigation of the relationships between selected acoustic environments and sound, an element of learning style, as they affect sixth grade students' reading achievement and attitudes.* Doctoral dissertation. New York: St. John's University.

Reyes, D. J. (1990). Models of instruction: Some light on the model muddle. *The Clearing House, 63*(1), 214–216.

Romberg, T. A. (1983). *Allocated time and content covered in mathematics.* Paper presented at the annual meeting of the American Educational Research Association, Montreal, Canada.

Romberg, T. A., & Carpenter, T. P. (1986). Research on teaching mathematics: Two disciplines of scientific inquiry. In M. C. Wittrock (Ed.), *American educational research association handbook of research on teaching* (3rd ed.). New York: Macmillan.

Schville, J., et al (1983). Teachers as policy brokers in the content of elementary school mathematics. In L. S. Schulman and E. G. Sykes (Eds.), *Handbook of teaching and policy.* New York: Longman.

Shavelson, R. J. (1984). Review of research on teachers' pedagogical judgments, plans, and decisions. Los Angeles: Rand Corporation and University of California. In R. L. Egbert and M. M. Kluender (Eds.), *Using research to improve teacher education* (pp. 132–133). Lincoln, NE: American Association of Colleges for Teacher Education/Teachers College, University of Nebraska.

Shavelson, R. J., & Stern, P. (1981). Research on teachers' pedagogical thoughts, judgements, decisions, and behavior. *Review of Educational Research, 51,* 455–498.

Shea, T. C. (1983). *An investigation of the relationship between preferences for the learning style element of design, selected instructional environments, and reading test achievement of ninth-grade students to improve administrative determinations concerning effective educational facilities.* Doctoral dissertation, New York: St. John's University.

Slavin, R. (1980). Cooperative learning. *Review of Educational Research, 50,* 503–527.

Slavin, R. E. (1989). On mastery learning and mastery teaching. *Educational Leadership, 46*(7), 77–79.

Snapp, J. C. & Glover, J. A. (1990). Advance organizers and study questions. *The Journal of Educational Research, 83*(5), 266–271.

Solomon, S. (1989). Homework: The great reinforcer. *The Clearing House, 63*(2), 63.

Stefanich, G. P. (1990). Cycles of cognition. *Middle School Journal, 22*(2), 47–52.

Stinnett, T., & Henson, K. T. (1982). see Chapter 16, The human equation and school reform. *America's public schools in transition: Future trends and issues.* New York: Teachers College Press.

Taba, Hilda. (1962). *Curriculum development: Theory and practice.* Orlando, FL: Harcourt Brace Jovanovich.

Thelan, H. (1960). *Education and the human quest.* New York: Harper & Row.

Trachtenberg, D. (1974). Student tasks in text material: What cognitive skills do they tap? *Peabody Journal of Education, 52,* 54–57.

Trump, J. L., & Miller, D. F. (1979). *Secondary school curriculum improvement: Meeting challenges of the times* (3rd ed.). Boston: Allyn & Bacon.

Tyler, R. W. (1984). Curriculum development and research. In P. A. Hosford (Ed.), *Using what we know about teaching.* Alexandria, VA: Association for Supervision and Curriculum Development.

Tyson, Harriet, & Toodward, Arthur (1989). Why students aren't learning very much from textbooks. *Educational Leadership,* 14–17.

Van Gulick, R. (1990). Functionalism, information, and content. In W. G. Lylcan (Ed.), *Mind and cognition.* Cambridge, MA: Basil Blackwell.

Von Glasersfeld, E. (1988). *Environment and communication.* Paper presented at Sixth International Congress on Mathematics Education, Budapest. In K. Tobin, K. Bugler, & B. Fraser (1990). *Windows into science classrooms: Problems with higher-level cognitive learning.* New York: Falmer Press.

Walter, L. J. (1979). How teachers plan for curriculum and instruction. *Catalyst, 2,* 3.

Walter, L. J. (1984). A synthesis of research findings on teaching, planning, and decision making. In R. L. Egbert & M. M. Kluender (Eds.), *Using research to improve teacher education,* Lincoln, NE: American Association of Colleges for Teacher Education.

Wellington, P., & Perlin, C. (1991). Palimpsest probability and the writing process: Mega-change for at-risk students. In R. C. Morris (Ed.), *Youth at-Risk,* Lancaster, PA: Technomic.

Wuthrick, M. A. (1990). Blue jays win: Crows go down in defeat. *Phi Delta Kappan, 71*(7), 553–556.

Zahorik, J. A. (1975). Teacher planning models. *Educational Leadership, 33,* 134–139. Lincoln, NE: Teachers College, University of Nebraska.

Zais, R. S. (1976). *Curriculum: Principles and foundations.* New York: Crowell.

# Chapter 11

# DEVELOPING TEACHING-LEARNING UNITS

## OBJECTIVES

This chapter should prepare you to:

- Develop a learning-teaching unit for a topic and grade level commensurate with your professional background.
- Write your own philosophy of education.
- Explain how your philosophy of education should work to guide the development of your curricula.
- For any given set of opposing views, clearly state a preference for one view over the other.
- Explain how your views toward youth should affect the design of your learning-teaching units.
- Give an example of how your views on the purpose of schools should affect your curricula.
- Contrast faculty psychology and stimulus-response theory.
- Contrast Gestalt psychology and connectionism.
- Contrast the views on learning held by developmental psychologists and those held by the structure of disciplines proponents.
- Give an example of the use of metacognition in school.
- Explain the role of a rationale statement in education.
- Contrast instructional evaluation and unit evaluation.

## INTRODUCTION

This book is based on four models: Taba's inverted model, Tyler's ends-means model, phenomenology (personal model), and a combination of the constructivist and concept models, and all four are important to this chapter. Taba's inverted model with its learning-teaching unit, is the focus, however, so let's begin by reviewing it.

## RATIONALE

Taba's inverted model has been discussed in earlier chapters in this book. A unique strength of this model is its inclusion of learning-teaching units. Another strength is the way in which Taba suggested that the units be developed and used.

Taba believed that learning-teaching units must be developed and used by teachers since teachers would then be (1) familiar with the units and (2) committed to making the approach succeed. Taba also believed that the unit had strength because it could be tested and revised. If based on research and theory, the unit could tie together theory and practice. By doing so, the unit could unite curriculum and instruction. Hill (1986, p. 7) explains the theory-to-practice function of the learning-teaching unit:

> Unit curriculum development and the tradition referred to as the emergent curriculum are the main approaches of which Taba has written so well. This tradition in the curriculum theory literature belongs in the domain of interactive theory or praxis theory. That is, the curriculum worker brings theory and practice together in the working setting and crafts the curriculum out of the interaction of real settings with a good grasp of concepts and constructs of his or her professional training. This interactive approach is described as making meaning from theory and practice.

This chapter explains a process teachers can use to develop learning-teaching units. Care is taken to ensure attainment of the potential benefits that Taba saw in the unit approach. But since this book is grounded in three other additional models, the Tyler model and the combined concept-constructivist model, and phenememological personal model, the unit development process suggested in this chapter will also capitalize on the strengths of those three models.

The Tyler ends-means model gives purpose to the curriculum development process by first identifying what the curriculum seeks to achieve and then designing it accordingly. This chapter will use a modified version of the Tyler ends-means model. Hill (1986, p. 7) explains the need for Taba's inductive model and Tyler's deductive model in curriculum development and curriculum evaluation:

> Curriculum evaluation must address curriculum, instruction, and learning in this tradition of Tyler and others because it is a widely accepted and useful method of working with school programs. Curriculum, instruction, and learning development and improvement require the feedback of a working curriculum evaluation system.

A second tradition in curriculum development derives from the inductive approach so well articulated by Hilda Taba (1962). Taba proposed a development of units of study for try-out based on eight steps which begin with a diagnosis of learner needs. This direct interaction with the learners is followed by formulation of objectives, selection of content, organization of content, selection of learning activities, organization of learning activities, selection of evaluation approaches, and a check of unit balance and sequence.

The Tyler ends-means model begins with a philosophy statement or a statement of the purposes of the curriculum. This statement can be adapted to the level of the learning-teaching unit. The philosophy statement enables the developer to identify the desired ends or outcomes for the unit.

Next, let's combine the four models into one. This can be done by developing a learning-teaching unit which has the major qualities of all of these components. Since the literature and research on concept teaching are convincing, the concept model will be blended with this new combination. This will be achieved through the selection of content. Broad content generalizations will be selected and related to previously learned content (knowledge).

The theoretical basis for this book is shown in the following:

A. The development of this book begins with Ralph Tyler's Ends-Means concept. The author's purpose for writing the book is to help the reader use the principles of curriculum development and the principles of educational foundations to meet current and future demands of educational reform. The entire book is designed to meet this goal. The purpose for including this final chapter is to ensure that these ends are met through providing the reader opportunities to use all the content introduced in this book.

B. The development and use of a learning/teaching unit as a vehicle to prepare for educational reform reflects Hilda Taba's Inverted Curriculum Model.

C. Through the development of learning/teaching units, the teacher is prepared to select the *most important concepts*, as opposed to small facts. The selecting of concepts and relating them to personal experiences reflects the constructionism model.

D. The teacher is prepared to select student activities that will help each student discover the concepts. This individual, *personal* approach to learning acknowledges the belief that each student learns differently and the belief that students understand that which they can relate to their accepted perceptions. This total focus on the learner as an individual and the viewing of learning as a behavior that must be integrated into the whole life experiences of the individual reflect the phenomenological and personal models.

## WRITING THE PHILOSOPHY STATEMENT

The first, and most important, step in writing a teaching-learning unit is to make a statement of your philosophy of education. This statement becomes the source for identifying the desired ends (aims, goals, and objectives) of the unit. Be sure that your philosophy statement is, indeed, *your* philosophy, and remember that you will tailor the following sample unit for your use in your own classes. Understanding your unit and being committed to it are essential to its ultimate success. Furthermore, the task of writing the unit will be easier if you write your own beliefs about each part of the unit.

To make your unit manageable and to aid its implementation in the classroom, try to limit each section to no more than two or three paragraphs. If one paragraph suffices for a section, that one paragraph will be fine.

Directions for writing each section of the teaching-learning unit are given in the following pages. A sample section from a unit developed by a student appears after each set of directions. Unless otherwise instructed, do not read the sample section until *after* you have drafted your section. After drafting your section and then reviewing the sample section, you may wish to revise your draft.

It is now time to select your topic and grade level. Do this *before* you begin writing. If the intended audience (class) is atypical in any way, explain the circumstances at this time in one or two paragraphs. Here are the topic and grade level of our sample unit.

## WHAT'S THE WEATHER? INTEGRATED SCIENCE LEARNING UNIT GRADES 4 TO 6

Begin writing your unit by developing your philosophy of education. Your unit cannot be better than your philosophy statement. The philosophy statement should answer the following questions:

1. What is the purpose of humanity?

2. What is the nature of a democratic society?

3. What is the nature of youth?

4. What is the purpose of schools?

5. What is the nature of knowledge?

6. What is the nature of learning?

7. What are your personal strengths and weaknesses?

## The Purpose of Humanity

For centuries, human beings have contemplated the meaning of their existence. Why are we on earth? Are we here by accident? According to the big bang theory, the earth is the result of a gigantic galactic explosion. If you believe this theory, explain how you think the earth became inhabited with people. Was that also an accident? Perhaps you subscribe to the theory of evolution. Or perhaps you believe that God made us and placed us here for a special purpose. Whatever you believe caused the earth to come into being, examine your beliefs about the reason(s) the earth is inhabited by humans. Write a paragraph or two expressing why human beings are on earth. Name this part of your philosophy The Purpose of Humanity. You may believe that there is more than one reason for our existence. If so, you may write more than one purpose. But to prevent your unit from becoming unmanageable, limit your number of reasons to two or three and limit this section to two paragraphs. *Only* after you have written this section should you review the sample Purpose of Humanity section that follows:

### The Purpose Of Humanity

All individuals who spend time on this earth have the opportunity to add to or take from the people and things around them. Individuals must select for themselves those things to which they can best apply their talents and abilities. All individuals have the opportunity and the corresponding responsibility to contribute a part of themselves for the "greater good" of humankind. For individuals to realize this goal, they must actualize themselves to the fullest extent possible. In a sense, then, self-actualization is the ultimate purpose of our existence, not only for our personal benefit but for the benefits that the complete person may yield to the family and future of humankind.

## The Nature of a Democratic Society

You have undoubtedly studied several different societies. Thanks to twentieth-century technology, you have been able to get a picture of a number of societies throughout the world. Perhaps you have read books and articles or have seen news clippings about German society during World War II. Maybe you have read about Anne Frank, who spent two years with her family and friends in hiding, afraid every moment that they would be killed. Finally, that is precisely what did happen to her and her family, as it did to over 6 million other innocent people.

Now, think about your own country. If you could tell people who know nothing about democracy just two or three facts to help them understand what it is like to live in a democratic society, what would you say? Write a paragraph or two expressing your perception of a democratic society.

When you have completed your section The Nature of a Democratic Society, compare it to the following example. You may wish to revise your section. If possible, limit your section to one or two pages.

### The Nature of A Democratic Society

A democracy is more than a form of government or the highest social ideal; it is a process which allows individuals to achieve as much as their abilities and efforts permit. In a democratic society, the welfare of the individual is paramount and the rights of the individual are protected from the will of the majority. Dogmatism has no place in a democratic society, where the "right to be wrong" is as important as the "right to be right." The intellectual integrity of each person must be guarded. Members of a democratic society find richness in diversity and poverty in sameness.

## The Nature of Youth

Think about the age-group you teach or would prefer to teach. Your statement on the nature of youth should address the following qualities or characteristics of this age-group. Although there are always going to be some exceptions, do you believe that young people are basically:

1. Lazy or industrious?
2. Honest or dishonest?
3. Social or independent?
4. Competitive or cooperative?
5. Curious or complacent?

Most of us would agree that for each of these sets of characteristics, youths display a little of both opposite qualities in each set. Although saying that you believe youth reflect all of these qualities would be an expedient way to answer these questions, it would not help you clarify your beliefs. So, for each pair of qualities, force yourself off the fence and come down on one side. When you cannot completely decide, write a paragraph about each side. This will work *only* if you make a commitment to one side over the other, and only if you state your preferences in writing.

For example, suppose you are responding to the first item "lazy or industrious." And suppose you believe that the age-group for whom you have chosen to develop your unit is both lazy and industrious. You notice that these youths have a high energy level, and yet you also know that where academic assignments are concerned, some of these students require a jump-start. When faced with this paradox, just say that you believe this age-group is basically industrious but that many members require initial motivation. Once they are motivated, their high energy level takes over.

In the following example, you will see that the teacher who developed this sample unit perceived a unique quality that affects this age-group's initiative: she says that youths are self-centered. Pointing out this uniqueness is an excellent practice since this knowledge will guide the development of other parts of this unit. For example, the teacher who believes that this age-group is especially self-centered will want to select content and activities that revolve around these students' lives. This teacher also said that the child is always part of a larger environment. This teacher would also select content and activities that involve the learner's friends—activities that are enjoyed by this age-group. The bottom line here is that you should include any traits that you think are especially typical of the age-group for whom you are developing your unit.

After you have written your statement, examine the Nature of Youth statement in our sample unit.

### The Nature Of Youth

> Each child is a unique individual. Efforts to classify children according to "stages" or even "ages" often result in their being lumped into artificial categories. Children are in the process of becoming, but are not adults. There is more different about them than their size. Children, by nature, are self-centered. As their circle of knowledge expands, so does their realization that they are not the center of the universe. Children usually reflect the environment that surrounds them. While genetics may impose some type of upper limit to their aptitude, their environment usually is more predictive of what the child will be able to accomplish.

You may now wish to revise parts of your Nature of Youth statement.

## The Purpose of School

As a teacher, counselor, administrator, or other school employee, you have been hired because of your potential to contribute to the purpose of the school. The moment you stray from this mission, your school will suffer from failure to reach its maximum effectiveness. Stray too far, and you may jeopardize your position. In many districts the lack of adequate finances prohibits districts from adequately rewarding teachers, often leaving teachers feeling that their hard work is not appreciated. Those teachers who contribute substantially to the school's mission usually receive more personal and financial rewards than their counterparts get.

Before you begin to write this section you may wish to review the discussion of the purpose of school in Chapters 1 and 3. Schools have many purposes. Most people find it difficult to single out *the* most important purpose. Therefore, you may wish to focus on the *two* most important purposes of schools. Beyond this number, the task of identifying the purposes will become increasingly difficult.

Suppose the generally accepted views on the purposes of schools and your perception of the purposes of schools do not match. Most successful teachers do not try to make radical changes in the overall mission of their schools. Rather, they find a common ground between their own desires for their students and the school's mission. Rather than using their energy to fight the system, effective teachers find ways to capitalize on their own strengths. If you are to do this you must understand your own perceptions of the purposes of schools. If you cannot reconcile the differences between your perceptions and others', you should either leave the school or stay and earn the trust of your administrators and fellow teachers—and then work to change the school's mission.

After writing your own statement of the Purpose of Schools, examine the following sample.

## The Purpose of School

It is the purpose of the school to give to children the opportunity to experience the joy and power of knowing and learning to know. The school has the responsibility to accept all children at whatever point they are in their social, emotional, physical and intellectual development and to view their education as a coherent system rather than as isolated episodes. The school must recognize the pervasive influence of realities beyond the school and equip the child to deal with them. For the individual, the school must provide the skills necessary for the transition from dependence to independence and for society, the school must assist in developing responsible, self-directing citizens. The school should assist students in the process of recognizing that they must accept responsibility for themselves. The intrinsic worth and dignity of every person should be upheld and each student's potentialities should be discovered, developed, and equally valued. Through the process of formal schooling, children should come to realize the traits and abilities necessary for the building of a better society, and they must learn to value cooperation as well as competition.

What aspect of the sample Purpose of School statement do you consider noteworthy? If you were told that this unit was developed prior to the first educational reform report, *A Nation at Risk*, you might find it surprising that "student empowerment" was a major thrust of this unit, a topic that is just now becoming very prominent in the literature, especially in the education reform reports. Actually, this sample statement was a good choice because this teacher could have argued that the schools exist to develop citizenship instead of developing the individual. But, rather than argue, she very wisely chose to align her beliefs in the development of students with the development of the nation. Such behavior is the essence of *human development*, that is, developing the nation through providing for all individual students to develop to their full potential.

## The Nature of Knowledge

Prior to writing this section, you may wish to review the discussion of knowledge in Chapter 7. Also, remember from Chapter 7 that although used interchangeably by laypersons, *knowledge* and *information* are different. Information is the raw product from which knowledge is made. Before it is refined, information is as useless as crude oil. This does not mean that it is worthless, but it does mean that the value of information increases enormously when it is changed into knowledge.

Few events in life are more stimulating than the confrontation between the human mind and knowledge. This is what makes teaching the richest profession of all. The business of the teacher is to set up an environment which challenges all students to master knowledge. Few professions could make a better gift to their clients than the discovery of the satisfaction of a duel between the learner and the learner's adversary—raw information which, like the gold that lured the forty-niners, is there for the taking, in unlimited supply.

Sometimes people find it difficult to get the writing of this section underway. You may choose first to examine the statement in the sample unit.

### The Nature Of Knowledge

Knowledge is power. In the absence of knowledge, the individual is powerless to make any decisions or exercise any control over his environment. Knowledge is not the memorization of facts but the possession of the skills needed to use facts for some benefit. Knowledge is not absolute and does not consist of a given set of facts. It is dynamic and requires the constant attention of those involved in its pursuit. Neither students nor teachers nor those in the larger society ever "arrive" at a state of finality in their acquisition of knowledge. There will always be more to learn, more to understand, and more to apply.

The teacher who developed this sample unit focused her statement on the ability that knowledge has to empower its owner. She also addresses the limitless nature of knowledge. She also could have mentioned that the more knowledge you acquire, the easier it is to acquire. This leads to the next philosophy section, The Nature of Learning.

## The Nature of Learning

### *Faculty Psychology*

During the twentieth century, our understanding of how we learn has grown remarkably. At the turn of the century, the dominant theory was *faculty psychology*, which held that the brain is a large muscle whose growth requires vigorous exercise. The faculty psychologists believed that the best exercise was memorizing lengthy recitations and dull and difficult topics.

## Stimulus-Response Theory

By about 1920, faculty psychology gave way to E. L. Thorndike's *stimulus-response (S-R) theory*. Thorndike believed that information should be given in small units followed by rewards. Originally, he had thought that all behavior could be described in terms of stimuli followed by responses. Indeed, thought Thorndike, when given a certain stimulus, the subject had no choice but to respond accordingly. This meant that instead of making learning unpleasant, teachers should reward it. Quite an improvement over faculty psychology! Later, Thorndike realized that each individual is different, and the particular way an organism responds is affected by the uniqueness of the organism. Thus, the S-R theory became known as the *S-O-R* theory, the added "O" representing the uniqueness of the organism.

## Connectionism

Embedded in Thorndike's learning theory was a concept called *connectionism*, which held that by connecting each part of the information to be learned, the learner would find that mastering the next part would be simplified. Even today, evidence that curriculum developers acknowledge the importance of order is to be found in college prerequisites. As discussed in Chapter 5, ordering content from the simple to the complex is one of several rules used by curriculum developers to sequence content and activities.

## Developmental Psychology

*Developmental psychology* is concerned with the effects that growth has on behavior in general. Learning is one area developmental psychologists study. They tell us that a prerequisite to learning is readiness; that is one cannot learn until reaching a point of developmental maturity. Perhaps the best known of the developmental psychologists was Jean Piaget, who proposed the following stages of development:

Sensor-motor birth to age 2—earliest stage of development

Preoperations (2 to 7 years)—stage at which children focus on only one characteristic, lacking the ability to think logically

Concrete operations (7 to 14 years)—stage preceding the ability to think abstractly; roughly covers the elementary school years

Formal operations (12 and over)—highest level of thinking; involves abstractions

## Structure of Disciplines Theory

Another group of learning theorists, the constructivists, focuses its study of learning on the *structure of the disciplines*. Perhaps the best-known leader in this group was Jerome Bruner, who was mentioned in Chapter 3 in connection with the Woods Hole Project. Bruner and his peers tell us that each discipline has its own unique structure, and mastering the discipline requires understanding its structure. In sharp contrast to the developmental psychologists' theory of readiness, Bruner (1966) has said that, when correctly structured, any information can be taught to any age-group in some intellectually honest form.

## Gestalt Theory

*Gestalt theory* had its beginnings in Germany, where experiments with apes revealed that the mind sees things in terms of patterns. These patterns give meaning to otherwise meaningless information. Thus, Gestalt psychologists tell us that the whole we see and understand in its collective pattern is often more than the sum of its parts.

Gestalt psychologists say that these whole pictures often surface in a moment of revelation, as was the case with Archimedes, who for some time had been perplexed about the properties known as buoyancy and displacement. As the story goes, when Archimedes sat down in his bathtub, the water overflowed. He was so excited by his discovery that he jumped up and ran down the street in his birthday suit shouting, "Eureka!" [I've discovered it]. This sudden coming together of a mental pattern is called *insight*.

## Learning Styles Theory

During the past two decades, educators have begun to realize that each individual learns in unique ways. In other words, as individuals, each of us has a preferred learning style. What facilitates learning for one individual may totally block learning for another.

David Hunt, Kenneth Dunn, Rita Dunn, and Joseph Renzulli have spearheaded the learning styles theory movement.

## Metacognition

Also of current interest to many educators is the technique of studying one's own learning processes. Perhaps in your own educational experiences you have discovered methods that help you make learning an easier and more efficient process. In elementary or middle school, you may have learned to use acronyms such as *Roy G. Biv*, which has helped many students remember the colors of the spectrum. In anatomy, biology, physiology, or zoology, you may have learned to remember the parts of the nervous system by using the limerick: "On Old Olympic's Tiny Top a Finn and German Viewed Some Hops." The first letter of each of these words is the same as the first letter of the name of a part of the nervous system.

Or you may have learned that you are more productive when you study at a particular time of day rather than at another time. You may know that study cards work very well for you but outlining doesn't, or vice versa. Perhaps you have passed on some study tips to your students. You may wish to include metacognition activities in your activities section, or you may believe that the whole idea of metacognition is an exaggeration and that time is better spent focusing on the content to be learned. If so, you may wish to ignore metacognition as you write this section.

After writing your own statement, examine the sample unit's section on the nature of learning.

### The Nature Of Learning

Children learn as a total organism. The physical, cognitive, and affective domains of the child cannot be dissected to fit the aims, goals, or objectives of a particular teaching plan. The learning that a child experiences is dependent upon both internal and external factors. Learning may be enhanced or inhibited by past experiences and genetic makeup as well as by the prescribed learning environment within the walls of the school.

As you read about each of the perspectives on learning, perhaps you found that you agreed with some parts of each theory. Such an eclectic approach is neither uncommon nor bad. On the contrary, there is strength in the ability to see some good in each theory and in the ability to employ some concepts from each theory in designing learning-teaching units.

## Personal Strengths and Limitations

Effective teachers know that they are better in some areas than in others. Most teacher decisions are made during the course of the day; yet long-term decisions affect learner attainment more than short-term decisions do. An important advantage of the learning-teaching unit approach to planning is that it provides teachers with opportunities to examine their own strengths and to design curricula to maximize the effects of those strengths. Likewise, the unit approach allows teachers to acknowledge their limitations and to design curricula that circumvent or minimize the damage that their limitations might do to their lessons.

Your philosophy statement should end with a section titled Personal Strengths and Limitations. Begin this section by specifying one or two of your special strengths. These may include your expertise in your subject, special physical skills, or personality traits that have the potential to contribute to your teaching effectiveness. After listing these strengths give a strategy for capitalizing on each strength.

Now write a paragraph identifying one or two of your limitations. You may be a poor artist. You may have a weak voice or poor vision. Or, perhaps you have a deficiency or two in your understanding of your content area. Most of us do. Identify these limitations and explain how you can minimize their negative effect on your teaching. After you have written your own statement, examine the sample statement on Personal Strengths and Weaknesses.

### Personal Strengths And Limitations

As a teacher, or instructional leader, I feel that I will share the children's curiosity and enthusiasm for learning. I believe that the teacher's attitudes toward all aspects of education are highly contagious and are predictive of later student feelings toward school. I believe each student has the right to benefit from high expectations, and I will expect my students to perform in accordance to the way I will teach.

On the other hand, I realize that my lack of actual classroom teaching experience causes me to have a certain amount of naíveté. My love for the children may cause me to become too involved and concerned about situations over which I have no control (e.g., poverty, parental neglect). I plan to put a large measure of mental and physical energy into planning and executing learning experiences for the children, and I will expect them to reciprocate. I realize that I will be disappointed when, for whatever reason, they do not exert the required effort to obtain maximum benefit from what I have planned.

## RATIONALE STATEMENT FOR A TEACHING-LEARNING UNIT

Every day, students of all ages enter their classrooms greeting their teacher with the all too familiar question "Why do we have to study this stuff?" Teachers who love their subjects may not welcome this question, yet it is a legitimate question and it deserves a convincing answer. Let this question guide your writing of this section. Keep the perspective of the student in mind. "To prepare you for college or for the next grade" is not a good response. Remembering that young people are self-centered and live in the present, try to get into their world. Youngsters are very "now" oriented.

Examine the rationale statement in the sample unit.

### Rationale For Studying The Weather

Let's think together about a perfect day. I want you to call out words that describe what you think of as a perfect day, and I'm going to write them on the board. (Construct a "perfect day" web of the suggestions.) Of all the things we could think of, most often we mentioned words that concern the weather. Chances are that when you got up this morning, you consulted a weather report before you decided what to wear. That report could have come from your parents, from radio or TV, or from your own observation as you looked out of your window. Then, as you planned what you would do today, you had to consider the weather. If it is pouring rain, do you bring your baseball glove to school? No, no game today. If it is freezing outside, you might hurry and get ready so that you can ride a bus to school instead of riding your bike. Can you think of other ways we have to plan around the weather?

It appears that weather is a pretty important subject, doesn't it? We certainly think about the weather a lot and talk about it a lot, but how much do we really know about what we call weather? Sometimes people may claim to "know what the weather is" just because they can tell you whether it is raining, or whether it's windy or whether snow has been predicted. But, do we know what wind is, why it is, or where it comes from? Do we know what causes lightning or hurricanes or hailstorms?

Weather is a condition that is caused by the interaction of a lot of different things. Learning what makes up the weather will help us understand weather reports and forecasts. Studying weather conditions around the world will help us to better understand the different ways that people live and work in other places. Through weather folklore we will see that weather has its own history, and the study of natural disasters like hurricanes and tornadoes will help us better understand how people can survive tragedy and work together as a community.

Weather is something that is shared by everyone. You can't escape it, and for the most part, you can't change it. But we can understand it, and after this unit of study, we will all know what we are talking about when we talk about the weather.

With your philosophy statement and rationale statement written, it is now time to write the aim(s) for your unit.

# WRITING AIMS

The aim(s) for your unit should spring from your philosophy statement. Remembering that an aim is so broad that it can never be fully attained, examine your philosophy statement. Now write one or two aims that capture the most important role(s) of the school. Keep your aims statements short and simple. Begin by limiting each to a short sentence or sentence fragment. Examine your statements. Next, examine the aims in the sample unit.

### Unit Aims

  I.  Development of a positive self-concept
 II.  Preparation for citizenship
III.  Promotion of the joy of discovery
 IV.  Transmission of knowledge and skills

# WRITING GOALS

Educational aims might be interesting to talk about, but by themselves they will not lead to anything useful. To make aims useful, curriculum developers must draw from the aims some goals, which, unlike aims, are attainable, although they are seldom obtained. For example, consider the following goals:

- By graduation, all students at Douglas High School will be performing at or above the national mean in mathematics.
- By the end of the year, all third-graders will have developed a commitment to keeping the environment clean.
- Upon completing their unit on wildlife conservation, all biology students will be committed to protecting the food chains.
- By the end of their junior year, all band members will have learned to direct their classmates as they play a simple arrangement.

Notice that unlike aims, which can never be attained, goals are time-specific. Each goal should always have a targeted time for attainment. Next, examine the goals statements in the sample unit.

## Unit Goals

1. To develop a working knowledge of the following process of science: observation, measurement, experimentation, communication, prediction, and classification (related aims: II, III, and IV).
2. To understand the basic knowledge related to the study of weather.
3. To encourage the child's curiosity about weather phenomena (related aims: I and III).
4. To provide the child with opportunities to develop as an independent and creative learner (related aims: I, II, III, and IV).
5. To develop the skills necessary for effective group participation (related aims: I, II, and IV).
6. To enable the child to develop effective skills in communication and self-expression (related aims: I and II).
7. To understand the relationship between weather and economics.
8. To be able to apply the knowledge of weather to better understand the past, present, and future of our culture and other cultures around the world (related aims: II and IV).
9. To reduce the child's fear concerning severe and unexpected weather events through an understanding of the concepts (related aims: I and IV).

Contrast these goals with the preceding ones. Which list do your prefer? Why?

Your unit should have at least one goal from each of the educational domains. Do not overload your unit by including too many goals. Remember that each goal should be accompanied by a few objectives.

As noted earlier, by themselves aims are likely to remain empty statements unless they are converted into goals. Perhaps you also recall that each aim should have one or more corresponding goals. To ensure that all aims do indeed have corresponding goals, a table of specifications can be used. Following is the aims-goals table of specifications from the sample unit.

**Table 11.1 Using a table of specifications to ensure that each and every unit aim has one or more corresponding goals.**

| | AIMS | | | |
|---|---|---|---|---|
| Goals | Pos. self-concept | Citizenship | Discovery | Knowledge/skills |
| 1. Processes | | ✔ | ✔ | ✔ |
| 2. Knowledge | | | ✔ | ✔ |
| 3. Curiosity | ✔ | | ✔ | ✔ |
| 4. Independence | ✔ | ✔ | ✔ | ✔ |
| 5. Group Part. | ✔ | ✔ | | ✔ |
| 6. Communication | ✔ | ✔ | | |
| 7. Economics | | ✔ | | ✔ |
| 8. Culture | | ✔ | | ✔ |
| 9. Reduce fear | ✔ | | | ✔ |

Notice that each goal in the sample unit is followed by a key identifying the particular aim(s) which that goal serves. Make a similar designation by each of your goal statements.

This unit has four aims. This is about as many as any unit can successfully use.

This unit has nine goals. Table 11.2 lists key words (verbs) to represent these goals. To assure that these goals become realities in this curriculum, Table 11.2 lists the unit objectives and a check is made in each cell showing to which goal each objective belongs. Notice that these objectives are represented by action verbs. Each unit objective is a simple statement and these are the actual verbs that are in the unit objectives.

Throughout this text concern has been expressed over excessive emphasis on the recall level of the cognitive taxonomy. To ensure that the curriculum takes students beyond this lowest level of thinking, and also that affective and psychomotor objectives are addressed, the table of specifications shown in Table 11.3 records the domain and respective level of each objective.

These are just three brief examples of ways that tables of specifications can be used. This same teacher may wish to add a fourth table of specifications to ensure that learning activities are included for each objective, including some multipurpose activities that would address (help students reach) several objectives.

**Table 11.2 Using a table of specifications to ensure that each unit goal has one or more objectives.**

GOALS

| OBJECTIVES | 1. Processes | 2. Knowledge | 3. Curiosity | 4. Independence | 5. Group part. | 6. Communication | 7. Economics | 8. Culture | 9. Reduce fear |
|---|---|---|---|---|---|---|---|---|---|
| 1. Apply symbols | ✔ | ✔ | | | | | | | |
| 2. Iden. terms | | ✔ | | | | | | | |
| 3. Write para. | | ✔ | | ✔ | | | | | ✔ |
| 4. Record weat. | ✔ | ✔ | | ✔ | | | | | |
| 5. List effects | | | | | | ✔ | | | |
| 6. Iden. clouds | ✔ | ✔ | | ✔ | | ✔ | | | |
| 7. Design mural | | | | | ✔ | | | | |
| 8. Research clim. | | | | ✔ | | | ✔ | ✔ | |
| 9. Complete act. | ✔ | ✔ | ✔ | ✔ | | | | | |
| 10. Apply symbols | ✔ | ✔ | | | | | | | |
| 11. Complete eval. | ✔ | ✔ | | | | | | | |
| 12. Re–supply ctr. | | | | ✔ | ✔ | | | | |
| 13. Perform in gr . | | | | | ✔ | | | | |
| 14. Label meas. | ✔ | ✔ | | | | | | | |
| 15. Interview | | | | ✔ | | ✔ | | ✔ | |
| 16. Record fore. | | | ✔ | | | | | ✔ | |
| 17. List machines | ✔ | | | | | | ✔ | | |
| 18. Construct inst. | ✔ | | | ✔ | ✔ | ✔ | | | |
| 19. Write quest. | | | ✔ | | | | | | |
| 20. List rules | | | | | | | | | ✔ |
| 21. List services | | | | | | | ✔ | | ✔ |
| 22. List variables | | | | | | | ✔ | | |
| 23. Make graph | ✔ | ✔ | | | | | | | |
| 24. Make puppets | | | | ✔ | | ✔ | | | |
| 25. Write letter | ✔ | | ✔ | ✔ | | | | | ✔ |
| 26. Write story | | | ✔ | ✔ | | ✔ | | | ✔ |
| 27. Create game | | | | ✔ | ✔ | | | | |
| 28. Write review | | ✔ | ✔ | | | | | | ✔ |
| 29. Develop problem | ✔ | | | | ✔ | | | | |
| 30. Constuct satellite | | ✔ | | | ✔ | ✔ | | | |

**Table 11.3 Using a table of specifications to ensure that the unit addresses higher levels of all domains of the educational taxonomies**

| Objectives | Knowledge | Comprehension | Application | Analysis | Synthesis | Evaluation | Receiving | Responding | Valuing | Organization | Characterization | Reception | Set | Guided Response | Mechanism | Comp. Overt Resp. | Adaption | Originzation |
|---|---|---|---|---|---|---|---|---|---|---|---|---|---|---|---|---|---|---|
| 1. Apply symbols | ✔ | | | | | | | | | | | | | | | | | |
| 2. Iden. terms | ✔ | | | | | | | | | | | | | | | | | |
| 3. Write para. | | | ✔ | | | | | | | | | | | | | | | |
| 4. Record weat. | | ✔ | | | | | | | | | | | | | | | | |
| 5. List effects | ✔ | | | | | | | | | | | | | | | | | |
| 6. Iden. clouds | | | ✔ | | | | | ✔ | | | | | ✔ | | | | | |
| 7. Design mural | | | ✔ | | | | | ✔ | | | | | ✔ | | | | | |
| 8. Research clim. | | ✔ | | | | | ✔ | | | | | | | | | | | |
| 9. Complete act. | | | ✔ | | | | | | | | | | | | | | | |
| 10. Apply symbols | | ✔ | | | | | | | | | | | | | | | | |
| 11. Complete eval. | | ✔ | | | | | | | | | | | | | | ✔ | | |
| 12. Re-supply ctr. | | | | | | | | ✔ | | | | | | | | | | |
| 13. Perform in gr. | | | | | | | | ✔ | | | | | | | | | | |
| 14. Label meas. | | ✔ | | | | | | | | | | | | | | | | |
| 15. Interview | | | ✔ | | | | ✔ | | | | | | | | | | | |
| 16. Record fore. | | ✔ | | | | | ✔ | | | | | | | ✔ | | | | |
| 17. List machines | | ✔ | | | | | | | | | | | | | | | | |
| 18. Construct inst. | | | | | ✔ | | | | | | | | | | | | | ✔ |
| 19. Write quest. | ✔ | | | | | | | | | | | | | | | | | |
| 20. List rules | ✔ | | | | | | | | | | | | | | | | | |
| 21. List services | | ✔ | | | | | | | | | | | | | | | | |
| 22. List variables | | ✔ | | | | | | | | | | | | | | | | |
| 23. Make graph | | ✔ | | | | | | | | | | | | ✔ | | | | |
| 24. Make puppets | | | ✔ | | | | | | | | | | | | | ✔ | | |
| 25. Write letter | | ✔ | | | | | | | | | | | | | | | | |
| 26. Write story | | | | | ✔ | | | | | | | | | | | | | |
| 27. Create game | | | | | ✔ | | | | | | | | | | | ✔ | | |
| 28. Write review | | ✔ | | | | | | | | | | | | | | | | |
| 29. Develop problem | | | | | ✔ | | | | | | | | | | | ✔ | | |
| 30. Construct satellite | | | ✔ | | | | | | | | | | | | | ✔ | | |

## WRITING OBJECTIVES

Since a step-by-step description of objectives in all domains at all levels, was presented in Chapter 6, you may wish to review Chapter 6 at this time and keep it nearby for reference. You might begin your review by noting that, unlike aims, which never can be fully attained, and goals, which require months or years to attain, and still are rarely attained, objectives are daily expectations. And unlike aims and goals, which are written for groups, objectives are written for individuals. You might begin by noting the choice of verbs for each objective. The verb should describe an action that is observable and measurable. At a minimum, each objective should include a statement of desired student behavior, a description of the conditions under which you expect the student to perform, and a minimum acceptable level of performance.

Using these guidelines, write at least two or three objectives for each of your goals. You may wish to write several objectives for each goal. Try to include objectives in each domain, and although writing an objective for each level of each domain might be an overwhelming prospect, for each domain be sure that your objectives represent various levels.

Having written the objectives, check each objective to ensure that each verb describes an action that is observable and measurable. Even if it does, you may think of a more precise verb. If so, substitute the better verb. For example, suppose that your verb was *to discuss* or *to describe*. These verbs connote action, but they have a quality of ambiguity. When such verbs are used, curriculum developers should break down the objective into specifics. For example: "Discuss what is meant by progressive reporting and list three types of materials that might be part of a progress report." Often, the double verb approach can help to make the objective more specific and yet let the students express themselves. Once you have drafted your objectives, share them with your students, inviting them to add objectives to the list. This approach may produce some additional useful objectives; it definitely will garner student support for the unit. Now examine the objectives in the sample unit.

### Unit Objectives

1. After completing the activities in the weather forecasting center, the student will, when given a forecast, apply the correct weather symbols to a map with 80 percent accuracy. (goals: 1 and 2; cognitive: knowledge).

2. Given a multiple-choice test, the student will identify 25 weather terms with 80 percent accuracy (goal: 2; cognitive: knowledge).

3. After a related discussion by a meteorologist, the student will write a paragraph from the following starter: "A meteorologist is someone who. . . " (Goals: 2, 4, and 9; cognitive: analysis).

4. After viewing the filmstrip "Weather Changes and Their Causes," the student will record weather conditions every day for the remainder of the unit and include them in a personal journal (goals: 1, 2, and 4; cognitive: application).

5. After class discussion, the student will list 6 of the 10 economic effects of weather (goal: 7; cognitive: knowledge).

6. After participating in the cloud-making experiment and instruction, the student will identify the type of clouds in the sky and draw or paint artwork illustrating the concept (goals: 1, 2, 4, and 6; cognitive: analysis; psychomotor: set; affective: responding).

7. After instruction, the student will participate with the group in the design and creation of a cloud mural (Goal: 5; cognitive: analysis; affective: responding; psychomotor: set).

8. After viewing the film "Weather and People," the student will research the climate of another country (of student's choice) and write a description of the climate that includes temperature and rainfall (goals: 4, 7, and 8; cognitive: application; affective: receiving).

9. During the unit, the student will complete 60 percent of the activities available at each learning center (goals: 1, 2, 3, and 4; cognitive: analysis).

10. After completing the activities in the weather forecasting center, the student will, when given a forecast, select the appropriate symbols, draw them, and apply them to the map (goals: 1, 2, and 9; cognitive: comprehension).

11. After performing independent experiments, the student will complete an evaluation form for each experiment (goals: 1, and 4; cognitive: application; psychomotor: complex overt response).

12. After working in a center, the student will resupply the center with materials and arrange the elements for the next user (goals: 4, and 5; affective: valuing).

13. When assigned to a group, the student will perform his or her function without teacher intervention 80 percent of the time (goal: 5; affective: valuing).

14. After completing the assigned experiments, the student will label measurements from three weather instruments with 85 percent accuracy (goal: 1, and 2; cognitive: comprehension).

15. After interviewing an older person about weather folklore, the student will list the ideas and share them with the class (goals: 4, 6, and 8; cognitive: analysis; affective: responding).

16. After a class discussion of weather reports, the student will watch the evening news report and record the forecast to share with the class (goals:

3, and 6; cognitive: comprehension; affective: responding; psychomotor: guided response).

17. After participating with the class in the experiments about air weight and pressure, the student will list three machines that require air weight and/or pressure to operate (goals: 1, and 7; cognitive: application).

18. After participating with a group in the weather station, the student will construct an original weather instrument using the materials in the center (goals: 1, 4, 5, and 6; cognitive: synthesis; psychomotor: origination).

19. After the first day's activities, the student will write three questions about weather that he or she would like to learn the answer to (Goal: 3; cognitive: knowledge).

20. After a presentation by local civil defense personnel, the student will list four safety rules to follow during a tornado warning (goal: 9; cognitive: knowledge).

21. After a field trip to the weather station at the airport, the student will list three services the weather station performs for the community (goals: 7, and 9; cognitive: comprehension).

22. After a presentation by a county agent concerning the importance of the study of weather to agriculture, the student will list three weather variables that farmers cannot control (goal: 7; cognitive: comprehension).

23. After keeping a record of the daily temperature for two weeks, the student will make a graph of the information (goals: 1, and 2; cognitive: comprehension; psychomotor: guided response).

24. After reading a weather book from the reading list, the student will make and use stick puppets to tell a part of the story (goals: 4, and 6; cognitive: analysis; psychomotor: complex overt response).

25. While working in the publishing center, the student will write a letter to a travel bureau in another state requesting information that includes the topic of climate (goals: 1, 3, 4, and 9; cognitive: application).

26. While working in the publishing center, the student will write an original story entitled "The Day the Weather Changed My Plans" (goals: 3, 4, 6, and 9; cognitive: synthesis).

27. After completing the activities in the game center, the student will (as a part of a group or individually) create an original game, or a "weather adaption" of a familiar game, for use in the center by other students (goals: 4, and 5; cognitive: synthesis; psychomotor: complex overt response)

28. While working in the reading center, the student will read and review in writing an article from a weather magazine (goals: 2, 3, and 9; cognitive: comprehension).

29. While working in the measurement and observation center, the student will develop a new problem card for use by other students (goals: 1, and 5; cognitive: synthesis; psychomotor: complex overt response).

30. After watching the film "How Weather Is Forecast," the student, as a part of a group, will construct a weather satellite from materials provided and discuss with the class one function of weather satellites (goals: 2, 5, and 6; cognitive: analysis; psychomotor: complex overt response).

Just as a table of specifications can be used to ensure that the necessary goals are included in your unit, a list of goals and objectives can be used to ensure the inclusion of the necessary objectives.

Notice, too, that the unit objectives can be used to ensure that all domains are included and that there are upper-level objectives in each domain. For any single goal, to attempt to write objectives at all levels of all domains is unnecessary and unwise since this practice could result in superficial objectives. Yet, as a whole, the unit should contain objectives at all levels of all three domains.

## CONTENT SELECTION

Before you begin selecting the content for your unit, review Chapter 7 and then your own philosophy statement. At this point you are ready to incorporate the other models into your unit—the concept and constructivist models.

You should select content based on your objectives. For each objective, choose the major generalizations which are basic to or prerequisites for achieving the objective. Consider also the question What broad understandings and what specific content are essential to understanding this discipline? Perhaps you will recall from Chapter 4 that Albert Einstein said that the concept is the center of all thinking. Choose your content carefully. But, first, examine the content generalizations and concepts in our sample unit. Notice that each content generalization is broken down into concepts. This helps ensure coverage of the pertinent concepts in each discipline. Share these content generalizations and concepts with your students and invite them to add to the list.

### Content Generalizations and Concepts

I. Weather is the condition of the atmosphere at a given time.
   A. Atmospheric ocean
      1. Troposphere
      2. Stratosphere
      3. Thermosphere
      4. Exosphere

    B. Weather fronts
       1. Air masses
       2. Condensation
       3. Humidity
    C. Weather conditions created by people
  II. Weather is caused by the interaction of the sun, air, and water
    A. Sun
       1. Energy
       2. Earth's rotation
    B. Air
       1. Contents
       2. Conditions
    C. Water cycle
 III. Water vapor in the air can form clouds and also cause precipitation
    A. Condensation
       1. Fog
       2. Frost
       3. Dew
    B. Precipitation
       1. Snow
       2. Hail
       3. Sleet
       4. Rain
    C. Clouds
       1. Cirrus
       2. Cumulus
       3. Stratus
       4. Nimbus
 IV. Special combinations of weather conditions form different kinds of storms.
    A. Tornadoes
    B. Thunderstorms
    C. Hurricanes
    D. Winter storms
  V. Wind is the movement of air over the surface of the earth.
    A. Uneven heating by the sun
       1. Shape of the earth
       2. Different rates of heat absorption and radiation
    B. Daily cycle
       1. Day-night cycle
       2. Ocean-land winds
 VI. Weather analysis and prediction are accomplished by using special instruments, professional expertise, geographical facts, and historical patterns.

A. Meteorologists
B. Weather stations
C. Weather instruments
   1. Thermometer
   2. Anemometer
   3. Wind vane
   4. Hygrometer
   5. Barometer
   6. Rain gauge
D. Weather maps
E. Weather history
   1. Documented history
   2. Folklore
VII. The social and economic development of any area depends
    largely upon the weather and climate.
   A. Difference in weather and climate.
   B. Importance of climate in economic development
      1. Transportation
      2. Occupations
      3. Production of food
   C. Climate affects lifestyle
      1. Recreation
      2. Clothing
      3. Housing

Review the content generalizations in the sample unit and then write the content generalizations and concepts needed to achieve the objectives for your unit.

## SELECTING CONTENT AND ACTIVITIES

Teachers base their selection of content and activities on many and varied criteria. As discussed in Chapter 7, some of the most frequently used criteria are indefensible, including the way one was taught (Marshall, 1991), the teacher's degree of expertise and corresponding level of comfort with the topic, and the textbook. Teachers can and must improve on their criteria for selecting content and activities.

McNeil (1990) gives five types of criteria for selecting activities: philosophical, psychological, technological, political, and practical. *Philosophical selection* is based on values, pairing the ideal with reality. *Psychological criteria* are based on learning theories, some of which are contradictory. *Technological criteria* have a single goal: increasing test scores. *Political criteria* originate in pressure groups whose purposes are sometimes legitimate, and sometimes not. *Practically based criteria* are usually concerned with anticipated cost.

Recent reform reports reflect some of these criteria more than others. For example, political criteria seem foremost in educational reform reports. Application and Practical are often the rhetoric in these reports, and are also often silent decision makers. The accountability dimension of educational reform often stresses technological criteria. For example, test scores for an entire state may appear in major newspapers. Clearly, the covert goal is to have each school and each district outscore the competition.

As you select the content and activities for your unit, remember from Chapter 3 the impact Francis Parker made by involving students in decision making. Your students may think of quality content and activities to add to the unit. Giving students such an opportunity is a sound practice.

## SELECTING ACTIVITIES

Prior to writing this section, reexamine your philosophy statement. Next, examine your objectives. Your task is to decide on a strategy for teaching each topic that is based on your perception of the teacher's role in learning. You can determine this strategy by examining your beliefs about the purpose of school and the nature of learning. Next, review your strengths and weaknesses. This is your opportunity to use your strengths to enrich your unit and to cushion your unit against possible damage from your weaknesses.

Select teacher activities that facilitate learning. If you get bogged down before all teacher activities are identified, don't become discouraged. Proceed to the next section and come back to this after finishing that section. Your activities should complement student activities, and switching between writing teacher activities and student activities will help ensure this complementary relationship.

The activities in the sample unit follow. Examine them and share them with your students. Then write your own unit activities. Permit your students to add activities to the list.

### Activities, Experiments, and Related Resources

The following activities and experiments are resources to be used to teach the content and concepts related to the study of weather. By no means do they exhaust the possibilities for teaching this subject. Many experiments may be done independently by the students. Others require the supervision of an adult, and with younger children might best be used in demonstration. The age and "chemistry" of each class must be the determining factor in the selection of appropriate and profitable activities.

### Experiments

- Does air take up space?

Materials: handkerchief, drinking glass, pot of water

Procedure:

Stuff the handkerchief into the glass. Place the glass upside down into the pot of water. Remove the glass from the water. Is the handkerchief wet or dry? Why?

(After the glass has been removed from the water, the handkerchief will be dry. Since air takes up space in the glass, there is no room for the water to get inside and wet the handkerchief).

- Does air have weight?

Materials: two balloons, string, yardstick, pin
Procedure:

Blow up the balloons so that they are as equal in size as possible. Tie each one with a string. Then tie one balloon to one end of the yardstick, and one balloon to the other end. Balance the yardstick on a chair or table. Use the pin to prick one balloon just below the knot of the string so that air escapes slowly. What happens to the yardstick? Why?

(The end of the yardstick to which the leaking balloon is attached will rise because the weight of the other balloon will be greater.)

- How can you show that air has pressure?

Materials: Empty screw-top can , hot plate, gloves or mittens, pan of cold water
Procedure:

Pour about one-half cup of water into the can. Heat the can until steam rises from the top. (*Caution*: Do not heat the can with the top on.) Put the gloves on and remove the can from the heat. Screw the top on tightly. Put the can in the pan of cold water.

What happens to the can? Why?

(The can is crushed because the air pressure outside the can is greater than inside the can.)

- Does air have pressure?

Materials: match, piece of paper, empty milk bottle, hard-boiled egg
Procedure:

Set the paper on fire with the match and drop the paper into the empty milk bottle. Quickly place the hard-boiled egg on the mouth of the bottle. The egg will be pushed into the bottle. Heat from the burning paper makes the air in the bottle expand and rise. The air pressure inside the bottle drops. The greater air pressure outside the bottle pushes the egg inside the bottle. To get the egg out of the bottle, tilt the bottle and blow hard into it. Then hold the bottle away from your mouth. Blowing causes air pressure in the bottle to rise and push out the egg.

- Is air heavy?

Materials: Several widemouthed gallon jars, strong plastic bags with no holes, several feet of string.
Procedure:

Ask students to fill the plastic bags with air (by blowing or "catching"). Then tie the mouth of an air-filled bag over the mouth of a jar tightly with a string. Ask students to press down on the bag, lean on it, or rest a book on it. Why doesn't the bag go down? (The air takes up space.) What other things act in this way? (Balloons, tires, etc.) Next, ask students to remove the bag and tie the bag over the jar again, but this time with the bag pushed down inside the jar. Ask the students to pull out the bags. Why won't they come up easily? To pull a bag up, one small part must be "plucked up" at a time. The plastic bag has air resting on it—air that extends up for hundreds of miles. A pupil cannot lift this much air—it weighs several hundred pounds!

- How does unequal heating produce wind?

Materials: large shoe box, plastic wrap, candle, match, two lamp chimneys, tightly rolled paper towel
Procedure:

Cut a large rectangular hole in one side of the shoe box and cover the hole with clear plastic wrap, pressing the wrap securely onto the box. Cut two holes about 4 centimeters (1 1/2 inches) in diameter, one near each end of the box. Place the box, open end down, over the lighted candle so that the candle is directly under one of the cutout holes. Now put a lamp chimney over each hole. Produce smoke by lighting the paper towel. Hold the smoking material directly over the chimney that does *not* have the candle under it. The smoke will be carried down the chimney, across the box, and up the other chimney. This movement occurs because the air above the candle is heated, and thus expands and becomes lighter. The warmer, lighter air is pushed up by the cooler, heavier air around it, causing a convection current. Winds in the atmosphere of the earth are formed in a very similar way.

- How is the earth heated unequally by the sun?

Materials: two small, shallow boxes, two thermometers, equal amounts of soil for each box, 4-inch-square wood block
Procedure:

Put equal amounts of soil into each box. On a sunny morning or afternoon place both boxes in the sunlight. Place one box level so that the sun's rays strike the soil on a slant, and prop up the other box so that the sun's rays strike it directly. Place thermometers that have the same reading into each box, inserting each thermometer into the same depth of soil. Take temperature readings every 10 minutes. The soil that receives the direct rays will become warmer. Point out that the equator receives direct rays, whereas the rays are more slanted in the northerly and southerly latitudes. Also point out that the air above the earth will be heated unequally as well.

- Do all surfaces absorb the same amount of the sun's energy?

Materials: two cans of the same size and shape, sand, water, two thermometers
Procedure:

Fill one can half full of sand. Fill the other half full of water. The temperature of the sand and water should be the same. Put both cans in the sun and leave them there for a half hour. Put a thermometer in each. Make a chart showing the temperature of each at 10-minute intervals for 1 hour. Which one is cooler? Why? Next, place the cans in a dark place away from the sun. Record the temperatures at 10-minute intervals for 1 hour. Which one holds the heat? (Water takes longer to heat, but it absorbs more heat and holds heat longer.) Relate these observations to the formation of land and sea breezes.

- What happens when air is heated?

Materials: balloon, soft drink bottle, pan of hot water
Procedure:
   Put the opening of the empty balloon over the neck of the soda bottle. Is there air in the balloon? Is there air in the bottle? Next, stand the bottle in very hot water. What happens to the balloon? Why? Is air coming into the bottle and going up into the balloon? Something must be happening to the air in the bottle to make the balloon larger. Do you know what it is? (Air expands when it gets warmer.) There is no more air in the bottle than there was before. But the air in the bottle takes up more room now. Heat has made the air expand and move into the balloon. This air causes the balloon to expand.

- What happens when air is cooled?

Materials: balloon, string, marker, refrigerator
Procedure:
   Blow up the balloon. Tie it tightly with string. Measure around the circumference of the balloon with the piece of string. Mark the measurement on the string. Put the balloon in a freezer or refrigerator. Do you think the balloon will change its size? In an hour, measure it again. What has happened?

- What factors increase evaporation?

Materials: two narrow-mouthed jars, two widemouthed jars, water, caps for one of each type of jar, tape
Procedure:
   Fill the jars with identical amounts of water. Mark the water line with masking tape. Cap one of each type of jar, leaving the other two open. Place all four jars on a windowsill. Record the amounts of water left in each jar at the beginning of the experiment and after one, three, and five days. Keep a chart of the changes. What conclusions can be drawn? Refill the jars evenly (or use additional jars) and place them near a source of wind (a fan), near a source of heat, and in a cool place. What does this experiment demonstrate about the effects of temperature on evaporation, the effects of surface area on evaporation, and preventing evaporation (capping the jars)? Relate the results to what happens to the class terrarium.

- Do winds help to dry out land?

Materials: two flowerpots, soil, electric fan, scale
Procedure:
   Fill the two flowerpots with soil dug up immediately after a rain. Both flowerpots, filled with soil, should weigh the same. Place one in a protected area such as a closet, and the other directly in front of a small electric fan. Weigh both at the end of the day. What has happened? Why? How do the results relate to the water cycle?

- Why does evaporation cause lower temperatures?

Materials: water, alcohol, hand lotion
Procedure:

Ask students to dip one index finger in water and one index finger in alcohol and then blow on their hands. Which finger feels cooler? Why? (The alcohol will evaporate more quickly because its molecules move faster at the same temperature. Because alcohol evaporates more quickly, it takes heat away from the hand more quickly, and the finger with the alcohol on it will feel cooler). What happens when you put lotion on one finger? Is the lotion designed *not* to evaporate quickly? Why or why not?

- What is condensation?

Materials: shiny can, water, ice cubes, spoon
Procedure:

Fill the can to the halfway point with water. Add ice cubes and stir. Soon a thin film of tiny droplets of water will form on the outside of the can, as the air containing water vapor is cooled and the molecules of water vapor move more slowly and come close enough together to become water again. The thin film will gradually form large droplets. In the summer, the humidity may be so high that the water vapor will condense without ice cubes having to be added. In winter, the humidity may be so low that salt will have to be added to the cold water and ice cubes to get the water vapor to condense.

- Why do you feel uncomfortable on hot, humid days?

Materials: water glass, water, Celsius thermometer, paper towels, string, clock or watch.
Procedure:

Measure and record the temperature of the room. Fill a glass with water at the same temperature as the room. Tie a piece of paper towel over the bulb of the thermometer. Put the thermometer in the glass. Measure and record the temperature after 5 minutes. Pour half the water out of the glass. Line the inside of the glass with a paper towel. Swirl the water around so that the paper towel gets wet and sticks to the glass. Pour out the rest of the water. Place the thermometer with the wet paper toweling on it inside the glass. Measure and record the temperature after five minutes. What happened when the wrapped thermometer was placed in water? What happened when the glass was lined with the paper towel? Do you think the humidity increased? How can this activity help explain why hot, humid days are uncomfortable?

- What is the dew point?

Materials: shiny can, water, thermometer, ice
Procedure:

Fill the can half full of water. Slowly add pieces of ice, stirring regularly with the thermometer. When a thin film of water appears on the outside of the can, the dew point has been reached. Record the temperature at this point. (Be careful not to breathe on the sides of the can.) Repeat this procedure on days with different weather conditions. Does the temperature vary with the weather conditions?

• What is fog?

Materials: dry, narrow-necked bottle, very hot water, ice cubes
Procedure:
  Fill the bottle with the hot water (add the water slowly to avoid cracking the glass). Then pour out most of the water, leaving about 5 centimeters at the bottom (2 inches). Put an ice cube on the mouth of the bottle and hold the bottle between you and the sunlight or the light of a lamp. A fog will form in the bottle as the warm, humid air is cooled by the ice cubes and the cool air below the ice cube, and the water vapor will condense in tiny droplets that float in the air inside the bottle.

• How is rain formed?

Materials: hot plate, large pot, ice cubes, water, shallow pan with handle
Procedure:
  Fill the pot with water and heat it on the hot plate until the water is boiling. Fill the shallow pan with ice cubes and hold the pan about 10 centimeters (4 inches) above the pot. "Rain" will be produced as the water vapor from the boiling water is cooled by the cold bottom of the shallow pan, causing droplets of water to condense on the bottom of the shallow pan and drop into the water in the pot.

• How do cold air and warm air mix?

Materials: two baby food jars, hot water, cold water, red food coloring, blue food coloring, index card
Procedure:
  Fill one jar with hot water and one with cold water. Put several drops of red food coloring into the jar of hot water and several drops of blue food coloring into the jar of cold water. Cover the opening of the hot water jar with an index card, invert the jar, and carefully place it over the mouth of the cold water jar. Slowly slide the card out and observe what happens. (Nothing: hot water is lighter than the cold water and will remain on top.) Next, repeating the process, put the card back on the hot water jar and put the cold water jar on top of the hot water jar. Remove the card. The colder, heavier blue water will sink into the warmer, lighter red water. In the same way, a cold air mass will push under a warm air mass to create a cold front. A warm air mass will climb over a cold air mass to form a warm front.

• What is lightning?

Materials: two small, oblong balloons for each student
Procedure:
  Blow up the balloons and tie knots in the ends. Turn off the lights in the room. Rub the balloons back and forth against your clothing or across the covering of a chair. Bring the balloons together so that they almost touch. Small flashes of light will be seen as electricity jumps between the balloons, and there will be a faint "crackle" sound.

• How are clouds formed?

Materials: small-mouthed gallon jug, one-hole rubber stopper, short piece of glass or plastic tubing, water, chalk dust, bicycle pump
Procedure:

Pour enough water at room temperature to cover the bottom of the jug. Allow the water to stay in the jug for about 20 minutes to let some of the water evaporate into the air inside the jug. Shake a little chalk dust into the jug. Fit the stopper tightly into the jug and connect the rubber tubing of the pump. Pump air into the jug using no more than five or six strokes and then remove the stopper quickly. A cloud will form in the jug, which can best be seen by holding the jug up to the sunlight. If the cloud does not form, add a little alcohol to the water and repeat the experiment.

When air is pumped into the jug, the air inside the jug is compressed. When the stopper is removed, the air expands. When a gas expands, it becomes cooler. The air is cooled below the dew point by the sudden expansion, and the water vapor in the air condenses on the particles of chalk dust, forming a cloud. Real clouds are formed the same way.

• Are frost, snow, sleet, and glaze all formed the same way?

Materials: tall metal can, table salt, cracked ice, wax paper, water
Procedure:

Fill the can with alternating layers of cracked ice and salt. Each ice layer should be twice as thick as the salt layer. Pack the mixture down firmly. Put some drops of water on a piece of wax paper. Use enough water to make one large drop high enough to touch the bottom of the can. Set the can on top of the wax paper. Some dew may form on the sides of the can and then freeze, but frost will also form as the temperature of the air inside the can falls to below freezing. After the sides of the can are well covered with frost, remove the can from the wax paper. The large drop of water will have frozen into ice. Point out that frost and snow are formed when water vapor condenses directly into ice crystals, whereas sleet and glaze are formed when raindrops freeze.

## Construction Activities

• Make a barometer

Materials: milk bottle or glass jar with a medium to narrow mouth, balloon, rubber band, soda straw, rubber cement, wooden match stick, piece of cardboard.
Procedure:

Cut off the dome-shaped end of the balloon and stretch it tightly across the mouth of the jar, fastening it securely with a rubber band. Flatten both ends of the soda straw and cut one of the ends into a sharp point. Place rubber cement or glue on the flattened end of the straw and attach it to the center of the stretched piece of balloon. Cut a tiny piece of the match stick and glue it to the edge of the piece of balloon so that the straw rests on top of the wood.

When air pressure in the room increases, the piece of balloon will be pushed down, making the straw move up. When the air pressure in the room decreases, the greater air pressure inside the bottle will push the piece of balloon up, making the straw move down. Place a cardboard scale with barometric marks next to the straw pointer. Chart the changes. Keep the barometer in a place as free from temperature changes as possible. Students can check the accuracy of their barometer by comparing the readings to an actual instrument in the room.

- Make a thermometer

Materials: Pyrex flask, water, red food coloring, long plastic or glass tube, one-hole rubber stopper, index card
Procedure:
Pour water that has been colored red into the flask until the flask is almost full. Insert the tube into the stopper and fit the stopper tightly into the mouth of the flask. Adjust the amount of water in the flask so that, when the stopper is inserted, the colored water will rise about one-third to one-half of the height of the part of the tube that extends above the stopper. Make two slits in the index card and slide the card over the tube. Mark the original height of the water in the tube.

When the temperature of the room becomes warmer, the water is heated, expands, and rises up the tube. When the temperature drops, the water is cooled, contracts, and falls down the tube. Keep a daily record of temperature changes by marking the levels on the index card. Compare the marks on the index card with the daily readings on a standard thermometer.

- Make an Anemometer

Materials: two small rubber balls (different colors, each cut in half), two small sticks or dowels cut the same length, a slightly larger stick, a nail or screw
Procedure:
Nail one-half of each ball to each end of both small sticks. Use the same color ball on a stick so that the colors will alternate when the sticks are crossed. Cross the sticks and attach the point where they cross to the larger stick so that the sticks can turn freely (avoid friction with this instrument). Place the anemometer in a place where the wind is unobstructed. Students can count the number of rotations per minute and record the findings on a chart. They can also compare the wind speed from day to day.

- Make a wind vane

Materials: straws, sticks, pins, nails, screws, cardboard, tagboard, glue
Procedure:
Many wind vanes shown in science books will not work because they are poorly designed. This problem can be turned into a learning experience for the students. Ask them to find pictures of several different wind vanes and make their own variations using the materials listed here. Then, go outside when the wind is brisk to see which ones work. Allow students to hypothesize about the factors that make one instrument successful and another not. Make compasses available so that the students can determine the direction of the wind.

- Make a wet-and-dry-bulb thermometer

Materials: two chemical thermometers with Fahrenheit scales, two hooks, a strip of wood, white woven cotton shoelace, small cup filled with water
Procedure:

Attach the hooks to the strip of wood, placing them a few inches apart. Suspend the thermometers from the hooks. Wind part of the shoelace snugly around one of the thermometer bulbs and insert the end of the shoelace into the cup of water. Fan both thermometers, either by hand or with an electric fan for a few minutes to blow away the air next to the shoelace and keep it from being surrounded by a layer of saturated air.

To find the relative humidity, read both thermometers and determine the difference in temperature between the two thermometers. Use this temperature difference and the temperature of the dry-bulb thermometer to find the relative humidity.

- Make a rain gauge

Materials: Large kitchen funnel, glass jar with a mouth exactly the same diameter as the rim of the funnel, a ruler, a narrow bottle such as an olive jar, paper, permanent ink marker, tape, water, large can
Procedure:

Pour exactly 1 centimeter or 1 inch of water into the jar, using a ruler to get the exact depth. Then pour the water into the narrow bottle, using strips of tape to hold the paper in place. With the marker, mark the strip of paper to indicate the point the centimeter or inch of water reaches. From this point to the bottom of the water in the jar, make additional marks on the paper, each one accounting for a centimeter or an inch of water. Now divide the space between each mark into 10 smaller marks so that each smaller mark represents 1/10 of a centimeter or 1/10 of an inch of water. Pour out the water from the narrow bottle.

Put the narrow bottle in the large can to keep the wind from blowing the bottle over. Put the funnel into the neck of the narrow bottle and place the can outdoors in an open area. The funnel will collect the rain, which will be collected in the narrow bottle, where the amount of rainfall can be measured.

## Other Activities

### Student Disaster Teams

Students can sign up to be on a disaster team. Each team can be assigned a particular kind of weather disaster (tornado, hurricane, ice storm, flood) to investigate and report about to the class. Members of local rescue and emergency organizations can be used as resources. If time permits, the group can stage a "disaster" and handle the "rescue." This process will probably require out-of-class time and parent involvement. It is a good option for extra credit.

### Special Days

Near the conclusion of the unit, as a reward for excellent work, "rainbow day," "balloon day," or "kite day" can be planned. These days can include activities just for fun, planned by the class around the selected theme.

Examples of activities are outside relay races and games, picnics, and special art projects.

**Guest Speakers**

> Pilot
> Agriculture service
> Civil defense personnel
> "Old-timer"
> Meteorologist

**Field Trip**

Weather station at the airport

**Addresses**

> Superintendent of Documents
> U.S. Government Printing Office
> Washington, DC 20402
> U.S. Department of Commerce
> Weather Bureau
> Washington, DC

## Music

Creative movement and dance activities can be organized for the children during this unit. There are a number of songs that are appropriate also (see copies). The record "Weather Songs" by Tom Glazer (Motivation Records, New York City), has a great many songs that may be used.

## Classroom Terrarium

During the unit, the class can construct and maintain a terrarium. Different groups should be responsible for it each week and should keep records of temperature and changes. The class can use the terrarium to learn about the water cycle and the effects of sun, wind, and rain on the environment.

**Reflection**

Notice that the sample unit activities are all student activities. Imagine that you are introducing each of these activities and supervising each activity. For each activity, add an introduction and then describe your role as you supervise the activity. Remember to include in the introductions opportunities for students to relate the content and activities to their previously acquired knowledge.

## EVALUATION

As stated in Chapter 9, to be fully effective, curriculum evaluation must be continuous and comprehensive. This means that the evaluation process for a teaching-learning unit must include both formative and summative evaluations of the instruction and that the evaluation of every unit must also include an evaluation of the overall unit.

### Instructional Evaluation

Traditionally, teachers have used summative product evaluation almost exclusively, evaluation that occurs *after* the instruction is completed (6-week tests, semester tests, etc.—tests that measure what the students remember). But as discussed earlier, such practices result in little achievement beyond the recall of facts.

This limitation can be avoided by giving short formative tests at short intervals during the learning period (for example, daily or weekly quizzes).

### Unit Evaluation

An evaluation of the unit described in this chapter involves evaluating the process as much as, or perhaps more than, the product. For this reason, a learning contract will have more direct relationship to the stated goals of the unit than will pencil and paper tests. Because certain facts and ideas are critical to the student's ability to use the processes in this unit, however, an examination is included in the contract.

To assist students in gaining proficiency in the processes during the course of the unit, it is critical that a system of formative evaluation be used to guide the student's learning. The teacher checklist shown in Figure 11.1 and the student self-progress report shown in Figure 11.2 are both types of formative evaluation that will be used. The checklist will be completed by the teacher and discussed with the student during the course of the unit. Figure 11.3 shows a sample grade contract. Figure 11.4 is a sample learning contract. Figure 11.5 is a sample test and Figure 11.6 is a unit evaluation.

Name_____

(+ excellent, O satisfactory, − needs improvement)

### Learning Centers

_____ Cooperates with others in the center

_____ Follows directions

_____ Uses materials properly

_____ Completes tasks

_____ Uses time productively

_____ Shows originality

### Experiments

_____ Follows directions

_____ Follows safety rules

_____ Completes tasks

_____ Is careful with materials

_____ Works cooperatively in the group

### Written Assignments

_____ Turns work in on time

_____ Work is neat and orderly

_____ Shows originality

_____ Shares work with class

_____ Takes pride in accomplishments

**Comments:** _____

_____

_____

**Plans for needed change:** _____

**Figure 11.1** Teacher Checklist

1. Is my journal up to date?_____
2. Has my group completed at least one project?_____
3. How many research questions have I answered?_____
4. Have I worked in every center?_____
5. How many activities have I completed in the following areas?
   Art_____ Publishing_____ Reading_____ Measurement_____
   Weather station_____
6. How many experiments have I written up?_____
7. Am I preparing for the exam?_____
8. What book(s) have I read?_____
   Have I discussed them with my teacher?_____
9. Am I working on an additional project?_____

Name_____ Date_____

**Figure 11.2** Student Checklist

**Grading** Student grades for this unit will be based on the grade contract. No student will be allowed to contract for a D or an F, but low grades will be given if the assigned work is not completed in a satisfactory manner. It is important that students believe that they earn their grades. However, the grade should not get in the way of learning by becoming the focus of the unit.

**Grade Contract**
   Student name_____ Date_____
   Contract for A, B, C (circle one)
   Personal journal:      Daily entries_____
                          Role in group projects_____
                          Self-evaluation of learning_____
                          Weather charts and predictions_____
                          Vocabulary words_____
                          Research questions_____
   Worked effectively in assigned group: Yes_____ No_____
   Centers:               Art_____
                          Publishing_____
                          Reading_____
                          Game_____
                          Measurement and observation_____
   Experiment forms:_____
   Books read and discussed_____
   Additional project (A contract only)_____
   Examination grade:_____
   Comments:_____
   Signed (Teacher)_____ (Student)_____

**Figure 11.3** Grade Contract

**To the Students** We are going to have a great many different kinds of learning experiences during our unit on weather. You will be participating in experiments, teamwork, outside investigation, and creative art and writing. Your grade for the unit will depend on how much you do on your own and in class and how well you do it. Read the requirements for each grade. Before the unit begins, you must decide what grade you are going to work toward, complete this form, and return it to me.

**To the Parents** Next week we will begin our unit on weather. This is a very exciting topic for the children, and many learning and enrichment activities are planned. In order to help your child to get the most benefit from this experience, I have decided to assign grades based on a "contract" system. I have discussed this with the class, and they have agreed that this is a reasonable way to grade their work on this unit. Attached are the contracts for A, B, and C grades. No student will be allowed to contract for less than a C, but lower grades will be given if a student does not fulfill the work required. Please read over the contracts and discuss with your child the choice he or she makes. If you have questions, please feel free to call me.

For a grade of C you must:

1. Compile a personal journal containing at least 80 percent of the activities.
2. Participate with your assigned group in the projects you choose.
3. Answer 10 or more research questions.
4. Work in each center at least one day.
5. Complete at least two activities from each center.
6. Turn in at least five experiment forms.
7. Score 70 or higher on the exam at the end of the unit. You will have two chances to take the exam.
8. Read and discuss one or more books from the reading list.

This is the grade I plan to earn during our study of weather. I understand that all of my work must be my "best" and must be finished by the end of this unit. I have discussed this with my parents, and they understand what I am expected to do.

Signed_____ Date_____
For a grade of B you must:

1. Compile a personal journal containing at least 90 percent of the activities.
2. Participate with your assigned group in the projects you choose.
3. Answer 15 or more research questions.
4. Work in each center at least two days.
5. Complete at least three activities from each center.
6. Turn in at least six experiment forms.
7. Score 80 or higher on the exam at the end of the unit. You will have two chances to take this exam.
8. Read and discuss two or more books from the reading list.

**Figure 11.4** Learning Contract

This is the grade I plan to earn during our study of weather. I understand that all of my work must be my "best" and must be finished by the end of this unit. I have discussed this with my parents, and they understand what I am expected to do.

Signed_____ Date_____

For a grade of A you must:

1. Compile a personal journal containing all of the activities.
2. Participate with your assigned group in the projects you choose.
3. Answer 15 or more research questions.
4. Work in each center at least two days.
5. Complete at least three activities from each center.
6. Turn in at least seven experiment forms.
7. Score 90 or higher on the exam at the end of the unit. You will have two chances to take this exam.
8. Read and discuss two or more books from the reading list.
9. Complete an additional project that you plan yourself. You must get an OK from me before beginning this project.

This is the grade I plan to earn during our study of weather. I understand that all of my work must be my "best" and must be finished by the end of this unit. I have discussed this with my parents, and they understand what I am expected to do.

Signed_____ Date_____

**Figure 11.4** Learning Contract (Continued)

## Sample Test Related to Study Questions, Chapter 14

Instructions: Read each question carefully. Choose the best answer from the choices given. Circle your answer.

1. The temperature is rising. The barometric reading is stable. There are cumulus clouds in the sky. What is the forecast?
   a. Rain on the way
   b. Fair weather to continue
   c. Thunderstorms likely
      [Cognitive: application]
2. The weight of air pushing on the earth is known as:
   a. Air pressure
   b. Temperature
   c. Moisture
      [Cognitive: knowledge]
3. When air pressure increases, water. . .
   a. Turns into a gas (fog or a cloud)
   b. Stays a liquid
   c. Freezes

**Figure 11.5** Sample Test

[Cognitive: comprehension]

4. A barometer measures:
   a. The amount of moisture in the air
   b. The amount of rainfall
   c. The amount of air pressure
   [Cognitive: knowledge]

5. Clouds are made from:
   a. Ice, snow, and dew
   b. Dust and water droplets
   c. Thin air
   [Cognitive: comprehension]

6. A covering of minute ice crystals formed from frozen water vapor is:
   a. Dew
   b. Rain
   c. Frost
   [Cognitive: knowledge]

7. Match the lettered terms below to the numbered words that follow.
   a. Dew
   b. Rain
   1. Precipitation
   2. Condensation
   [Cognitive: application]

8. A long narrow band of changing weather between two kinds of air masses is:
   a. A storm
   b. A cloud
   c. A front
   [Cognitive: knowledge]

9. The temperatures for a week in June are listed below. What was the average temperature for that week?

| Monday: 88 | Thursday: 82 | Saturday: 84 |
| Tuesday: 85 | Friday: 88 | Sunday: 85 |
| Wednesday: 79 | | |

   a. 84.4
   b. 79
   c. 89
   [Cognitive: comprehension]

10. A tornado warning has just been issued for the school. What would be the *best* thing to do first?
    a. Try to get all the students home at once
    b. Call everyone's parents and tell them about it
    c. Move everyone to the hall quickly
    d. Assemble all students in the gym
    [Cognitive: evaluation]

**Figure 11.5** Sample Test (Continued)

1. Was I enthusiastic about the subject?
2. Was I well prepared for each lesson?
3. Did the students accomplish the desired objectives?
4. Were the students interested in the activities?
5. Did the students work well in groups?
6. Was the classroom atmosphere conducive to learning?
7. Did all the children complete their journals?
8. Were the parents helpful? Why or why not?
9. Should the speakers be invited again?
10. What should I do differently with this topic next time?

**Figure 11.6** Unit Evaluation—Summary

This evaluation will be useful as you improve your unit in preparation for the next time you teach it. Remember that a major strength of the unit, as perceived by Taba, is the teacher's ability to revise and improve it each time it is used. Remember, too, that good curriculum revision is continuous. As you read the professional literature, you will gain information and skills constantly. Add the improvements you read about to your unit as quickly as you discover them.

## SUMMARY

Most teacher decisions concern the activities of the day, but such short-term decisions do not affect learning nearly as significantly as long-term decisions do. Success in the classroom requires teachers who understand the curriculum and who are committed to making the curriculum succeed. All these needs can be met through teacher-developed learning-teaching units. Such units should reflect the teacher's philosophy.

The actual act of writing out of one's philosophy can clarify thinking, but only when teachers are willing to make a greater commitment to some theories and beliefs than others. A teacher's philosophy should purposefully shape all other components of that teacher's curriculum. A good philosophy statement encompasses the teacher's views on the purposes of humanity and the schools, and it also covers the teacher's views on the nature of knowledge, youth, democracy, and learning.

By identifying their strengths and weaknesses, teachers can use their strengths to improve their units and minimize any ill effects their limitations might cause.

## QUESTIONS

1. What are multipurpose activities, and why are they important in a curriculum?
2. In what way(s) is stimulus-response learning theory superior to faculty psychology?
3. What are two common uses of tables of specifications?
4. How should developmental psychology's contribution to the understanding of the learning process affect curriculum?
5. What is a rationale statement, and why should every unit have one?
6. What are curriculum components and, specifically, what are the components in the model that undergirds this text?
7. Why should teachers make a commitment to one side of a controversial issue such as Are youths complacent or curious?
8. What is meant by an eclectic view, and how does it relate to unit development?
9. What are the relationships between information, knowledge, and content?
10. Why shouldn't teachers be required to write objectives at all levels of all domains?

## SUGGESTED FURTHER ACTIVITIES

1. Focusing on each part of your newly developed learning-teaching unit, describe the type of classroom that will accommodate your curriculum.
2. Interview a professor who teaches learning theory. List the suggestions this professor makes to enhance classroom learning. After the interview, review this list and note the suggestions that you are willing to employ in your classes.
3. Review your statement of strengths and weaknesses and your strategy for using your strengths and for compensating for your weaknesses. Now, put this strategy into action in your class.
4. Select one of the learning theories introduced in this chapter (or another learning theory) and read at least five articles and/or book chapters on that theory. Make a list of six important content generalizations or concepts that will help others understand this theory.
5. List at least three learning theories in their order of chronological development and, for all but the first theory, explain how each has advanced our understanding beyond the earliest theory.

## BIBLIOGRAPHY

Bloom, B. S. (1956). *Taxonomy of educational objectives. Handbook I: Cognitive Domain.* New York: David McKay.

Bruner, J. S. (1960). *Toward a theory of instruction.* Cambridge, MA: Harvard University Press.

Henson, Kenneth T. (1993). *Methods and strategies for teaching in secondary schools* (2nd ed.). New York: Longman.

Hill, J. C. (1986). *Curriculum evaluation for school improvement.* Springfield, IL: Charles C. Thomas.

Kohlberg, Lawrence (1984). *Recent research in moral development.* New York: Holt, Rinehart, & Winston.

Krathwohl, D. K. (1956). *Taxonomy of educational objectives. Handbook II: Affective domain.* New York: David McKay.

Mager, R. F. (1961). *Preparing instructional objectives.* Palo Alto, CA: Fearon.

Marshall, Carol. (1991). Teachers' learning styles: How they affect students' learning. *The Clearing House, 64*(4), 225–227.

McNeil, J. D. (1990). *Curriculum : A comprehensive introduction* (4th ed.). New York: HarperCollins.

Taba, Hilda (1962). *Curriculum development: Theory and practice.* New York: Harcourt, Brace, and World.

Tyler, Ralph W. (1949). *Basic principles of curriculum and instruction.* Chicago: The University of Chicago Press.

# REFORMING AMERICA'S PUBLIC SCHOOLS

*Recent years have seen a rash of national task force reports on the status of American schools. Too many of them have political motives and are designed to alarm, rather than inform.*

KENNETH T. HENSON

When public anxiety is aroused by war, inflation, depression, civil unrest, or whatever, Americans look for someone to blame. That's good, because the one unfailing sign of a vital, healthy climate is the public's vigorous desire to participate in criticisms and give suggestions for reforms. Frequently, the easy target is the tax-supported neighborhood school. America's public schools are not the perfect instruments that some would like us to believe they are. There is much room for improvement, and there always will be.

However, many attacks on schools, teachers, and administrators are unfair, and many are just plain faulty. For example, in the past, our schools have been criticized heavily for lack of discipline. Over the last 15 years, the Gallup Poll of Public Attitudes Toward the Public Schools has found the number-one concern to be lack of discipline. In the 1984 poll, over three-fourths of the population rated discipline in the schools as a serious problem. Yet, before we blame teachers for this problem, we should hold up a mirror to society. Violence is running rampant in our communities. During our entire involvement in Vietnam, more Americans were killed on the streets of American cities by handguns than were killed on the battlefields in Southeast Asia.

In America, violence is a way of life. Recently, on national television, the police commissioner of a major city warned residents to purchase guns, carry them, and learn how to use them if they are interested in protecting themselves and their families.

Even our youth are not safe from violence. Each year, over 300,000 American children are abused in their own homes by family members. According to Marvin Wolfgang, director of the Center for Studies in Criminology and Criminal Law at the University of Pennsylvania, "Americans tend to legitimize violence by glorifying war, buying guns, and supporting the use of physical punishment." The worsening condition of school discipline is reflected in the changes in our perceptions of discipline problems over the past four decades. The effect has been that today's students have to commit a far more serious act than did their earlier counterparts to even have it considered a discipline problem. An examination of the top problems in public schools today compared to those of 1940 reflects this change. In 1940, they were talking, chewing gum, making noise, running in the halls, getting out of turn in line, wearing improper clothing, and not putting paper in wastebaskets. By 1982, the worries were radically different, focusing on rape, robbery, assault, arson, murder, suicide, vandalism, extortion, drug and alcohol abuse, pregnancy, abortion, and venereal disease.

Do the school teachers cause the discipline problems?—of course not. In fact, they are often the victims of them. Annually, over 50,000 teachers are physically attacked by their students and by other members of our society who just walk into their classes from off the streets. How many critics of our schools realize that, in this country, more teachers are attacked each year than are policemen? In 1978, the National Institute of Education reported that 5,200 junior high school teachers were attacked each month over a 10 month period—totaling 52,000 attacks on teachers, compared to 49,079 attacks on policemen during the same period.

Other critics load their guns with test scores, blaming the schools and teachers for doing a poorer job than their predecessors. There are at least two major errors here. First, since the 1950's, our schools have constantly increased their holding power so that two-thirds of those who were dropping out at that time are now remaining in school long enough to take the standardized exams. In other words, while it is true that the national test scores have steadily declined for several years, we are now testing a large percentage who earlier would have been drop-outs. In reality, our decline in test scores has been much less than our increase in holding power.

This introduces a second major error in blaming the schools for poorer academics. American students are competing with students of other nations, but the percentage of American students who pursue formal education long enough to take those tests is far greater than that of schools of other countries throughout the world. Recently, when the top nine percent of American students was compared with the top nine percent of students of other countries, our students held their own. It is remarkable that our schools and teachers can prepare these top performers so well while simultaneously educating a far larger portion of its youths than do schools of any other country.

In the U.S., high school graduation has become a national norm. Eighty-six percent of adults aged 25–29 hold a diploma, an increase of 50% since 1950. Our schools are often criticized for failure to provide adequate defense for the nation. They are accused of being weak in the hard sciences such as math and languages. Yet, the number of Nobel prizes earned by Americans shows a different picture. In fact, since the Nobel prizes were first awarded in 1901, Americans have won one-third of *all* that have been awarded. This is approximately seven times as many as have been won by the Soviets and twice as many as any other nation.

# A TONE OF PANIC

Recent years have seen a rash of national task force reports on the status of American schools. Too many of them have political motives and are designed to alarm, rather than inform. For example, the most popular of all was "A Nation at Risk"(1983). If the title of this report lacks sensationalism, the report itself doesn't. Words are carefully selected and sentences carefully constructed to exaggerate the popular myths that many Americans hold about their schools. For example, consider this sentence: "If an unfriendly foreign power had attempted to impose on America the mediocre educational performance that exists today, we might well have viewed it as an act of war."

A similar report, "Action for Excellence" (1983), appeared at about the same time. This report also carries a tone of panic. It speaks of "a need for survival" and uses such terms as emergency and urgency. Through the use of exaggeration and inflammatory language, these and similar reports of the 1980s mislead the public. Most of these reports are the products of groups who may have very little knowledge about the total role that American schools have played and must continue to play if America is to continue as a free, democratic nation. The purposes of our schools can not become so narrow that they exist only to sustain a healthy economy or only to provide national defense. Although these are worthy goals, the American school must continue its much broader purposes—to prepare citizens for living in a democracy and to challenge each student to become everything that student is capable of becoming, whether it be a computer scientist or an artist, an astronaut or a teacher. A brief look at each of these reports shows both reason for hope and reason for concern.

**"A Nation at Risk"** was written by the U.S. Department of Education's National Commission on Excellence. It recommends requiring all students to take four years of English; three years of mathematics, science, and social studies; and one-half year of computer science. These are good recommendations, but how about the fine arts, vocational subjects, and the performing arts? The report does recommend that these should be offered, but such a recommendation does little to assure that they will become part of the curriculum. Even if they do find their way into the curriculum, those students who need them most may be the least likely to elect to take them.

"A Nation at Risk" recommends that both the school year and the school day be lengthened. Adopting these actions would likely increase both the level of teacher burn-out and the number of discipline problems. Neither increase would be apt to improve the amount of learning in the classroom. Of perhaps far more benefit is the Commission's suggestion that the time already available should be more efficiently used. Currently, only 75% of class time is spent on instruction, and an overwhelming majority of that time is spent by the teacher giving factual material to be recalled.

**"A Place Called School"** was based on a study of 38 schools in seven states. John I Goodlad's 1983 report in many ways runs in total opposition to the other reports. For example, Goodlad points out that merely adding more sterile hours to the school day will not likely result in more learning. Rather, he suggests that we should make better use of the existing school hours. Perhaps the most valuable and yet overlooked contribution of any of the reports involves Goodlad's suggestions for improving some of the current practices. Specifically, he suggests that, rather than adding facts to the curriculum, for each subject we should include a set of concepts. Each student's curriculum should include a common set of concepts, principles, and skills. Goodlad recognizes that this will require additional planning time for teachers.

"A Place Called School" recognizes that any substantial improvement in schooling must begin with the result from the work of teachers. Goodlad recognizes that this will require cooperation among teachers. Although he says that the principals' heavy work load precludes their being instructional leaders, he proposes that, in small schools with no curriculum supervisor, each building principal will be the kingpin in organizing the teachers and providing the leadership needed to make generic improvements throughout the school.

## High School

Based on a field study of 15 high schools, the Coleman Report, and Goodlad's *A Study of Schooling*, Ernest Boyer's 1983 book, *High School*, agrees with all of the panel reports which say that we are asking too little from our students and too little from our schools. Unlike most other reports, Boyer recognizes that our best schools are among the best in the world. He perceives communication skills as the area of greatest need, recommending language proficiency as a prerequisite for admission to high school (summer schools would be used for remediating those who lack this proficiency). Boyer recommends a core curriculum with arts, foreign language, history, science, mathematics, and technology. A requirement that stands out is art. Most of the recent panel reports have not emphasized any of the fine arts. On the contrary, some reports have deleted all humanities and fine arts in favor of increased math, science, and foreign languages. Like Goodlad, Boyer sees no value in having a separate vocational track. Career education and vocational education should be a concern of all teachers and can be achieved through the general education program.

## The Paideia Proposal

Mortimer Adler's (1982) report, based primarily on discussions of 22 educators, recommends beginning with lectures and textbooks; moving to skills-producing exercises such as reading, writing, speaking, calculating, problem-solving, measuring, and observing; and then on to Socratic questioning and discussions of books, art, music, and drama. Adler sees no benefit in specific vocational education. In many ways, "The Paideia Proposal" is the antithesis of "A Nation at Risk," which excluded the arts in its required curriculum. Adler elevates the arts to an important part of the curriculum. Unlike "A Nation at Risk," which emphasized the use of textbooks, "The Paideia Proposal" does not emphasize the use of textbooks. On the contrary, it recommends the use of books other than textbooks. The report gives similar positive emphasis to the use of lectures and other teaching methods.

**"Action for Excellence"** (1983) is the work of the Education Commission of the States' Task Force on Education for Economic Growth. It seems natural that this task force—which includes 41 business leaders, educators, legislators, and governors—would perceive school improvement as a responsibility of business persons and others outside the education community. Technological advancements should be used to their maximum potential.

An impressive recommendation was the strengthening of all disciplines, not just math and science. An even greater and more unique recommendation was the emphasis given to motivation. While many of the reports speak of education as something which happens to students, "Action for Excellence" seems to recognize that the students themselves are the key to improvement. Complementing this strength was the emphasis given by this report to "learning to learn" skills.

Not so impressive are this report's recommendations for considering longer school days and longer school years. Although the role that teachers play in providing excellence in education was recognized, the report placed teachers in a somewhat receptive, rather than active, role. Instead of improving teacher skills through providing more preparation periods, it recommended increasing teacher selection standards, teacher certification standards, and teacher dismissal standards.

Although many significant discrepancies exist among the recommendations found in these reports, their authors agree on some major issues. All see the need for vast improvement in the high school curriculum, especially in mathematics, computer education, languages, and the sciences. All agree that vast improvement in the qualifications of teachers is mandatory. There is strong feeling that mastery of a core of common knowledge should be required of all students. These needed improvements apply to all students, not just to the gifted or the handicapped or other minority groups. Those reports that were produced by noneducators have a noticeable lack of concern with improving the process of learning. Rather, they emphasize external routes to achieving their goals. Many reports recommend the development of career ladders, better pay, and other programs aimed at increasing teacher incentives.

As one might expect, the recommendations of each of these programs reflects the goals of the individuals or groups who wrote the reports. For example, an economic group stressed goals that are linked to improving the nation's economy; a group appointed by the President recommended goals that are concerned with national security; and proposals written by educators show deep concern for improving the learning process in the classroom. In general, each report obviously reflects the concerns and biases of its authors. These concerns may or may not be appropriate goals for schools.

## EFFECTS OF REPORTS

The flurry of reports on education is affecting the schools. State legislatures and departments of education are responding to these reports. Some of the resulting reforms are good, but many bring severe detriments to American education. For example, most of the reports call for a reduction in the number of electives students will have in their curricula. Indeed, some recommend the abolishing of all electives. Almost none of the reports mention the fine arts or the need for a broad-based liberal arts curriculum.

What the reform proposals are eliminating from the curricula is only part of the damage. Of equal concern is what they are adding to the programs. In response to these reports, seven states have extended their school year and 14 more are considering this move. Thirteen states have lengthened their school day and eight others are considering the same. Twenty states have devised yet other ways of increasing time and 18 are considering doing the same. All of these changes are based on the assumption that increased instructional time will increase learning. Many recent time-on-task studies have found this to be untrue. When will we ever learn that just forcing kids to sit in classrooms for longer periods and more days will not do the job? It takes more. It always has. Disinterested students don't soak up knowledge by osmosis. Almost none of the reports address motivation or the need for the ability to assemble facts into broad general understandings which make sense to students.

Rather than improving teaching methods, one of the major 1983 reports actually calls for a return to lecture and recitation. This approach is based on the turn-of-the-century belief that the brain is a muscle which must be exercised rigorously with difficult and boring assignments if it is to grow in capacity and self-discipline. Contemporary teachers know that their role goes beyond all of the ideals and goals espoused in these reports. While they must contribute to the maintenance of national defense, a sound economy, and all other concerns that plague our country, today's teachers know that they are also responsible for unlocking the human mind and challenging all of our students to go beyond their previous limits.

# WHY OUR OPEN CLASSROOMS FAIL

Kenneth T. Henson

American education has experienced a decade of criticisms that have come mainly from within its own ranks. Indeed, a brief visit to the nearest library or bookstore will turn up many books (most written by American teachers) with titles such as *Crisis in the Classroom* (Silberman, 1970), *Death at an Early Age* (Kozol, 1967), *Deschooling Society* (Illich, 1970), *How Children Fail* (Holt, 1964), *The Underachieving School* (Holt, 1970), and *The Way It Spozed to Be* (Herndon, 1975). Supportive evidence is beginning to emerge carrying the all-too-familiar note, "I told you so." Scholastic Achievement Test scores have declined for ten continuous years (Newsfront, 1979). A decade of testing by the National Assessment of Educational Progress (NAEP) reports that our elementary pupils' achievement is down in four major areas (Neill, 1979). More than 70,000 teachers are assaulted physically every year in classrooms and hallways (Armstrong, 1978) and a staggering $600 million worth of school property is destroyed each year, an increase of 66 percent a year since 1977 (Kratcoski, Kratcoski, & Peterson, 1978).

Whether our schools really are responsible for our national energy crisis, inflation, pollution, unemployment, poverty, and other societal problems is a philosophical question of little consequence. The fact remains: Americans are disenchanted with their schools and, according to a recent national survey, are no longer willing to support them (Gallup, 1979). Ironically, as public opinion of schools declines, the cost of educating each child rises 7 percent annually (Lublow, 1978).

These are the conditions that have caused American educators to search beyond their own realms for answers. But why the British schools? After all, if England's schools were held accountable for that country's current state of economic, social, labor and political affairs, they would fare even less well. The sterling pound has hit all-time lows repeatedly in the past three years. In most areas that are used as indexes of national welfare, Great Britain's problems are equal to or greater than those of the United States. Its airline, bread, and coal strikes have kept its unemployment rate considerably higher than the unemployment rate in America. Former Prime Minister James Callaghan's rapport with the Queen has been so poor that he even declined an invitation to attend a social hosted by Her Majesty, an unprecedented gesture in a country that has always prided itself in following traditions and social graces. Englishmen are spending numerous hours standing on a box in Hyde Park affirming that the country can no longer afford the two million dollar annual budget for a figurehead who actually has no authority.

In the storm of national problems, as though to announce the state of British affairs, on August 5, 1976, even the clock in Big Ben, a symbol of steadiness and strength for the past 170 years, screeched, clanged, screamed, and stopped. It is indeed strange that with all of Britain's current national problems, America is still looking at British schools. But the peculiarity disappears as one closely examines the schools that are revolutionizing our own schools. These are the world renowned British Infant Schools, which enroll children from age five to age seven.

The British have different expectations for their schools. Unlike Americans, the British do not hold their schools responsible for their society's conditions. In fact, the British people rarely interfere with their schools at all. Parents may offer to assist, but they almost never interfere. While many assist daily with supervising the playgrounds and swimming pools, and help children dress and undress for swimming, they do not become involved in planning the school program. Members of the Parent-Teacher Association provide service by raising money for the schools, but even they do not get involved in decisions about how the school is run.

Unlike American schools, which resemble large, cold factories, the British Infant School carries the personality of its headmaster or headmistress, who has complete autonomy to run the school as he or she sees fit. The respect for the head carries on into the school, where every teacher perceives the principal as a master teacher. Indeed, that is the true meaning of "head" or "head teacher." One can quickly see that this difference runs below the title surface, since the British heads continue to teach throughout their careers as heads of the schools. Of course, this affects their relationship with each child, since they know every child by name, a nearly impossible task for American principals of schools with enrollments numbering in the thousands.

The closeness of the British head with the pupils sets the stage for discipline in British schools. As one head recently explained, "I don't use corporal punishment because I don't need to." This contrasts sharply with the attitude toward corporal punishment in America. The 1979 Gallup Poll (Gallup, 1979) found that Americans still feel that lack of discipline is the number one problem in American schools. The head explained, "When a child is sent to me for discipline, by the time he reaches my office he has already been disciplined."[1] Because each child knows the head personally and vice versa, and because the

---

[1]Taken from a personal interview with Mr. Alan Dixon, headmaster of St. Barnabas & St. Philip's School in Kensington, London, England, May 13, 1976.

head is respected, the child is humiliated by having to appear before the head for misbehavior. Usually, a brief talk between the two is all that is necessary to admonish the undesired behavior. In rare instances where the child has repeated an offense, the head will delay the meeting, leaving the child to sit alone and think about the misbehavior for some time before they begin their talk. This approach is called the "mellowing period."

The warmth between the British head and each pupil is passed on to the teacher-pupil relationship. Rarely does one see a British infant teacher admonish a child. Even during conflicts among pupils, the teacher is reluctant to interfere. The teacher views misbehavior as a temporary and self-correcting thing that will soon pass by itself if left alone. In the meanwhile, others, including peers and teachers, must be willing to tolerate it. If the children do not correct their behavior in a reasonable length of time, the teacher will move over close and may even place a hand on a child's shoulder, offering comfort and security.

The prevailing attitude is that the British teacher's time is too valuable to be spent reprimanding pupils and could be better spent planning experiences for them. This concept is reflected throughout every British Infant School. Each classroom is different and unique. The walls are covered with school programs, each designed by the teacher in that room. One wall might have a "Sherlock Snoopy" theme with a picture of Snoopy the dog in his Sherlock Holmes cap searching with his magnifying glass for missing parts of speech. Another room may have pupils learning to cook or to keep house.

These roles and relationships are basic to the underlying philosophy in British education, which espouses the concept that school is not a preparation for life. School *is* life. Therefore, the quality of life in school is all important. School faculty and staff share the responsibility of helping each child learn to enjoy school life. Family grouping (multi-age grouping) helps the younger and older children learn to cooperate and learn from each other. Groups of near equal ability, called "houses," compete for trophies, as opposed to our system, which often forces individuals to compete with others of infinitely more ability. The absence of tests and letter grades further increases the enjoyment of school life. Having no report cards with which to compare children with their peers is another positive factor, for it removes the fear of disappointing one's parents at reporting periods.

We Americans must remember that Silberman's comprehensive study of American schools, which led to his book *Crisis in the Classroom*, reported that the single variable that correlates highest with students' success in American schools is not the children's I.Q.s or how seriously they apply themselves; it is the income level of each child's family. No wonder we parents insist on A's and B's. They don't reflect our children's success in school; they reflect *our* success in life.

The belief in quality of life is borne out of the experiences that make up the British Infant School day, experiences that are built around those activities that children naturally enjoy. A visit to any British Infant School reveals a flexible climate where children are allowed to pursue activities of their own choice. For example, all children like to play in water and sand, and all children love to play with animals. This manipulation of concrete objects is consistent with the world renowned learning theorist Jean Piaget, who says that children are unable to deal with abstractions until about age twelve. Actually, ". . . formal stage thinking emerges in adolescence (and even then only) as a potentiality only partially attained by most and fully attained only by some" (Dulit, 1979). Some people actually never mature enough cognitively to deal with the abstractions that we demand of our children. In fact, 25 to 75 percent of all adults have not achieved formal operations (Good, 1979).

To provide their pupils with the necessary manipulative-type experiences, the British Infant Schools have a physical plant design called "indoor-outdoor planning." This physical environment is complemented by the attitude of the British teachers, who are willing to allow pupils the necessary freedom to pursue their own interests, either in groups or individually.

Unfortunately, the operation of British Infant classrooms appears deceptively simple to the casual observer, who may notice only the physical openness of the room itself. This is exemplified by the American open classroom, which has emerged as a modification of the British Infant School classroom. Many such schools house a traditional program in an open building. These classes are often accurately described as noisy, unruly, and chaotic. While the British Infant School may appear free and unstructured, a great deal of planning and structuring is necessary to make the system succeed. Some open classrooms in this country are highly successful. These, like their British counterparts, operate on the common beliefs that:

The child is an active agent in his own learning.

One child may learn differently from all others.

The teacher is responsible for helping each child discover how he learns best.

The function of the school is to encourage exploration.

The child has rights as well as obligations.

The teacher is a trained observer, diagnostician of individual needs, consultant, and facilitator [Rathbone, 1971].

American educators have learned much from the British Infant School, but only when seen in its total perspective does it offer much improvements for American schools. True improvements require willingness to adopt the basic philosophy that undergirds the British Infant School system. This philosophy must be accepted by the teachers and principals. Success without open classrooms will be increased if parents, too, understand the underlying philosophy.

Letter grades are for parents; they are against children. Parents should become involved with every opportunity to work with the school. Quietness and stillness aren't always best. Whether the climate is traditional or modern, each child must know the goals he or she is pursuing. Parents should share the responsibility of helping their children learn to enjoy school and feel successful in school each day.

Some open schools in this country have succeeded in achieving these goals. Such success has followed sacrifices by teachers who are willing to invest a lot of hard work in planning and to risk a lot of their own security by yielding many responsibilities to students. The greatest success has come when parents have been willing to trust in the nature of experimentation, in the expertise of their children's teachers, and in the capabilities of their children.

## BIBLIOGRAPHY

Armstrong, O. K. The scandal in our public schools. *The Saturday Evening Post*, May 1978, p. 40.

Dulit, E. Adolescent thinking á la Piaget: The formal stage. *Journal of Youth and Adolescence,* New York: John Wiley and Sons, 1979, p. 202.

Gallup, G. H. The Eleventh Annual Gallup Poll of the Public's Attitudes toward the Public Schools. *Phi Delta Kappan*, 1979, *61*, 33–45.

Good, R., et al. Piaget's work and chemical education. *Journal of Chemical Education*, 1979, *56*(7), 426–430.

Herndon, J. *The way it spozed to be.* New York: Simon and Schuster, 1975.

Holt, J. *How children fail.* New York: Pitman, 1964.

Holt, J. *The underachieving school.* New York: Pitman, 1970.

Illich, I. *Deschooling society.* New York: Harper and Row, 1970.

Kozol, J. *Death at an early age.* Boston: Houghton Mifflin, 1967.

Kratcoski, P. C., Kratcoski, L. D., & Peterson, D. The crisis of vandalism in our schools. *USA Today*, 1978, *107*(2398), 15–16.

Lublow, A. Ohio's troubled schools. *Newsweek*, September 25, 1978, p. 105.

Neill, G. Washington report. *Phi Delta Kappan*, 1979, *61*, 157.

Newsfront. Oops! SAT scores still falling. *Phi Delta Kappan*, 1979, *61*, 155.

Rathbone, C. H. The open classroom: Underlying premises. *The Urban Review*, September 1971, pp. 4–10.

Seligman, J. Empty-desk blues. *Newsweek*, April 24, 1978, p. 94.

Silberman, C. E. *Crisis in the classroom.* New York: Random House, 1970.

# A MODULE ON MODULES

Module #113
Estimated Time Units: 4.0

## OBJECTIVE(S)

The purpose of this module is to enable the student (teacher) to write and understand the component parts of a module by being able to:

1. Write one or more behavioral objectives on a topic of his or her choice

2. Write a rationale which supports the objectives

3. Write a module guide which provides a step-by-step procedure for working through the modules

4. Identify any preassessment measures which will allow the pupil to test out of the module

5. Design appropriate instructional activities which will enable the pupil to realize the objectives

6. Write the evaluation procedures in objective terms

7. Provide for any necessary remediation

Evaluation of the prepared module will be based on the module resource person(s) assessment using the evaluation checklist provided in this appendix.

The prepared learning package may be used in the classroom, but such activity is not required for this module.

## RATIONALE

Modules can be defined as a type of teacher-learning packet which includes:

1. A list of competencies that a student (teacher) is expected to have at the end of a unit.

2. An explanation of any teacher or learning activities that are designed to help the individual to achieve what is expected of him or her.

3. Statements of how each student's performance and progress are to be evaluated.

4. Standards each student must meet in order to complete or master those things expected of him or her.

The nature of teaching is determined by what the pupil is to be taught to learn and how he or she best may learn it. The nature of the acquisition process by which teaching competence is acquired is determined by what the teacher is to learn and how he or she may best learn it. The rationale for competency-based teacher education pertains to the latter. The former determines its content.

The rationale for competency-based programs derives from concepts about the nature of what is to be learned (in this case, teaching competency) and from a model of a system most likely to enhance this acquisition.

Learning modules are becoming popular educational tools in schools today. This module is designed to help a student (teacher) learn about modules by going through a self-instructional module on the concept of modules.

Module Guide

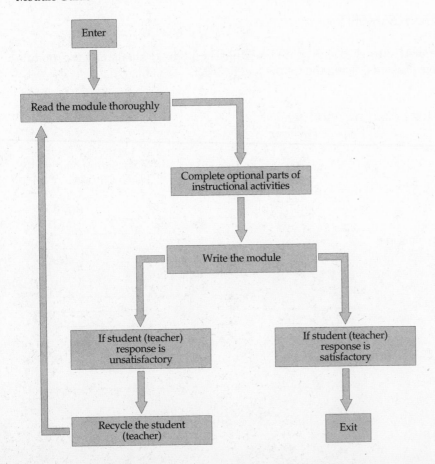

## PREASSESSMENT

None

## INSTRUCTIONAL ACTIVITIES

The following activities are optional but are designed to help the student (teacher) complete the module satisfactorily.

1. Read *Preparing Behavioral Objectives* by Robert Mager.
2. Study other modules in Project ESCAPE to learn types of content—the component parts.
3. Study the categories on the postassessment check list.
4. Read Measuring Instructional Intent by Robert Mager.

## POSTASSESSMENT

The student's (teacher's) prepared module should be evaluated by the module resource person(s) using the following checklist.

## Evaluative Checklist for Learning Modules

Name of Evaluator_____

| | Yes | Not Sure | No | If Not Sure or No, Please Comment |
|---|---|---|---|---|
| I. Objectives | | | | |
| 1. Specifies what is to be done | ___ | ___ | ___ | _____ |
| 2. Identifies condition | ___ | ___ | ___ | _____ |
| 3. States how it is to done | ___ | ___ | ___ | _____ |
| 4. Provides criteria for completion | ___ | ___ | ___ | _____ |
| II. Rationale | | | | |
| 1. Identifies relevant research | ___ | ___ | ___ | _____ |
| 2. Shows relationship to topic | ___ | ___ | ___ | _____ |
| 3. Is consistent with objective(s) | ___ | ___ | ___ | _____ |
| 4. Shows importance of objective(s) | ___ | ___ | ___ | _____ |
| III. Module Guide | | | | |
| 1. Identifies prerequisites | ___ | ___ | ___ | _____ |
| 2. Identifies procedures for completing module | ___ | ___ | ___ | _____ |
| IV. Pre-assessment | | | | |
| 1. Consistent with objective(s) | ___ | ___ | ___ | _____ |

2. Allows student to test out
of module     \_\_\_\_\_    \_\_\_\_\_    \_\_\_\_\_      _____

V. Instructional Activities

1. Consistent with stated objective(s) \_\_\_\_\_    \_\_\_\_\_    \_\_\_\_\_      _____
2. Reasonable amount of time
required     \_\_\_\_\_    \_\_\_\_\_    \_\_\_\_\_      _____

VI. Remediation

1. Procedure to be followed in event
of unsatisfactory progress     \_\_\_\_\_    \_\_\_\_\_    \_\_\_\_\_      _____

Suggestions for improvement (additional prerequisites, instructional activities, etc.)

_____

_____

_____

_____

# REMEDIATION

Recycle the student (teacher) if parts were not completed satisfactorily.

# BIBLIOGRAPHY

Houston, W. Robert (1974). Exploring Competency Based on Education. Berkeley, CA: McCutchan.

Mager, Robert Frank (1970). Analyzing Performance Problems. Belmont, CA: Fearon.

Mager, Robert Frank (1973). Measuring Instructional Intent. Belmont, CA: Fearon.

Mager, Robert Frank (1962). Preparing Behavioral Objectives. Belmont, CA: Fearon.

# THE PROS AND CONS OF PERFORMANCE-BASED TEACHING

## ACCOUNTABILITY AND PERFORMANCE-BASED PROGRAMS IN EDUCATION: SOME PROS AND CONS

*Performance-based teaching may prove to be one of the big advancements of education in this century.*

Kenneth T. Henson

For many decades, education in the U.S. has been compared unfavorably to industry. Education has been adjudged by many to be inferior in its operating procedures because its product, unlike industry's, cannot be measured on a piecemeal basis, and because quality control is not possible. The obvious answer toward improvement, then, would be to find a way to measure the quality and quantity of the educational work. Thus was born the concept of "accountability" in education. Accountability means "the ability to deliver as promised."[1] In education, it is "a means of holding an individual or group responsible for a level of performance or accomplishment for specific pupils."[2] If each school system, each school, and each teacher could be held accountable for the level of performance, there would be no reason why education could not operate as efficiently as do business and industry.

---

[1] Medill Bair, "Developing Accountability in Urban Schools," *Educational Technology*, 11:39, January, 1971.

[2] William C. Miller, "Accountability Demands Involvement," *Education Digest*, 38:14, October, 1972.

No doubt, we need some system for measuring the effectiveness of the current practices in education. In his major message on educational reform, Pres. Nixon said: "To achieve this. . . reform, it will be necessary to develop broader and more sensitive measurements of learning than we now have—new measurements of educational output."[3] If we could install in each classroom a type of teaching which could be measured, much of the waste of time and money in our schools throughout the country would be eliminated. This is what the public wants. The Gallup survey found that, "by a margin of 49% to 28%, American citizens favor performance contracting because it introduces efficiency and accountability, no results—no pay."[4] However, teachers do not favor it. Of those who have feelings either for or against performance contracts, 37.9% favor and 47.7% oppose it. A closer look at these two groups shows that, while only 7.5% strongly support performance contracting, 22% strongly oppose it.

The concept of accountability and performance-based teaching continues to dominate the literature. Why is it such a controversial issue? Certainly, the magnitude of its apparent impact is evidence that performance-based teaching does possess significant potentials. Likewise, opposition by so many educators shows that performance-based teaching contains some important disadvantages. The following is an account of the development of this movement and some of the pros and cons of performance-based teaching, along with a discussion of possible ways of changing some of the disadvantages into advantages.

**Pros**

*Performance-Based Teaching:*
1. Clarifies the objectives of teaching, assuring purposeful teaching directed toward the attainment of definite goals.

**Cons**

*Performance-Based Teaching:*
1. Is primarily concerned with cognitive learning; therefore, it does not account for the development of the whole child—emotionally and socially.

Concern that current attention to cognitive development will ignore other important areas of child or adolescent development is unfounded. Actually, the forces of this emphasis, if properly directed, can be utilized to improve the guidance of social, emotional, and attitudinal growth. The use of performance-based activities which are built around activities which involve students will provide opportunity for the teacher to observe how students work with others (social and emotional growth) and to talk with students about their school and nonschool interests. In the future, insight into cognitive goal-identification and

---

[3] Quoted in Foster J. Watkins and James D. Hughes, "Accountability in Schools of Education," *School & Society*, 100:159, March, 1972.

[4] Charles Blaschke, "Performance Contracting Cost, Management Reform, and John Q. Citizen," *Phi Delta Kappan*, 53:245, December, 1971.

measurement of cognitive growth should provide information applicable to noncognitive areas.

| Pros | Cons |
|---|---|
| 2. Enables the student to know what he is working toward, making learning meaningful and enjoyable, enabling each student to work together and independently toward visible, pre-identified goals. | 2. Does not account for difference in potential among students. It demands the same achievement from the least capable as from the most capable. Will result in the gifted student achieving below his potential. |

Fear that PBT will limit the gifted student is based on the supposition that every student will have the same number of same experiences. While all students will share some of the same experiences, additional, more sophisticated experiences can be provided to challenge the gifted student to go beyond those minimum objectives expected of all.

Because success is important to them, high achievers insist on knowing why they are studying X curriculum and need to know how they are progressing toward their goals. PBT can provide continuous feedback which will encourage them to move further and faster.

| Pros | Cons |
|---|---|
| 3. Will help the teacher to become organized, providing efficient use of time and energy, releasing the teacher to give attention to individual students. This can help bring humanization back into the curriculum. | 3. Will result in teachers' concern for their own welfare at the expense of ignoring the welfare of students. As in programmed instruction, the effects will be a dehumanizing process |

PBT aims to improve the quality of learning by students. Teachers who feel threatened by such a program should remember that, so long as their first interest remains that of teaching, there is no conflict between their objectives and those of PBT. In fact, some teachers who primarily are concerned with their own well-being rather than with student progress may be encouraged to provide more help and encouragement to students.

| Pros | Cons |
|---|---|
| 4. Has subject content and activities which are selected by experts and the curriculum does not depend on the creativity and imagination of every classroom teacher. | 4. Has lesson content and activities determined outside the classroom which may be unrelated and unmeaningful to the locale of any particular school. |

Many PBT programs are being initiated by organizations outside the local school systems. Some systems are contracting for the installation of complete PBT systems in all subject areas, at all grade levels (K–12). Since the designers of PBT programs are experts, programs will be sound in most respects. However, each local system is responsible for making certain that the objectives of the program are in harmony with its locale and specific objectives.

| **Pros** | **Cons** |
| --- | --- |
| 5. PBT is a means of identifying excellence in teaching; therefore, it can provide a means for rewarding outstanding teaching. | 5. PBT can be used by education systems as a means of economizing, making concern for learning secondary. |

The criterion for adoption of curriculum innovation should be whether it will improve learning experiences enough to justify its costs, rather than whether it will save money. PBT programs, implemented as they should be, probably will be expensive.

To reach its objective of improving teaching, PBT must provide a system for identifying, recognizing, and rewarding objective teaching.

| **Pros** | **Cons** |
| --- | --- |
| 6. Places the student in an active role. Can be much more motivating than the teacher-dominated lesson. | 6. Is content oriented and, therefore, teaching and learning may be artificial, resulting in rote memorizing which will become boring and soon will be forgotten. |

PBT should provide students with a means of escape from passive, teacher-dominated roles. Whether this actually will happen will depend on when and if the teacher adjusts to a less-dominating role and assumes the more-helpful role of advisor and assistant.

| **Pros** | **Cons** |
| --- | --- |
| 7. Provides a means of exposing incompetent teachers and motivating toward excellence those teachers who otherwise would be mediocre. | 7. Is an instrument which can be misused by administrators to dismiss or otherwise to penalize teachers. |

Administrators' use of performance-based teaching as a punitive device would cause all teachers to suspect, fear, and eventually abhor the entire concept of PBT. Such misuse is analogous to teachers using assignments of additional work (which should be enjoyed) for punishment.

| **Pros** | **Cons** |
|---|---|
| 8. Curriculum decisions will become a topic of much attention and discussion by all faculty members. | 8. Curriculum decisions are not made at the local level, which could lead to bureaucratic and political control of schools by forces which are not aware of the schools' operational procedures. This may result in unreasonable pressure on local administrators and teachers to incorporate practices which are rushed into without adequate time for planning. |

Because teachers and administrators usually are kept so busy just keeping the program working smoothly, there is a dangerous tendency for this to become the total objective of the school. Performance-based teaching's demand for attention to curriculum content and experiences will bring in new experiences and content and delete obsolete curriculum to the degree of the administrator's willingness to keep communications open.

| **Pros** | **Cons** |
|---|---|
| 9. Provides time for teacher to plan for creative student activities. | 9. Limits educational gains to teacher set objectives; does not account and provide room for student imagination and creativity. |

To avoid letting PBT limit student progress to preestablished objectives, teachers must encourage and regard achievement in areas outside the program objectives. As the program provides time for the teacher, the teacher must provide time for each student to explore his own interest areas.

| **Pros** | **Cons** |
|---|---|
| 10. Has so much thrust that it will result in significant improvement in education. | 10. Is another utopian fad which bandwagoners will misuse and overuse until it seriously damages the educational system in this country. |

Whether PBT will be misused and overused is uncertain. That it will produce some important findings about teaching and learning is definite. Whether these findings will be recognized and used depends on openminded teachers and administrators.

The potential gains from performance-based teaching will be limited by the skills possessed by its users. When misused, the performance-based approach can produce undesirable effects which can lower the quality of experiences provided by any school.

Positive or negative results will depend largely on the local school system. Rapid implementation of this innovation probably will produce little success. However, if the system first provides the in-service training essential for familiarizing each teacher with the new program, and provides time for pilot programs, performance-based teaching may prove to be one of the big advancements of education in this century.

# STATE MANDATED ACCOUNTABILITY PROGRAMS: ARE THEY EDUCATIONALLY SOUND?

*Curriculum theory and practical curriculum development are interdependent, despite the all-too-common belief to the contrary, say these writers. They describe Mississippi's statewide accountability program to illustrate the need for a sound theoretical base for instruction.*

## Kenneth T. Henson and Thomas H. Saterfiel[1]

State Departments of education across the country—often in conjunction with universities—are initiating accountability programs aimed at increasing student gains on standardized tests. Elsewhere, college professors are writing curriculum textbooks which provide theories and axioms for use in developing curricula.

Unfortunately, it is commonly assumed that theory and practice are unrelated events. A second and even more unfortunate assumption is that theory and practice are somehow opposite forces. The result is that teachers accuse professors of being theoretical and unaware of the real world, while professors may fail to demonstrate clear applications of the theory they espouse.

An analysis of an existing statewide accountability program in terms of curriculum axioms presented in one of the popular textbooks may help to dispel these faulty assumptions. The program selected for analysis is Mississippi's Accountability and Instructional Management (AIM) program.

---

[1]Kenneth T. Henson is head, Department of Curriculum and Instruction, University of Alabama, Tuscaloosa. Thomas H. Saterfiel is in the Bureau of Educational Research and Evaluation, Mississippi State University, Mississippi State.

The curriculum axioms are taken from *Developing the Curriculum*, by Peter F. Oliva.[2]

## OVERVIEW OF THE PROGRAM

In 1979, Mississippi mandated a statewide curriculum development program which was by law to be implemented throughout all of its 150 public school districts. In effect, every school district in the state was given five years (or until November 1, 1984) to have in full operation a districtwide curriculum that covered grades 1 through 12. Kindergarten was to be added by 1985. Each program was to include all of the components shown in the figure.

| Objectives | Content | Teacher Activities | Student Activities | Materials | Evaluation |
|---|---|---|---|---|---|

All objectives were to be written in terms of expected student behavior. The content was to emphasize broad generalizations, not just facts. And several test items were to be included for each of the hundreds of objectives.

Now, as the five-year development period draws to a close, many Mississippi teachers realize that more curriculum development is possible than they had once thought. These possibilities and the positive outcomes of the AIM program are not at all unrelated to the curriculum axioms which undergird this program. The following is an analysis of this program based on curriculum axioms found in the current literature.

## PROGRAM ANALYSIS

### Axiom 1. Curriculum change results from changes in people.

A common question among Mississippi teachers has been "Why doesn't the state department of education develop the curriculum?" As Hilda Taba pointed out some 30 years ago, only when teachers are involved in making changes will they be willing to and capable of implementing those changes.

Of all the advantages to be derived from this (or any other) accountability program, perhaps the greatest advantage of all is the change that takes place within the individual teachers who, upon completion of this program, will be infinitely better prepared to write behavioral objectives, select activities and content to attain these objectives, and develop test items to evaluate student progress in terms of these objectives. Equally important is the change in attitude that occurs when teachers participate for such a long period of time in

---

[2]Peter F. Oliva, *Developing the Curriculum* (Boston, Mass.: Little, Brown and Co., 1982).

such a systematic curriculum development process. In the future, these teachers will automatically plan in terms of objectives, sequence, scope, and balance.

### Axiom 2. The curriculum planner starts from where the curriculum is, just as the teacher starts from where the students are.

At no point in its development has Mississippi's AIM program suggested that teachers throw away their existing lesson plans. On the contrary, consultants for the AIM program frequently advise teachers to start their curriculum development by stating their existing practices. This posture was in many instances the single force that enabled many teachers to accept the new mandate.

### Axiom 3. Curriculum changes made at an earlier period can exist concurrently with newer curriculum changes.

One of the most disappointing things that can happen to a teacher who has invested considerable time and energy to improve a curriculum is to learn that by the time all of the kinks are worked out of the new innovation and it begins to operate smoothly, an administrative decision is made to eliminate the innovation. Many teachers in the AIM program had invested time and energy in earlier programs but, fortunately, most of these teachers have been able to keep their existing programs.

For example, many reading teachers had previously adopted prepackaged reading programs which included textbooks, objectives, activities, and even daily lesson plans. In most instances, these teachers were encouraged to continue these programs and to use those objectives and activities in the new AIM curriculum.

### Axiom 4. Systematic curriculum development is more effective than trial and error.

Mississippi's AIM program holds each school district accountable for the new curriculum. While it provides districts with the flexibility of letting each school develop its own segment of the program, it does require systematic curricula development at the school and district levels. Those systems which let each school develop its own curriculum must show how these separate curricula fit together to form a districtwide curriculum with scope, sequence, balance, and continuity.

### Axiom 5. Curriculum improvement is effected as a result of cooperative endeavor.

This program has proved to Mississippi school teachers that the level of curriculum continuity, balance, scope, and sequence needed to produce a meaningful, correlated education experience cannot be attained through individual, isolated teacher efforts. Interestingly, in each group a few very competent teachers quickly emerged as catalysts for their respective groups, but the total team, complete with the administrative leadership, was required to develop the system needed to produce such large-scale curriculum change.

## Axiom 6. Curriculum development is basically a decision-making process.

As is true of any program that requires change, the teachers who have participated in the AIM program have experienced their share of frustrations. One of the most difficult and frustrating features of this program is the decision-making responsibility it places on teachers.

During the last quarter of the nineteenth century, Col. Francis Parker introduced the practice of involving teachers in curriculum planning. Were he alive today he would surely be pleased with both the extent and level of involvement of teachers in the AIM program. These teachers have frequently been charged with making decisions about such operational questions as:

- How are we going to divide the work load?
- Will we form teams for each discipline, or will we form interdisciplinary teams?
- Will each school operate as a team or will an elementary faculty, a junior or middle school faculty, and a high school faculty unite to form a working team?

While such questions tend to produce frustrations, this basic level of decision making is the core of sound curriculum development.

## Axiom 7. Curriculum development is a continuous process.

As Mississippi's AIM program continues to develop, a common question among many teachers is, "When will it end?" The answer, of course, is never. Once the deadline for these programs is reached, the Mississippi State Department of Education will begin a continuous process of evaluating the AIM program. More exactly, in the future each accrediting visiting team will have one or more individuals who are charged with evaluating the AIM program. Additional evaluations will be made randomly between accreditation visits by special AIM evaluation teams.

## Axiom 8. Curriculum not only reflects but is a product of its time.

By observing Mississippi teachers as they work on the AIM program, many contemporary features—both conceptual and concrete—can be seen. An example of a modern conceptual feature in this program is the use of formative test items. Throughout the history of our schools, testing has been almost exclusively limited to summative tests which come at the end of the instructional process. These tests are designed to determine who passes, who fails, who receives a diploma, and who becomes licensed or certified.

In contrast, formative tests are given prior to instruction for placement purposes, and during instruction to help the teacher and students make needed adjustments. Put simply, the purpose of formative tests is to improve teaching and learning.

The AIM program has made teachers sensitive to the potential that evaluation holds for improving teaching and learning. The process of writing objectives for every lesson and test items for every objective has led these teachers to think and plan in terms of objectives. The evaluation component has made them aware of the use of advance organizers (frequently formative test items), making all lessons correspond with the intended learning outcomes.

## Axiom 9. Change is inevitable and necessary.

To suggest that Mississippi's AIM program has not faced opposition would be a grossly misleading statement. From the beginning, many teachers had to be sold on the idea that change was needed. This is not to suggest that their curricula were inferior to others, but rather to acknowledge that there is always room for improvement. Further, planned change which involves everyone is more likely to succeed than are abrupt decisions made by external parties without involving those who will be most affected.

## SUMMARY

Too often the content of college textbooks and that which happens in school classrooms are considered to be separate and unrelated. Yet, direct involvement with the AIM program in public schools and awareness of the axioms found in contemporary curriculum development textbooks bring similarities that cannot be dismissed.

It would seem reasonable to suspect that many other state accountability programs are consistent with the theory taught in college classrooms. Certainly, investigations comparing these two variables will lead to a better awareness of the validity of the theory and of the need for a sound theoretical base.

## What Are the Reading Basics?

What are the "basics" when it comes to literature? What literature should all high school students be familiar with?

William J. Bennett, chairman of the National Endowment for the Humanities, recently asked hundreds of educators, authors, businesspersons, and politicians that question. Their responses form the basis of the following list:

1. *Macbeth, Hamlet*—Shakespeare
2. American historical documents, particularly the Declaration of Independence, Constitution, and Gettysburg Address
3. *Huckleberry Finn*—Twain
4. *Bible*
5. *Odyssey, Iliad*—Homer
   *Great Expectations, Tale of Two Cities*—Dickens
6. *The Republic*—Plato
7. *Grapes of Wrath*—Steinbeck
8. *Scarlet Letter*—Hawthorne
   *Oedipus Rex*—Sophocles
9. *Moby Dick*—Melville
   *1984*—Orwell
   *Walden*—Thoreau
10. *Collected Poems*—Frost

# GLOSSARY

This book has emphasized the perspectives of the constructivists and phenomenologists, acknowledging that each individual's perceptions are unique, based on prior experiences. The book has further emphasized that our conceptualizations are continuously shaped and refined as we continue to gather more experiences. In this spirit, the following glossary is offered, not as a list of definitive definitions, but as opportunities for the readers to refine their existing perceptions of these terms.

As an experienced educator, you may already have a basic level of understanding of all of these terms. Still, you may wish to compare and contrast your definitions with those offered here, paying particular attention to the ways in which your definitions of many of those terms are changing.

**achievement test** Standardized test designed to measure how much has been learned about a particular subject.

**affective domain** The part of human learning that involves changes in interests, attitudes, and values.

**AIM** Accountability in Instructional Management program. The first of the 1980s state-wide reform programs.

**aims, educational** Aspirations so broad that they can never be fully achieved.

**algorithm** Step-by-step procedure for solving problems.

**alignment, curriculum** Matching learning activities with desired outcomes, or matching what is taught to what is tested.

**articulation** The flow (absence of disruptions) of a curriculum, either vertically or horizontally.

**authentic tests** Tests that are designed and administered throughout the year to cause students to develop those skills that are valued.

**axiology** The philosophical structure concerned with pursuing the study of values and ethics.

**balanced curriculum** Equal emphasis on disciplines; for example the Arts and Sciences, or vocational courses and college preparatory courses.

**Boston English Classical School** The first public high school in America, established in 1821.

**broad-fields curriculum** Curricula designed to replace the subject-centered curriculum and lead to understanding the broad content generalizations that spread among two or more subjects.

**Cardinal Principles of Secondary Education, Seven** The National Education Association's aims for elementary and secondary schools.

**catechisms** Religious rhymes used extensively in Colonial times to teach morality.

**CIPP model** A curriculum evaluation model that focuses on the content, input, process, and product.

**coercive power** Power based on the ability to punish or give rewards.

**cognitive domain** The part of human learning that involves changes in intellectual skills, such as assimilation of information.

**cognitive objectives** Instructional objectives that stress knowledge and intellectual abilities and skills.

**coherence, curriculum** The fitting together or meshing of curriculum components.

**components, curriculum** Any of the following: aims, goals, objectives, philosophy statement, student activities, teacher activities, content, and tests.

**computer-assisted instruction (CAI)** The use of computers to present programs or otherwise facilitate or evaluate learning.

**computer literacy** Knowledge of a computer's basic operations, potential, and limitations. Usually includes such skills as the ability to write simple programs, use databases, and use spread-sheets.

**computer managed instruction** The use of a computer system to manage information about learner performance.

**computer phobia** Self doubt in the ability to learn how to use computers.

**concepts** Those major understandings within each discipline characterized by recurring patterns such as a common physical characteristic or common utility.

**concrete operations level of development** Stage in Piaget's developmental learning theories that precedes the ability to think abstractly; roughly includes the elementary school years. Ages seven to eleven.

**connectionism** A learning theory which says that the most effective approach to learning and therefore to curriculum development is to connect newly acquired information to prior understandings.

**connectionists psychologists** Psychologists who perceive learning as occurring in a step-by-step fashion.

**consortium, educational** A group of schools that join together usually led by a university or other organization. By pooling their resource, these schools can afford programs that, by themselves, none of the schools could afford.

**content, curriculum** Information which has been selected for inclusion in the curriculum.

**constructivism** A theory of learning that holds that new information is made meaningful by tying it to prior understandings.

**constructivists** Psychologists who believe that new information must be related to previously acquired understanding (knowledge) before it can become meaningful.

**continuity, curriculum** The quality of a curriculum that links parts together in a sequence for easier learning. Vertical articulation.

**core curriculum** A curriculum design that has a common core of content and/or activities required of all students and other content and activities that are electives.

**criterion-referenced evaluation** Evaluation that measures success by the attainment of established levels of performance, individual success is based wholly on performance of the individual without regard to the performance of others.

**criterion-referenced test** Measure of a student's performance with reference to specified criteria or to that individual's previous level of performance.

**cultural diversity** The existence of several different cultures within a group; encouraging each group to keep its individual qualities within the larger society.

**cultural pluralism** Cultural diversity.

**culture** The capacity for constantly expanding the range and accuracy of one's perception of meanings. An attempt to prepare human beings to continuously add to the meaning of their experiences.

**curriculum** The total experiences planned for a school or students.

**curriculum alignment** Matching learning activities with desired outcomes, or matching what is taught to what is tested.

**curriculum compacting** Strengthening parts of the curriculum for gifted students.

**curriculum guide** A written statement of objectives, content, and activities to be used with a particular subject at specified grade levels; usually produced by state departments of education or local education agencies.

**dame schools** Private homes where the Colonial mother taught her children and her neighbors' children. Also called *kitchen school*.

**deductive logic** Reasoning that starts with the general and moves to the specific.

**dilectic logic** Reasoning that begins with a thesis, goes to an antithesis, and then to synthesis.

**dissatisfier** A factor that is a prerequisite to the operation of motivators but which itself does not motivate.

**eclecticism** Incorporating into a learning-teaching unit ideas from several learning theories.

**education** The process through which individuals learn to cope with life.

**educational taxonomy** A hierarchial system for classifying educational objectives.

**effective schools** Those schools whose students are high academic achievers.

**effective teaching** Teaching which results in high learner achievement.

**empowerment, teacher** Giving teachers a broader role in the operation of the school.

**epistemology** That structure which pursues the study of truth.

**essentialism** That structure which focuses on the knowledge that is needed for a successful adult life.

**evaluation** Making measurements plus providing value judgments.

**existentialism** That structure that focuses on the present. Life is only what you make of it. Live for the moment.

**expert power** Power that derives from the possession of specialized skills or knowledge.

**faculty psychology** A learning theory that considers the brain as a muscle whose growth requires rigorous and boring exercise.

**formal operations level of development** Piaget's highest level of thinking, involving abstractions. Usually begins from age 11 to age 16.

**formative evaluation** Evaluation that occurs before or during instruction and whose sole purpose is to promote learning by improving study skills, instructional strategies, or the curriculum.

**Franklin Academy** A pragmatic school that by the end of the Revolutionary War replaced the Boston Latin Grammar School as the most important secondary school in America.

**generalizations** The broad understandings required to master any given field of study; also called *content generalizations*.

**gestalt psychology** A learning theory that says that we learn by seeing new patterns or insights.

**global education** Study about and learning to care about and protect the welfare of the world.

**goal displacement** Inadvertently letting the attainment of the goal replace the purpose for having the goal.

**goals, educational** Desired learning outcomes stated for a group of students and requiring from several weeks to several years to attain.

**Goals for 2000** A list of six goals set by the president and governors in 1990 to be reached by all American schools by the year 2000.

**grading** The act of using a combination of types of student performance that encompasses a student's overall level of success.

**hornbook** A board with Biblical rhymes (catechisms) and other simple curriculum content, covered by a thin, transparent material, used in the dame schools.

**human development** The idea that schools should improve society by improving individual learners.

**hypothesis** A statement of predicted outcomes.

**idealism** A belief that reality lies in ideas and that there are universal truths and values.

**inductive logic**  Reasoning that moves from the specific to the general.

**information**  Rather random facts which have not been connected to the learner's prior knowledge.

**in-service teachers**  Teachers who have graduated and are teaching full time.

**insight**  Learning that occurs when an individual perceives new relationships.

**integration of disciplines**  Uniting two or more disciplines through the use of conceptual themes.

**Kalamazoo Case**  A law passed in 1874 giving state legislatures the right to levy taxes to support schools.

**knowledge**  Meaningful information that the learner has related to prior understandings.

**knowledge base**  The research-derived knowledge and other knowledge that supports the practice of a profession.

**Latin Grammar School**  Forerunner of modern high schools which prepared young men for entrance to Harvard College.

**learning**  More or less permanent change in behavior as a result of experiences.

**learning activities**  Ways to involve students in the curriculum to help them relate newly acquired information to prior knowledge.

**learning experiences**  Student activities that are made meaningful by tying these activities to prior experiences.

**learning unit**  A curriculum plan that usually covers 1 to 2 weeks of elementary study or 6 to 18 weeks of a middle school or high school program.

**legitimate power**  Organizationally sanctioned ability to influence others.

**mastery learning**  Technique of instruction whereby pupils are given multiple opportunities to learn using criterion-based objectives, flexible time, remediation, and instruction that matches the learners' styles.

**measurement**  The nonqualitative part of evaluation.

**metanalysis**  An organized process for analyzing many studies on a common topic.

**metacognition**  Knowledge of how one's mind works; thinking about ways to improve one's own ability to think and learn. The study of one's own learning processes.

**metaphysical**  Knowledge gained through nonscientific means and which cannot be proven empirically.

**metaphysics**  The philosophical structure that studies the supernatural. Also called ontology.

**microcosm**  A small version of a much larger system.

**mission statement**  A statement of an institution's purpose.

**model**  A written or drawn description used to improve the understanding of its subject.

**multicultural education** Educational goals and methods that teach students the value of cultural diversity.

**multiethnic education** Multicultural education.

**multipurpose activity** An activity that serves to attain two or more objectives.

**naysayers** A group of workers who oppose all changes, especially those that would require them to retrain to improve their job performance.

**need hierarchy model** Abraham Maslow's model of human motivation; it assumes that people are primarily motivated by a desire to satisfy specific needs, which are arranged in a hierarchy.

**norm-referenced grading** A student's performance is evaluated by comparing it to the performance of others.

**normal learning curve** A symmetrical, bell-shaped curve that shows the distributions of learners' abilities.

**Northwest Ordinance of 1787** A law requiring that one section (one-sixteenth) of every township be set aside to be used to support public schools.

**objectives, educational** Desired learning outcomes stated for a single student, specifying a minimum acceptable level of behavior and the conditions under which the behavior must be demonstrated. Also called behavioral objectives, performance objectives, instructional objectives, or learning objectives.

**Old Deluder Satan Act** A Massachusetts Colony law passed in 1647 which required every town of 50 or more families to hire a teacher and every town of 100 or more households to build a school.

**ontology** The philosophical structure which studies the super-natural. Also called metaphysics.

**open education** Curriculum that stresses student activity and student freedom, multiage grouping, self-selection, and individualized teaching. Also called *open classroom*.

**operational objective** Objective written with active verb and specified criteria; also called behavioral objective and performance objective because it requires the student to perform specific behaviors.

**perennialism** That structure that focuses on that knowledge that continues to return through the years.

**pertinent concepts** Those concepts whose understanding is a prerequisite to understanding the discipline being studied.

**philosophy** The love, study, and pursuit of wisdom.

**portfolio, learners'** A diversified combination of samples of a student's quantitive and qualitative work.

**pragmatism** The structure that emphasizes the practical.

**praxis theory** Curriculum theory that brings together theory and practice.

**preoperations stage of development** That state in Piaget's learning theory when children attend to or focus on only one characteristic. The period when language development is the most rapid. Two to seven years.

**progressive education era** From the early 1920s to the early 1940s when the curriculum was student-centered and activities-centered.

**psychomotor domain** The part of human learning that involves motor skills.

**punishment power** The ability to punish others who fail to comply with your requests.

**Quincy System** One of the nation's first school district's to use a child-centered curriculum.

**rationale, curriculum** A statement that uses students' values to convince them of the worth of a topic of study.

**readiness** The stage of development required to perform mental and physical operations.

**realism** The belief that people should pursue truth through using the scientific method.

**reconstructionism** That philosophical structure which is dedicated to using education to rid society of its ills.

**referent power** The ability to influence others because they identify with you or want to be like you.

**research-based teaching** Using methods that are research validated.

**restructuring** Changing a school's entire program and procedure, as opposed to changing only one part of the curriculum.

**reward power** The ability to reward others when they do what you want them to.

**satisfier** Motivator.

**scientific method** A systematic approach to pursue truth through using the five senses.

**scope, curriculum** The breadth of a curriculum.

**Scopes Trial** A 1925 court case in which John Thomas Scopes contested the right to teach evolution in a Tennessee secondary school.

**sensorimotor stage of development** Piaget's earliest stage of development. Birth to age two.

**sequence, curriculum** The order in which content and activities in a curriculum are arranged.

**spiral curriculum** A curriculum that introduces the same topic at different levels because students were not able to deal with some of the abstractions at a lower level (younger age).

**stimulus-response psychology** A learning theory that views all behavior as responses to stimuli.

**structure of disciplines learning theory** A learning theory that emphasizes the need to understand the unique structure of the discipline being studied.

**structure of knowledge** The unique organization of each discipline.

**subject-centered curricula** Curricula consisting of specific courses usually delivered by using lectures and textbooks.

**summative evaluation** Evaluation that occurs following instruction and is used to determine grades and promotion.

**Taba's Inverted Model** A curriculum model that begins with teachers who design learning units; considered opposite or inverted from traditional top-down models.

**table of specifications** Chart to assure coverage of varying levels of desired objectives, knowledge, and skills.

**teacher empowerment** An attempt, associated with education reform, to increase teachers' involvement in decisions that affect the entire school.

**technological competency** The presence of confident ability to use and extend present technologies and to adapt quickly to new technologies.

**technological literacy** *See* computer literacy.

**testing** Measuring student performance or measuring the degree to which students meet a curriculum's objectives.

**theory** a set of interrelated constructs (concepts), definitions, and propositions that present a systematic view of phenomena by specifying relations among variables, with the purpose of explaining and predicting the phenomena.

**transescence** Preadolescent development stage.

**Trump Plan** A curriculum design by Lloyd Trump which requires all students to use a combination of large group instruction, small group instruction, and independent study.

**Two-Factor Motivation Theory** Herzberg's theory that there is a set of factors that when absent can block performance but when present do not motivate performance.

**Tyler's Ends-Means Model** A curriculum model that begins by identifying desired learning outcomes and designing the curriculum accordingly.

**wisdom** The knowledge of things beautiful, first, divine, pure, and eternal.

**Woods Hole Conference** A meeting of 35 scientists, educators, and business leaders in 1959 to redesign the curricula in American schools.

# CREDITS

Chapter 1 pgs. 6–8
From *Developing the Curriculum* by Peter Oliva. Copyright © 1992 by HarperCollins, Inc. Reprinted by permission of HarperCollins Publishers, Inc.
From SUPERVISION FOR TODAY'S SCHOOLS, 4/e by Peter F. Oliva. Copyright © 1993 by Longman Publishing Group. Reprinted by permission.

Chapter 1, pgs. 13–14
Hodgkinson's , H. "Reform v. Reality, 73(1): 9–16. Copyright © 1991, Phi Delta Kappan, 1991. Used by permission.

Chapter 2 , pg. 29
Wirth, Arthur "Educational Worth: The Choices We Face." *Phi Delta Kappan*, Vol. 74, Issue 5, p. 361. Used by permission.

Chapter 2, pgs. 32–33
From *Curriculum: A Comprehensive Introduction*, Fourth Edition by John McNeil, pg. 4. Copyright © 1990. Reprinted by permission of HarperCollins College Publishers.

Chapter 2, pgs. 34–35
Lounsbury, John H. *Middle School Journal*, Vol. 23, Issue 2, 1991. Used by permission of the National Middle School Association.

Chapter 3, Fig. 3.1, page 71
Jenkins/Jenkins "The NMSA Delphi Report: Roadmap to the Future." *Middle School Journal* 22 (4) , March 1991. Used by permission of the National Middle School Association

Chapter 4, pgs. 100–101
From John Wright's comments in Tyson J.C. and M. A. Carroll, *Conceptual Tools for Teaching in Secondary Schools*. Used by permission of the author.

Chapter 4, pgs. 104–106
Excerpted from FOUNDATIONS OF BEHAVIORAL RESEARCH, Second Edition by Fred N. Kerlinger, copyright © 1973 by Holt, Rinehart and Winston, Inc., reproduced by permission of the publisher.

Chapter 4, pgs. 105–106, 111
Reprinted with the permission of Macmillan College Publishing Company from HISTORICAL PHILOSOPHICAL FOUNDATIONS OF EDUCATION, 4/e, by Howard Ozmon and Samuel Craver. Copyright © 1990 by Macmillan Publishing Company Inc.

Chapter 4, pgs. 108–109, 118–121, Fig. 4.3, and Fig. 4.4.
From SUPERVISION FOR TODAY'S SCHOOLS, 4/e by Peter F. Oliva. Copyright © 1993 by Longman Publishing Group. Reprinted by permission.

Chapter 4, Table 4.1, pg, 115
From Stefanich Piaget Table. *Middle School Journal*, 1979. Used by permission of National Middle School Association.

Chapter 4, pg. 122, Fig. 4.5
Saylor/Alexander: *Curriculum Planning for Modern Schools*. Copyright 1966. Reprinted by permission of the author.

# NAME INDEX

# SUBJECT INDEX